Human Rights in the South Pacific

This book looks at the challenges and contemporary issues raised by human rights in the island countries of the South West Pacific which have come under the influence of the common law – where the legal systems are complex and perceptions of rights varies widely.

Drawing on a wide range of resources to present a contemporary and evolving picture of human rights in the island states of the South Pacific region, the book considers the human rights aspects of constitutions, legal institutions and structures, social organisation, culture and custom, tradition and change. The materials provide legal, historical, political, social and cultural insights into the lived experience of human rights in the region, supported by illustrative material from case-law, media reports, and policy documents. The book also locates the human rights concerns of Pacific islanders firmly within the wider theoretical and international domain while at the same time maintaining focus on the importance of the unique identity of Pacific island nations and people.

Human Rights in the South Pacific will appeal to anyone interested in the region or in human rights, including international rights advocates, investors and developers, policy makers, representatives of government and civic society and those wishing to acquire a better understanding of what countries emerging from colonial rule face in developing but still retaining their identity.

Sue Farran is a Senior Lecturer at the School of Law, University of Dundee, Scotland and was formerly an Associate Professor of Law at the University of the South Pacific, Emalus Campus, Vanuatu.

Human Rights in the South Pacific

Challenges and changes

Sue Farran

Routledge·Cavendish
Taylor & Francis Group
LONDON AND NEW YORK

First published 2009
by Routledge-Cavendish
2 Park Square, Milton Park, Abingdon, Oxon OX14 4RN

Simultaneously published in the USA and Canada
by Routledge-Cavendish
270 Madison Avenue, New York, NY 10016

Routledge-Cavendish is an imprint of the Taylor & Francis Group

Transferred to Digital Printing 2009

© 2009 Sue Farran

Typeset in NewBaskerville by Keyword Group Ltd

British Library Cataloguing in Publication Data
A catalogue record for this book is available from the British Library

Library of Congress Cataloging in Publication Data
Farran, Susan.
  Human rights in the South Pacific : challenges and changes/
  Sue Farran.
    p. cm.
  Simultaneously published in the USA and Canada.
  ISBN 978-1-84472-109-2
  1. Human rights–Oceania. 2. Civil rights–Oceania. I. Title.
  KVC572.F37 2009
  323.0995–dc22   2008033871

ISBN 10: 1-84472-109-4 (hbk)
ISBN 10: 0-415-48997-0 (pbk)
ISBN 10: 0-203-88268-7 (ebk)

ISBN 13: 978-1-84472-109-2 (hbk)
ISBN 13: 978-0-415-48997-3 (pbk)
ISBN 13: 978-0-203-88268-9 (ebk)

To Bob Hughes, University of the South Pacific, who gave me a job and opened a door, and who died in March 2007.

Contents

Preface

In 1996, as a Visiting Scholar to the University of the South Pacific, I was asked to create a human rights course for undergraduate law students. Finding any Pacific sources to support the course was, to say the least, a challenge. Many of the official series of law reports had ceased at independence, copies of legislation were hard to come by and library holdings were incomplete. There was very limited legal academic comment on the region and even less international focus. Today much has changed and considerably more information is available and accessible. Increasingly, the international community is becoming aware of the region and Pacific island countries themselves are publishing more information. However, many of the sources are scattered and not always easily located. This book provides an opportunity to bring together a range of these resources and to critically address a number of human rights issues which are relevant to the region.

The perspective is unavoidably and unashamedly that of a white, female, non-Pacific islander. My understanding of the topics which follow has been shaped by my own experiences while living and working in the Pacific, conversations with many Pacific islanders and the views and opinions of others who have researched and written on such matters. All understanding is coloured by the lens through which information is viewed, the language by which it is translated and communicated and the time and place at which it is acquired. During the period of research and writing, there have been developments and changes concerning human rights in the region. If the subject matter contained herein does nothing more than provoke contrary views or debate then one of its aims will have been achieved. If it makes readers realise that human rights in the Pacific region are a subject worthy of closer scrutiny and from which much can be learned, that too, will be good. And finally, if this book helps to mainstream Pacific concerns in the international community, then it will be a success.

This book has been made possible through the support of my current university, the University of Dundee, Scotland; the inspiration and contacts engendered by my previous university, the University of the South Pacific, and first-hand experience of some of the challenges facing human rights though working with NGOs and others in the region. Funding to present a paper on some of the issues raised in Chapters One and Two was provided by the British Academy and funding to undertake research relevant to Chapter Four was provided by the Society of Legal Scholars. Financial support to attend the 2008 human rights symposium in Apia, Samoa, was provided by the Commonwealth Secretariat, New Zealand Aid, the Government of Samoa and the Federal Republic of Germany Foreign Office.

I am grateful to a number of people for their opinions and comments, in particular my former colleague and mentor Emeritus Professor Don Paterson, University of the South Pacific; Dr Guy Powles, Monash University; Associate Professor Peter MacFarlane, University of the South Pacific; Professor Tony Angelo, University of Victoria, Wellington; Dr Jennifer Corrin Care, T.C. Beirne School of Law, Queensland; Professor Janet MacLean, University of Dundee, and Dr Tony Crook from St Andrews University. I am also grateful to staff at the University of Dundee library, the Emalus campus library at the University of the South Pacific and at the Pacific Institute for Legal Information. Research assistance on the early stages of this work was provided by Dundee student Dianne Kay and Teaching Assistant Andrew Woodcock. Finally, I am grateful to those who have desisted from asking how I was getting on with the book, they will be glad to know they can now ask me.

Cases cited

All Pacific cases are taken from the electronic data base PacLII except where otherwise indicated. Country abbreviations are as follows: CK – Cook Islands; FJ – Fiji Islands; FM – Federated States of Micronesia; KI – Kiribati; MR – Marshall Islands; NR – Nauru; PNG – Papua New Guinea; SP – Solomon Islands; WS – Samoa (or WSNZCA for cases heard by the New Zealand court or ASHC prior to the division of Samoa into Western and American Samoa); TO – Tonga; TV – Tuvalu; VU – Vanuatu.

Table of legislation

Where possible the PacLII reference has been given. Full references can be found in the text.

Abbreviations and acronyms

ACP	African, Caribbean and Pacific Countries (as in EU-ACP)
AOSIS	Alliance of Small Island States
AusAID	Australian Government's Overseas Aid Programme
Cap	Chapter in a consolidation of legislation as found in a number of Pacific Island Countries
CAFOD	Catholic Agency for Overseas Development
CAT	Convention against Torture and Other Cruel, Inhuman or Degrading Treatment or Punishment
CEDAW	Convention for the Elimination of All Forms of Discrimination against Women
CERD	International Convention on the Elimination of all Forms of Racial Discrimination
CESCR	International Covenant on Economic, Social and Cultural Rights
CHOGM	Commonwealth Heads of Government Meeting
CJC	Chief Justices' Conference
CLEA	Commonwealth Legal Education Association
COC	Christian Outreach Centre
CRC	Convention on the Rights of the Child
CRMW	International Convention on the Protection of the Rights of All Migrant Workers and Members of their Families
ECANSI	Environmental Concerns Action Network of Solomon Islands
ECHR	European Court of Human Rights
ECREA	Ecumenical Centre for Research, Education and Advocacy
EEZ	Exclusive Economic Zone
EKT	Ekalesia Kelisiano Tuvalu
EPA	Economic Partnerships Agreement
EU	European Union
FAO	United Nations Food and Agriculture Organisation
FPRTS	Forum Principles on Regional Transport Services
FWCC	Fiji women's crisis centre
FWRM	Fiji women's rights movement
FSM	Federated States of Micronesia

GATT	General Agreement on Trade and Tariffs
GDP	Gross Domestic Product
GEF	Global Environment Facility
HIV/ AIDS	Human Immune Virus/ Acquired Immune Deficiency Syndrome
ICC	International coordinating Committee of National Institutions for the Protection and Promotion of Human Rights
ICESCR	International Covenant on Economic, Social and Cultural Rights
ICCPR	International Covenant on Civil and Political Rights
ICJ	International Commission of Jurists
ICRC	International Committee of the Red Cross
ICTSD	International Centre for Trade and Sustainable Development
IMO	International Monetary Fund
LAWASIA	Law Association for Asia and the Pacific
NGO	Non-government Organisation
MOX	Mixed Oxide
NTF	National Tidal Facility
NHRIS	National Human Rights Institutions
NZAid	New Zealand Government's Overseas Aid Programme
OHCHR	Office of the High Commission for Human Rights
PACER	Pacific Agreement on Closer Economic Relations
PacLII	Pacific Legal Information Institute
PANG	Pacific Network on Globalisation
PASO	Pacific Aviation Safety Office
PIANGO	Pacific Islands Association of Non-Government Organisations
PICCAP	Pacific Islands Climate Change Assistance Programme
PICTA	Pacific Island Countries Trade Agreement
PIDP	Pacific Islands Development Programme
PIFFA	Pacific Islands Forum Fisheries Agency
PIPSO	Pacific Islands Private Sector Organisation
PILON	Pacific Islands Law Officers Network
PRAN	Pacific Regional Assistance to Nauru
RAMSI	Regional Assistance Mission to the Solomon Islands
RRRT	Regional Rights Resource Team
RTFP	Regional Trade Facilitation Programme
SIDT	Solomon Island Development Trust
SOPAC	Pacific Islands Applied Geoscience Commission
SPARTECA	South Pacific Regional Trade and Economic Cooperation Agreement
SPC	Secretariat of the Pacific Community

SPEC	South Pacific Bureau of Economic Co-operation
SPREP	Secretary of the Pacific Regional Environmental Programme
SPTO	South Pacific Travel (formerly South Pacific Tourism Organisation)
TRIPS	Trade-related Aspects of Intellectual Property Rights
UN	United Nations
UNDP	United Nations Development Programme
UNESCO	United Nations Educational, Scientific and Cultural Organisation
UNICEF	United Nations Children's Fund
UNPFII	United Nations Permanent Forum on Indigenous Issues
US/USA	United States of America
USP	University of the South Pacific
USSR	United Soviet Socialist Republic
WAC	Women's Action for Change
WHO	World Health Organisation
WTO	World Trade Organisation
WWF	World Wide Fund for Nature. Since 2000 known as WWF – 'For a Living Planet'

Introduction

This book is about human rights in a particular region of the world: the island countries of the South West Pacific. However, this topic cannot be divorced from a wide range of other topics such as constitutions, legal institutions and structures, social organisation, culture and custom, tradition and change, especially in the Pacific region where the legal systems are complex and perceptions of what rights are or should be varies widely. Consequently, although a range of issues are discussed in separate chapters, in fact they are closely related, and indeed sometimes difficult to separate. The inclusion of certain matters in one chapter rather than in another is therefore somewhat artificial; it could be done differently. It should also be borne in mind that this book looks at the human rights of a region, not just one country but many; each of which has its own unique characteristics, languages, history, people and culture. Some assertions and examples therefore will not be applicable to all countries in general but only to a few; however it is not proposed to take each country separately but to consider shared themes. In some cases, these are best illustrated by examples drawn from a limited range of jurisdictions or even a sole jurisdiction, while with others a wider range of examples may be both applicable and available. The region does not exist in isolation – although many islands in it are isolated – but in a broader global framework. Because of this there will also be reference to international influences, and the comparative experience of countries which may share some of the characteristics of, or challenges faced by, Pacific island countries.

The Pacific island countries considered here are both a part of and apart from the international discourse and experience of human rights. The region represents and illustrates a number of issues and challenges that are not restricted to that region alone. In particular, the countries considered are examples of relatively young countries emerging from colonial rule. While seeking to assert their national and unique identity, they also want to take their place in the international community and, because they are weak economically and often politically unstable, may be powerless to resist international demands or constraints or they may be vulnerable to the consequences arising from compliance with these.

They are also countries where concerns about indigenous rights are at the forefront because in most of these countries indigenous people are in the majority but not necessarily immune from the pressures and influences of non-indigenous powers. It is a region facing considerable and rapid change while retaining many examples of traditional social organisation and economic activity. It is also a region where legal systems are plural, with laws introduced under colonial administration operating alongside customary laws and increasingly international laws. Sometimes these various sources of law are in conflict or are contradictory or inconsistent. Often there will be uncertainty as to which laws apply and inequalities of outcome. In a number of countries, differences in emerging political and economic aspirations have led to conflict, instability and unrest, jeopardising peaceful development and growth and leaving these countries at risk of interference from elsewhere. Political instability and shaky economies have also meant that the environment has not always been conducive to fostering human rights and that even today there are problems in getting governments to focus on rights issues when there are other competing concerns.

What are the human rights issues of the region?

Human rights in the region give rise to both theoretical and practical issues. On the theoretical level, there are debates about the nature and form of human rights and the relevance or not of these in the Pacific region. There is a view that human rights are not indigenous but alien to Pacific people and that human rights advocacy and the pressure to comply with international standards is merely another form of imperial domination in which small island states lack a voice, while large states set the agenda and standards without necessarily observing these themselves. Alternatively, there is a view that human rights pre-date any contact with western liberal theories or globalisation and are indigenous to the region and given effect in traditional values and customs. That the international community cannot recognise this is the failure of that community not Pacific island states. A middle view is to endeavour to negotiate a common ground between Pacific human rights and international human rights, to identify similarities and resolve differences.

These theoretical viewpoints are not distinct from practical issues but integral to them. For example, in 1985, at a conference in Fiji, Pacific island delegates identified the following human rights concerns: the colonial background and recently acquired sovereignty of many island countries with its related consequence of having to resolve issues of self-determination; the historical social and economic problems which needed to be addressed when considering development; issues of cultural identity, especially for ethnic and indigenous minorities; the rights of women in the region; nuclear issues affecting the region; rights concerning the use and preservation of the cultural identity of ethnic and indigenous groups and the relationship of traditional values to changing life styles (Deklin 1992). These concerns, while perhaps not very significant on a global scale, are probably not unique to people of the Pacific countries.

The Pacific region is one that rarely attracts the attention of the world press or world leaders, certainly not for human rights abuses. Indeed, it has been stated that 'the human rights record of this region is, comparatively speaking, quite good' (Hyndman 1992: 101). However, in the course of the last decade a slightly different picture has emerged. The regional office of the United Nations Office of the High Commission for Human Rights indicates in its 2008–2009 programme statement that:

> Some of the most pressing human rights issues in the region include widespread poverty, violence against women and children, lack of judicial independence and ill treatment in detention. These issues are compounded by political and social instability and weak justice systems. There are also significant instances of racial discrimination. Processes of social reconciliation and peace-building in the Solomon Islands, civil unrest and emergency rule in Tonga, and a political crisis in Fiji all affect those nations' key institutions.[1]

In fact, despite the positive picture indicated by Hyndman in 1992 she did indicate that there were concerns regarding: the self-determination of people; the rights of indigenous people and of cultural minorities; the status of women; the rights of children, youth and the elderly; and the right to participate in democratic decision-making. More recently a number of non-governmental and intergovernmental organisations have highlighted similar concerns. For example, concern about the exploitation of children for purposes of pornography, prostitution, adoption and sexual assault, including incest, prompted a visit by a special rapporteur of the United Nations to Fiji in 1999. Her findings concluded that 'There is urgent need for strong political will to implement legislative reform and to formulate policies for the protection of children, in order to bring Fiji into line with its obligations under the Convention on the Rights of the Child' (OHCRH 1999). In 2007, the Commonwealth Youth Programme held a regional caucus in Solomon Islands. Writing to heads of governments the caucus drew attention to the following facts:

> Children as young as ten years old are engaged in sexual services on ocean-going vessels; Young people are entering marriage before reaching 16 years of age. This is affecting their health and impeding their education; Single mothers are denied legal autonomy thereby limiting their ability to provide for themselves and their dependents;

Young people found guilty of minor offences are subject to punitive detention without opportunity for rehabilitation (Commonwealth Secretariat 2007).

UNICEF has highlighted the risk of an HIV/AIDS epidemic in the region due to poverty, illiteracy, sexual exploitation of children and the prevalence of unsafe sex practices. Its report on countries of the region indicates an increase in the number of sex workers in the region, a rise in the number of teenage pregnancies, continuing high figures for infant mortality and 'an overall decline in living standards for women and children'. It also draws attention to the high number of children dropping out of school because parents cannot afford fees.[2]

Women too continue to be the victims of human rights abuses. In 2005, a World Health Organization Multi-country Study on Women's Health and Domestic Violence Against Women found that of the two Pacific countries included in the study – Japan and Samoa – Samoa had the highest prevalence rates for gender-based violence – including violence against pregnant women. The study went on to comment:

> The alarmingly high rates of non-partner physical and/or sexual gender-based violence (62% lifetime prevalence) and partner physical and/or sexual gender-based violence (46.1% lifetime prevalence) in the only (South Pacific) country which has been subjected to a total population study, Samoa, suggests the urgent need to establish reliable data from large-scale prevalence studies in other countries in the Region to see if they too have a 'hidden' epidemic (of domestic violence)
>
> (WHO 2006: 5).

Research from Fiji also reflects high incidences of domestic violence, including violence against pregnant women (Fiji Women's Crisis Centre 1997/1998) and there are similar concerns in Vanuatu, Kiribati, Federated States of Micronesia and Papua New Guinea (US Country Reports 2007). In a report published in 2006, the Asia Pacific Director of Amnesty International stated that 'Violence against women is endemic in Papua New Guinea: it affects the majority of women and girls in some parts of the country' (Sen 2006). The human rights of women and children in the region, therefore, are a cause for concern.

Civil unrest and ethnic violence have also led to human rights being abused and placed at risk. This has occurred most recently in Solomon Islands in 1998–2003, in Fiji in 2002 and 2006 and in Tonga in 2006. In Papua New Guinea, tribal fighting continues to take place especially in more remote areas. Where such unrest has occurred, property has been destroyed, lives lost, people displaced, dispersed and detained, and freedom of expression and association curtailed. Although the extent of these rights' abuses is poorly documented, in some of these countries the International

Red Cross has been involved in bringing relief to displaced persons and visiting those detained in prison as a result of their involvement in the unrest (ICRC 2006: 224). Human Rights Watch has expressed concern, in letters to the interim Prime Minister and the President of Fiji, concerning arbitrary detention and abuse of human rights activists following the 2006 military coup, and called for assurances that fundamental human rights would be restored to the citizens of Fiji (Human Rights Watch 2007). The International Commission of Jurists has expressed similar concern in its press statement on the Fiji military regime (ICJ 2006). Human Rights Watch has also reported concern about the involvement of child soldiers – children under eighteen – in the ethnic conflict of 2001 in Solomon Islands.

More specific human rights violations have also occurred. In 1998, following a state of emergency, Amnesty International conducted a visit to Vanuatu prisons and reported a series of human rights abuses (Amnesty International 1998). Concern about prison conditions and treatment of prisoners has been expressed about other countries in the region as well, for example, Marshall Islands and Papua New Guinea (US Country Reports 2007). In 2001 Amnesty International reported on police in Papua New Guinea killing protesters seeking to petition the Prime Minister (Amnesty International 2001). In 2002 the same organisation called on the Fijian authorities to investigate the torture by the military of suspected mutineers, four of whom died as a result of their beatings (Amnesty International 2002). In 2007 a report published by a non-governmental organisation in Tonga indicated the extent of unlawful detention and police and military brutality used against those arrested following the civil disturbances in the capital of Tonga in late 2006 (McLean 2008).

Regional case law and local media reports also indicate that there are other areas of concern ranging from religious intolerance to suppression of the press. A number of these will be considered in the course of this book. There is moreover a more general perception that there are a variety of factors in the region that mitigate against the successful advocacy, enhancement or enforcement of human rights which need to be considered. These include a continuing perception that human rights are foreign and therefore incompatible with indigenous concepts of rights; lack of political will to commit to either national, regional or international statements of rights; lack of explicit national policies and goals in respect of human rights; assertions of tradition and culture against claims of equality, modernisation or globalisation and the dichotomy between civil society and state institutions. There are also external forces at work which combine to shape and sometimes frustrate the agenda of rights. Relations between Pacific island states, their regional neighbours and the wider international community determine the priorities of governments and the development policies which are pursued. Sometimes these are favourable to human rights, sometimes they are not.

Bearing in mind not only the concerns expressed by Pacific islanders in 1985, but also subsequent examples of human rights abuses and developments in the intervening period, the aim of this book is to consider the present state of human rights in Pacific island countries, taking into account the challenges that have to be confronted and the changes that have occurred in taking rights forward in the region.

In order to do this, a fairly broad thematic approach has been adopted supported by a number of detailed illustrations. Not all human rights are addressed nor are all avenues of analysis explored. The topics selected are ones which illustrate a number of the human rights challenges and changes occurring in the region but these are by no means the only topics which could have been chosen. At the outset the specific Pacific environment within which rights operate is considered by looking at the region itself and describing something of its composition, location and structures in order to better understand why there may be problems and obstacles in respect of human rights. Consideration is then given to the distinctive quality of rights as human rights and the various sources of law which are relevant to shaping and securing rights in the region in Chapter Two. Chapter Three considers the theoretical hurdles, looking at differing perspectives of human rights and the significance of these for small independent island states and explores the possibility of finding a middle ground which meets domestic and international demands. Chapter Four considers the tensions between group rights and individual rights as illustrated by changing approaches to property rights and the challenges posed by the pressures of development in island countries with limited resources. Against a background of introduced rights and international expectations attention is then given to the challenges faced by claims of custom, especially in relation to social ordering, the changing identity of Pacific island people and the clamour for equality. To do this Chapter Five examines the sometimes conflicting relationship between custom and human rights with particular focus on the rights of women and the challenges which can arise in rapidly adjusting societies. Chapter Six considers the experience of human rights where identities are being redrawn and freshly examined as a result of international influences. In particular this chapter looks as discrimination on various grounds, including ethnicity and religion. The pursuit and advocacy of rights is then reviewed in Chapter Seven, which considers the various players in the rights arena. This chapter examines the role of the courts in adjudicating rights' claims and affording access to justice, other existing mechanisms and organisations which could or do champion human rights in the region and the success or otherwise of these. The concluding chapter speculates on the way ahead, and the possibilities that present themselves when considering the development or demise of human rights in South Pacific island countries. The book concludes with some personal views on the future of human rights in the region.

Notes

1 OHCHR Pacific Regional Office 2008–2009, Chttp://www.ohchr.org/EN/Countries/AsiaRegion/Pages/PacificSummary 0809.aspx (accessed 6 June 2008).
2 UNICEF Information by Country: East Asia and the Pacific, http://www.unicef.org/infobycountry/index.html (accessed 6 June 2008).

1 The region of the Pacific

Introduction

While some readers will be familiar with the region, others will not. The purpose of this chapter is to establish the regional environment in which human rights operate. This requires some awareness of the geographical parameters of the area under consideration, the composition of its people and forms of social organisation, the nature of its political and constitutional structures, the relationship of Pacific Island countries with other powers and the economic environment. All of these elements contribute to shape the experience of human rights in the Pacific region and to explain some of the obstacles and challenges that confront them. Given the diversity and complexity of the region, never mind its expanse, it is impossible to do more than to sketch this environment in order to build a foundation upon which further detail can be added through consideration of specific human rights issues and incidences in subsequent chapters.

The region under consideration

Composition and location

The 'South Pacific' is not a precise term, what is meant and understood depends on the situation in which it is used. From the perspective of countries such as the United States of America, Japan and the European Union, there may be a tendency to regard the South Pacific as meaning that area and the countries south of themselves. From this viewpoint, the Federated States of Micronesia, Guam, Hawaii, Marshall Islands, Northern Marianas and Palau, are seen as being in the South Pacific, even though they are all the north of the Equator. Literally, South Pacific refers to the tropical island nations and territories south of the equator in the region of the Pacific Ocean. However, for the Pacific Islands, South Pacific often includes islands north of the equator, on the basis of cultural and constitutional similarities rather than on geographical grounds.

Defining the region is not only a problem of perception. There are different groupings for different purposes. In 1947, a South Pacific Commission was established in Australia by the Canberra Agreement, signed by Australia, France, Netherlands, New Zealand, the United Kingdom and the United States of America. The Commission then became the Secretariat of the Pacific Communities in 1998. The Secretariat currently has twenty-two member countries and territories. These are: American Samoa, Cook Islands, Federated States of Micronesia, Fiji Islands, French Polynesia, Guam, Kiribati, Marshall Islands, Nauru, New Caledonia, Niue, Northern Mariana Islands, Palau, Papua New Guinea, Pitcairn Islands, Samoa, Solomon Islands, Tokelau, Tonga, Tuvalu, Vanuatu, and Wallis and Futuna. In addition, there are four founding countries: Australia, France, New Zealand and the United States of America.[1] Clearly not all of these are located in the South Pacific region.

By contrast the South Pacific Forum which was established in 1971 has fewer members, thereby excluding some countries brought together under the Secretariat. Member countries of the Forum are: Australia, Cook Islands, Federated States of Micronesia, Fiji, Kiribati, Nauru, New Zealand, Niue, Palau, Papua New Guinea, Republic of the Marshall Islands, Samoa, Solomon Islands, Tonga, Tuvalu and Vanuatu. Meanwhile, the University of the South Pacific, established in 1968, has twelve member countries. Marshall Islands joined as a recent member regardless of its geographical location which is north of the equator. The rest are from the south of the equator: Cook Islands, Fiji, Kiribati, Nauru, Niue, Samoa, Tuvalu, Tokelau, Tonga, Solomon Islands and Vanuatu.[2] However, students from other Pacific Island countries such as the Federated States of Micronesia and Palau also attend the university.

These differences of affiliation have significance for the development of regional initiatives and can also cause confusion as to which countries are actually being referred to.[3] For the purposes of this book, it has been decided to focus primarily on those countries which came under the direct or indirect colonial administration of Britain and therefore the influence of the common law. That is: Cook Islands, Fiji, Kiribati, Nauru, Niue, Samoa, Tuvalu, Tokelau, Tonga, Solomon Islands and Vanuatu,[4] together with Palau, Papua New Guinea, Pitcairn Islands, Federated States of Micronesia and Marshall Islands. Most, but not all, of these countries are now independent or have a degree of independence.[5]

Having established which countries are to be considered, it is necessary to locate these globally. They all lie in the largest of the world's oceans, the Pacific. This expanse of sea has an area which is greater than all the dry land on the planet. It occupies more than one-third of Earth's surface – as much as the Atlantic, Indian and Artic oceans combined. It is the largest geographical feature in the world. The area it covers is about 165,384,000 sq km (16,000 km wide and 11,000 km long) with an average depth of 4,000m. It is believed that there are more than 30,000 islands in the Pacific basin.

The Pacific basin includes all the countries on the rim of the Pacific Ocean and the island states and territories within the ocean. The area under consideration is not quite so extensive.

For the purposes of this book the region stretches from north to south and east to west. In the north lie the Federated States of Micronesia – latitude 6 degrees, 55 minutes north, longitude 158 degrees, 15 minutes east of the Equator, and the Marshall Islands – latitude 9 degrees north, longitude 168 degrees east of the equator. The southern limit is the Polynesian state of Tonga – latitude 20 degrees south and longitude 175 degrees, west of the equator. In the East the limit is the Pitcairn Islands – latitude 25 degrees, 0 minutes south, longitude 130 degrees 6 minutes, west of the equator. The western boundary is Papua New Guinea, latitude 6 degrees south, longitude 147 degrees east of the equator.

The people

There are three major groups of people and culture in the region: the Melanesians, Polynesians and Micronesians. Melanesian people are found in Papua New Guinea, Solomon Islands, Vanuatu, and parts of Fiji. They are also found in the French territory of New Caledonia.[6] Polynesians are found in the central south Pacific in Tuvalu, Tonga, Tokelau, Samoa, Niue and Cook Islands, but also in French Wallis and Futuna. In the northern Pacific, Polynesians are found in Hawaii, in the East Pacific in French Polynesia and in the south in New Zealand. Small communities of Polynesians are also found in parts of Vanuatu – notably the Banks Islands, Rotuma and some of the eastern islands of Fiji, in Ontong Java, Tikopia, Anua, Rennel and Bellona in Solomon Islands, and in Pohnpei in the Federated States of Micronesia. Micronesians are found in the western Pacific region, in Marshall Islands, the Federated States of Micronesia, Nauru, Kiribati and Palau. There are also small populations of Micronesians in Tuvalu.

There is considerable variation in the population composition between the three major races in the region. Ninety-one per cent are Melanesian, 4.45 per cent are Polynesian and 4.35 per cent of the total population are Micronesian. Papua New Guinea itself contains 70 per cent of the total population. The smallest indigenous population in the region is that of Tokelau with about 0.02 per cent of the total population.[7] Island countries of the Pacific are grouped according to their predominant population type. Out of the total land area, Melanesia contains about 99.4 per cent, Micronesia 0.17 per cent and Polynesia 0.42 per cent. The high percentage which is Melanesia is attributable to Papua New Guinea which has the largest land mass.

In addition to the three major races there are other ethnic minority groups of European and Asian descent scattered across the region. In Fiji, for example, the population of Indians brought in by the colonial administration as indentured labourers to work in the sugar plantations now constitutes about 40 per cent of the Fiji Islands total population although in 1982 it represented over 50 per cent of the population.[8] Throughout the region there are small numbers of people of European origin as well as Chinese and Vietnamese. There are also groups of Pacific islanders living in countries which are not their country of origin. For example, as a result of high population growth rate between 1950s and 1960s, British colonial administration resettled Kiribati people in Fiji and Solomon Islands. Therefore, there are i-Kiribati descendants residing in Fiji and in the Western part of the Solomon Islands.

The three groups, Melanesians, Micronesians and Polynesians, display different customs, languages, cultures and social organisation. Despite the diversity of cultures, Polynesians and Micronesians have some aspects in common. The Melanesian societies are less homogenous. They are known for the diversity within their own societies and differ considerably from Polynesians and Micronesians. The Melanesian societies are less socially stratified and are more egalitarian. The Polynesian and Micronesian societies are traditionally stratified and hierarchical (Sahlins 1963). This means that in Polynesia status is often prescribed at birth so that the members of a society are classified as commoners, elders, chiefs, high chiefs and so on with limited opportunity for change of status. This traditional structure has been described as 'pyramidal' while that of Melanesia as 'segmental' (Sahlins 1963: 287). The former is politically, although unequally, integrated, while the latter is politically unintegrated. While this is changing under the influence of modern values of education, personal accomplishment, the accumulation of wealth and political influence it has by no means disappeared. In Melanesian societies there is less stratification of classification and an individual may acquire status – or lose it – according to personal merit. Nevertheless, there are some Polynesian societies within Melanesia that display Polynesian social structure, for example, Tikopians, and people from Renell and Bellona in the Solomon Islands. Similarly, where the chiefly system is intact in the Melanesian societies such as Short Lands, Choiseul and Central Islands in Solomon Islands there are some forms of stratification, while elsewhere in Solomon Islands there is less stratification and a more variable and sometimes shifting social structure. The situation in Fiji is different and needs to be treated separately. Fiji is regarded as the island country where Melanesian and the Polynesian influences and people meet. Physically, Fijians share Melanesian features; however, culturally Fijians are more closely linked to Polynesians. Even within Fiji Islands however there are differences. Fiji Islands is also distinct on account of the large percentage of the population which is not indigenous.

Population

The population growth rate of the island countries of the South Pacific varies. Since Melanesia contains 91 per cent of the total population of the region, its population growth rate is high compared to the Polynesian countries. The maximum population growth rate is 2.91 per cent in the Solomon Islands, followed by Papua New Guinea with 2.39 per cent. Kiribati also has a high anticipated population growth rate of 2.3 per cent. However, in Fiji Islands and Vanuatu the population growth rate is less than 1.7 per cent and possibly as low as 0.7 per cent in Fiji Islands. Tonga's population is barely growing at all and Niue and Cook Islands are estimated to have falling populations.[9]

Within the region the Polynesian countries have the lowest population growth rates. One or two may have negative population growth rates, for example, Samoa and Tokelau. One reason why Polynesian countries have very low or negative population growth rate is partly because of the high number of Polynesians migrating to New Zealand, Australia and United States due to domestic land pressure and links with these countries brought about either by a history of migration and settlement or because of trade and government links. Better education has also led to higher aspirations which may not be met by staying in the home country. This is particularly the case for Cook Islands and Niue with respect to New Zealand. Indeed, there are estimated to be three times more Niueans in New Zealand than in the country itself. In 2001, Niuean people made up 9 per cent of New Zealand's Pacific Island population (291,000 Niueans), with 70 per cent of these having been born in New Zealand.[10] There is also significant outward migration in Tonga and Samoa.[11] In 2001, 50 per cent of the total Pacific islander population in New Zealand was Samoan, of whom 58 per cent were born in New Zealand, representing an increase of nine per cent over a 10-year period. Tongans represented 18 per cent of the total Pacific people in 2001, marking an increase in the total number of Tongans of 30 per cent in the period 1996–2001. In the 2006 New Zealand Census, Pacific peoples' ethnic groups increased by over 14 per cent from the 2001 Census, up to a total 265,974. Writing in 1999 Cook stated that:

> Demographically, Pacific people in New Zealand are characterised by high fertility, rapid miscegenation, a high population growth rate and a youthful population ... their age structure, even half a century on, will remain more youthful than the current New Zealand structure, and this could have direct implications for the labour market dynamics and New Zealand Society as a whole.
>
> (Cook *et al.* 1999)

He also pointed out that while the number of Pacific people in New Zealand was likely to increase this would be due to population growth among those within New Zealand – a fact born out by recent statistics – rather than migration to New Zealand, largely due to the limited size of populations in the Pacific. For example in 1996 there were 47,019 Cook islanders in New Zealand and an estimated 19,000 in Cook Islands.[12]

Ultimately, therefore, increases in migration would see net losses to populations in Pacific Island countries. For the moment, however, the pace of migration continues so that in 2001, for example, 93,285 respondents to the Census in New Zealand gave the Pacific Islands as their birth place.[13]

Emigration

The availability of dual citizenship or foreign passports is a significant and discriminating influence on emigration patterns. For example, in the Federated States of Micronesia, the 1986 Compact of Free Association with the United States included the right to migrate to the United States and its territories, such as Guam and Hawaii. In 2000, it was estimated that 12–16 per cent of the total population of the Federated States of Micronesia lived outside the Federation (Grieco 2000). In Cook Islands, Cook islanders are New Zealand citizens so that migration – and with it access to social welfare and the other benefits available – to New Zealand and sometimes onwards to Australia is easy. Similarly, Niueans and Tokelauans are New Zealand citizens under section 29 of the Citizenship Act 1977/61 (NZ). While there is a long and steady pattern of migration to New Zealand from these countries, internal crises can substantially increase outward flows. For example, failure of government-led and aid-backed development plans in the 1990s led to the migration of 25 per cent of the Cook Island population between 1996 and 2001 (Marsters *et al.* 2006: 34). Other countries have seen more limited outward migration but in some there have been rapid increases in the numbers of those either migrating or being born overseas. For example, between 1996 and 2001, the number of Tuvaluans making up the Pacific Island population in New Zealand rose from 900 to 2,000; 1,400 of whom had been born outside Tuvalu.[14]

In contrast, in countries such as Papua New Guinea, Vanuatu and Solomon Islands it is comparatively difficult for indigenous people to acquire foreign citizenship unless they are born abroad or move abroad and marry there. While there have been some discussions to promote the use of migrant labour in neighbouring countries such as Australia, and recently legislation has been passed to facilitate this,[15] these initiatives are unlikely to result in large numbers of permanent emigrants unless they remain as overstayers or repeated renewals of labour contracts confer sufficient periods of residency in the host country to entitle migrant labourers to remain (Inglis 2003). Historically a number of Melanesian labourers did remain in Australia under the now notorious 'blackbirding': the forced recruitment of unskilled labour for agricultural development in Queensland.[16] While – as will be indicated – emigration may generate valuable remittances to the home country, it can also lead to a drain on valuable human resources. This has been experienced in Fiji.

Here large-scale emigration has been triggered by political unrest. Fiji has experienced coups in 1987, 2000 and 2006. Outward migration has resulted in a large number of Indo-Fijians emigrating, to the extent that whereas prior to 1987 about 52 per cent of the population were Indo-Fijian, today it is less that 40 per cent.[17] Whereas annual emigration figures between 1978 and 1986 averaged 2,300, between 1997 and 1996 this increased to 5,005, the overwhelming majority of whom were Indo-Fijians, many of whom were engaged in professions much needed by Fiji such as medicine, education, architecture, engineering and accounting (Lal 2003). Similarly as a result of unrest and civil disturbance in Tonga in November 2006, it is estimated that 200 or more Chinese Tongans expressed a wish to leave Tonga. As the Chinese community own around 70 per cent of the businesses in Tonga, especially in the capital, Nuku'alofa, their departure could have severe economic repercussions (Misa 2006).

Emigration is one way of balancing population growth, but can have negative effects in the long term because it may either reduce the overall population and lead to a situation where there is increasing dependency on remittances or overseas aid, or it may reduce the (predominantly male) working population who leave to seek employment opportunities abroad, so that while the population may remain stable or indeed be increasing, it is composed of a large percentage of children and the elderly. These demographic dynamics present economic challenges for island governments. Population growth is related to a number of factors, not the least of which is overseas intervention, especially in the provision of health care. For example, as part of the Compact of Free Association with the Federated States of Micronesia, mentioned above, considerable economic aid was offered to the Federation in return for the United States securing exclusive use of its land, airspace and territorial waters for military purposes. One consequence was a rapid growth in population. In 2000 over half of its residents were under twenty years old. Similarly, in Marshall Islands, where the United States have also poured in economic aid in return for military privileges there is an estimated population growth rate of 1.6 per cent over the decade 2004–2015.[18]

In general, it can be said that the population is growing rapidly in Melanesian and Micronesian countries and decreasing in the Polynesian countries. For countries such as Kiribati, Nauru and Marshall Islands, with very high population growth rates compared to their land masses, there will be the serious threat of over population in the near future unless there is considerable and sustained outward migration. This, however, may leave the country with insufficient able-bodied people to work the land and support the agricultural and other development needed to sustain these countries. The other problem is that in a number of countries a high percentage of the population are young. In 2006, the estimated median age of people in Marshall Islands, Solomon Islands, Vanuatu, Federated States of Micronesia, Samoa and Tokelau was under twenty.[19] This not only places a strain on education and health resources but it gives rise to a large youth population, who, in rapidly changing societies, may have needs and expectations that Pacific Island governments are unable to meet.

Overseas Pacific islanders and remittances

Although many Pacific islanders live outside their countries of origin they also maintain contact through visits and remittances.[20] Brij Lal describes these Pacific islanders – including the many Indo-Fijians who have left Fiji – as transmigrants, who play an important role in the social, economic and political development of the region, through their networks, remittances to family members who remain in the islands, fund-raising for disaster relief or for local projects and as a conduit to the wider world (Lal 2003). The practice of remittances also provides an important cushion against the deficiencies of domestic state welfare provision, especially for the elderly, or for specific categories of persons, such as Indo-Fijian students wishing to attend university.[21] At the same time, however, reliance on remittances can have negative effects. Not only do remittances allow state governments to avoid their social welfare responsibilities, they may also diminish the relevance of the state and its structures to individuals. For example, Marsters *et al.* (2006: 35) suggests that in the Cook Islands, following the failure of grandiose government development plans backed by foreign aid in the 1990s, Cook islanders turned to their own personal, often international, networks for resources and to support development, thereby severing personal future development from national initiatives. While remittances may support localised development, they may also cultivate a culture of dependency among recipients and can be a considerable drain on the provider. The culture of remittances maintains notions of communal support and distribution rather than the accumulation of individual wealth and as such may limit certain aspects of development. Indeed, it is not unknown for Pacific islanders to seek to escape from home in order to be relieved of the endless demands on their resources by family members. Alternatively, those that stay behind often to look after family land or aging parents, while appreciating the remittances may resent the intervention of non-resident family members in land management decisions.

The importance of Pacific diaspora is not limited to material benefits. Not only are networks with family and place maintained and nurtured, but also language and culture. Contacts with Pacific islanders elsewhere inform the world view of those residing in the islands. Young people in particular travel to visit relations in the United States, Australia or New Zealand, or attend university or further training abroad. There is therefore a continual exchange of information and experience between the developing and developed countries not only within the region but beyond its boundaries. This is significant for human rights awareness and advocacy and also for informing opposition to certain developments in human rights. For example, opposition to greater freedom of the press which may conflict with traditional notions of respect for leaders; or for enhanced rights for homosexuals which may conflict with strongly held religious – largely Christian – beliefs.

Traditional social organisation

A degree of caution is necessary when commenting upon traditional social organisation. This is for a number of reasons. First, whatever is traditional is malleable and changing either due to the passage of time or to suit the agenda of the claimant or both. There are many influences which shape the discourse of 'chiefs' or traditional leaders in the Pacific region, including the influence of international agencies, for example, the United Nations Permanent Forum on Indigenous Issues. Second, the interpretation of traditional structures is coloured by the lens through which they are viewed. In many cases the early interpreters of traditional social structures in the Pacific region were missionaries and foreign anthropologists. Subsequent commentators have been historians, geographers, government advisers and others. Some have been indigenous to the region some have not. Today the interpretation is often that of modern political leaders who may wish to adopt and enhanced traditional perceptions of 'chiefly' power for their own ends, or may wish to regulate and reduce the power and esteem given to chiefs (White and Lindstrom 1997: 3). Third, there is a danger that the general excludes the specific or that the specific is taken to be the general. In homogenous societies this danger is perhaps less than in those societies which may be much more diverse and/or widely scattered geographically. Thus there are many differences encountered in Solomon Islands, Vanuatu, the Federated States of Micronesia, and perhaps fewer differences encountered in Samoa or Cook Islands. Field studies from which information is draw are often restricted in scope, and while they may be true of a particular time and place may be limited in value for supporting any general assertions. Fourth, what is claimed as 'traditional' may in fact be quite modern or recent. In particular it may be a product of colonial administration or of independence rather than a legacy from the pre-colonial or pre-contact period. Missionaries and others who provided the first 'western' contact with the islands frequently sought out or were greeted by chiefs. The identification – and in the case of missionaries, the conversion – of such people was important for establishing mission stations and later for supporting effective colonial administration. If there were no clearly identifiable chiefs then the colonial authorities appointed them to provide links between the indigenous population and the incoming foreigners. The construction and emergence of chiefs in this way is still apparent in the esteem afforded to church leaders. For example, in Tuvalu it has been stated 'The Church leader on the island is deemed to be a Chief and his power although not of the *Ulu Aliki* (traditional chief) has the equivalent status' (Duckworth 2002). Similarly, colonial administrators gave official standing to certain social groupings, such as clans, or tribes, regardless of whether these reflected traditional groupings. Finally, there may be some disparity between what is claimed to be traditional and what actually exists, especially in societies which have undergone rapid modernisation and development. What is claimed to be traditional may be coloured by nostalgia or by the conscious or unconscious recognition that grounding current conduct or policies in past values can have practical and political advantages.[22] With these cautions in mind, what follows is a simplified overview of some traditional structures which, as will be seen during the course of this book, can have an impact on the interpretation and implementation of human rights in the region.

The family or group

As found elsewhere in subsistence economies, central to the survival of Pacific Island people was, and often still is, the family or clan. The size of this group varied depending on available resources, the extent to which its members could be controlled, and the degree to which more remote kin observed allegiance to it. Leadership was vested either in individuals or a collection of individuals such as a group of elders. The extent to which small closely knit groups were democratic in their decision making is not clear. This may have been the case with respect to daily life but as so much depended on the management of shared resources and co-operation within the group, it is likely that decisions in the case of dispute were made and enforced by a limited number of people. Marriage and warfare maintained the balance and links between kin groups. In Polynesia these groups tended to be larger than in Melanesia. Often those who had power combined temporal with spiritual power or relied on the favourable support of those who had the latter. No group could survive without access to land, although this might include reefs and coastal areas. The power to acquire or grant land was therefore important, as was the power to defend it from competing groups. Those who lost land due to natural disasters or conquest became dependent on the land and benevolence of others. Group formation and social organisation was therefore probably subject to considerable fluctuation. The arrival of missionaries and later other settlers often disrupted and impacted on this. For example, mission stations established permanent residential locations for those who converted, while settler plantations took land out of general use by indigenous people. What remains significant, however, is the importance of the integration of the individual within the collective.

Leadership

Historically the attainment of leadership status varied through the region. This variation persists today although there is considerable blurring of the distinctions. What is important is the contemporary reliance on 'traditional' power structures to justify claims to leadership or status.

The traditional power structure in Melanesia was achieved through individual success. Theoretically this meant that any individual could accomplish political power through individual exertion. Units of political affiliation therefore tend to be small, starting with immediate family and kin groups and then extending to the locality. The individual who became a 'Big-Man' or chief had to work at it and had to be both deserving of support and able to reward it. The retention of personal power was, and remains, therefore, precarious. 'Big-Men' or elected chiefs could fall from power and then have to re-build their power base. This traditional structure is reflected in the dynamics of contemporary politics in Melanesia, where small chiefs to Prime Ministers may be demoted but re-emerge. It also explains why there are so many disputes about who is rightly entitled to a title or rightly entitled to represent particular group interests, for example, to negotiate timber logging contracts, mining concessions or to alienate or develop land.

In Polynesia, the power base was generally ascribed. This meant that the role and status of members of a society was pre-determined prior to birth – often because of links with ancestors which conferred spiritual strength on any claim. Consequently, authority passed from one generation to another through hereditary means and usually, but not always, through the same blood line. Power, therefore, was inherent and determined by societal rank not only within one genealogy but also between genealogies, with royalty and paramount chiefs at the apex of the pyramid. This acceptance of ascribed authority has persisted in Polynesia. Although it has been subject to some adaptation as different qualities are afforded greater recognition – for example, education.

In Micronesia, in Marshall Islands, a distinction was made between royal blood and commoners. Paramount and lesser chiefs appear to have been recognised as well as lineage heads.[23] It has been suggested that, prior to the present Constitution and the introduction of constitutional guarantees of equal rights to all citizens, that 'the Iroij had virtually complete domination over their subjects.'[24] Under Japanese administration many customary forms and titles appear to have been suppressed. They have since been revived.[25] Today the appointment of representatives to sit in the Council of Iroij seems to be a mixture of eligibility and election. Their power is diminished, not only because the elected President is not an Iroij but also because – as will be seen, constitutionally they play a limited role.

In the Federated States of Micronesia, Yap remains the most traditional society,[26] with a rigid caste system and a clearly defined class of leaders. In Pohnpei the traditional kingdoms are also still recognised,[27] while elsewhere western contact seems to have eradicated traditional leadership forms.

Throughout the region, prior to western contact, chiefs wielded considerable and sometimes brutal power. For example, in Tuvalu it has been stated that:

> (The) Chief dominated the island and had the power to take such decisions as were felt necessary for the running and control of the island. That included dealing with all administrative matters including the right to dispense justice and punishment in the manner necessary.
>
> The Chief tended to pass down through descent and go from one generation to the next. In this way, the chiefly system was preserved within a family and promoted certainty. However, this did cause problems with intrigue and jealousy. Early Tuvaluan history records a large number of deaths of those who were Chiefs and their descendants by those who were envious of their position and power (and who took control).
>
> (Duckworth 2002)

Inter-clan warfare, rivalry between potential leaders and conflict over land meant that, even where hereditary chiefs claimed entitlement by birth, their positions were often precarious and they maintained power by forming strategic alliances, military power and murder if necessary.

The intervention of missionary influence, which disapproved of traditional practices such as head-hunting, cannibalism, polygamy, marriage between close relatives and warfare, changed the ways in which traditional leaders could assert their power and maintain their status. In some cases, it meant that traditional leaders lost both, and that new forms of status and leadership emerged. In others, traditional leaders retained power and esteem by adapting and adopting some of the indicators of esteem introduced under colonial influence.[28] In some countries, colonial administrators sought to reduce the powers of chiefs or local leaders which they saw as undermining the centralised state; elsewhere it was recognised that utilising such influence was the only way in which colonial administration could work, especially in rural and more remote areas. It is therefore too simplistic for the post-colonial period to claim that in Polynesian society status is ascribed while in Melanesian society it is acquired. Often a combination of individual success or aptitude, combined with considerations of birth or genealogies, determine individuals of status even in Polynesian counties. For example, the *matai* in Samoa and those who are the sons or even daughters of 'Big Men' or chiefs in Solomon Islands or Vanuatu are more likely to have the opportunity to move up the hierarchical ladder than those who start without this advantage.

The more coherent power structure of Polynesia, with its acceptance of hierarchy, appears to have accommodated post-colonial notions of state more easily than in Melanesia, although this may have required either that the highest ranking genealogies were crushed,[29] or that they were sufficiently incorporated so as to make the modern structure acceptable to traditionalists.[30] In some Pacific Island countries, as will be seen, the traditional authority and power accorded to those of high rank has been incorporated into the formal power structure post-independence but often in a diluted form.

It is also the case today that political influence is often closely linked to traditional status, with the latter being used or acquired to promote or maintain political standing. A striking example of this is found in Samoa where, in order to be a member of parliament it is necessary to have a traditional *matai* title. This has resulted in a proliferation of such titles.[31] Similarly, in Vanuatu it is very unusual to find a Cabinet Minister who is not a chief – although they may have acquired their title on the way up the political ladder. In Tonga, members of the royal family wield considerable power through the executive roles they hold in government. In Fiji commoners may become members of the political elite but they will need to curry the patronage of chiefs if they are to succeed (Lawson 1997: 108).[32] In today's ideals of democratic government, the interrelationship of political power and traditional power leads to criticisms of corruption, nepotism, the intimidation or bribery of voters and the unequal distribution of government funded aid and development programmes.[33]

The relationship between traditional leadership and the exercise of power in western-style governments introduced into the region can also create challenges for human rights. For example, in Fiji, there has been tension concerning the power wielded by the Great Council of Chiefs, particularly as this body does not represent Indo-Fijians. Conversely, in Vanuatu, there has been concern at the lack of power conferred on the Council of Chiefs. Calls for greater democracy or wider participation in government may be seen to threaten the *status quo*. Similarly, advocacy of equal rights, the right to freely express criticism of the government or freedom of movement may all be seen as potentially undermining traditional structures and forms of organisation. An example can be seen in Tonga.

In Tonga, the traditional social structure dates back to 1845 when King Tupou 1 enacted laws to constrain the powers of chiefs – and thereby strengthen his own position. In 1862 a new landed aristocracy was created and the 1875 Constitution provided for twenty nobles, selected from traditional chiefs to be granted hereditary estates. Although this number was increased in 1880 by another ten and later a further three, the number of nobles holding hereditary estates, and who can in turn make grants of land from those estates to commoners, has remained small, elite and male. In Tonga many vestiges of traditional social organisation and status attribution appear to be preserved today. Both within households and civil society there were and are strict hierarchies. Within families the wife and children are subordinate to the father who is the head of the family. There are strict taboos between members of the opposite sex especially within the same family, and although girls have precedence over brothers, Tongan society is essentially patriarchal (James 1997: 49, 50). Moreover, unlike the situation in Samoa, the head of the family group is not be elected by family members; birth and descent are fundamental to status, social organisation and politics.[34] Although commoners are no longer solely dependent on nobles to grant them land,[35] the persistence of a feudal structure has provoked considerable disquiet and unrest in Tonga.[36] Many holders of hereditary estates are now absentee land lords – having had the benefit of overseas education and opportunities – and where all the land is in the hands of commoners holding allotments, respect for the nobility is waning, especially among younger, urbanised and educated Tongans. Consequently there have been calls for constitutional reform and associated with this, repression of the most outspoken critics of the current structures (Campbell 2005: 91).

The incorporation of traditional government in contemporary structures

As has been indicated, what may appear to be 'traditional' forms and forums of government in the region were in some instances modified or shaped by colonial administrators – sometimes with the assistance of social anthropologists, or missionaries – in order to facilitate that administration.[37] Thus clans, kinships groups, forms of succession to chiefly title and the nomenclature of chiefs established by independence are not necessarily historically traditional but have become so over a period of time. In many cases today it is increasingly difficult to distinguish pre-contact traditional forms of leadership or social organisation and those which emerged following contact. Indeed one of the problems in distinguishing traditional forms of leadership from 'western' forms of democratic leadership is due to the failure of colonial government to establish the foundations of the latter prior to independence. The manipulation of traditional forms of leadership to serve colonial purposes meant that at independence continuity with the past was achieved through the retention of these forms, while at the same time independence from colonial rule provided an opportunity for clarifying what the role and function of traditional leaders was to be. Moreover the assertion of a new nationalism fostered claims of indigenous tradition which became a post-colonial neo-tradition.

Today, traditional government in the form of individuals having chiefly status, group leaders – whether heads of clans or families or households, elders and other title holders, continue to play a significant role in the contemporary Pacific, either because they are perceived as being representative of the nation or a significant group within the nation; or because they represent local government for a centralised state; or because they provide a focus and forum which is an antithesis to the centralised state; or a combination of these.

Formal 'traditional' government

In a number of countries, traditional forms of government, or forms of government that seek to draw on traditional structures and roles, are formally included in the written constitutions acquired on independence. For example, in the Cook Islands the House of Ariki is to 'consider such matters relative to the welfare of the people of the Cook Islands as may be submitted to it by [Parliament] for its consideration, and it shall express its opinion and make recommendations thereon to [Parliament]; and ... have such other functions as may be prescribed by law'.[38] In Marshall Islands the Council of Iroij may consider 'any matter of concern to the Republic of the Marshall Islands, and it may express its opinion thereon to the Cabinet ... (and) may request ... the reconsideration of any Bill affecting the customary law, or any traditional practice, or land tenure, or any related matter, which has been adopted ... by the Nitijela'.[39] Under this provision a copy of every bill which has been adopted at a third reading has to be submitted to the Council for consideration. The Council only has seven days in which to consider the bill and comment. If it does express a view on the proposed law then the Nitijela may take that view into account – or not.[40] In Vanuatu the Constitution makes provision for the Council of Chiefs – the *Malvatamauri*,[41] which has 'a general competence to discuss all matters relating to custom and tradition and may make recommendations for the preservation and promotion of ni-Vanuatu culture and languages ... (and) may be consulted on any question, particularly any question relating to tradition and custom, in connection with any bill before Parliament.'[42]

In Fiji this has been addressed more vigorously but not without political upheaval. The Great Council of Chiefs – *Bose Levu Vakaturaga*, was constituted under the Fijian Affairs Act 1945 (Cap 120). Membership was originally by election, nomination or appointment as determined by the Governor General. The powers of the Council were

> to submit to the Governor-General such recommendations and proposals as it may deem to be for the benefit of the Fijian people, and to consider such questions relating to the good government and well being of the Fijian people as the Governor-General or the Board may from time to time submit to the Council, and to take decisions or make recommendations thereon.[43]

It was also provided that the Council might have additional powers or duties conferred on it. The 1970 independence constitution gave the Great Council of Chiefs the right to nominate senators in addition to those nominated by the Prime Minister and the Leader of the Opposition. Moreover, where any proposed amendment to the law affected Fijian or Rotuman land, customs or customary rights, the majority in the Senate had to include at least three quarters of the nominees of the Great Council of Chiefs and the Council of Rotuma. Following a military coup in 1989, a new Constitution was drafted in 1990 so as to afford greater protection to indigenous interests at a time when Indo-Fijians out-numbered Fijians. This Constitution enlarged the powers of the Great Council of Chiefs. Not only were they to be consulted on any matters concerning Fijian and Rotuman economic, social, educational, cultural, traditional and other interests, but also the Great Council of Chiefs was given the right to appoint the President and to designate the two people entitled to act in that office when necessary. It also required the President to consult with the Great Council of Chiefs and the Council of Rotuma before nominating 25 of the 34 Senators and required that they were Fijian or Rotuman. Thus although the Great Council of Chiefs did not form a political party it was likely to have considerable influence in the Senate.[44] When a commission – the 1995 Reeves Commission – was drawn up to review the 1990 Constitution its terms of reference

> required the Commission to ensure that the new arrangements would recognise, protect and guarantee the rights, paramountcy of interests and concerns of the indigenous Fijian and Rotuman people, guarantee protection and security for the land rights, fishing rights and resources of indigenous Fijians and Rotumans and recognise the Great Council of Chiefs.[45]

The Council of Chiefs was involved, along with others, in the deliberations leading to the 1997 Constitution of Fiji, which had to be approved not only by both houses of Parliament but also to be endorsed by the Great Council of Chiefs. It was this 1997 Constitution which the 2000 coup, led by George Speight, sought to overthrow, claiming that it did not sufficiently protect indigenous Fijian interests. Following the 2000 coup it was the Great Council of Chiefs that swore in the interim President. Ultimately the 1997 Constitution was reinstated and continues to ensure that the involvement of the Great Council of Chiefs in a number of constitutional functions is an added safeguard against any action that may prejudice the rights of the indigenous population.[46]

In Tonga and Samoa, traditional structures have been incorporated into the fabric of government. In Samoa only those who hold *matia* titles (chiefly titles) may sit in Parliament. Indeed until the Electoral Amendment Act 1990 only those who held such titles could vote for members of Parliament.[47] This has now changed so that all adult Samoan citizens are enfranchised. One of the consequences of this close association between chiefly titles and government however has been a proliferation of titles and consequently what many see as the abuse of the *matai* system and its debasement. At a local level traditional leaders continue to be highly influential and to yield considerable power under the Village Fono Act 1990. This legislation validates and empowers the exercise of authority by the assembly of the

Alii ma Faipule of a village over those who reside in the village, and sanctions the exercise of 'any power or authority ... in accordance with the custom and usage of that village' without stipulating what the custom of usage is.[48] As will be seen the powers of village *fono* in Samoa may be extensive and the exercise of them may conflict with human rights.[49]

In some countries, the exact status of traditional leaders is unclear. For example, in Tuvalu it has been held that:

> The authority of the matais is founded in the values and cultures of Tuvalu. It is the linch pin of the life and laws of Tuvalu protected by the Constitution. The authority of the matais requires them to make decisions to guide the people and foster their welfare. This means that ... in Tuvalu the matais necessarily and legitimately exert great influence and their decisions carry great weight.[50]

In a recent case it was recognised that 'the decision making role of the Falekaupule is part of the traditional manner of guiding the community and caring for the people's welfare'.[51] Yet the court held that the resolutions of the Falekaupule – which is a traditional body formalised by legislation – did not have the status of law. Similar confusion has arisen in Kiribati where the High Court has held that customary leaders (male elders) do not represent an organ of the state,[52] despite the Constitution stating that the people of Kiribati would continue to 'cherish and uphold the customs and traditions of Kiribati,'[53] so that an action brought against them by an individual for breach of fundamental rights cannot succeed.

In Palau, traditional leaders are incorporated into the constitutional scheme of things but not necessarily given great power at a formal level. For example, section 1 of Article V of the Constitution which deals with traditional rights states:

> The government shall take no action to prohibit or revoke the role or function of a traditional leader as recognized by custom and tradition which is not inconsistent with this Constitution, nor shall it prevent a traditional leader from being recognized, honored, or given formal or functional roles at any level of government.

A similar provision is found in the Constitution of the Federated States of Micronesia.[54]

In Vanuatu (as indicated,) the National Council of Chiefs is integrated into the Constitution under Articles 29–32 but the role is essential advisory and for some time there has been dissatisfaction expressed by the chiefs themselves and by others that they do not have a more active role.[55] Recently however, the powers of this body have been potentially strengthened through the National Council of Chiefs Act 2006 which puts the Council on a statutory footing and creates a hierarchy of chiefly councils at different levels. While its role remains essentially advisory and supervisory this new status may provide a springboard for a more influential Council.

In Vanuatu and elsewhere in the region the role, status and identity of chiefs is in a state of flux. Often there is uncertainty and dispute about who is entitled to be a chief or what the hierarchy is among different chiefs in the same locality. The confusion of political status with chiefly status, and inherited status with achieved status, creates disunity among chiefly supporters.

For example, Lal has suggested that:

> Among Fijians, the era of the dominance of paramount chiefs with overarching influence across the whole spectrum of indigenous Fijian society, tutored for national leadership by the British in the post-war years has ended. The paramounts are gone.
>
> (Lal 2003: 342)

They have been replaced, he suggests, by individuals who have insufficient training for leadership and who are more concerned with cultivating a regional or provincial power base than a national one.

The cultivation of individual following and the shift to provincial or regional focus is experienced elsewhere. In Vanuatu the proliferation of individuals standing for national elections and the ease with which elected members change parties suggests that political affiliation to a particular agenda is less important than affiliation to a particular individual. As indicated, in Samoa the proliferation of *matai* titles to qualify holders to stand for political seats led to disrespect for the traditional system. While in Solomon Islands there has been increasing demand for greater de-centralisation and the expansion of the power of local, provincial government. Thus the political prize is not so much a seat in central government – which is seen as weak and ineffective – but at the local level. Traditional polities are therefore being adapted to take advantage of new ones.

The State

Traditional foundations of power and contemporary experiences of government can create difficulties for human rights at a number of levels. International human rights instruments impose obligations on the national government of a state to put in place measures to give effect to the rights articulated in such instruments. Thus the central government, members of which relate to the external world, is expected to give internal effect to these obligations. However, the members of central government may have less interest in passing laws which give effect to the State's obligations than laws which meet their own obligations to their supporters. This is turn may explain why members of parliament are ready to 'cross the floor' to support other parties, or form new alliances or pass votes of no confidence in the government of the day.

Alternatively central government may be very keen to be seen by the external world as giving effect to the State's international obligations but incapable of implementing these obligations away from central government because of the autonomy of local or provincial government, often influenced by more traditional forms of government at the grass roots level. Another possibility is that central government identifies closely with a particular sector of society and while supportive of measures which strengthen that sector will be less supportive of measures which undermine it. Proposals to change electoral boundaries, voting systems or the number of seats reserved for particular classes of people, for example nobles in Tonga, are measures which attract this type of opposition.

Similarly, national constitutions impose obligations on the state to carry out certain functions including the effective implementation and observation of fundamental rights stated within those constitutions. The role of the state in this sense is something of an anathema in the Pacific region. While clearly independence recognised the autonomy of Pacific Island nations, the location of the state and its relationship with individual citizens is more problematic. This is not only because some new 'states' emerged, for example, Kiribati and Tuvalu from the Gilbert and Ellice Islands, and Palau from the western Carolinas, but also because under colonial administration there was no state. In most countries land became vested in the Crown so that even where native title was recognised and retained, the power to allocate or alienate land was limited. Government was by representatives of the colonial power and the policies which shaped colonial government were remote. For most Pacific islanders the experience of government lay either in their local traditional form of government or the administrative officials of the introduced colonial administration. As a consequence, for many governments and states in a western sense equated with the representatives of this administration. This dysfunctional relationship between individuals and the state persists. For many the state equates with the public sector, which is a significant employer in the region, and with central government located in the capital. Poor publicity or inadequate media coverage of government policy and initiatives means that many people are unaware of the activities of central government. For most people it is their experience with public sector institutions which shapes their perception of the state, for example, contact with the courts, the police, the tax office or the immigration authorities; or through state owned and run utilities and services. Further from urban centres and among more isolated communities this state-society interaction will be less frequent and often very minimal.

Moreover, the public sector is not the only influence on the quotidian experience of Pacific islanders. As important often is civil society: churches, sports clubs, trade unions and non-government organisations, as well as kin and clan groups (Larmour 1992). In some respects these have emerged as a consequence of the failure of state – for example, to provide social welfare benefits, access to the formal legal system or efficient health services, but they also have historical roots, especially the churches. Indeed, it is among civil society that human rights advocacy may be strongest – for example, among women's or youth groups. Civil society, however, only has limited political power. It may be effective at lobbying, or its members may have other power bases – for example a chief may also be a lay preacher or the member of an influential non-governmental organisation, but generally civil society, while advocating human rights needs the power of others to implement any changes. Civil society can however act as bridge between state and non-state, depending on the degree to which the institutions of civil society are independent from the state, and between individuals and the state. The importance of these various players in the arena of human rights will be considered later in this book.

The difficulties of accommodating the modern state within the more traditional forms of government – and *vice versa*, and the distribution of power between central and local authority and between elected and non-elected representatives continues to pose problems in the region. Differences between actual power and notional power bases can have consequences for human rights because, while international and/or domestic rights instruments may impose obligations on central government, the disjunction of this and regional government, and between modern democratic government and traditional government may mean that little can be achieved at a national level. This in turn impacts on human rights at a regional level and within the international arena.

National Governments

The political systems of the countries in the region are modelled on the standard political systems of those metropolitan powers which had an influence in the region. Apart from Tonga, all Pacific Island states underwent a process of colonial administration prior to independence, and some have not yet reached the end of that journey.[56] Tonga was exceptional in that it was never a colony. The former Friendly Islands were united into a Polynesian kingdom in 1845 and became a constitutional monarchy in 1875. In 1900 it became a British protectorate and ceased to be a protectorate in June 1970.

The impetus for conferring independent status on the colonial territories of the Pacific region was the British Prime Minister Macmillan's 'wind of change' address in 1960. Although made in the context of the growing demand for African countries to self rule, it marked a change in colonial policies for Britain. The United Nations was also calling for the move towards self-government. In accordance with the purposes and principles of the Charter of the United Nations, on 14 December 1960 the United Nations General Assembly passed the Declaration on the Granting of Independence to Colonial Countries and Peoples – resolution 1514 (XV). Consequently, not only is the right to self-determination of peoples a fundamental principle of international law, it is also enshrined in article 1 of the International Covenant on Economic, Social and Cultural Rights and article 1 of the International Covenant on Civil and Political Rights, as well as in other international human rights instruments. The United Nations envisaged several different forms of self-government: free association with an independent State, integration into an independent State, or independence.[57]

The first country to gain independence was Western Samoa (now Samoa). Formerly a colony of Germany in the period 1900–1919, it was then brought under the mandate of New Zealand by the League of Nations mandate from 1919 to 1945. Following the end of the Second World War it became a United Nations trust territory of New Zealand until it gained independence in 1962.

In 1968, the Republic of Nauru – formerly Pleasant Island – gained its independence from its former status as a United Nations Trust Territory, under the combined administration of Australia, New Zealand and the United Kingdom. In 1970, Fiji became independent after 96 years of colonial administration which had been in place since 1874 when it was ceded to Britain. Papua New Guinea became independent from Australia in 1975, and in 1976 Solomon Islands attained self-governing status. Two years later Solomon Islands became independent under its Constitution of 7 July 1978. In the same year, Tuvalu, which had formerly been part of the British protectorate of Gilbert and Ellice Islands, governed by the High Commissioner of the Western Pacific, and then the British colony of Gilbert and Ellice Islands, gained its independence and a year later Kiribati, also formerly part of the Gilbert and Ellice Islands, became independent. In the same year the Federated States of Micronesia, formerly a part of the Trust Territory of the Pacific Islands, formed its own constitutional government on 10 May 1979. In 1980 the Republic of Vanuatu, formerly the New Hebrides and ruled by an Anglo-French Condominium government from 1906–1980, achieved independence on 30 July. It was not until 1986 that Marshall Islands gained independence from the United States of America administration of the country as a United Nations Trust Territory. In the same year a Compact of Free Association with the United States – which had been signed in 1983, entered into force. Under the Compact, the country is fully sovereign in domestic and foreign affairs, but gives responsibility for defence to the United States.

In 1994 the Republic of Palau became independent, having resolved not to become part of the Federated States of Micronesia in 1973. A Compact of Free Association with the United States was approved in 1986, but not ratified until 1993 and did not come into force until 1994. In 2006 the people of Tokelau decided not become self-governing and the country remains a territory of New Zealand, which has been its status since 1925 when it ceased to be a British protectorate.[58] Pitcairn Islands remains a British dependent territory.

The forms and structures of government achieved at independence were largely based on the Westminster model. In most of the South Pacific countries the prime minister is the head of the cabinet but countries such as Kiribati and Nauru have a presidential system, although unlike the American system, the President is elected and can be removed from office following a vote of no confidence. The head of government, either the prime minister or president in the case of Nauru and Kiribati, is responsible for appointing cabinet ministers. The exception is Tonga, where the King is responsible for appointing members of the cabinet, the prime minister and the legislative assembly. The members of parliament are elected by the electorate although different electoral systems are found. Some countries, such as Fiji and Tonga, have two houses in the legislative assembly, others, such as Samoa, Solomon Islands, Niue and Nauru have a unicameral parliament. In Tokelau each of the three islands has a separate government for local matters. Some of the countries of the region have declared themselves to be republics. Fiji became republic after a coup in 1987. Kiribati, Nauru, Palau and Vanuatu declared themselves republics at the time of their independence.

In the self-governing countries of Cook Islands and Niue, under an agreement of free association with New Zealand, the two countries are responsible for the administration of their internal affairs and New Zealand is responsible for military and foreign affairs in conjunction with the advice of the two governments.[59] Had there been the necessary two thirds majority of the referendum in Tokelau its relationship with New Zealand would have been similar to that of Cook Islands and Niue, under a compact of free-association (Gregory 2006). Although Tonga is the only monarchy in the region other countries retain the British monarch as the honorific head of state. These countries are Cook Islands, Niue, Solomon Islands and Tuvalu. In Fiji and Vanuatu an elected President is Head of State. In these countries the President, although not involved in the day to day affairs of government, has some significant powers. For example, in Vanuatu the approval of the President is required for an act of parliament to become law, and in Fiji the President determines who is to be Prime Minister.

Table 1.1 presents a summary of the key political features of the island countries under consideration.

In principle, the island countries of the South Pacific region respect the separation of powers between the legislative, the executive and the judiciary based on the colonial powers administrative structures. The separation of powers is enshrined in the constitutions of all these countries. In the case of Solomon Islands, Papua New Guinea and Vanuatu, a form of provincial government system was adopted with the main objective of spreading development to the rural areas. In recent years there has been some pressure to increase the powers of the provinces at the expense of national government. In Papua New Guinea the region of Bougainville seceded

Table 1.1 Key features of Pacific Island countries

Country	Status with date of acquisition of such	Size (Land sq. km)[a]	Population[b]	Government
Cook Islands	Self-governing in free association with New Zealand (1965). Queen Elizabeth II is chief of state	237	14,000	Unicameral with an advisory council of chiefs – the House of Ariki
Federated States of Micronesia	Self-governing (1979) with a Compact of Free Association with the US (1986)[c]	701	112,700	Unicameral
Fiji Islands	Self-governing republic (1970)	18,272	836,000	Bicameral – Senate and House of Representatives. The Great Council of Chiefs which advises the President on the appointment of 24 of the 34 senate seats
Kiribati	Self-governing republic (1979)[d]	811	93,100	Unicameral
Marshall Islands	Self-governing with a Compact of Free Association with US (1986)[e]	181	55,400	Unicameral with an advisory Council of Chiefs
Nauru	Self governing republic (1968)	21	10,100	Unicameral
Niue	Self governing in free Association with New Zealand (1974)	259	1,600	Unicameral
Papua New Guinea	Constitutional monarchy (1975). Queen Elizabeth II is chief of state represented by a governor general	462,840	5,695,300	Unicameral
Palau	Self-governing (1978) in free association with the US[f]	488	20,700	Bicameral – Senate and House of Delegates
Pitcairn	Overseas territory of the UK. Queen Elizabeth II is represented by the UK High Commissioner to New Zealand	39	46[g]	Unicameral Island Council
Samoa[h]	Self-governing republic with an elected head of state	2,935	182,700	Unicameral

Continued

Table 1.1 Cont'd

Country	Status with date of acquisition of such	Size (Land sq. km)[a]	Population[b]	Government
Solomon Islands	Self governing parliamentary democracy with Queen Elizabeth II as chief of state (1978)	28,370	460,100	Unicameral
Tokelau	Administered by New Zealand (1925) as a colony but voting on self determination 2006[i]	12	1,500	Unicameral General *Fono* with limited legislative power[j]
Tonga	Hereditary Constitutional Monarchy (1875)	650	98,300	Unicameral legislative assembly
Tuvalu	Constitutional monarchy with Queen Elizabeth II chief of state represented by a Governor (1978)	26	9,600	Unicameral House of Assembly
Vanuatu	Parliamentary republic (1980)	12,190	215,800	Unicameral with an advisory National Council of Chiefs

a. Statistics taken from Pacific Islands Populations 2004, Secretariat of the Pacific Community. These statistics vary slightly from those found elsewhere.
b. As above. These are mid-year estimates.
c. Compact of Free Association, 3 November 1986, amended May 2004.
d. Formerly known as the Gilbert Islands which were granted self-rule by the UK in 1971. Until 1979 the US claimed the Phoenix and Line Islands but relinquished these to Kiribati in 1979.
e. Amended in 2004.
f. Compact of Free Association approved in 1986, entered into force 1994.
g. This estimate is taken from the CIA World Fact Book on Pitcairn, http://www.cia.gov/cia/publications/factbook/geos/pc.html#People (16/01/06).
h. Until 1997 Samoa was known as Western Samoa – to distinguish it from American Samoa.
i. Currently Tokelau is administered under the Tokelau Islands Act 1948 (amended in 1970). Queen Elizabeth II is chief of state and the UK and New Zealand are represented by an Administrator.
j. Tokelau Amendment Act 1996.

from centralised government and acquired its own constitution in 2004. In Solomon Islands a 2004 Bill envisages a federal constitution which would divide Solomon Islands into separate semi-autonomous states.[60] At present this Bill does not seem to be tabled before Parliament and therefore its future is currently uncertain (Corrin 2007).

In Federated States of Micronesia a federal government system was put in place after the Compact of Free Association with the United States came into force in 1986. In some respects this federal system is similar to the provincial system adopted by the Melanesian countries. However, the difference between the two systems is that with the provincial system the power is centralised at the national government, whereas in a federal system the states are responsible for internal administration of their own states, the national government is only responsible for external matters and then only to the extent that it has autonomy in these. So, for example, in the Federated States of Micronesia most matters of government except for defence and foreign affairs are carried out at state level. Indeed, each state has its own distinctive constitution. Representatives of each state meet in the Congress of the Federated States of Micronesia.[61] Each State also has its own constitutional government with three co-equal branches of government consisting of the executive, legislative, and judicial branches.

In Tonga the situation is quite different. The King as the Head of State controls the government. In other words, the administrative structure in Tonga is not free or independent. There is the possibility of interference in the three components of the government by the Head of State. The persistence of this political structure has had a profound impact on the development of democracy in Tonga and the experience of human rights. Things may however be changing. In 2005 elected Members of Parliament were appointed to the Cabinet, marking a break from the pervious practice whereby Cabinet Ministers had been hand-picked from outside Parliament by the King. In November 2006 King Tupou V promised greater democracy in government, which is meant to be given effect in 2008.[62]

One of the on-going concerns debated in the region is whether the constitutional provisions and structures inherited at independence are appropriate or even workable in the Pacific context (Deklin 1992; Ghai 1988). A number of the key features of the forms of government found in the Pacific appear not to work very well or fall short of the standards expected by external agencies and often their own citizens. Among these are ideas of democracy, accountability and transparency of government, efficiency and integrity in the public service, free and fair elections and good governance.

These are not solely matters of political concern at the domestic, regional and international level. They impact on the economic welfare of Pacific Island countries, the esteem in which they are held by the international community, and in turn the strength or weakness of human rights of the region as well as of individual states.

The relationship between customary structures and systems and received systems and structures in the politico-legal systems of the region is also often unclear and uneasy. At times these two spheres seem to operate in parallel. For example, in Vanuatu provincial boundaries cut across islands, but each island has its own council of chiefs as well as its own languages, culture and land tenure systems. Similarly, electoral boundaries may be drawn so as to divide those who have shared interests or may force together those who have little in common and may indeed be traditional enemies. Even when these different systems and structures operate together there may be inconsistency and confusion as regards spheres of authority and responsibility (Hughes 2005). While this may be partially a legacy from colonialism, when the state represented the alien, the introduced and sometimes the repressive, post-independence it can be argued that this should no longer be the case and certainly the opening declarations in the constitutions of the region resonate with a sense of ownership by Pacific islanders for the governance of their country. Nevertheless there is also a sense of disjuncture between the identity of the state and the identity of individuals, although as Lamour suggests, this is not necessarily a problem restricted to Pacific Islands (Larmour 1992: 116, 117).

Foreign influences

One of the unifying themes determining the selection of the countries considered in this book is the influence – either directly or indirectly – of English common law. There have however been a range of external influences in the region particularly during colonial government. Fiji Islands, Solomon Islands, Kiribati, Tuvalu, Tonga and Vanuatu all came under British influence, while the latter also came under French influence under the joint Anglo-French Condominium rule of the New Hebrides – as Vanuatu was before independence. Papua New Guinea and Nauru came under Australian influence, while Samoa, Cook Islands and Niue were under the influence of New Zealand. Some of these countries also came under the trusteeship of the United Nations, for example, Samoa, Nauru, Papua New Guinea and the Marshall Islands, either in preparation for independence or as a result of political changes during the Second World War.

Nor should it be forgotten that other foreign countries had an influence in the region. For example, Samoa was annexed as a colony of Germany in 1899 and remained a German colony until 1914 when it came under military occupation by New Zealand. Germany also had an influence in Solomon Islands, with parts of the country coming under German control from 1885 until 1900. Nauru also came under German influence, being annexed and declared to be a colony of Germany in 1888 and was not liberated until the end of the First World War.

Asia-Pacific influences

A number of countries of the region came under Japanese occupation during the Second World War, for example, Nauru, Solomon Islands, and the German-held territories of what is now the Federated States of Micronesia. Although Japan lost its influence as a consequence of its defeat by allied forces, it is today an important player in the region, not only because of its place in the wider Pacific region but because of its investment and assistance to Pacific Island countries. For example, in 2002 Japan provided US$401,000 to the Pacific Islands Forum Secretariat for its annual projects. Since 1996 Japan has provided the Secretariat with US$6.1 million.[63] In 2006 Japan pledged 45 billion yen (US$399.5 million) to Fiji and other Pacific Island Forum member countries over the next three years.[64] Japan is also involved with matters such as fisheries projects in the Solomon Islands,[65] environmental training programmes in Samoa and Palau,[66] the preservation of cultural heritage in the Federated States of Micronesia,[67] contributions to the development of infrastructure in the region, for example, bridges in Papua New Guinea (Nicholas 2001), and grant assistance to the development of grassroots projects in Vanuatu.[68] Indeed a number of Pacific Island countries see Japan as a major benefactor of the region, not only providing export markets for agricultural and marine products but also funding a variety of projects regardless of the size of the country. Since 1997 there have been regular summit meetings between Japan and the Pacific Island countries and official visits by heads of state in both directions take place. In 2000 the annual meeting between government representatives of Japan and South Pacific Forum members (Australia, the Cook Islands, Federated States of Micronesia, the Fiji Islands, Kiribati, Nauru, New Zealand, Niue, Palau, Papua New Guinea, Republic of the Marshall Islands, Samoa, Solomon Islands, Tonga, Tuvalu and Vanuatu) held in Miyazaki, Japan, led to the 'Miyazaki Palm Declaration: Our Common Vision For The Future'. This sets out the mid to long term priorities for South Pacific-Japan co-operation. As will be seen, however, Japanese aid, although beneficial in many respects, also comes at a price, particularly with regards to some of the natural resources of the region. It has also been pointed out in the Cook Islands – which is sceptical of Japanese interest in the Pacific – that Japan's contribution to the Pacific Island countries may be motivated by the country's perceived need to counterbalance the influence of China in the region.[69]

Historically, China has had an interest in the Melanesian Islands of the Pacific. Chinese people are settled throughout much of the region and China exports around US$69 million in goods to the region. It also provides an export market for Pacific Islands products worth around $130 million (Seneviratne 2000). China became much more active in aid donations when Taiwan started to become interested in the region. For example, China has strong links with Papua New Guinea. In early 2007 it was report that

'Papua New Guinea is China's largest trading partner in the Pacific', with an annual trade value of US$518 million in 2006 (Yakham 2007).

In recent years, China's influence has been extended to other countries in the region. For example, in 2004 China had approved an aid package of $20 million for economic development in Tonga,[70] and in 2006 the Tongan government was seeking a loan of US$29.4 million from China for a package of measures.[71] Aid from China is welcomed because it is seen as having 'no-strings attached' according to the then Deputy Prime Minister of Vanuatu, Serge Vohoor, who received a cheque for US$313,589 from China in 2001.[72] Other countries have expressed some reserves. For example, in Papua New Guinea it has been suggested that aid – as opposed to trade – may not come without political strings. Indeed caution has been expressed about having such close dealings with a country which is communist, has a poor human rights record and lacks the democratic freedoms enjoyed in Papua New Guinea.

In April 2006 the first China-Pacific Leaders Forum was held in Nadi, Fiji. The aim of the conference was to launch a Chinese proposal for regular ministerial level meetings to discuss trade and economic development for Fiji and other Pacific Island countries.[73] However, those countries that recognise or trade with the Chinese government in Taiwan tend to be viewed less favourably that those who support China's 'One China Policy'.

As long as Taiwan remains active in the Pacific region it is likely that China will seek to match or better any offers made by Taiwan, particularly as a number of Pacific Island countries change their allegiance from time to time from China to Taiwan and back again, for example, Papua New Guinea, Vanuatu, Nauru, and in 2004 Kiribati. As stated in the Papua New Guinea press:

> The worldwide battle between China and Taiwan, with the latter seeking international recognition, has spilled over into our own region. Both the Chinese and the Taiwanese are doing everything within their power to win the political support of the South Pacific nations, particularly as expressed in world forums. And each group backs up that determination with hefty financial inputs for those countries whose political stance is clear and unequivocal.[74]

Manipulation of Pacific Island countries by donors is a concern. Academic commentator Professor Ron Crocombe has suggested that 'the Chinese are playing a long-term game for access to Pacific fish stocks which they already have and possible seabed mining opportunities. In Papua New Guinea, the Chinese are moving into investment in mining and gas extraction' (quoted by Keith-Reid and Pareti 2006).

Affiliation to contesting political entities is causing a rupture in the Pacific Forum. In April 2006, the Chinese Premier Wen Jiabou met with

Pacific leaders supportive of the 'One China policy' in Fiji. These were the prime ministers of Papua New Guinea, Samoa, Tonga, Cook Islands, Fiji and Vanuatu and the president of the Federated States of Micronesia – all countries which recognise China in return for economic aid. The Forum member countries which he did not meet with were those which recognise Taiwan: Tuvalu, Kiribati, Palau, the Solomon Islands, Nauru, Palau and the Marshall Islands. Although not recognised by Beijing, Taiwan enjoys formal relationships with many countries in the region.

South Korea is also active in the region, contributing financial and technical assistance in a number of ways. For example, it has been involved in strengthening fisheries legislation through assistance to the Pacific Forum;[75] in supporting improved use of forest and tree resources in the region through funding to the Secretariat of the Pacific Community;[76] in assisting Papua New Guinea with storm water drainage projects;[77] and in funding a trade policy advisor to the Pacific Forum Secretariat.[78] Korean overtures to the region continue, with for example Korea suggesting that Fiji should open an embassy in Korea in order to promote its tourism,[79] and in 2006 South Korea opened a consulate in Solomon Islands.[80]

Relations with the European Union

In contrast to the growing influence of the Asia-Pacific countries, Germany, France and indeed Great Britain are today far less influential in the region.[81] In 2004, Britain started the process of reducing its representation in the region, closing high commissions in Vanuatu, Kiribati and Tonga. For much of the region the European Union has now become almost the sole point of contact with Europe.

Formal relations with the European Community were established under the first Lomé Convention in 1975, which was a co-operation agreement between non-European states and the Community. These were countries from Africa, the Caribbean and the Pacific (ACP countries). In the Pacific Fiji, Tonga and Samoa were parties to the Convention and Papua New Guinea, Solomon Islands, Tuvalu, Kiribati and Vanuatu joined subsequently. Further Lomé conventions followed. The main aim of these was to facilitate favourable trade co-operation through preferential tariffs for ACP countries. In 2000 this framework was replaced by the ACP-EU Cotonou Agreement. This agreement encompassed not only the existing Pacific parties but also now included Marshall Islands, the Federated States of Micronesia, Nauru, Palau, Cook Islands and Niue. Pitcairn is included as an overseas dependent territory of the United Kingdom. While the Cotonou Agreement is still directed at facilitating trade through preferential trading terms to ACP countries, it aims to do this by assisting in the development of ACP countries with the ultimate purpose of integrating them into the world economy. Included within this goal is the intention to conclude economic trade partnership agreements which are compatible with World Trade Organisation criteria, and which remove trade barriers between the European Union and ACP countries and enhance cooperation in all areas relevant to trade. The aim was to commence putting in place these Economic Partnership Agreements in September 2002 and to conclude them by December 2007.[82] As part of the aim of facilitating development the European Union Development Fund has financed a number of projects in the region as well as providing technical co-operation. In the period 1975–2002 the fund provided €165 million to finance Pacific ACP regional projects.[83] Projects supported under the various Lomé Conventions included regional initiatives in telecommunications and human resource development; the development of regional transport, energy communications infrastructure and training; support for tourism development, and strategic sectors of agriculture and fisheries. In the last decade of Lomé new areas of intervention included support for projects directed as the environment and the sustainable development of natural resources. Under Cotonou a number of these projects have continued but there is also the objective of fostering a regional free-trade area among the Pacific Island countries.

Fiji in particular benefits from preferential trade arrangements with the EU under the Sugar Protocol and Special Preferential Sugar Agreement (Serrano 2007). However, recent political upheaval in Fiji may have jeopardised this.

Included within the stated aims of European Union policy towards ACP countries is to help to promote and sustain democracy, human dignity and social justice and pluralism, the full respect of human rights and fundamental freedoms, to develop and strengthen the rule of law and the professionalism and independence of the judiciary and to ensure transparent and accountable governance and administration in all public institutions.[84] In 2006 the Council of the European Union condemned the military take-over in Fiji and wrote to the President H.E. Ratu Josefa Iloilo, expressing its concern and in particular the breach of fundamental human rights and the respect for the rule of law that underpinned ACP-EU agreements. The Fiji government was invited to make representations to the Council in Brussels to address these concerns. It did so in April 2007. Although the European Union did not terminate all financial assistance to Fiji, it did make the continuation of some financial assistance conditional on the Fiji government meeting a number of its expressed commitments. For example, the finalisation of the Country Strategy Paper and National Indicative Programme for the tenth round of European Union Development Funding is now subject to the Fiji government meeting the commitments made with regard to human rights and the rule of law. The 2008 sugar allocation is dependent on sufficient evidence of preparations for new elections, while that of 2009 is dependent on a legitimate democratically elected government being in place.[85] The European Union has also indicated that it will continue to closely monitor the situation in Fiji.[86] It may be therefore that although some of the development initiatives supported by the European Union raise concerns regarding human rights, the financial pressure that the Council is able to bring to bear at government level could see an improvement in fundamental rights in extreme circumstances.

The economic environment

Even where Pacific Island countries are legally sovereign states many remain economically dependent on external support by way of trade, aid funding, scholarship programmes and other forms of association. In some cases it is difficult to see how this cycle of dependency will ever to broken. There are of course positive benefits from overseas aid funding, for example, improved health services or greater provision in education, but even these may have longer term negative consequences, for example, rapid population growth without commensurate economic development, or raised expectations of waged, skilled or professional employment which are likely to be frustrated or unfulfilled in many Pacific Island economies, prompting migration, or political unrest. Indeed, the growing divide between the material wealth of some urban dwellers, compared to the relative economic poverty of rural dwellers, can also lead to an increase in criminal activity and general dissatisfaction with the *status quo*.[87] While not all dissatisfaction with government will lead to political unrest or military coups, at a local level it can lead to civil disobedience, the break down in law and order and lack of respect for the rights of others. This in turn may contribute to threats to fundamental rights.[88] For example, in Vanuatu, increasing criminal activity in the urban areas of Vanuatu has led councils of chiefs to meet to consider the prime causes. Among these they see the right of free movement enshrined in the Constitution which facilitates urban drift and related problems of unemployment (Marango 2008).

Economic independence or dependence?

Dependency on foreign aid is linked to the economic health of the region. A number of the Pacific Islands under consideration are among the least developed countries of the world and although their relatively small population numbers may return a higher GDP than some African countries, many remain heavily reliant on imports, aid and remittances.

Table 1.2 gives an indication of the economic environment in the Pacific Island countries under consideration.

The statistics, even as estimates, indicate the imbalance between exports and imports and also explain why aid funding is likely to be required and desired for any major development initiatives. In some respects however the picture is misleading. The statistics may fail to take into account the large numbers of Pacific Island people, especially in more rural areas, who are

Table 1.2 The economic environment in the Pacific Island countries under consideration

Country	GDP (Purchasing power parity)	Exports	Imports
Cook Islands	$105 million (2001 est.)	$9.1 million (2000)	$50.7 million (2000)
Federated States of Micronesia	$277 million (2002 est.)	$22 million (1999 est.)	$149,000 (1999 est.)
Fiji Islands	$5,012 billion (2003 est.)	4609 million (2002)	$835 million (2002)
Kiribati	$79 million (2001 est.)	$35 million (2002)	$83 million (2002)
Marshall Islands	$115 million (2001 est.)	$9 million (2000)	454 million (2000)
Nauru	$60 million (2001 est.)	$18 million (2002)	$31 million (2002)
Niue	$7.6 million (2000 est.)	$137,200 (1999)	$2.38 million (1999)
Papua New Guinea	$11.48 billion (2003 est.)	$1.938 billion (2003 est.)	$967 million (2003 est.)
Palau	$174 million	$18 million (2001 est.)	$99 million (2001 est.)
Pitcairn Samoa	$1 billion (2002 est.)	$14 million (2002)	$113 million (2002)
Solomon Islands	$800 million (2001 est.)	$90 million (2002 est.)	$100 million (2002 est.)
Tokelau	$1.5 million (1993 est.)	$98,000 (1983 est.)	$323,000 (1983 est.)
Tonga	$236 million (2001 est.)	$27 million (2002 est.)	$86 million (2002 est.)
Tuvalu	$12,2 million (2000 EST.)	$1 million (2002)	$79 million (2002)
Vanuatu	$563 million (2002 est.)	$79 million (2002)	$138 million (2002)

Source: These figures are taken from The World Factbook, http://www.cia.gov/cia/publications/factbook

living subsistence economies, or the circulation of wealth within countries where one person's wages may support a number of family members in various ways. It is also not clear to what extent these figures include the value of remittances, both in cash and kind, sent back to Pacific Island countries by those living outside it, or the value of shared labour and non-monetary resources.

The assessment of economic development on the basis of externally imposed criteria is however relevant because it influences perceptions of development or lack thereof in the region and contributes to the pressure on Pacific Island countries 'to do better'. In response, national and regional development plans are directed at economic growth. An example can be found in the Pacific Plan of the Pacific Islands Forum Secretariat. The Pacific Plan lists as its economic priorities for the region for the period 2006–2008 the following:

- Expansion of market for trade in goods under the South Pacific Regional Trade and Economic Cooperation Agreement (SPARTECA), the Pacific Island Countries Trade Agreement (PICTA) and the Pacific Agreement on Closer Economic Relations (PACER), and with non-Forum trading partners
- Integration of trade in services, including temporary movement of labour within the Pacific Island Countries Trade Agreement framework (PICTA) and Economic Partnerships Agreements (EPA)
- Timely and effective implementation of the Regional Trade Facilitation Programme (RTFP)
- Investigation of the potential impacts under the Pacific Agreement on Closer Economic Relations (PACER) of a move towards a comprehensive framework for trade (including services) and economic cooperation between Australia, New Zealand and the Forum Island Countries
- Maximisation of sustainable returns from fisheries by development of an ecosystem-based fishery management planning framework; encouragement of effective fisheries development, including value-adding activities; and collaboration to ensure legislation and access frameworks are harmonised
- Intensified development of proposals or strategies for regional bulk purchasing, storage and distribution of petroleum
- Implementation of the Forum Principles on Regional Transport Services (FPRTS) including development of the Pacific Aviation Safety Office (PASO) and intensify focus on enhancing shipping services for Smaller Island States
- Intensified implementation of a regional digital strategy for improving information and communication technology
- Support of private sector mechanisms including through the Pacific Islands Private Sector Organisation (PIPSO).[89]

These are ambitious projects and not only require considerable political will on the part of Forum member countries but also resources to implement the necessary frameworks and personnel required to support such projects. Whether all or indeed any of these goals will be achieved in the time period indicated is questionable. It is also questionable whether all these initiatives are desirable or beneficial (Kelsey 2005). The Pacific Network on Globalisation (PANG) has been critical of PICTA, PACER and the EU economic partnership agreements. In particular the organisation is concerned that the Pacific countries are not forced into agreements that have negative impacts for Pacific societies, livelihoods, and culture. Similarly OXFAM has cast doubts on the economic agenda behind New Zealand's support of a free-trade zone in the Pacific (2007).

Potential challenges are highlighted in a recent Australian report. The report, entitled 'Pacific 2020: Challenges and Opportunities for Growth', published in May 2006, opens by stating

> The overall performance of the Pacific Island countries in the course of the past two decades has been poor. The region suffers from high unemployment and joblessness, and governments are failing to meet the expectations of their citizens. Several countries suffer from social or political instability, or serious crime. Some face daunting health or environmental challenges. Without an upturn in economic growth, the future for these countries is at best uncertain and at worst bleak.[90]

It goes on to indicate that four out of five Micronesian countries had negative economic growth and that in Melanesia only Fiji managed an economic growth rate over one per cent in the period 1990–2004 – although since 2006 Fiji's economy has declined. Throughout the region economic growth was lower than comparable developing countries. The report suggests that there are three economic possibilities facing the region: failure to achieve economic growth; maintenance of the *status quo* buoyed up by aid packages and outward migration; and rapid economic growth facilitated by major reforms. The report advocates the latter. It identifies as the major obstacles to positive economic growth: weak governance and poor functioning of government institutions; poor and insufficient infrastructure; insufficiently developed regional cooperation and economic integration and lack of commitment to implement reforms. The report focuses on five areas of productivity which it sees as needing development if economic growth is to be achieved. These are: agriculture, fisheries, forestry, mining and petroleum, and tourism.

These areas of activity are already being exploited and developed in the region, often with little thought being given to sustainability, the social and environmental impact on indigenous people, or the long-term impact on the survival of Pacific Islands subject to such exploitation. As will be seen in Chapter Four, the exploitation of what are primarily natural resources, while it might be good for the economy, can pose considerable difficulties and challenges for a range of fundamental rights. At the same time it is clear that near neighbours are encouraging Pacific Islands towards more rapid development and greater exploitation of resources.

In the meantime, the economies of most Pacific Island countries remain poor and subject to the detrimental effect of factors ranging from natural disasters to political coups. The Australian Government's statement on the Pacific on its overseas aid page states:

> The fragile states of the Pacific are especially vulnerable to developmental decline due to their small size, lack of economic diversity, remoteness

from major trade and commercial sectors, and weak governance frameworks.

Economic gains have been weak, volatile, and unequally distributed. Weak public expenditure frameworks have affected the quality and distribution of key services and infrastructure. Social instability has hampered growth ... Growing populations pose future challenges for sustainable development.[91]

Aid

In 2000, the United Nations established eight Millennium Goals. These are: to eradicate extreme poverty and hunger; achieve universal primary education; promote gender equality and empower women; reduce child mortality; improve maternal health; combat HIV/AIDS, malaria and other diseases; ensure environmental sustainability; and develop a global partnership for development.[92] Given that two-thirds of the world's poorest people live in the wider Asia-Pacific region it follows that these goals cannot be achieved without assistance from wealthier more developed nations. Indeed, to date, only two countries of the region, Fiji and Papua New Guinea, have even filed progress reports on the Millennium Development Goals.[93]

In the Pacific Island countries under consideration obstacles to economic growth, combined with internal and external pressures to develop monetary economies, mean continuing dependency on foreign aid and technical assistance. Sometimes this aid is channelled through large international organisations such as agencies of the United Nations, in other cases it is directed at specific countries or initiatives, for example, immunisation programmes, infra-structure construction or the provision of health centres, primary schools or hospitals. Often projects are co-funded by two or more aid donors.[94] This can facilitate the practical implementation of policies such as those articulated in the Pacific Plan. At the same time, however, it can compromise the autonomy or Pacific Islands countries and also lead to the problem, identified in the 2020 Report referred to previously, of lack of national ownership of initiatives and related to this failure to maintain or follow through projects beneficial to the national economy. Outstanding loan repayments or failure by national governments to meet their commitment of a funded initiative may also prove a stumbling block, as may the limited involvement of local people in the conception or management of such projects.

Table 1.3 illustrates the role of foreign aid in the region.

The largest regional donor is probably Australia which in 2002 gave AU\$175.80 million to Pacific Island countries, followed by Japan which gave AU\$ 164.0 million and then New Zealand which gave AU\$79.2 million.[95] Actual aid received or given in any period is difficult to pinpoint accurately. A number of the figures given are estimates; events and circumstances since the aid period indicated may have seen an increase or decrease

Table 1.3 The role of foreign aid in the region

Recipient country	Aid period	Amount of aid in US$	Donor country(ies)
Cook Islands	1995	13.1 million	New Zealand largely
FSM	1986–2001	1.3 billion	United States
Fiji	1995	40.3 million	
Kiribati	2001	15.5 million	UK, Japan, Australia, New Zealand and China
Nauru	2000	2.25 million	Australia
Niue	2002	2.6 million	New Zealand
Marshall Islands	1986–2000	1 billion	United States
Papua New Guinea	1999	400 million	
Palau	1994–2009	700 million	United States
Samoa	1995	42.9	
Solomon Islands	2001	21 million	Australia
Tonga		5.5 million 2.3 million	Australia
Tokelau	Annually	4 million	New Zealand
Tuvalu	1999	35 million	Tuvalu International Trust Fund – Australia, New Zealand, Japan, South Korea and UK
Vanuatu	1995	45.8 million	

Source: CIA World Factbook, http://www.cia.gov/cia/publications/factbook/geos/ps.html

in aid. For example, the Federated States of Micronesia have experienced a reduction in foreign aid with the ending of the original aid commitment under the Compact of Free Association with the United States in 2001. However, a new Compact was negotiated in 2003 under which the United States will provide $1.8 billion economic assistance over a period of twenty years. Also engagement with the European Union under the Cotonou Agreement now gives the Federated States of Micronesia access to European Union Development Fund monies.

The roller-coaster of economic growth experienced in the region is illustrated by Nauru. Exploitation of Nauru's phosphate resources, first by the Pacific Phosphate Company (a German-British consortium) in 1907 and then later by an Australia, New Zealand and UK consortium – the British Phosphate Company – over a 90-year period has left all but 10 per cent of the country a wasteland denuded of top soil and with very limited fresh water supplies. Once the wealthiest country of the region, with one of the highest GDP per capita in the world, in recent years it has been bankrupt.

Nauru's bankruptcy has rendered it increasingly dependent on Australia and in a weak bargaining position when it comes to intergovernmental negotiations. The creation of two asylum detention camps on Nauru in 2001 for more than 1,500 illegal immigrants seeking asylum is an example (Barutciski 2005: 11). In return for substantial aid Nauru – and Papua

New Guinea – agreed to the setting up of detention centres for refugees seeking asylum in Australia. Indeed, it appears that the asylum seekers were re-routed to Nauru in the Norwegian ship *MV Tampa* before the official inter-governmental arrangements were even concluded.[96,97] Nevertheless, the funding received by Nauru in return has been a welcome contribution to Nauru's weak economy.

Australia also subsidises Nauru's over-staffed public service. In a recent Asian Development Bank Report, it has been stated that continued aid funding for public services is essential for keeping Nauru's economy afloat (ADB 2008). While some improvement in the economy may be expected from a limited resumption in phosphate mining, the closing of the Australian asylum seekers camp on the island will bring to an end that source of revenue. In the longer term economic growth potential includes offshore fishing, long-line fishing, small-scale local agriculture and services such as construction, finance and insurance, and tourism. Whether Nauruans, who have become accustomed to a diet largely dependent on imported foodstuffs, will embrace these ideas remains to be seen. Tourism, however, is unlikely to flourish until there are better public utilities and competitive regular flights to Nauru.

It is not only in the case of Nauru that economic assistance or other aid may be provided at a price. For example, aid to Palau is in return for the provision of military facilities, while a considerable portion of aid to Marshall Islands is in the form of compensation for nuclear testing and the continued hosting of key installations in the United States missile defence network. Aid provided to the Federated States of Micronesia under the original Compact of Free Association was in return for exclusive American use of the country's airspace, territorial waters and land.

Aid or assistance can take a number of forms. The region has also seen military intervention by outside agencies on a number of occasions, most recently with the deployment of Australian and New Zealand forces in Tonga following a spate of attacks on business premises – a number of which were owned by the King or important Ministers – by local people (Sevele 2006). While the rioting may have been an opportunity for criminal conduct it is also believed to be a symptom of frustration among many Tongans who support the pro-democracy movement in Tonga. The swift response of the combined foreign forces at the invitation of the Prime Minister, whose government has made few concessions to the pro-democracy movement, raises questions about the human rights priorities of these external powers.

While Australia refused to provide troops to intervene in the 2006 Coup in Fiji at the request of the threatened government – although it had troops on standby – it has been less reluctant on other occasions. For example, in Solomon Islands the Regional Assistance Mission to the Solomon Islands (RAMSI) which was deployed in 2003 has seen a substantial increase in Australian intervention in Solomon Islands, albeit with assistance from other Pacific Island Countries. While the aim of the Mission is to enable Solomon Islands to return to stability, peace and economic development, many key posts remain occupied by ex-patriates especially in the police and justice sectors and there have been some concerns about abuse of human rights by RAMSI personnel.

Conclusion

The purpose of this chapter has been to establish the context in which human rights operate in the region. There are many factors at play here. While, as will be seen in the next chapter, there are clear statements recognising and endorsing the rights of Pacific Islands' people to certain fundamental rights and a number of structures and institutions which can protect and uphold these, there are also obstacles which can undermine or negative such rights, such as lack of resources, conflicting hierarchies of values and lack of political will or effective power. The civil, political and economic rights of Pacific Island people are all influenced by the social, political and economic environment found in the region and this environment impacts on the success or otherwise of rights claims. It is against this background that specific rights and future possibilities have to be considered.

Notes

1 The United Kingdom was a founding member but withdrew for the second time (the first being 1996–1998) in 2005.
2 Papua New Guinea has its own university. There is also a National University in Samoa as well as a campus of the University of the South Pacific.
3 Further reference is made to these various organisations and regional initiatives in Chapter Nine.
4 Vanuatu also came under the influence of French civil law under the Condominium, but post independence, due to a number of factors, this has largely fallen into disuse – see Farran (2004a).
5 Pitcairn and Tokelau are not self-governing.
6 In New Caledonia – which lies outside the region under consideration – indigenous *Kanaks* are currently outnumbered by French colonial settlers.
7 Pitcairn has a smaller population – under 50 persons – but these are the descendants of Anglo-Polynesians.
8 Vital Statistics in Fiji, 1981–1982, 1983.
9 Estimated poulation growth rates 2006–2010, http://www.spc.int/demog/en/stats/2006/Pacific%20Island%20Populations%202006-2015%20-%2030%20Oct%2006.xls (accessed 29 May 2007).
10 New Zealand Statistics, http://www.stats.govt.nz/cmsapp/templates/system/migration.aspx?NRMODE=Pubis (accessed 1 February 2006).
11 One avenue of migration sometimes overlooked is religious affiliation. It has been estimated for example that over 10,000 Mormon Tongans live in the United States of America, and given that 30 per cent of the Tongan population

is reportedly Mormon this emigration path seems likely to continue (Franco 1997: 80). Mormonism is also strong in Samoa.

12 Table One Demographic Trends 1999.
13 Personal communication with the Information Officer, Statistics New Zealand (01/02/06).
14 New Zealand government statistics. This information is taken from the 2001 Census of Population and Dwellings.
15 In Vanuatu the Seasonal Employment Act No 23 of 2007.
16 It is estimated that around 62,000 Pacific islanders were brought to Australia under this form of labour recruitment, http://www.premiers.qld.gov.au/ About_the_department/publications/multicultural/Australian_South_Sea_ islander_Training_Package/history/australia/recruiting/ (accessed 15 March 2006).
17 Lal (2003) indicates that in 2002 indigenous Fijians were projected to make up 53.5 per cent of the total population and Indo-Fijians 39.8 per cent. Today this percentage is likely to have decreased further.
18 Pacific Island Populations 2004, Part 1, Secretariat of the Pacific Community 2004.
19 As above.
20 For example, 6,000 Tokelauns live in New Zealand, according to a press release on the Official site of the Tokelau Government, http://www.tokelau.org.nz/ (accessed 2 November 2005).
21 There is considerable literature on the role of remittances. See, for example, Borovnik (2006: 151); Marsters, Lewis and Freisen (2006: 31) and Brown and Connell (2006: 135).
22 This is what Lawson (1997: 109) calls the 'reification of "tradition"'.
23 Customary Law (Declaration) Act 1990.
24 *RepMar v ATC et al. (3)* [2001] MHSC 2.
25 See, for example, the Customary Law (Restoration) Act 1986. The establishment of a Customary Law Commission under the Customary Law and Language Commission Act 2004, may see a further revival in the recognition of traditional leaders.
26 See Yap Constitution, Article 111, which provides for the role of traditional leaders.
27 Pohnpei Constitution, Article 5.
28 For example, they converted to Christianity and formed alliances with representatives of the church, or they became quasi-civil servants carrying out functions of colonial government. See in particular the close relationship between Samoan *matai* and missionaries and the local government role of *matai* under colonial government, in Macpherson (1997: 19–24).
29 As happened in Tonga where three Tongan royal titles were merged under King Taufa'ahau Tupou in the period 1820–1845 and the power of many chiefs was removed in 1862.
30 As has happened in Samoa with the reservation of Members of Parliament to *matai* title holders.
31 Government of Western Samoa (1975: 2).
32 An example is the rise of Sitveni Rabuka in Fiji.
33 See, for example, the reports of Transparency International (2006–2007) and (2002).
34 James (1997: 65) indicates that traditionally hereditary leaders were chosen by an electoral college of family members as much for personal qualities as birth rank.
35 The 1882 Land Act provided for allotments of land to be granted directly by the King and registered with the State. However, in 1915 the law was amended making it necessary for commoners to get permission from the holder of the hereditary estate before they could register their allotment.

36 The pro-democracy movement in Tonga is gaining ground, not always at grass roots level but among the educated Tongans.

37 For example, in the Solomon Islands paramount chiefs were recognised because they played an important role in exercising powers devolved from central colonial administration in the provinces, even if, as has been suggested, paramount chiefs were not recognised as such prior to colonial administration (Keesing 1997: 253). Keesing suggests that 'paramount chiefs are good to westernise with' (1997: 260) and indeed post-colonial law reports suggest a proliferation of 'paramount' chiefs.

38 Section 9, The Constitution of the Cook Islands and House of Arikis Act 1966. An *Ariki* is defined as 'a person who has been invested with the title rank or office of Ariki in accordance with ancient custom prevailing in each of the Cook Islands'.

39 Article III, Constitution of the Marshall Islands.

40 See section 3(7) of the Article.

41 Article 29, Constitution of the Republic of Vanuatu.

42 Article 30.

43 Section 3(2) as amended .

44 See comments by Amet JSC in a dissenting opinion in *In Re the Constitution, Reference by HE The President* [2002] FJSC1.

45 *Republic of Fiji Islands v Prasad* [2001] FJCA 2.

46 See section 116, Constitution (Amendment) Act 1997.

47 A discriminatory provision upheld by the Court of Appeal in *In re the Constitution, Attorney-General v Olomalu* [1982] WSCA 1.

48 Section 3.

49 See, for example, *Leituala v Mauga* [2004] WSSC 9 and *Sefo v Lands and Titles Court* [2000] WSSC 46.

50 *Alama v Tefasa* [1987] SPLR 385, Donne CJ at 393.

51 *Teonea v Kaupule* [2005] TVHC 2.

52 *Teitinnang v Ariong* [1987] LRC (Const) 517.

53 Principle 4 of the opening paragraph to the Constitution.

54 Article V, Section 1, Constitution of the Federated States of Micronesia.

55 See, for example, comments by Lunabeck (2004: 33).

56 For example, Tokelau and Pitcairn Islands. Cook Islands and Niue, although self-governing, exist in free association with New Zealand which remains at least partially responsible for their external affairs. Marshall Islands has a Compact of Free Association with the United States of America as does the Federated States of Micronesia.

57 Resolution 1541 (XV) 1960.

58 The Tokelau Islands were made a British protectorate in 1889 and formed part of the Gilbert and Ellice Islands Colony between 1916 and 1926. Registration for voting on Tokelau Referendum for self-determination commenced on Monday 26 September 2005, http://www.paclii.org/tk/government.html (accessed 2 November 2005). The outcome of the referendum held on 17 February 2006 was that the people of Tokelau by a narrow majority voted to remain dependent on New Zealand and not to change the *status quo*.

59 Although Cook Islands acts autonomously in some international transactions.

60 Draft Federal Constitution of Solomon Islands

61 Chuuk has six seats, Pohnpei four and Yap and Kosrae each have two seats. See Art IX of the FSM Constitution.

62 'Tonga Kings Vows More Democracy', BBC News, 23 November 2006, http://news.bbc.co.uk/1/hi/world/asia-pacific/6177522.stm (accessed 16 March 2007).

63 'Japan Funds Pacific Islands Forum Secretariat Projects', Pacific Islands Forum Secretariat Press Statement, 15 April 2002, http://archives.pireport.org/archive/2002/april/04-16-21.htm (accessed 16 March 2007).

64 'Japan Pledges $400 Million To Pacific Aid', May 29 2006, *Fiji Times*, http://www.fijitimes.com/ (accessed 16 March 2007).

65 'Japan gives Solomons $9.5 million for Fisheries', Solomon Islands Broadcasting Corp, March 7 2005, www.sibonline.com.sb (accessed 16 March 2007).

66 'Japan supports Palau, Samoa Regional Environmental Projects', Pacific Island News Association, 22 August 2001, http://www.pinanius.org (accessed 16 March 2007).

67 'FSM-Japan ties strengthen during President Falcam's meeting with Japan PM Koizumi', FSM Information Services, February 1 2002, http://archives.prieport.org/archives/2002/february/o2-04-11.htm (accessed 16 March 2007).

68 'Vanuatu projects get $633,000 from Japan', *Vanuatu Daily Post*, 17 December 2005, http://www.vanuatudaily.com (accessed 16 March 2007).

69 'Cook Islands have 'issues' with Japan Largesse', *The Cook Islands Herald*, 3 June 2006, http://www.ciherlad.co.ck/Times.htm (accessed 16 March 2007).

70 'Tonga King Cites $20 Million China Aid Package', *Matangi Tonga Magazine*, 11 November 2004, www.matangitonga.to/home/ (accessed 16 March 2007).

71 'Tonga Seeks $29 Million Loan From China', *Matangi Tonga Magazine*, 1 May 2006, www.matangitonga.to/home/ (accessed 16 March 2007).

72 'Vanuatu praises China's Way of Giving Aid', 18 September 2001, *Vanuatu Trading Post*, http://www.pinanius.org (accessed 16 March 2007).

73 'Chinese Premier Wen Jiabao To Visit Fiji', 24 January 2006, *Fijilive*, http://www.fijilive.com (accessed 16 March 2007).

74 'Png Must Keep Watchful Eye On China's Benevolence', *The National*, 25 April 2006, www.thenational.com.pg/ (accessed 16 March 2007).

75 http://archives.pireport.org/archive/1998/august/08-14-17.htm (accessed 27 February 2008).

76 http://archives.pireport.org/archive/1998/september/09-08-16.htm (accessed 27 February 2008).

77 http://archives.pireport.org/archive/2004/may/05-21-11.htm.

78 http://archives.pireport.org/archive/2000/april/04-04-21.htm.

79 http://archives.pireport.org/archive/2007/august/08-13-17.htm.

80 http://archives.pireport.org/archive/2006/january/01-27-23.htm.

81 For example, in Samoa German law applied from 1900 – see *Samoan Public Trustee v Collins* [1961] WSNZCA 1, while in Vanuatu, although notionally French law continues to be applicable under the Constitution Article 95(1) and (2), it is rarely used. See Farran (2004a).

82 2000:2001. 2000 PITSE 13. At the time of writing only Vanuatu seems to have formalised an ACP-EU Partnership Agreement, Act No 22, 2001.

83 http://www.delfji.ec.European Union/en/European Union_and_country/regional_partnership.htm (28/02/08).

84 http://www.delfji.ec.European Union/en/EU_and_country/cotonou.htm.

85 Council Decision of 1 October 2007 on the conclusion of consultations with the Republic of the Fiji Islands under Article 96 of the ACP-EC Partnership Agreement and Article 37 of the Development Cooperation Instrument (2007/641/EC) Official Journal of the European Union 5.10.2007, L 260/15.

86 Press Release by the Council of Europe Luxembourg, 1 October 2007, 13383/07 (Presse 214).

87 Looting and attacks on shopkeepers during periods of unrest – as in Tonga and Fiji – or escalating property crimes are examples of this dissatisfaction.

88 See, for example, comment by the editor of Vanuatu Daily Post suggesting private vigilante groups and road blocks to protect ex-patriate people and properties (Neil-Jones 2008).
89 Final Pacific Plan, 5 November 2006.
90 http://www.ausaid.gov.au/publications/pdf/pacific2020.pdf p.1. (accessed 28 February 2008).
91 Australia's Pacific Regional Aid Strategy 2004-2009 can be seen at http://www.ausaid.gov.au/country/southpacific.cfm (accessed 9 May 2008).
92 http://www.un.org/millenniumgoals/goals.html# (accessed 9 May 2008).
93 Fiji in 2004 and Papua New Guinea in 2005. These are accessible at http://www.undg.org/index.cfm?P=87&f=S.
94 See, for example, the Asian Development Bank Annual Report 2000: 72-79, http://www.adb.org/Documents/Reports/Annual_Report/2006/ADB-AR2006-Pacific.pdf (accessed 20 June 2008).
95 Attachment C Pacific Regional Aid Strategy, p. 38, http://www.ausaid.gov.au/country/southpacific.cfm (accessed 28 February 2008).
96 BBC News 'Pacific states step into the breach', 3 September 2001, http://news.bbc.co.uk/1/hi/world/asia-pacific/1520388.stm (accessed 12 March 2007).
97 This was done in the Australia-Nauru Memorandum of Understanding, 9 December 2002. Subsequent amendments to this followed. It was intended that the agreement would terminate in 2005. As of 18 July 2005 it was reported that 32 people were still detained in Nauru camps, http://www.nauruwire.org (accessed 10 February 2007).

2 Rights and the laws that give effect to them

Introduction

Having established the environment in which human rights are to be considered, it is next important to have some idea of the subject matter: 'human rights' and the way in which these rights are articulated in law. This immediately raises two basic interrelated questions. The first is what is understood or interpreted as a 'right' in the context of 'human rights' and the second is what is meant or recognised as 'law'. Both these questions are important because lack of clarity or agreement may account for some of the misunderstandings which surround human rights discourse in the region and undermine the effectiveness of rights advocacy. It may also be the case that in the plural legal systems of Pacific Island countries certain interpretations or understanding of human rights may be incompatible with the application and observation of certain laws. This chapter explores some of the difficulties in arriving at a satisfactory answer to the first question and by examining possible answers to the second question aims to throw some light on the first.

What are 'human rights'?

While it is not the purpose here to explore all the philosophical and jurisprudential theories of rights, the question is asked because in part the difficulties encountered by advocates of human rights in the Pacific region are due to different definitions and perceptions of 'human rights'. All too often the argument raised is that human rights are an alien concept which is ill-adapted to meet or reflect Pacific needs and priorities.

Rights, however, can be understood or perceived in a number of different ways. One perception is that rights are simply the beneficial corollary of duties. These latter may be moral, religious, legal or a combination of these. Sometimes these duties are non-justiciable but are encouraged because of perceived positive benefits to society. For example, in Vanuatu Article 7 and 8 of the Constitution of Vanuatu lists a number of duties which individuals are expected to observe and which the State has a duty to encourage.

Included among these are the duty of a parent to 'to support, assist and educate all his children, legitimate and illegitimate, and in particular to give them a true understanding of their fundamental rights and duties and of the national objectives and of the culture and customs of the people of Vanuatu', while in return children have a duty to respect their parents. Similarly, the Constitution of the Independent State of Papua New Guinea lists a number of 'Basic Social Obligations' which everyone owes 'to themselves and their descendants, to each other, and to the Nation'. The enjoyment of the Basic Rights listed subsequently in Division 3, are subject to these obligations as well as to the National Goals and Directive Principles established in the opening provisions of the Constitution. In the Republic of Palau positive duties are imposed on the state in Article VI of the Constitution, which states that:

> The national government shall take positive action to attain these national objectives and implement these national policies: conservation of a beautiful, healthful and resourceful natural environment; promotion of the national economy; protection of the safety and security of persons and property; promotion of the health and social welfare of the citizens through the provision of free or subsidized health care; and provision of public education for citizens which shall be free and compulsory as prescribed by law.

Similarly, the government of the Marshall Islands has a constitutionally endorsed obligation to 'to take every step reasonable and necessary' to provide the people of Marshall Islands health care, education, and legal services (Section 15, Article II).

Sometimes compliance with duties may conflict with the exercise of rights. For example, in Tonga there is a duty, sanctioned by law, to respect the King and the Royal Family.[1] On occasion this has led to conflict with the freedom of the press and attempts by government to stifle publications critical of the present regime, including the use of Orders in Council.[2]

The importance of duties is not necessarily diminished by the emergence of rights. The enjoyment of any rights set out in the various 'Bills of Rights' found in the region, is invariably subject to the duty to respect the rights and freedoms of others. This too can create a conflict, especially where a claim to individual rights appears to conflict with a duty that individual may have in respect of collective rights. Examples encountered in the region arise in the context of freedom of religion, freedom of association and freedom of movement, especially where considerable power is wielded by community organisations at a local or village level.[3]

The term 'rights' can also be used to refer to those 'rights' which are considered to be the entitlement of all people regardless of their status, location, legal system or any other context. This understanding of rights may not fit easily with highly stratified or hierarchical societies such as those found in parts of the Pacific, where inequalities of power and rights have a long history. Moreover, to claim that human beings have rights by virtue of being human does not take us very far, nor does it necessarily distinguish various categories of rights. If rights are to be protected or freedoms preserved then the content and nature of these needs to be identified and the means by which they might be given effect need to be understood. This is an evolving process in which the detail of broader principles has to reflect and adapt to new circumstances and environments. This is particularly true of the interpretation and experience of human rights in the Pacific region, where the body of received law has to be applied in a variety of contexts and situations, some of which will be very different from the environment in which such ideas were originally engendered, while indigenous law may have to adapt to accommodate non-indigenous concepts of human rights.

Although rights may be understood in an abstract, philosophical or moral sense, the modern concept of human rights is largely a legal one. Historically modern discourse on rights emerged as a result of power struggles between those who wielded power and those who were subject to it. For individuals to claim rights or liberties is meaningless unless those who govern are prepared to exercise their power(s) taking into account those claims or freedoms. Thus the early emergence of rights discourse is against a background of political change, notably, the struggle between Crown and subjects culminating in the Bill of Rights in 1689 in England, the American Declaration of Independence in 1776, and the French Revolution of 1789. These political changes reflected the relationship of individual rights and governing power and the idea that there was a social contract between the power that ruled and those who were ruled, under which the natural rights of the latter would be upheld and observed by the former. Bad government violated this contractual understanding and justified civil disobedience. Theories of rights – which are considered in the next chapter, therefore, needed practical recognition, either by way of non-interference or restriction with certain liberties, such as freedom of association, religion or movement; or by way of positive measures such as criminal prosecution for infringements to the right to life, or civil law protection of the right to property. In the Pacific region, while power struggles led to independence from colonial rule, the statements of rights and freedoms found in the constitutions of these new states were as much a legacy of colonial rule as an affirmation of freedom from it. As a result of colonial influence, the historical struggles indicated above are echoed in the forms of government, in the separation of powers and the parliamentary systems put in place at independence in Pacific Island Countries. Whether the articulation of rights in the constitutions of the region accurately reflect the values and aspirations of Pacific islanders is less certain.

The idea of the freedom of the individual from oppression, which is associated with Western style democracies, finds expression in the advocacy of civil liberties and the belief that people are free to do or act as they like, provided the law does not forbid or restrict such conduct or activity and provided the civil liberties of others are not infringed. So, for example, freedom of expression is a liberty provided its exercise does not infringe laws relating to defamation, blasphemy or breach of confidence. The exercise and enjoyment of freedoms unhindered by state restriction or intrusion is an important check on the exercise of power where the state has the ability to intrude into the lives of individuals, and the language of 'fundamental freedoms' is found throughout the region. Often, however, in Pacific Island Countries it is not the state that restricts the exercise of such freedoms but customary practices, local chiefs, church or community leaders. Indeed, outside the major metropolitan areas the state may have minimal influence on the daily lives of Pacific islanders.

In a sense, however, freedoms impose no duty on the State to promote or safeguard rights, simply to refrain from interference. An illustration can be found in the case of privacy. Historically, it has been the case that in English law there is no right to privacy. There are freedoms to take photos of private citizens or celebrities, publish stories about them and peer through their windows, provided various civil and criminal wrongs are not committed such as defamation, trespass, assault or watching and besetting. Thus, it has been held that no wrong was committed when journalists intruded into a hospital ward to take photographs of a seriously ill actor, or when an aerial photographer flew over a person's home and took photographs; or when a radio commentary of a race meeting was broadcast from a tall tower overlooking the racecourse on neighbouring land.[4] Since the incorporation of the European Convention on Human Rights and Fundamental Freedoms into English domestic law by the Human Rights Act 1998, however, there is a right to privacy.[5] In some circumstances therefore, a written Bill of Rights confers new rights or declares as rights what were formerly liberties, such as the right to peaceful assembly or to express a variety of views. Alternatively a written declaration of rights may simply confirm freedoms or liberties, frequently providing circumstances in which the state may justifiably curtail or restrict these. Often there is a combination of rights, and freedoms. Sometimes the one without the other is meaningless.

For example, in the region the freedom to express oneself in traditional dance, song, language and costume is supported in a cultural environment which values customary usage and traditions – as indicated in many of the preambles of the written constitutions.[6] These freedoms, which were often repressed under the influence of missionaries and colonial administration, may be particularly important post-independence as an expression of unique cultural and national identity. However, as will be considered in a later chapter, freedom of cultural expression may not be enough to protect these interests, more may be required, states and indeed the international community may need to take positive measures if these freedoms are not to be infringed. It is also the case that rights and freedoms may be differently interpreted in different contexts. So, for example, in English law it may not be an important aspect of the right to privacy that details concerning entitlement to land or titles is kept confidential and out of the public domain, whereas in Samoa this may be very important. Similarly, the transfer of knowledge may be surrounded by secrecy in Papua New Guinea, but widely publicised elsewhere in the name of freedom of expression and the right to access information.

The emergence of 'rights' under the influence of international rights instruments has come to mean more than just tolerance of liberties or non-interference by the state or governing body. Rights today are increasingly associated with positive duties on the part of the state and sometimes other individuals, non-observance of which may give rise to an expectation of a remedy. Understood in this way these rights are more closely akin to other legal rights. For example, the right to protection of property may include both public and private rights. The former requires the state to provide compensation frameworks for any public requisition of property but also to provide a legal system which supports the individual who claims this right, for example by facilitating registration of title or providing for the adjudication of land claims.

The state therefore, may be expected to provide a facilitative and regulatory framework as well as means of redress should these rights be infringed or unduly restricted. Indeed, the idea of a partnership between those that govern and those that are governed requires this. This imposes not only obligations on the state, but also powers.

The right to exercise such powers is another form of right. Such powers may be conferred on an individual or office holder, an organisation or an authority. Examples of such powers are the right of a local authority to licence places of entertainment, bars or hotels, or the power of the police to permit or refuse the holding of marches or demonstrations. In this sense, rights may not be generally enjoyed by all citizens but limited to a few. Provided those few that hold power are accountable and exercise their power within prescribed limits, with appropriate sanctions where these are overstepped, this right to exercise powers is compatible with the preservation of fundamental rights and freedoms. However, as will be seen, the exercise of powers in the Pacific is not always proscribed in this way, so the balance is not preserved. Violations occur.

Finally, a right may provide a defence to conduct which might otherwise attract sanction. An example which is found in a number of democratic societies is the idea of parliamentary privilege, whereby members of parliament have the right to say what they like within the confines of parliament or the legislative assembly without fear of being sued for defamation. Similarly, individual liberties or rights may be curtailed or restricted where it is found necessary and justified to do so in the interests of the greater good, for example in the interest of national security, public health, public order, or because the rights and liberties of others are at risk. The way in which these justifications are interpreted is crucial to preserving the balance between upholding rights and freedoms and repressing them. For example, the continuation of mining in Papua New Guinea has been justified in a number of Acts as being a matter of 'urgent national importance' even though it is recognised that the continuation of mining activities at Ok Tedi pose a variety of environmental and human rights risks.[7]

All these interpretations of rights are relevant in the Pacific region and indeed may enlarge or enhance those 'human' or 'fundamental' rights for which specific provision is made. In some of the constitutions both rights and freedoms are listed, for example, Cook Islands, Kiribati, Nauru and Solomon Islands. In others the focus is on rights, for example, Marshall Islands, Palau, Samoa and Tuvalu. In Vanuatu the emphasis is on rights and duties, while in Papua New Guinea rights are divided into those that are fundamental and those that are qualified.

In the context of human rights any of these interpretations may apply, or a combination of these depending on the right under consideration. For example, if a person charged with a crime has a right to a fair trial, that person does not have to pursue any particular course of conduct. Here the right could be interpreted as a claim, which the machinery and process of justice is expected to satisfy. However, the concept behind the right claimed goes further than this because it requires those who have the right to exercise certain powers to do so in a particular way. So, for example, the police and prosecuting authorities may be expected to act fairly and expeditiously and legislation governing evidence and procedure might be expected to reinforce this obligation. Moreover, the person accused of a crime may believe that he or she has the right to conduct themselves in the way complained of, that is has the freedom or liberty to do so, unless this clearly conflicts with or impinges upon another person's freedoms. This claim of liberty may be raised as a defence. So, for example, a parent may believe that he or she is free to chastise his or her own child without interference. However, concern about the welfare of children, an increase in the number of incidents of physical abuse of children within the home, and changing attitudes towards parental disciplining of children, may limit or prohibit this by making certain forms or degrees of chastisement unlawful. At the same time, in order to preserve the remaining freedom of parents to raise their children as they think best there must be procedural safeguards to ensure that parental rights are not curtailed arbitrarily, unreasonably or haphazardly. Thus, a parent may claim immunity from challenge for some acts of discipline and not others, or may retain the power to discipline children in ways which do not amount to abuse. The boundaries between rights and liberties, powers and immunities may not always be clear and certainly they may vary from one legal context and jurisdiction to another.[8] They may also vary within different cultural and social contexts.

How then may human rights, which are deemed to be fundamental – that is unchallengeable and non-derogable by the State – be distinguished from other rights, such as the right to property, or the right to enter into contracts, or the right of the state to penalise criminal activity? The notion of human rights is underpinned by a moral or normative code which holds that there are certain aspects of being human which the state or those who have power over others should respect and not abuse. What those aspects are is arrived at by consensus based on various philosophical and political theories and also the particular moment at which claims to certain rights are being urged. This last is important because the history of human rights demonstrates that the various instruments that advocate human rights have resulted from periods of oppression, abuse of power by those in control and suffering by large numbers of ordinary individuals. In some cases the statement of rights arrived at has been a consequence of the oppressed achieving greater power,[9] in other cases the statement of rights has been articulated outside national boundaries by multi-national agencies.[10] Whatever the consensus as to those rights which are deemed to be important is, clearly there is a close connection between political structures and the articulations of rights. In dictatorships there is unlikely to be any democratic process involved in determining what rights are important and will be upheld and what rights are not important and will not be protected. By contrast, in a democracy it is to be expected that the electorate have a greater say in the formulation of rights statements. This is not always the case, however, especially where constitutional structures are imposed rather than freely selected by the people who are to be governed by them. This happened in a number of countries emerging from colonial rule and, although in the years since independence constitutional changes have occurred, many, particularly in the Pacific, retain constitutional structures acquired at independence. The role of Pacific islanders in the formulation of national rights statements has, therefore, in a number of countries, been limited.

The observance of the rights of individuals or groups by the governing powers of a state is not, however, solely a matter for domestic or national concern. Increasingly the sovereignty of states in these matters has been invaded, influenced and perhaps abridged by the views, standards and sanctions of external agencies, not primarily in the form of other states – although individuals from these may be deployed, such as peace-keeping forces of the United Nations or election observers appointed by Transparency International – but international organisations, notably the United Nations, but also the Commonwealth, the International Red Cross, the World Bank, the International Court of Justice, the European Union and others, whose mandates are to standardise state activity in accordance with goals and standards established by themselves and sanctioned by the international body. The environment in which human rights operate today is therefore one which is globalised as well as domestic; which is legal as well as political; moral as well as aspirational; and in which many of the key players have very little common ground except the rhetoric of rights. Indeed, it has been suggested that the emergence of international rights statements, starting with the Universal Declaration of Human Rights in 1949

> profoundly changed the international landscape, scattering it with human rights protocols, conventions and treaties and derivative declarations of all kinds so that there is now not a single nation, culture or people that is not in one way or another enmeshed in human rights regimes.
>
> (Morsink 1999: x)

Sources of rights

The legal environment of human rights in the South Pacific region is made up of two main sources: those contained in individual constitutions, and those found in international human rights treaties and conventions to which Pacific Island states are signatories or to which states have given effect in domestic law.[11] These latter are important for a number of reasons. First, they represent a culmination of rights advocacy at an international level. Second, and increasingly, they inform international expectations of state players. Third, they influence domestic legislation and judicial reasoning. There are also three other sources, the importance of which will vary depending on the jurisdiction under consideration. These are customary international law, principles of common law and equity introduced into the region and principles of customary law which are indigenous to many Pacific Island Countries.

International human rights

Although not solely a modern phenomenon (Hoffman and Rowe 2006: 19),[12] today's international advocacy of human rights – that is an agreed body of rights to which different nations subscribe – emerged as a result of particular historical circumstances which occurred in Europe (Civic 1995–1996: 285).[13] Prior to this international law had been primarily directed at regulating the relations between states and was not concerned with individuals within those states. Although international humanitarian law had begun to emerge in the latter part of the nineteenth century, with the formation of the International Committee of the Red Cross in 1863, the Geneva Convention of 1864 (which was aimed at encouraging the humanitarian treatment of soldiers wounded in battle), and the 1899–1907 Hague Conventions on the treatment of prisoners, these were directed at states. There was no international intervention against the domestic government of a country if it persecuted its own nationals or those within its borders unless these were foreign nationals, so the persecution and oppression of persons on the grounds of religion, race or sex was not usually of international concern.

This incidentally meant that colonial authorities were left to administer the various countries and regions which came under their control – including those in the South Pacific – largely unhindered by international opinion or pressure.

During the course of the two World Wars in the first half of the twentieth century, a number of large-scale persecutions and atrocities against mankind took place, most notably – although certainly not solely – by the Nazi regime in Germany against Jews and other minority groups such as gypsies, the mentally handicapped and people of colour.[14] This was not the first time that persecutions had taken place, indeed these have been a recurrent theme of history throughout the world. What was perhaps different was the coming together of a number of different major powers in the aftermath of the two wars to articulate a policy which was intended to provide an international statement acknowledging that all people had certain rights and agreement to put in place a human rights framework which was essentially directed at restraining governments from exercising unchecked power. The articulation of these rights in international instruments, especially the Charter of the United Nations[15] and the Declaration of Human Rights,[16] was integral to the idea of democracy, good governance, and humanity. The early international rights instruments were soon followed by others such as the International Covenant on Civil and Political Rights[17] and the International Covenant on Economic, Social and Cultural Rights.[18]

In Europe the United Nations Declaration of Human Rights influenced the drafting and adoption of the European Convention for the Protection of Human Rights and Fundamental Freedoms in 1949, which came into force in 1950. Originally this Convention was directed at preventing infringements of the rights contained therein by signatory states. However, under Article 25 there was provision for a state to recognise the jurisdiction of the European Commission on Human Rights in the case of individual petitions. This right of individual petition became effective on 5 July 1955 after six of the High Contracting Parties made declarations recognising the competence of the Commission to receive individual petitions. It is now the case that petitions brought by individuals against their own country far outweigh inter-state cases.

In the Pacific region, these international initiatives and those in Europe are significant for several reasons. First, as the island countries of the Pacific gained independence and became members of the United Nations, so they became either expressly or by implication subscribers to the ideas and values of that international body. A number of states inherited treaty obligations as a colonial legacy. For example, Fiji is a signatory to the International Convention on the Elimination of all Forms of Racial Discrimination (CERD) by succession to the treaty obligations undertaken prior to independence; Solomon Islands succeeded to obligations under the International Covenant on Economic, Social and Cultural rights (ICESCR) on 17 March 1982 and to CERD on the same date.

In some newly independent states the constitutions specifically incorporated reference either to specific treaties or to international law, for example, the Tuvalu Constitution states

> In determining whether a law or act is reasonably justifiable in a democratic society that has a proper respect for human rights and dignity, a court may have regard to ... international conventions, declarations, recommendations and judicial decisions concerning human rights.
>
> (Section 15(5) (c))

Similarly, in Papua New Guinea, in determining whether a restriction or limitation on a fundamental right is justified in a democratic society, a court may have regard to:

> the Charter of the United Nations; and ... the Universal Declaration of Human Rights and any other declaration, recommendation or decision of the General Assembly of the United Nations concerning human rights and fundamental freedoms; and ... the European Convention for the Protection of Human Rights and Fundamental Freedoms and the Protocols thereto, and any other international conventions, agreements or declarations concerning human rights and fundamental freedoms; and ... judgements, reports and opinions of the International Court of Justice, the European Commission of Human Rights, the European Court of Human Rights and other international courts and tribunals dealing with human rights and fundamental freedoms.
>
> (Section (39)(3) (b)–(e))[19]

Other Pacific Island Countries used their new status to become signatories to various international treaties, particularly the Convention on the Rights of the Child (CRC) and the Convention for the Elimination of All Forms of Discrimination against Women (CEDAW).

Table 2.1 reflects the treaties to which Pacific Island states are parties.

However, although post-independence a number of Pacific Island states have signed up to international treaties, they have been rather less enthusiastic about giving these effect in domestic law. At present, the Convention on the Rights of the Child and the Convention on the Elimination of all Forms of Discrimination against Women have the greatest support in the region, while the International Covenant on Civil and Political Rights has only one signatory – Nauru, although Cook Islands and Niue are party to this as a result of New Zealand's ratification. The International Covenant on Economic, Social and Cultural Rights (ICESCR),[20] the Convention Against Torture and Other Cruel, Inhuman or Degrading Treatment or Punishment (CAT),[21] the International Convention on the Protection of the Rights of All Migrant Workers and Members of their Families (CRMW),[22] the Convention on the Rights of Persons with Disabilities

Table 2.1 Treaty status of Pacific Island countries

Country	Convention on the Rights of the Child (CRC)	International Covenant on Civil and Political Rights (CCPR)	Convention on the Elimination of all Forms of Discrimination against Women (CEDAW)	International Convention on the Elimination of all Forms of Racial Discrimination (GERD)
Cook Islands	06 Jul 1997	(28 Dec 1978)[a]	11 Aug 2006[b]	(22 Nov 1972)[c]
Fiji	13 Aug 1993		28 Aug 1995	11 Jan 1973[d]
Kiribati	11 Dec 1995		17 Mar 2004	
Marshall Islands	04 Oct 1993		2 Mar 2006	
Federated States of Micronesia	05 May 1993		1 Sep 2004	
Nauru	27 Jul 1994	12 Nov 2001[e]		12 Nov 2001
Niue	20 Dec 1995	28 Dec 1978[f]	10 Jan 1985[g]	(22 Nov 1972)[h]
Palau	04 Oct 1995			
Papua New Guinea	01 Mar 1993		12 Jan 1995	27 Jan 1982
Samoa	29 Nov 1994	15 Feb 2008[i]	25 Sep 1992	
Solomon Islands[j]	10 Apr 1995		06 May 2002	
Tonga	06 Nov 1995			17 Mar 1982
Tuvalu	22 Sept 1995		06 Oct 1999	16 Feb 1972
Vanuatu	07 Jul 1993	29 Nov 2007[k]	08 Sep 1995	

a. The International Covenant on Civil and Political rights was ratified on behalf of Cook Islands by New Zealand on this date but not enacted as part of the law of Cook Islands and is therefore of no legislative effect. *In Re Section 201 of the Income Tax Act 1997, Application by Smith* [1999] CKHC 1.

b. Cook Islands was previously included by express extension by New Zealand's ratification in January 1985.

c. It is unclear whether Cook Islands remains bound by this treaty as a result of New Zealand's ratification since no reports are filed for Cook Islands by New Zealand, and in recent years Cook Islands has acquired greater autonomy in its international relations.

d. This is by succession. Fiji has made reservations to this particularly in respect of Fijian land interests.

e. Signatory only.

f. By virtue of New Zealand's ratification although New Zealand does not appear to file reports for Niue under this treaty.

g. By virtue of New Zealand's ratification and express extension to Niue.

h. By virtue of New Zealand's ratification but, as in the case of Cook Islands, New Zealand no longer files reports for Niue so its status is uncertain.

i. Samoa has ratified this treaty.

j. Solomon Islands is also a signatory to the Optional Protocol to the Convention on the Elimination of All Forms of Discrimination against Women (CEDAW-OP) (06 Aug 02), as is Vanuatu.

k. Signatory only.

(Disability Convention),[23] and the International Convention for the Protection of All Persons from Enforced Disappearance (the Disappearance Convention) have similarly little or no support.[24] Only Samoa and Vanuatu have shown an interest in the Disappearance Convention,[25] and to date only Vanuatu has signed the Disability Convention.[26] Nauru is the only country under consideration to have signed the Convention against Torture and Other Cruel, Inhuman or Degrading Treatment or Punishment.[27] These initial moves, while they may be indicative of an intention to ratify at a later date, impose no obligations on the signatory states other than not to take positive moves to frustrate the purpose and intent of the respective Conventions. Thus the *status quo* in respect of disabled people or victims of torture can remain. Lack of practical and positive commitment to international treaties has been a matter of concern in the region (Jalal 2006).

In October 2005, the Pacific Island Forum members endorsed 'The Pacific Plan'. Among its initiatives is one which states that member states are to 'where appropriate, ratify and implement international and regional human rights conventions, covenants and agreements' (Pacific Plan 2005 Initiative 12.5). The time frame for putting this priority into effect was 2006–2008. It would appear that this rather short time-frame was over optimistic.

The picture thus presented is one of partial or incomplete commitment to the international framework of human rights. This operates at two levels. First, there is the reluctance of Pacific Island Countries to fully commit to these international treaties by ratification. Second, there is the reluctance of Pacific Islands Countries to give internal effect to the treaty obligations they have assumed under those treaties to which they are party. This second step is required because Pacific Island countries which came under the influence of the common law have dualist systems, whereby an international treaty does not automatically become part of domestic law but needs to be incorporated,[28] either in whole – for example, by a ratification Act, or by introducing new legislation which gives effect to the major principles of a convention,[29] or in a piecemeal fashion by modifying existing legislation – for example, by removing provisions which discriminate against women. The consequences of non-implementation of existing treaty obligations is illustrated by a number of issues considered later in this book.

There is no doubt a range of reasons why Pacific Island Countries are reluctant to take on more treaty obligations (Baird 2007; Jalal 2006). Not only are the international mechanisms for monitoring the implementation of these treaties resource intensive,[30] there is also the question of how effective this monitoring is. There are also conceptual, historical and cultural barriers which may make international treaties unattractive to Pacific Island States,[31] combined with the fact that hitherto Pacific Island countries have played virtually no part in the formulation or drafting of these international instruments.[32] Moreover, the procedures in place for treaty ratification in most Pacific Island countries may have meant that there has been very little internal consultation as to the ramifications of the consequent obligations. Either countries have 'inherited' treaty obligations by way of succession from former colonial powers, or ratification has been undertaken by the executive arm of government.[33] As Pacific Island governments are often volatile the act of a particular Minister of Foreign Affairs or Attorney-General may not necessarily be supported by his successors. Unless ratification is implemented through a domestic democratic process it is hardly surprising that ordinary citizens perceive international conventions to have little bearing on their lives. Thus it is all very well for the international community, or the Office of the High Commissioner for Human Rights, to call on states to ratify the various treaties but until this is taken up by Pacific communities and countries themselves such ratification may be at best a token gesture, or undertaken for motives which are not directly for the benefit of a country's citizens but for political or economic gain.[34] As will be considered in a later chapter, where civic society is involved in lobbying for convention rights and recognises and advocates the value of these, international conventions may be more successful.

The reasons for not giving effect to existing treaty obligations within domestic law may be linked to similar issues and obstacles which arise in respect of the above but which may also be due to more complex internal difficulties, such as the need to preserve a balance between the stability of the *status quo*, which is often upheld as reflecting tradition and custom and finds support among conservative leaders within the domestic framework, and demands for change to conform with new standards and aspirations expressed by emerging articulate, middle class and less conservative elements of society. As will be indicated in the chapters which follow, this domestic struggle between giving positive effect to rights and justifying their restriction or limitation is a constant one and operates in a variety of ways.

Customary international law and human rights

Customary international law is that body of law to which nations subscribe without necessarily being parties to the treaties which give rise to it or, in the case of unwritten customary international law, the jurisdictions from which it originally emanates. As independent states, there is a presumption that Pacific Island Countries subscribe to a body of norms which are shared by other states and which inform recognised and accepted inter-state practice, for example, international customary law regarding torture, war, slavery, genocide and crimes against humanity. It has also been suggested that parts of the Universal Declaration of Human Rights have become integrated into customary international law because of the international acceptance of the standards advocated in that Declaration (Lillich 1984: 116). Certainly, the Vienna Convention which codified much customary international law recognised the human rights elements of the Charter of the United Nations.[35]

Customary international law is accepted as being a source of law applied by the International Court of Justice established under the Charter of United Nations.[36] By implication therefore customary international law is part of the legal systems of those countries which are members of the United Nations.

An advantage of customary international law over treaty law is that customary international law norms are binding on all states, while treaties only bind those states which have ratified them. This is of some significance in the Pacific region because of the varied signatory status of the different countries, as indicated above.

Customary international law operates in two ways. First, there is the shared practice of a number of states over a period of time which emerges as a common customary law between nations, and then there is the recognition by individual states that observation of the shared practice is necessary or desirable and should be given formal legal effect. The first element of the definition is commonly referred to as 'state practice' and the second as '*opinio juris*'. Evidence of state support of certain customary international law practices may be established by a range of sources, including domestic legislation, regulations, treaties, judicial decisions, diplomatic communications, and the policies and operations of non-governmental and intergovernmental organisations. This support does not have to be manifested by actual conduct, unless the customary law is one which requires action. There also has to be evidence of the *opinio juris* – the recognition of the obligation on a state to observe customary international laws. This may be found in any of the above or, and more tellingly perhaps, in the judgments of the courts and communications of the executive.

What exactly the rules of customary international law are is not always clear, and while it is agreed that there must be a consensus among states for a practice to become customary it is not clear where states which have not been part of that consensus – because their statehood is relatively new – fit into that process. This was an issue raised by newly independent states following de-colonisation in the 1960s, and is a question of relevance to Pacific Island Countries.

There is also the question of how far, and to what extent, customary international law applies to those countries in the Pacific which do not have autonomy in their foreign or inter-state affairs, for example, Cook Islands, Niue, Marshall Islands and the Federated States of Micronesia. Thus in some Pacific Island jurisdictions it could be argued that customary international law is part of the body of law which can be taken into account, while in others this may be more doubtful.

It has also been suggested that regional versions of customary international law may emerge and develop as a result of the member countries of regional organisations subscribing to a shared set of norms or standards on matters which affect the region as a whole. For example, support of statements made by the Pacific Islands Forum, which are often framed in normative language by members of this inter-governmental organisation, may be viewed as regional customary international law (Boister 2005: 55, 56). One of the counter-arguments is that often these statements are merely aspirational and there is no obligation on Forum member states to give effect to these aspirations in domestic law and indeed the policy of the Forum is to encourage rather than impose or sanction. Lack of enforceability of Forum resolutions would not necessarily be fatal to the emergence of a regional customary international law. After all the Universal Declaration of Human Rights is itself aspirational and not enforceable but has been held to be part of customary international law. Distinctively however the Forum is not founded on a treaty.[37]

Even if the validity of a regional customary law is questionable, there is no doubt that for some purposes there is reference to customary international law in the region, particularly with reference to maritime zones, where rights to control fishing within state exclusive economic zones is crucial to many Pacific Island countries.[38] The law of the sea, much of which is determined by customary international law, is therefore of considerable importance to all Pacific Islands countries.

Closer to shore however, customary international law may conflict with local customary law. For example, in the Solomon Island case of *Allardyce Timber Company v Laore* [1990] SBHC 96, a customary land claim to the reefs and seabed challenged the notion of state sovereignty over these areas. Within the twelve mile territorial waters zone municipal law may be able to accommodate such claims (Tom'tavala 2000), beyond these however freedom to navigate on the high seas may not always be in the best interests of Pacific islanders.[39]

Customary international law has also been called on to protect the rights of individuals. For example, in the Papua New Guinea case of *Application by Ireeuw, Wawar, Ap and Wakum* [1985] PNGLR 430, the applicants, fearing for their own safety, had crossed into Papua New Guinea from West Irian. They sought to rely on the customary rule of international law of non-refoulement of refugees. However, it was held that this rule – even if accepted as being part of customary international law, was not incorporated as part of the law of Papua New Guinea under the Constitution, because it was contrary to the provisions of the Migration Act.[40] It was also inconsistent with an earlier decision by a national court of *Premdas v Independent State of Papua New Guinea* [1979] PNGLR 329, in which Prentice CJ, cited with approval the case of *Attorney-General for the Dominion of Canada v Cain* [1906] AC 542, where it was said

> One of the rights possessed by the supreme power in every State is the right to refuse to permit an alien to enter that State, to annex what conditions it pleases to the permission to enter it, and *to expel or deport* from the State at pleasure, even a friendly alien.
>
> (at 546. Emphasis added by Cory J)

It may also be the case that Pacific Island courts may draw on international human rights jurisprudence. Whether this body of law can be properly called customary international law is uncertain. Nevertheless it may prove a valuable source of law, especially where there are a limited number of national or even regional precedents. For example, in Fiji, human rights decisions from Europe have been called on to support a claim that trial by General Court Martial under Military law would amount to a breach of the right to a fair and impartial hearing.[41] The Constitution of Fiji provides that in giving effect to the Bill of Rights contained within it 'the courts must promote the values that underlie a democratic society based on freedom and equality and must, if relevant, have regard to public international law applicable to the protection of the rights set out'.[42]

In the case in question, the Court accepted that it was obliged in the process of interpretation to consider public international law including law coming from other international human rights tribunals such as the European Court for Human Rights. In particular the Fiji court considered the cases of *Findlay v The United Kingdom* (110/1995/616/706 SCHR) and *Coyne v The United Kingdom* (124/1996/743/1942) but found them to be distinguishable. It placed more emphasis on *Morris v The United Kingdom* (38784/97 ECHR) where it had been held that

> a military court can, in principle, constitute an 'independent and impartial tribunal' for the purposes of Article 6(1) of the Convention ... However, the Convention will only tolerate such courts as long as sufficient safeguards are in place to guarantee their independence and impartiality.
>
> (Para 59)

and *Cooper v United Kingdom* (Application No. 48843/99 judgment 16 December 2003), in which the court found that the ECHR had accepted that military courts have a place, and that they should remain provided the process was fair. As the Fiji Constitution allows a law to limit a right or freedom, and a law that does so

> is not invalid solely because the wording of the law exceeds the limits imposed by this Chapter if the law is reasonably capable of a more restricted interpretation that does not exceed those limits. In that case, the law must be construed in accordance with the more restricted interpretation.
>
> (Section 43(3))

the Court held that it was not convinced that the applicant's right to a fair and impartial trial would be infringed if he were tried under Military Law by a General Courts Martial.

While the willingness of Fiji courts to look to customary international law – especially human rights law – is facilitated by the enabling provisions of its Constitution, there is hope that this trend will become more widespread through the region as judges, lawyers and litigants become more aware of the international jurisprudence.

National human rights instruments

Although most of the countries of the region are now independent,[43] their constitutional structures are not uniform. While it is not the purpose of this book to closely comment on the various constitutions of the region, as this has been done elsewhere,[44] the content of these constitutions and their interpretation, especially by the courts, shapes and determines the protection and enjoyment of human rights, not least because it is here, in the Constitutions, that these rights are set out and it is the Preambles of the Constitutions and the structures which are provided for therein, which can either facilitate or present obstacles to human rights. In all of the countries under consideration where there is a written constitution this is the primary source of law.

Preambles and general principles

The authoritative statements of rights found in the Constitutions may be constrained or restricted by the preambles which precede them or may be enlarged by these where they are taken to be not merely preambles but substantive statements of rights. The question is one of interpretation (Corrin Care *et al.* 1999: 86). For example, the Constitution of Nauru contains a preamble to the statement of Fundamental Rights and Freedoms which states:

> Whereas every person in Nauru is entitled to the fundamental rights and freedoms of the individual, that is to say, has the right, whatever his race, place of origin, political opinions, colour, creed or sex, but subject to respect for the rights and freedoms of others and for the public interest, to each and all of the following freedoms.

Similarly, in the Constitution of Kiribati the preamble to the declaration of rights states:

> ... every person in Kiribati is entitled to the fundamental rights and freedoms of the individual, that is to say, the right, whatever his race, place of origin, political opinions, colour, creed or sex, but subject to respect for the rights and freedoms of others and for the public interest, to each and all of the following, namely ...

the provisions of this Chapter shall have effect for the purpose of affording protection to those rights and freedoms subject to such limitations on that protection as are contained in those provisions, being limitations designed to ensure that the enjoyment of the said rights and freedoms by any individual does not prejudice the rights and freedoms of others or the public interest.

Provisions in the Solomon Islands are similarly worded.

If these sections are interpreted as merely preambles and not as substantive statements then it could be held that they do not determine the scope of human rights provisions. It has been pointed out that the courts (including the Judicial Committee of the Privy Council) are divided over the status and effect of these preambles (Care *et al.* 1999: 87).

In some cases, the Preamble includes rights which do not appear to be listed elsewhere. For example, the Nauru preamble stated above includes a reference to the right to family life but this is not indicated in the list of rights which follow.[45] Similarly, in Fiji, the Preamble to the 1997 Amended Constitution emphasises the value of the family by reaffirming: 'our recognition of the human rights and fundamental freedoms of all individuals and groups, safeguarded by adherence to the rule of law, and our respect for human dignity and for the importance of the family', but there is no right to family life specified under the fundamental rights. Case law considering these anomalies has not been consistent in determining whether or not the preamble confers substantive rights or not.[46] This was a matter requiring consideration in the Solomon Island case of *Folotalu v Attorney-General* [2001] SBHC 149, where it was argued that increasing the deposit required for Parliamentary candidates breached not only the fundamental rights of freedom of association and assembly and discriminated against those from rural communities, but infringed the national objectives and purposes set out in the Preamble to the Constitution. It was held by Palmer ACJ, following earlier Solomon Island authority,[47] that the Preamble was to be viewed as an integral part of the Constitution which in particular reflected the 'jurisprudential philosophy or underlying principles or beliefs by the people as the basis of the new nation'. It could be referred to as an aid to interpretation of more specific provisions in the Constitution where there was ambiguity but not where such provisions were clear and unambiguous. This approach has been adopted elsewhere in the region, for example, in Papua New Guinea Schedule 1.3 of the Constitution provides that 'recourse may be had to the preamble as an aid to interpretation in cases of doubt'.[48] In Tuvalu the Interpretation and General Provisions Act (Cap 1A) section 7, provides that the Preamble to the Constitution 'shall be used to assist in explaining the purport and object of the law' and section 4(2) of the Constitution provides that '(I)n all cases, this Constitution shall be interpreted and applied consistently with the principles set out in the Preamble'. In Solomon Islands the Preamble has been relied on to establish the basic democratic structure of government, whereby the rights of the public are vested in the people and not in the Crown, so that *locus standi* for relator actions is distinguishable from that in the common law.[49]

In Fiji, it has been held that the Preamble to the Constitution is non-justiciable, but that the specific mandates set out in the Constitution must be placed within the wider context established by the Preamble which reflects the spirit and purpose behind the Constitution.[50] A similar approach has been followed in Samoa where it has been held that

> Although the Constitution is the supreme law and although it is to be read generously, the Courts do not have the power or ability to go beyond the clear and unequivocal words used. General words in the Preamble are not a mechanism whereby the Courts can extend beyond the clear boundaries contained in the Constitution. The Preamble sets the scene within which the powers and responsibilities established by the Constitution are to be exercised, but they are not a general licence to avoid the clear words which have been employed.[51]

Elsewhere the Preamble may appear to contradict rights provisions, for example, in Tuvalu the principles enumerated under the Preamble clearly indicate that traditional and group values are to prevail in Tuvalu. Indeed, the intended impact of the Preamble in Tuvalu on substantive law is clear in section 13 of the Constitution, which states 'The Principles set out in the Preamble are adopted as part of the basic law of Tuvalu, from which human rights and freedoms derive and on which they are based'. A consequence of this is that while private parties may bring an action against each other for alleged breaches of rights, in deciding the outcome group or traditional rights may prevail over individual rights.[52]

The scope of the Preamble in the Constitution may go beyond the provisions of the Constitution itself. For example, in Fiji it has been argued (unsuccessfully on appeal) that the Preamble emphasises the enduring influence of Christianity and its contribution, along with that of other faiths, to the spiritual life of Fiji. This in turn justifies the criminalisation of homosexuality in the Penal Code (Cap 17), even where homosexual acts are consensual and in private.[53] In Vanuatu provisions which stipulate Melanesian values and Christian principles found in the Preamble have been used to justify the condemnation of adultery and as justification for ordering the payment of damages by the offending party or parties where this is a ground for divorce.[54] In Solomon Islands reference to 'the worthy customs of our ancestors' in the Preamble has been relied on to emphasise how wrong the violation of a child is in customary law in Solomon Islands, especially where committed by close kin,[55] while the Preamble right of Solomon Island people to the natural resources of their country has been relied on to expand the scope of the Customs and Excise Act (Cap 58) to include birds under prohibited exports,[56] and to vest the ownership of illegally mined gold in the Crown.[57] In the Federated States of Micronesia it has been suggested that in interpreting the law the courts should be mindful of the values established in the Preamble when turning to the law of other nations. So that, although there has been a long tradition of referring to American law, reference to external sources 'should reflect sensitive consideration of the "pertinent aspects of Micronesian society and culture," including Micronesian values and the realities of life here in general and the nation-building aspirations set forth in the Preamble of the Constitution, in particular'.[58]

Preambles, therefore, may or may not assist in the protection and promotions of human rights depending on their status, content and interpretation.

Constitutional rights statements

The written constitutions granted at independence included – with the exception of Niue – statements of fundamental rights which were granted to individuals.[59] These in turn were modelled on codes of rights taken from elsewhere or influenced by ideas from beyond the region. For example, in Fiji Islands, Kiribati, Nauru, Samoa, Solomon Islands and Tuvalu the statements on fundamental rights and freedoms are modelled on those found in the European Convention for the Protection of Human Rights and Fundamental Freedoms and the Universal Declaration of Human Rights, whereas those found in the written constitutions of Cook Islands and Vanuatu follow the Canadian model (Corrin Care *et al.* 1999: 85).[60] Countries such as Marshall Islands and the Federated States of Micronesia are influenced by the American Declaration of Rights. These models not only influence the content and expression of the rights contained therein but also the interpretation of them. For example, rights set out in the Constitutions of Cook Islands and Vanuatu are relatively brief and are expressed in general terms – as are the exceptions to them, whereas those found in the Constitutions of countries such as Fiji Islands and Samoa are much more detailed. These rights are listed either in a 'Bill of Rights',[61] or in a section entitled 'Fundamental Rights and Freedoms' which is the nomenclature used in Kiribati, Nauru, Cook Islands and Solomon Islands. The Federated States of Micronesia and Samoa use the term 'Fundamental Rights' as does Palau. Kiribati and Solomon Islands refer to the rights and freedoms of the 'individual' while elsewhere the place of the individual in the framework of rights is enlarged upon in the preamble to the rights (see above) or in the rights themselves.

While the style, scope and detail of the constitutions vary considerably, especially as regards the provisions for human rights contained therein, the actual rights vary less; the additional detail usually pertains to the ways in which these may be restricted or limitations justified. Some of the rights listed are quite brief. Cook Islands, for example, lists eight basic rights,[62] while Fiji indicates twenty-one.[63] Some, but not all, of these rights will be considered in later chapters.

Interpretative approaches

Whatever the wording, however, these instruments have to be interpreted and applied in factual situations. The interpretation and application of such rights falls to the courts of the region and much depends on the approach taken by judges. It has been suggested in English law that fundamental rights provisions based on the Universal Declaration of Rights and the European Convention on Human Rights should be subject to a liberal interpretative approach.[64] While the interpretation of written constitutions may require particular approaches,[65] it has been suggested elsewhere that

> Basic or fundamental rights of individuals which presently stand formally incorporated in the modern constitutional documents, derive their lineage from, and are traceable to the ancient Natural Law. They require to be construed in consonance with the changed conditions of the society and must be viewed and interpreted with a vision to the future.[66]

In the Pacific region, a variety of interpretative approaches have been adopted by the courts, often with extensive reference to interpretative approaches used elsewhere. For example, in Cook Islands it has been held that, in construing enactments so as to comply with the fundamental human rights set out in the Constitution, a 'generous and purposive construction' should be used.[67] Indeed, sub-clause (2) of Art 65 of the Constitution requires all Acts and their provisions to be construed purposively and 'to receive such fair, large, and liberal construction and interpretation as will best ensure the attainment of the object of the enactment according to its true intent, meaning and spirit'. A 'fair and liberal' construction approach has also been approved in Samoa,[68] while in Vanuatu the claim that that the fundamental rights 'should be construed "with all the generality which the words used admit" ...' finds support.[69]

The need to be 'dynamic and creative, sensitive to popular expectations and democratic values' has found support in Fiji, especially with reference to the role of the judiciary in interpreting and applying fundamental rights.[70] See similarly the approach in Papua New Guinea in the case of *NTN Pty Ltd and NBN Ltd v The State* [1992] PGSC11, where it was held that in determining whether a law that restricted a fundamental right was justifiable in a democratic society – here a law to prohibit television because of its adverse effects – the test should be objective, and considered within the context and subject matter of each case.[71]

In Solomon Islands however, a more restrictive interpretation has been adopted, partly to avoid the horizontal application of the statement of Fundamental Rights found in the Constitution, and it has been held that a 'literal interpretation' is to be preferred.[72] Similarly, in the Federated States of Micronesia it has been held that if the words 'are clear and permit only one possible result, the court should go no further'.[73] In Tonga it has been held that looking at the actual words used is only the first step. A literal or rigid interpretation should be avoided. The court must go further than this. Following principles established in an earlier case,[74] Chief Justice Webster came up with a set of guidelines which the courts in Tonga should adopt when considering the interpretation of constitutional provisions regarding fundamental rights.[75] These are that the court should, first, pay proper attention to the words actually used in context and must not construe the Constitution as partly written and partly not; second, avoid doing so literally or rigidly – which is especially important for the protection of human rights; construe any derogation narrowly, but not so narrowly as to amount to misconstruction, and in doing so the court must beware of imposing the judge's own values; third, look at the whole Constitution; fourth, consider the background circumstances when the Constitution was granted in 1875; fifth, bear in mind established principles of international laws; and finally, be flexible to allow for changing circumstances.

The path between a broad and purposive approach and one where the court reads ' its own predilections and moral values into the Constitution'[76] can be a difficult one, and, where written constitutions place the courts in a position to review the constitutionality of legislation place considerable responsibility on judges.[77]

Bills of Rights and their application

One of the interpretative questions which the courts are faced with is whether constitutional provisions for human rights have a vertical or horizontal effect. That is whether they are only enforceable against the State, or its agents and representatives, or whether they can be relied on in litigation against other individuals or private parties. This is an issue which has caused debate elsewhere (Leigh 1999; Brinktrine 2001; du Plessis and Ford 2004), but has received relatively little attention in the Pacific region (Corrin 2007).

If fundamental rights are enforceable between individuals or private parties then there needs to be a correlative duty imposed on one private party in respect of the other asserting the right. For a right to be enforceable the party infringing it must either take some positive action which breaches the right or refrain from doing something which should have been done to give effect to the right. In many cases private parties lack the power to take the positive action required to give effect to rights. However, if rights are the entitlement of all private parties then at the very least there is a duty to respect the rights of others and to exercise one's own rights with the rights of others in mind. In practical terms the question may be whether, if one's right is infringed by another private party, any action can be taken to hold that party liable.

In some countries of the region, provisions relating to rights are clearly stated to be of horizontal effect permitting an action to be brought by one private party against another. This is the case, for example, in Tuvalu where section 12(1) of the Constitution, referring to the scope of fundamental rights – states:

(1) Each provision of this Part applies ...

   (a) between individuals as well as between governmental bodies and individuals; and
   (b) to and in relation to corporations and associations (other than governmental bodies) in the same way as it applies to and in relation to individuals, except where, or to the extent that, the context requires otherwise.

Elsewhere, it is not clear whether the intention is that rights should only be enforceable against the State or also against individuals or private parties. For example, in Palau some of the fundamental rights provisions specifically state that '(T)he government shall take no action to deny or impair the freedom ...' and in others the reference is to 'every person'.

In Vanuatu, the fundamental rights are indicated as the entitlement of every individual and that '(A)nyone who considers that any of the rights guaranteed to him by the Constitution has been, is being or is likely to be infringed may, independently of any other possible legal remedy, apply to the Supreme Court to enforce that right.' (Article 6(1) read with Article 5(1)). However, it is not clear if the infringement must be by the state or its representatives or could include an infringement by a non-state actor. Similarly, under the Human Rights Rules of Tokelau, 2003, rights are framed as individual rights and any person who considers that one of their rights has been infringed can apply for protection of that right to the 'Council of the Ongoing Government for protection of that right' and the Council can make whatever order it thinks appropriate. So that although the government or its representative is seen to be the adjudicator and enforcer of rights it appears that an individual could complain about the infringing action of another private party.

In Cook Islands the Constitution recognises that

   every person has duties to others, and accordingly is subject in the exercise of his rights and freedoms to such limitations as are imposed, by any enactment or rule of law for the time being in force, for protecting the rights and freedoms of others or in the interests of public safety, order, or morals, the general welfare, or the security of the Cook Islands

and that all written laws should 'be so construed and applied as not to abrogate, abridge, or infringe or to authorise the abrogation, abridgement, or infringement of any of the rights or freedoms recognised and declared' (Article 64(2) and (65(1)), suggesting that both horizontal and vertical effect may apply.

In other countries, there are equally clear statements that rights are only enforceable against the State or its agents as in Fiji where the Constitution of Fiji Islands section 21(1) states

This Chapter (the Bill of Rights) binds:

(a) the legislative, executive and judicial branches of government at all central, divisional and local; and
(b) all persons performing the functions of any public office.

However, this type of statement does not necessarily exclude horizontal effect especially if the judicial branch of government is included within the ambit of responsibility. If the courts have a duty to give effect to the State's obligations to uphold the fundamental rights and freedoms of parties before them, then indirect horizontal effect may be achieved in a number of ways. First, a court may find that the legal environment created by legislation put in place by the State infringes a fundamental human right and therefore is in breach. Second, the courts may interpret and shape unwritten law so as to best give effect to a private party's fundamental rights whether these are being asserted against the state or another private party. In the Pacific region this exercise may entail judicial interpretation of introduced principles of law or customary law or a combination of both.

The role of the courts is also important where it is unclear or ambiguous whether fundamental rights are to have vertical or horizontal effect. For example, in Samoa and Solomon Islands it is not clearly stated. The courts however have held that in some circumstances there may be horizontal effect.[78]

Even if fundamental rights are only enforceable against the state as represented by its agents there is still the question of who are the agents of the state. While in some situations this will be obvious and uncontroversial, for example, Ministers and staff in government departments, in others it will not be so clear. In the region, this uncertainty may be particularly relevant in determining the role and status of customary leaders and traditional sources of authority who continue to exercise considerable power over the lives of individuals.

The role of custom, customary law and customary institutions is pervasive throughout the region. Customary courts and the officials of those courts may also be formalised within the court system, either as lower courts or as parallel courts for certain matters.[79] Elsewhere they may be acknowledged within a formal system but left to administer their own affairs in a largely unregulated fashion.[80] Sometimes, however, it is not clear if a person or institution is acting as a representative of the state or not. This is particularly so where local leaders or private parties operate outside any official mandate but are nevertheless accommodated within broader statements of principle in the Constitution or accepted as part of the informal but necessary government of the country.

Among the more ambivalent 'officials' who may make decisions or carry out actions which impact on the lives and rights of private parties are church leaders and representatives, school teachers, parliamentary candidates, land owners and employers.

If there is no horizontal application of rights then there is the possibility that acts of the above can take place with impunity, or at least free from rights' sanctions. For example, in the Kiribati case of *Teitinnang v Ariong* [1986] KIHC 1, the plaintiff sought to bring an action against village elders who had denied the plaintiff access to his land and his children access to the primary school in the village because he had commercially harvested and sold pandanus thatches. The court held that he could not bring an action against the village elders on the grounds that 'no duty can be owed by an individual or group of individuals to another individual under the fundamental rights provisions of the Constitution'. However, the plaintiff had a right to sue in private law for unlawful interference with the exercise of his legal rights.

While, as in the above case, there may be recourse to other forms of legal action, if fundamental rights are only applied vertically then there is the danger that certain abuses of rights will be unprotected. This is particularly a concern where these take place away from the public arena (Forsyth 2005). Some of these issues will be considered in further chapters.

The role of the Constitution in the hierarchy of laws

As has been indicated, throughout the region written constitutions are the primary source of law. It follows therefore that the provisions for human rights within these constitutions should take precedence over other legislation and law. Indeed, this has been held to be so in a number of cases, some of which will be considered later in this book. However, the superiority of the constitution also means that other considerations besides fundamental rights may enjoy constitutional protection, thereby creating an internal conflict, the resolution of which may not always be in favour of human rights. This conflict may be between customary law and human rights; between entrenched protected positions and human rights; or between broadly encompassing provisions and the more specific provisions of human rights. It might therefore be queried whether the constitutions help or hinder human rights?

The incorporation of bills of rights into constitutions has the advantage that these statements of rights are less vulnerable to legislative change than would be the case were they simply in a statute – as, for example, is the case in the United Kingdom or New Zealand. Most constitutions have particular and often complex procedures for amendment. This can be both an advantage and a disadvantage. It is an advantage in so far as it may restrict the arbitrary whims of government – especially in times of political upheaval or crisis.[81] It is also an advantage in so far as the constitution is the highest source of law and, therefore, even in the absence of specialised constitutional courts, means that the highest courts can rule that the principles of the constitution must be upheld in preference to any subordinate legislation. It is, however, a disadvantage in so far as it may be a very difficult process to change aspects of a constitution which are no longer acceptable or in conformity with contemporary rights expectations or standards. For example, where inequalities based on race or sex or status are entrenched in a constitution.

A further concern is that the protection of human rights within a constitution is based on the premise that the structures put in place by that constitution will function so as to provide an effective means of protecting those rights. Thus there may be assumptions about the separation of the arms of government, observance of the rule of law, accountability and transparency in the workings of government and responsible exercise of power by a representative and freely elected government. This has not always been evidenced by the experience of Pacific Island counties.

However, formal statements of rights – whether in international treaties or in written constitutions – are not the only relevant influence, and it might be argued that even without these, the countries of the region would not be devoid of certain rights and freedoms.

Rights in Common Law

Even if there had been no statement of rights included in the written constitutions of the countries of the region under consideration, as in Niue, it is evident that the laws introduced into the region, either under colonial law or subsequently via customary international law or international treaties, have brought a number of principles of fundamental rights into the legal systems of Pacific Island countries. In other words, a bill of rights or constitutional statement of rights is not essential for claiming that certain fundamental rights exist, although these various sources may complement each other. This assertion is supported and illustrated by Australia, which, until fairly recently, had no bills of rights, and where judges are expected to interpret and apply the law in such a way as to safeguard the rights and freedoms of the individual (Gibbs 1982–1983).[82] Similarly, in the

United Kingdom, where there is no written constitution and only recently an authoritative statement of individual rights.[83]

Most Pacific Island countries are in the position of having both written constitutions incorporating declarations of rights and a residual legacy of common law introduced into the region and not yet fully replaced or repealed. Common law rights are, consequently, a feature of these legal systems. Some of these rights have emerged from written agreements between the ruler and the ruled, others from unwritten sources.

Foremost among documented rights which are still relevant in the Pacific region are those that were established by the *Magna Carta* 1215, and the Bill of Rights 1688. The most important, formerly unwritten right, is that of *habeas corpus*.[84] It has been suggested that *Magna Carta* and *habeas corpus* were 'the greatest bastion of individual liberty' in English common law (De Smith *et al.* 1995: 619 and 636). Indeed, Dicey expressed the view that the Habeas Corpus Acts – which replaced the unwritten common law from 1679 – were 'worth a hundred constitutional articles, guaranteeing individual liberty'(Dicey 1959: 199). While these common law rights are limited and vulnerable to being abrogated or removed by domestic legislation, they should not be overlooked when considering the protection of human rights in the Pacific region.

The legacy of Magna Carta *and the Bill of Rights*

Following revolt from his barons, King John of England agreed to sign the *Magna Carta* of 1215. In this charter, he guaranteed to this powerful lobby of landowners – and only incidentally to less important people – certain rights, including the right that there should be no punishment without a lawful judgement or according to the law of the land. *Magna Carta* also limited the power of the King, emphasising that the ruler should rule according to the law. In 1225 Henry III re-issued the 'Great Charter', as did Edward 1 in1297.[85] It received further statutory confirmation in 1351, 1354, and 1368.[86]

While many of the provisions of *Magna Carta* dealt with grievances which were prevailing at the time it also established certain important constitutional principles, including that the King – as Britain was then ruled by a King, does not have unlimited power but can be controlled by a written agreement. Today that power is controlled by written constitutions in many countries, including those of the South Pacific. *Magna Carta* also established certain protected rights to property (including water rights);[87] for the fair hearing of complaints against the Crown or its officials; for the observance of due process in court proceedings; and for proportionality between punishments and crimes. In particular it provided that

> No free man shall be seized or imprisoned, or stripped of his rights or possessions, or outlawed or exiled, or deprived of his standing in any

other way, not will we proceed with force against him, or send others to do so, except by the lawful judgment of his equals of by the law of the land.

(Paragraph 39 British Library Translation)[88]

It also stated that '[T]o no one will we sell, to no one deny or delay right or justice' (Paragraph 40).

Although the *Magna Carta* marks a moment in history considerably removed both in time and location from the contemporary Pacific, it remains relevant. Not only has it been incorporated into the law of the region but it has also been referred to in the courts of the region – see below. The principles it expounds are also relevant to a more fundamental question that arises in plural legal systems, if an individual should not be punished except according to the law of the land, what is that law, and in particular what is the role and status of custom and customary law in Pacific legal systems?

Magna Carta is not the only legacy of the common law to be relevant to the region. In the seventeenth century Britain experienced a civil war between royalists – who supported the King and parliamentarians – who wanted a more democratic form of government. This spanned the period 1642–1651. Ultimately the monarchy was secured but with considerably reduced powers. The Act Declaring the Rights and Liberties of the Subject and Settling the Succession of the Crown (The Bill of Rights 1688) came into effect in 1689 and established the constitutional monarchy still found today in the United Kingdom and of significance to those Pacific Island countries for which the English monarch is still Head of State.[89] Further curbs on the powers of the monarchy were found in the 1701 Act of Settlement.[90] The 1689 Act stated the positive rights which citizens should have in a free and democratic society.[91] In particular it emphasised the rights inherent in the relationship of the people and their representatives in Parliament, for example: the process of free elections; the right of citizens not to be taxed without the due process and approval of a representative parliament; freedom of speech in Parliament (now known as 'parliamentary privilege'); freedom from cruel and unusual punishment; freedom from the imposition of penalties and forfeiture of property without trial. In effect the Bill of Rights read with the *Magna Carta* came to be interpreted as establishing a range of civil and political rights for citizens and these became integrated into the common law, helping to shape not only the political structure of a Westminster Parliament – forms of which were introduced into the Pacific, but also the relationship of the citizen with the law makers and law enforcers. These basic constitutional rights were further strengthened by the Act of Settlement 1701 and the Parliament Acts of 1911 and 1949. Although the 1701 Act was passed primarily to govern succession to the English throne, it also established the importance of judicial independence.[92] It is part of the constitutional law of those countries which retain the British Monarch as the Head of State. The Parliament Acts are restricted in application to the United Kingdom and therefore of little relevance to the Pacific region.

Many of the principles established by these historical events in English law are of continuing relevance in the Pacific region. They are part of the legacy of colonies either settled by or ceded to the British. For example, in New Zealand it was presumed that these early constitutional enactments were part of the inheritance of New Zealand (Joseph 2001: 18). The schedules of the Imperial Laws Act 1988 (NZ), which is the definite statement of which British statutes apply to New Zealand, listed *Magna Carta*, the Petition of Right 1627 – which affirmed due process and prohibited taxation without representation,[93] the Bill of Rights 1688,[94] parts of the Act of Settlement 1700 and the Habeas Corpus Acts of 1640, 1679 and 1816.[95] Indeed, in New Zealand in 1976 the Bill of Rights was relied on by the Chief Justice to declare that the Prime Minster had acted illegally in purporting to abolish a superannuation scheme before Parliament had passed legislation to that effect.[96] In Australia it has been argued that the 1688 Bill of Rights has continued to play an important part in the protection of human rights in the country in the absence of a bill of rights in the Constitution (Gibbs 1982–1983), although there is not always consensus on this.

In Cook Islands it has been held that the Bill of Rights 1688 forms part of the law of the Cook Islands by virtue of section 615 of the Cook Islands Act 1915, which incorporates into Cook Islands '[T]he law of England as existing on the 14th day of January in the year 1840 ... save so far as inconsistent with this Act or inapplicable to the circumstances of those islands'. Provisions of the Bill of Rights which have been relied on include Article 9: 'That the freedom of speech and debates or proceedings in Parliament ought not to be impeached or questioned in any Court of place out of Parliament;[97] and Article 1, which provides that 'election of members of Parliament ought to be free.'[98] Similarly, in Niue, Article 9 has been held to be fundamental to democratic government and freedom of speech in the legislative assembly.[99] In Fiji the Bill of Rights and its prohibition on 'the raising or keeping of a standing army within the Kingdome in a time of peace unless it be with consent of Parliament is against law' has been referred to in the context of military law and trial by court martial of those involved in the Speight led coup of 2000.[100]

It is not only the Bill of Rights that remains of relevance in the region. In Tonga and Vanuatu *Magna Carta* is incorporated into the legal systems of both countries via the notes to section 6 Civil Evidence Act 1968, which was a law of general application.[101] Elsewhere the courts have made reference to *Magna Carta* to support the principle that any fines levied on an offender should be within that offender's ability to pay; that no courts can be created except by law;[102] that ordinarily arrests should not be made without the sanctity of a warrant;[103] that a person is entitled to be tried without undue delay;[104] and that fair trial should not be prejudiced by adverse media coverage.[105] There is evidence therefore that not only have Magna Carta and the Bill of Rights been important influences in the evolution of fundamental rights in English common law but continue to be used to support rights in the contemporary Pacific.

Habeas corpus

Also of importance is one of the most important fundamental rights of longstanding in English law: the right to *habeas corpus* in the case of wrongful or unjustified detention. The right to bring an action on the basis of *habeas corpus* allows a demand to be made to a court that just cause is provided for that detention. Originally a prerogative writ,[106] it is an action available against the State or its representatives and against private parties.[107] It is also available *ex parte* in clear cases of wrongful detention or deprivation of liberty falling short of incarceration.[108] In 1816 English law extended the application of *habeas corpus* to civil detention and provided grounds whereby the court could investigate the alleged reasons for detention.[109]

Habeas corpus was introduced into those islands of the Pacific that came under British influence via the Western Pacific (Courts) Order in Council 1961.[110] Today this common law remedy finds its place in written law and in the principles of common law applied by the courts, either as part of the adopted law,[111] or as integral to the general principles of law and equity. For example, it is found in the Federated States of Micronesia,[112] in Fiji, under Order 54 High Court Rules 1988,[113] in Papua New Guinea in the National Court Rules 1983,[114] and in Vanuatu – although the language is modernised, in the Civil Procedure Rules 2002, Rule 16 (3) and (4), where it is referred to as 'a claim for release'. Its application in the local context has been considered in a number of cases. For example, in Papua New Guinea in the case of *Aika v Uremany* [1976] PNGLR 46, it was held that when considering a claim of *habeas corpus* the local circumstances must be taken into account; in Samoa, the courts have had to distinguish *habeas corpus* from the right to bail; [115] in Tonga it has been used to secure the release of a person arrested without a warrant[116] and in circumstances where members of the legislative assembly were imprisoned by order of the Speaker of the Legislative Assembly.[117] In Marshall Islands it has been held that the right to *habeas corpus* is not ousted by the Immigration Act in the case of illegal immigrants,[118] and in Solomon Islands it has been used where police misinterpreted their powers of detention and calculation of sentence.[119] The availability of the writ of *habeas corpus* has therefore proved to be of considerable relevance in the legal systems of the region, especially in circumstances where ordinary legal rules and remedies are unavailable.[120]

Indeed, the writ of *habeas corpus* has been important in a number of contemporary situations, such as political coups and the detention of illegal immigrants or asylum seekers. Two examples illustrate this.

In 2004, refugee Afghan nationals being held in detention camps in Nauru while seeking asylum in Australia, applied for relief by way of *habeas corpus*.[121] The question was whether the detention of asylum seekers in these camps was unlawful as a form of 'extra-curial imprisonment'. In fact it was established in court that the gates of the camps were generally left open – although security personnel were in place to monitor movement. Nevertheless the court was satisfied that the applicants were in custody for the purposes of *habeas corpus* because they were confined to a particular location.[122] However, the detention was held to be lawful under the exercise of statutory powers delegated to the Principal Immigration Officer under the Immigration Act 1999 and the Immigration Regulations 2000 and as agreed between the government of Nauru and the Australian government.[123] The detention was non-punitive and directed as keeping aliens without the required entry permits or visas under supervision or control until their status was determined – which could take time. The applicants were free to leave and return to their country of origin whenever they liked, although anyone who has tried to travel to and from Nauru will know that the practicalities of doing this can be a challenge.

In Fiji, political arrest, which has manifested itself in several coups, has also been a context in which *habeas corpus* has remained relevant. In *Baleinamau v Commander of the Fiji Military Forces* [2001] FJHC 126, the question of the lawful detention of a non-civilian suspected of being involved in the military mutiny which took place in 2000, was challenged.[124] Powers of detention were exercisable under the Emergency Decree (No. 4) of 2000, the Rules of Procedure (Army) 1972, the Queen's Regulations for the Army 1975 and the Army Act (UK) 1955.[125] However, the detainee had been in custody without being charged for 277 days – a period considerably in excess of the statutory periods provided for. Referring to a previous decision – pertaining to the 1997 Fiji Coup,[125] the court held that although the detention was being exercised under a legislative framework applicable to non-civilians, *habeas corpus* was not excluded. The country was not – at the time of the application – under Martial Law, although the Emergency Decree remained operative. The 1997 Constitution remained in force and the civil courts still had jurisdiction.[127] *Habeas corpus* was granted.

There were further applications for *habeas corpus* in relation to other military personnel involved in the 2000 mutiny who were subsequently charged and detained for many months. Considering such an application in the case of *Ralumu v Commander, Republic of Fiji Military Forces – Reasons for Judgment*, Jitiko J, emphasising in particular the due process constitutional rights of the accused, stated:

> The applicants have been in detention awaiting trial for some 25 months as of today. No country that calls itself civilised, let alone democratic, can possibly allow this situation to continue. It is an intolerable situation. While they may have been charged with serious offences against the

State their rights as individuals and citizens of this country cannot be
ignored simply because the system is not able to bring them to trial early;
or there are unsubstantiated reports linking them to further disturbance
that happened recently.[128]

Habeas corpus was granted but frustrated because immediately notice of
the court order to release the detainees was served on the Director of Legal
Services at the Barracks, the men were taken back into detention under fresh
charges. A further application for *habeas corpus* was made. The same judge,
while critical of the tactics used by the Army, held the detention to be lawfully
exercised under military law – the United Kingdom Forces (Jurisdiction of
Colonial Courts) Order 1965 incorporated under s 70(4) Army Act 1955
(UK). This refusal to grant *habeas corpus* was upheld by a single judge sitting
in the Fiji Court of Appeal, on the grounds that any application unlikely to
be successful given the lawfulness of the present detention under the new
charges. An appeal to the Supreme Court under Constitutional provisions
which allowed special leave of appeal to the Supreme Court on matters of
general legal importance,[129] required the Court to consider and rule on the
fundamental rights of non-civilians. The 1970 Constitution granted to Fiji on
independence excluded from the ambit of its fundamental rights provisions
service personnel of the disciplined forces (naval, military or air force) who
were subject to the disciplinary law of that force. The right to personal liberty
was not however excluded for such persons. Similarly, the right to personal
liberty was not excluded in the later 1990 Constitution. Moreover the 1970
exclusions in respect of service personnel were not incorporated into the
present 1997 Constitution. Consequently, the Supreme Court found that an
application for *habeas corpus* could be made in respect of service personnel
detained for offences which may be subject to disciplinary law. Further, the
Supreme Court indicated that *habeas corpus* might be granted for wrongful
detention even though the detained person was simultaneously being
detained for another, lawful reason, or where – despite the grant of *habeas
corpus* – there were reasons, for example of public safety or for the safety of
the detainee, that release was not ordered – for example, where the detainee
was medically or mentally unfit to be released into the community.[130] The
Supreme Court held therefore 'that there were circumstances in which
habeas corpus might and should be granted although the issuance of the
writ would not lead to the applicant's release from detention'. So: '*habeas
corpus* may be granted for the release of a person from detention on one
basis when that person may lawfully continue in detention on another'.[131]
   Although the Supreme Court had clarified the law, the decision to refuse
the writ of *habeas corpus* on the facts of the case was upheld by a single
judge of the Court of Appeal, who held that the detained petitioners were
lawfully under arrest because the Commander of the Army was empowered
to charge a person who was the subject of military law with the offence of
murder provided that the victim was also military personnel.[132]

It is evident therefore that reliance on these ancient protections of certain rights remain important for the protection of fundamental rights in the region, especially where declarations of military law or a state of emergency may curtail certain rights set forth in written constitutions and hamper the efforts of human rights enforcement agencies to uphold such rights, as illustrated recently in the December 2006 coup in Fiji.

Fundamental principles

Although incorporated into statute in English law from the mid-seventeenth century, *habeas corpus* is one of a number of fundamental rights developed by the courts of common law. Others include the right to private property free from unlawful trespass by the State or its agents;[133] the right to be informed of the grounds for arrest where such an arrest is made;[134] and that no statute should have retrospective effect unless clearly intended to do so and even if so intended only so far as is necessary.[135]

These fundamental principles of common law and equity have also been incorporated into the legal systems of Pacific countries and may afford significant protection of human rights, especially where these principles have yet to be replaced by domestic legislation. For example, it has been held that the principle against double jeopardy in criminal cases should apply unless a statute expressly and specifically provides otherwise. Indeed in Cook Islands it has been held that

> it is a fundamental principle of interpretation that no statute should be so construed as to abrogate a fundamental principle of the common law. For that to happen there must be a clear and unequivocal expression of intention in any statutory provision that that should be so construed.
> (*Police v Ngau* [1992] CKHC 3 per Dillon J)

However, whether a general body of fundamental rights prior to the emergence of constitutional rights existed is less clear. This was a question raised in the Nauru case of *In re the Constitution, Jeremiah v Nauru Local Government Council* [1971] NRSC 5. The petitioner, a Nauruan, had been refused consent by the Council to marry a non-Nauruan. This consent was required under section 23 of the Births, Deaths and Marriages Ordinance 1957–1967. While the Constitution includes a right to freedom of respect for private and family life it makes no mention of the right to marry. The petitioner argued that this was a common law right implied in the right to family and private life. The court found that the right of every individual to the rights and freedoms subsequently listed in the Constitution appeared to assume that these rights and freedoms already existed but found that 'there is no statutory or common law basis for some of those enumerated'. The court concluded that 'the reference to ... an entitlement to fundamental rights and freedoms of the kinds stated is clearly not intended to refer to any pre-existing rights and freedoms but only to those set out in detail in (subsequent articles)'. It was not therefore prepared to accept that there was a body of pre-existing common law fundamental rights which could be implied to enlarge those rights which were expressly stated. Much, therefore, may depend on the willingness of the courts to admit general principles of rights where there is no clearly expressed right.

Customary human rights

Perhaps, however, international developments and initiatives are unnecessary. It may be that there is a sufficient body of indigenous rights' law already in the region. Two of the constitutions of the region, Federated States of Micronesia and Palau specifically refer to 'Traditional rights'. In the Federated States of Micronesia these rights take two forms. Primarily they are the rights of traditional leaders to exercise functions of government (Article V sections 1 and 3). In this sense these rights are powers to be exercised by a few, not rights to be enjoyed by all. Second, traditional rights are also preserved under Article V, section 2, to the extent that these may take precedence over other constitutional rights without being deemed to breach these. These rights may be protected or endorsed by statute at the expense of individual rights listed in the Constitution under Article IV. This could mean that in certain circumstances some rights will trump or take precedence over other rights. Both sets of rights may be claimable by the same people or certain right holders may be preferred over others.

In Palau, traditional rights also take the form of preserving the power of traditional leaders, provided the recognition and exercise of such powers is not unconstitutional (Article V section 1). However, the recognition of 'traditional power' under traditional rights envisages a possible conflict between the traditional law that confers the power, and statute law. The relevant provision, Article V section 2, states that where such a conflict occurs and both are equally authoritative, statute law shall prevail but only to the extent that it is 'not in conflict with the underlying principles of the traditional law'. This suggests that in practice, where there is a conflict, traditional law may well 'trump' statute law. In fact an example can be found in Tuvalu where the case of *Tepulolo v Pou* [2005] TVHC 1, provided an opportunity to weigh international human rights against Tuvaluan traditions and customary usage which found support in domestic law, notably the Native Lands Ordinance, section 20 and the Custody of Children Ordinance, section 3. In this case an unmarried mother sought to retain custody of her young son against the claim of the child's father. The father relied on the child's right to inherit land in accordance with native customary law, which entitled the father to claim custody of the child once he was two years old. The mother sought to rely on the non-discrimination provisions of the Constitution and the provisions of international conventions: the CRC and CEDAW. The father won.

The domestic legislation endorsed Tuvaluan custom and usage which was itself supported in a number of places in the Constitution. The court held that discrimination on the grounds of sex was permitted especially with reference to land, and the international covenants were not part of the domestic law (Farran 2005c).

While it is often difficult to escape from the type of conflict illustrated in the above case (Corrin Care 1999; Farran 1997), it has been suggested more recently that traditional rights, or ideas of rights in customary law, share some of the same underlying principles as introduced rights and that more should be done to explore and establish common ground.

The New Zealand Law Commission has suggested that fundamental rights are already observed in custom and customary law in the Pacific region as evidenced by certain forms of expected and approved conduct and the disapproval or punishment of other forms of conduct (New Zealand Law Commission 2006). In particular it is suggested that many of the values that inform customary practices and rules are similar across the region although they may be formulated differently from one place to another. These values include: individual dignity or worth, which in turn gives rise to an expectation of mutual respect between people; care towards others manifested by love, the observation of filial and family obligations, and the sharing of resources; benevolent leadership and community participation in decision making; mutuality and reciprocity in social exchanges; humility, generosity and wisdom.[136] Many of these values are informed by or share Christian principles and for that reason alone may be seen as having a commonality with the values and norms that have informed declarations of rights elsewhere.[137] Whether all these values are endorsed by all Pacific islanders or whether they are given positive effect in practice is uncertain, largely because of the lack of empirical research in this area.

There are also procedural and substantive difficulties. In many cases the manifestation of any body of customary fundamental rights is not formal but depends on the observation of daily life and social organisation. It may be difficult to establish whether certain conduct is a consequence or indication of respect for certain fundamental rights or due to some other cause. For example, displays of respect or deference may be due to fear or repression rather than recognition of the inherent value of all members of society. Similarly, apparent consensus or toleration may conceal the suppression of other fundamental rights such as freedom of expression, or association, or movement. It may also be the case that not all members of a society subscribe to the traditional norms or that these operate in direct conflict with more recently introduced fundamental rights. For example, young people educated outside their islands may challenge the unquestioned acceptance of decisions of heads of families or local chiefs; women may challenge their lack of voice or participation in decision making forums or the patriarchal ordering of land rights; new urban elites may not subscribe to the egalitarian sharing of resources. Moreover, in widely scattered communities where culture, language, customary usage and tradition are not homogenous it is probable danger that individual experiences of rights and freedoms will be very disparate.

This is not to suggest that custom and customary law does not operate within a normative framework. Clearly it does, and has to in order to be accepted. However it may be that this framework prioritises rights differently from those expressed in the written constitutions or in international treaties, or that the enjoyment of such rights sacrifices the individual's claim to the greater good of the wider group. It is clear however that if the lives of many people in the region are determined by customary law, then a body of traditional rights and duties cannot be ignored. The challenge is to understand how these different approaches can work together to create a positive framework of rights for everyone.

The New Zealand Law Commission (2006) suggests that there are direct parallels between some custom values and human rights ideals. For example, the Pacific endorsement of distributive equality and egalitarianism and international declarations on the important of equal rights both suggest the importance of caring and sharing resources (Para 6.5–6.6); the importance of community participation and reciprocity in decision making finds a similarity in freedom of expression subject to restrictions influenced by the need to show respect and the acceptance of authority (Para 6.7); while respect for the spiritual beliefs of others and the acceptance of missionary teaching demonstrates religious tolerance (Para 6.8). Whether this commonality between custom and human rights provides sufficient grounds for claiming that the two are 'converging currents' will be considered when looking at the practice rather than the rhetoric of rights in subsequent chapters. What is evident about custom values is that any exercise of individual rights tends to be subject to those of the group. This reflects the mutuality and inter-dependence of individuals and the group. This requirement of mutuality is found in international and national human rights statements, although usually in the context of the exercise of individual rights. There are however provisions for the recognition of group rights,[138] and often the claim of one individual will be representative of many others.[139] The extent to which the group can be accommodated within the framework of rights found in the region will be considered subsequently, as will the proposals of the New Zealand Law Commission. Suffice it to say at this point that there is a body of opinion which suggests that custom is sanctioning and endorsing fundamental rights without recourse to the written statements of rights in the various constitutions and that, therefore, either the written statements of rights are superfluous or, if they are to become wholly acceptable to Pacific Island people, they need to be integrated with these customary rights and not seen as something separate and alien. Certainly if custom is understood to define that which belongs to the people (in contradistinction to that which comes from outside or is alien) it is important that Pacific Island people see human rights as belonging to them.[140]

Conclusion

This chapter has explored the contemporary emergence of human rights. It is evident that a number of different influences have contributed to that body of rights which are loosely brought together under the broad heading of 'human rights and fundamental freedoms'. While the historical context in which they emerged in the international arena and the formulation of such rights by international instruments all pose problems and challenges for rights' discourse, implementation and observance in the Pacific region, it is clear that Pacific Island countries are brought within this web of rights' law in a variety of ways. It is suggested that the articulation of rights is not a totally alien concept in the region even if the international formulation of rights in the course of the twentieth century has shifted the emphasis. It is also evident that, even if Pacific countries had no written statements of rights, there would still be a body of rights' law which could be referred to and which continues to be drawn on. It is important to keep this in mind, not only because it means that for those countries without bills of rights there is still a rights' framework, but also in those countries with written statements of rights which appear to be ineffective, poorly protected or imperfectly upheld there are alternative avenues.

Notes

1 Constitution of Tonga 1875 Article 7, as amended in 1990 and 2003. See *Taione v Kingdom of Tonga* [2004] TOSC 47.
2 See, for example, *Lali Media Group Ltd v Lavaka Ata* [2003] TOSC 27; *Utoikamanu v Lali Media Group Ltd* [2003] TOCA 6.
3 See, for example, *Teonea v Kaupule* [2005] TVHC 2 where the local *Falekaupule* refused to allow the establishment of a new church, and similarly *Lafaialii v Attorney-General* [2003] WSSC 8 where the local *Alii* and *Faipule* sought to prevent and banish a religious group.
4 See *Kaye v Robertson* [1991] 1 FSR 62; *Lord Berstein of Leigh v Skyviews and General Ltd* [1978] QB 479 and the Australian case of *Victoria Park Racing and Recreation Grounds Co Ltd v Taylor* (1937) 58 CLR 479.
5 Schedule 1, Human Rights Act 1998, Part 1, The Convention, Article 8.
6 See, for example, the preambles to the constitutions of Fiji, Federated States of Micronesian, Kiribati, Papua New Guinea, Samoa and Tuvalu.
7 Mining (Ok Tedi Mine Continuation) Ninth Supplement Agreement, Act 2001 s 1(4).
8 This is self-evident in the notion of national 'margins of appreciation' as applied in the context of the European Convention of Human Rights, particularly in respect of those rights which impinge on private lives.
9 The French Declaration of the Rights of Man 1789 is one such example, as is the American Bill of Rights 1791.
10 As was the case with most rights statements following the two World Wars and subsequently statements through the United Nations.
11 The main international human rights instruments with which this book is concerned are: the Universal Declaration of Human Rights (adopted on 10 December 1948); the United Nations Covenant on Civil and Political Rights (adopted 16 December 1966), the International Convention on the Elimination

of All Forms of Racial Discrimination (adopted 7 March 1966); the Convention on the Elimination of All Forms of Discrimination against Women (adopted 19 December 1979); and the Convention on the Rights of the Child (adopted 20 November 1989).

12 It has been suggested that Thomas Paine first coined the phrase 'human rights' in 1791 in a book entitled *The Rights of Man* (Hoffman and Rowe 2006:19). National statements of certain fundamental rights can be found much earlier, of course, in documents such as *Magna Carta* 1215, the American Declaration of Independence 1776, and the French Declaration of the Rights of Man 1789.

13 Civic (1995–1996) argues that it was a basic distrust of rulers and power derived from the hierarchical and essentially unaccountable structure of feudal Europe which led to the *Magna Carta* in England and the Declarations of Rights in France and America.

14 The predecessor of the United Nations, the League of Nations which was established in 1920 after the First World War 1914–1918, began the process of putting the rights of peoples in the international law arena. The League of Nations system of mandates for the former colonies of defeated nations applied to a number of Pacific Island countries.

15 Charter of the United Nations (the 'Charter'), opened for signature 13 February 1946, Res 22A(1) (entered into force 14 December 1946).

16 The Declaration of Human Rights was adopted by the United Nations General Assembly in 1948.

17 International Convention on Civil and Political Rights, opened for signature 19 December 1966 (entered into force 2 March 1976).

18 International Covenant on Economic, Social and Cultural Rights, opened for signature 19 December 1966 (entered into force 3 January 1976).

19 Section 39(3)(b)–(e). In Fiji 'public international law' (of which human rights instruments may be a part) is referred to as an aid to interpretation of the rights set out in Chapter 4 of the Constitution (Amendment) Act 1997, section 43(2).

20 [1966] PITSE 4, opened for signature New York, 16 December 1966, entered into force 3 January 1976.

21 [1984] PITSE 4, opened for signature 10 December 1984, entered into force 26 June 1987.

22 [1990] PITSE 19, opened for signature 18 December 1990, entered into force 1 July 2003.

23 [2006] PITSE 5, opened for signature 13 December 2006, entered into force 3 May 2008.

24 Cook Islands and Niue are parties to the ICESCR by virtue of New Zealand's ratification and Solomon Islands succeeded to this Convention so it can hardly be said that these are positive commitments on the part of their governments.

25 This is by signature only; both countries on 6 February 2007.

26 Vanuatu on 17 May 2007. This came into force on 3 May 2008 having achieved the requisite twenty signatures.

27 12 November 2001.

28 In the case of Vanuatu it could be argued that under French influence under the Condominium government of the New Hebrides, it has, or could elect to have a monist system but this path does not seem to have been followed.

29 As was done in Fiji with the Family Law Act 2003.

30 See comment by Baird (2007) on the reporting mechanisms and processes required under most of the core conventions and Jalal (2006) on the ramifications of implementing measures to comply with the obligations incurred under these conventions.

31 A number of these are considered in subsequent chapters.

32 While the larger and wealthier Pacific Island countries, such as Fiji and Papua New Guinea, are now becoming more involved in United Nations matters, the voices of smaller Pacific Island countries tend to be ignored.

33 Only in Vanuatu is the involvement of Parliament required (section 26 Vanuatu Constitution).

34 Whether this takes the form of attracting more aid funded projects, or facilitates inward investment or trade relations. These motives may also explain a greater enthusiasm for ratifying conventions of the WTO or the IMO.

35 Vienna Convention On The Law Of Treaties, signed at Vienna, 23 May 1969, entered into force 27 January 1980.

36 Article 38(1) International Court of Justice Statute.

37 http://www.forumsec.org.fj/pages.cfm/about-us/

38 See, for example, *Fa v Naniura* [1990] PGNC 97.

39 Examples are where nuclear waste is trans-shipped across the region despite objections being voiced by those Pacific Countries through whose waters ships pass.

40 1978, Ch No 16 especially sections 10 and 13.

41 *Naduaniwai v Commander, Republic of Fiji Military Forces* [2004] FJHC 8.

42 Section 43(2) and (3).

43 Independence was achieved as follows: Western Samoa (now Samoa) in1962; Nauru in 1968; Fiji (now Fiji Islands) in 1970; Papua New Guinea in1975; Tuvalu in 1978; Solomon Islands in 1978; Kiribati in 1979 (formerly part of the Gilbert and Ellice Islands with Tuvalu); Marshall Islands in 1986; Cook Islands in 1965; Niue in 1974; Federated States of Micronesia in 1986; Palau in 1978; Vanuatu (formerly the New Hebrides) in 1980.

44 See, for example, Ghai (1988); Ntumy (1993); Paterson (2000); Roberts Wray (1966); Sack (1982).

45 Article 3(c), Constitution of Nauru 1968, Preamble to Part 11, Protection of Fundamental Rights and Freedoms.

46 Compare, for example, *Jeremiah v Nauru Local Government Board Nauru Law Reports* [1971] NRSC 5 with *Fiji Waterside Workers Union v Reginam* (1977) 23 FLR 196.

47 *The Minister of Provincial Government v. Guadalcanal Provincial Assembly CAC No. 3* [1997] SBCA 1.

48 Approved in *Premdas v the State* [1979] PNGLR 329 where it was unclear what fundamental rights aliens were entitled to.

49 *Kenilorea v Attorney General* [1983] SBHC 30.

50 *Naba v The State* [2001] FJHC 127.

51 *In re the Constitution , Mulitalo v Attorney-General of Samoa* [2001] WSCA 8.

52 *Teonea v Kaupule* [2005] TVHC 2 is an example.

53 *Nadan v the State* [2005] FJHC 252 and *McCoskar v The State* [2005] FJHC 500.

54 *Maltok v Maltok* [2002] VUSC 70.

55 *R v Poloso* [2006] SBHC 33.

56 *Maetia v R* [1994] SBCA 4.

57 *Knight v Attorney General* [2005] SBHC 6.

58 *Semens v Continental Airlines Inc* [1985] FMSC 1.

59 These can be found as follows: Part IVA The Constitution of Cook Islands; Article IV, The Constitution of the Federated States of Micronesia; Chapter 4, Constitution (Amendment) Act 1997 Fiji; Chapter II, The Constitution of Kiribati; Article II, The Constitution of the Marshall Islands; Part II, The Constitution of Nauru; Article IV, The Constitution of the Republic of Palau; Division 3, The Constitution of the Independent State of Papua New Guinea; Part II, The Constitution of the Independent State of Western Samoa

(now known as Samoa); Chapter II, The Constitution of Solomon Islands; Part I, The Constitution of Tonga; Part II, The Constitution of Tuvalu; Chapter 2, Constitution of the Republic of Vanuatu. In Tokelau provision for human rights can be found in the Human Rights Rules 2003.

60 The 1964 Constitution of the Cook Islands made no such provision but this was amended in 1981 (Constitution Amendment Act (No. 9 1980–81) which provides for a bill of rights.

61 Bill of Rights is used in Fiji and Marshall Islands and 'Human Rights Rules' is used in Tokelau.

62 Part IVA, Cook Island Constitution Act 1964.

63 Chapter 4, Fiji Constitution 1997.

64 *Minister of Home Affairs v Fisher* [1980] AC 319.

65 *Hunter v Southam Inc.* (1985) 11 DLR (4th) 641 (SCC) at 649 per Dickson J.

66 *Nawaz Sharif v President of Pakistan* PLD 1993 SC 473.

67 *Police v Tutakiau* [2001] CKHC 1.

68 *Malifa v Sapolu* [1999] WSSC 47.

69 See *In re the Constitution, Timakata v Attorney-General* [1992] VUSC 9, citing the Australian case of *Queen v The Public Vehicle Licensing Appeal Tribunal of the State of Tasmania* (1965) 113 CLR 207 at 225 with approval.

70 See *Naba v The State* [2001] FJHC 127, which includes a comprehensive overview of approaches from other Commonwealth Jurisdictions and *Ali v the State* [2001] FJHC 123, which endorses a purposive approach.

71 Per Kapi DCJ, who amended his former subjective test in *Re Organic Law On National Elections* [1982] PNGLR 214. See also Prentice CJ in *Constitutional Reference No 1* [1977] PNGLR 362 at 373.

72 *Ulufa'alu v Attorney-General* [2001] SBHC 81.

73 *In Re Paul* [2002] FMCSC 16 and *Panuelo v Pohnpei* [1987] FMPSC 5.

74 *Tu'itavake v Porter* [1989] TOSC 3.

75 *Taione v Kingdom of Tonga* [2004] TOSC 47.

76 *Reyes v The Queen* [2002] 2 AC (PC) : 235: 246, per_Lord Bingham of Cornhill para 26, cited with approval in *Taione* (above).

77 See, for example, *Clarke v Karika* [1982] CKCA 1 and *In re the Constitution, Timaka v Attorney-General* [1992] VUSC 9.

78 *Loumia v DPP* [1985–86] SILR 158 and *Tuivaiti v Sila* [1980–93] WSLR 181. Compare however *Ulufa'alu v Attorney-General* [2001] SBHC 81.

79 See, for example, the Island Courts, or the Customary Land Tribunals in Vanuatu, the *Fono* and Lands Courts in Samoa or the *Falekaupule* in Tuvalu.

80 See, for example, the role of the councils of chiefs in Solomon Islands in determining land disputes: Local Courts Act (Cap 19).

81 Although this did not prevent the interim government in Fiji following the 2000 coup from introducing a new Constitution.

82 More recently written Bills of Rights have been adopted; notably in the Australian Capital Territory (2003) and Victoria (Charter of Human Rights and Responsibilities Act 2006).

83 The Human Rights Act 1998, which brings into the domestic law of England and Wales, Scotland and Northern Ireland, most of the rights and freedoms set out in the European Convention for the Protection of Human rights and Fundamental Freedoms.

84 This is a writ of great antiquity. Judge Pathik in Fiji cites the Earl of Birkenhead's reference to it having been used in the thirty-third year of Edward 1 in *Secretary of State for Home Affairs v O'Brien* [1923] All ER Rep. HL 442 at 444.

85 25 Edw. 1 (*Magna Carta*) (1297), Vol. 6. A translation of *Magna Carta* (which was originally written in Latin) can be found at http://www.bl.uk/treasures/magnacarta/translation.html.

86 (1351) 25 Edw 3 St 5 c 4; (1354) 28 Edw 3 c 3; (1368) 42 Edw 3 c 3.

87 Relied on in *Ulelio and Others v Nelulu Land Group, Registrar of Titles and The State* [1998] PGNC 19.

88 *Magna Carta*, British Library translation, http://www.bl.uk/treasures/ magnacarta/translation.html (accessed 2 March 2007).

89 For example, Cook Islands, Papua New Guinea, Pitcairn, Solomon Islands and Tuvalu.

90 The Act was originally passed by the Parliament of England and was later extended to Scotland by the terms of the Acts of Union 1707.

91 In Scotland – which at that time was a separate kingdom – the 1689 Claim of Right of the Scottish Estates had a similar effect but also established William and Mary as King and Queen of Scotland following the flight and abdication of James 11 of Scotland.

92 It was extended to Scotland by the Act of Union in 1707.

93 3 Cha 1 c 1.

94 1 Will & Mar Sess 2 c 2.

95 The Habeas Corpus Act 2001 (NZ) now makes specific New Zealand provision for *habeas corpus*.

96 *Fitzgerald v Muldoon and Others* [1976] 2 NZLR 615.

97 See *Advocate-General of the Cook Islands v Story* [1980] CKHC 2 and *Robarti v Privileges Standing Committee – Judgment 1* [1994] CKCA 2.

98 *Pokoati v Tetava* [1978] CKHC 2.

99 *Kalauni v Jackson* [1996] NUCA 1.

100 *Naduaniwai v Commander, Republic of Fiji Military Forces* [2004] FJHC 8.

101 The same Act also refers to the Bill of Rights.

102 *Qalo v Qaloboe* [2004] SBCA 5, in which the Court of Appeal of Solomon Islands held that s 10(8) of the Constitution of Solomon Islands was designed to give effect to the rule recognised in *Re Lord Bishop of Natal* (1864) 3 Moo PC 115 and 42 Edw 3, c 3, which confirmed *Magna Carta* and the provision that 'no man be put to answer without presentment before the justices of matter of record, and by due process and original writ, according to the ancient law of the land'.

103 *RepMar v Waltz* [1987] MHSC 12, in which it was held by the Supreme Court of the Marshall Islands that arrests without a warrant by Local Government Police were unauthorised and unlawful on the grounds that ancient common law rights going back to *Magna Carta* applied in Marshall Islands in the absence of any national provision.

104 *Pohnpei v Weilbacher* [1992] FMPSC 1, endorsing Sir Edward Coke's view of the fundamental importance of *Magna Carta*, especially paragraph 40.

105 *Guest v Reginam* [1978] FJSC 35.

106 *Richard Bourn's Case* (1620) Cro Jac 543; 79 ER 465.

107 Under the Habeas Corpus Act 1640 an English subject was guaranteed the right to *habeas corpus* against the king.

108 *Ex parte Mwenya* [1960] 1 QB 279 (CA).

109 1816 Habeas Corpus Act.

110 Order 61, Division 2.

111 As in Nauru under the Custom and Adopted Laws Act 1971. s 4(1).

112 The Chuuk Constitution Article III, section 7, applied in In *re Paul* 11 FSM Intrm. 273 (Chk. S. Ct. Tr. 2002).

113 *Baleinamau v Commander of the Fiji Military Forces* [2001] FJHC 126; *Keppel v Attorney General of Fiji* [1998] FJHC 16. *Taalili v Commissioner of Prisons* [1994] WSSC 28.

114 Order 17, rr 1–10.

115 *Taalili v Commissioner of Prisons* [1994] WSSC 28.

116 *Fifita v Fakafanua* [1998] TOCA 1.

117 *Minister of Police v Moala* [1997] TOCA 1

118 *Navarro and Velasco v Chief of Police* [1989] MHSC 24 (Cf the Fiji case of *In re Robert Hilton Bottamley* [2002] FJHC 79).

119 *Bitiae v Attorney General* [1995] SBHC 92.

120 See *R v Cowle* (1759) 2 Burr 834, 855 and *Crowley's Case* (1818) 2 Swan 1, 48) and *R v. Commanding Officer of Morn Hill Camp ex parte Ferguson* [1917] 1 KB 176 cited with approval in *Railumu v Commander, Republic of Fiji Military Forces* [2006] FJCA 7 para 15.

121 *Amiri v Director of Police* [2004] NRSC 1.

122 See *Yasmin Ali Shah v Attorney-General* [1988] SPLR 144.

123 Memorandum of Understanding 24 February 2004 between the two governments extended an earlier Australia-Nauru Memorandum of Understanding of 9 December 2002.

124 He had released weapons to members of his unit (the Counter Revolutionary Warfare Unit) which were subsequently used in the May 2000 military coup and possibly the mutiny against the authority of the commanding officer Commodore Bainimarama. Eight soldiers were killed during the mutiny.

125 This UK Act retains its force by incorporation into the Royal Fiji Military Forces Act (Cap 81) Vol 4, *Laws of Fiji* 1985, revised edition.

126 *Re Nikhil Naidu* [1987] FJSC 6.

127 After the 2000 Coup a new Constitution had been introduced. In *The Republic of Fiji, the Attorney-General of Fiji v Chandrika Prasad* [2001] FJCA 2 the Court of Appeal had declared that the 1997 Constitution had not been abrogated.

128 *Ralumu v Commander, Republic of Fiji Military Forces – Reasons for Judgment* [2004] FJSC 11 para 6.

129 Section 122, read with The Supreme Court Act 1998, section 7(2) and (3).

130 The Supreme Court drew on examples cited in Clarke and McCoy (2000).

131 The Supreme Court decision is reviewed in *Railumu v Commander, Republic of Fiji Military Forces* [2006] FJCA 7 Paras 7,8.

132 This interpretation of the law was subject to further appeal and a full bench of the Supreme Court allowed an extension of time for further hearings *Ralumu v Commander, Republic of Fiji Military Forces – Reasons for Judgment* [2004] FJSC11.

133 *Entick v Carrington* (1765) 19 St Tr 1029.

134 *Christie v Leachinsky* [1947] AC 573 (HL).

135 *Rua v Kimilia* [1997] CKCA 1.

136 Paras 4.42–4.54.

137 In order to make palatable the universality of international instruments to peoples of different faiths, this Christian dimension is not expressly articulated but given the background to the key players in the immediate post war Conventions, clearly informs the values behind these.

138 See Article 27 ICCPR and section 6 Fiji Constitution.

139 For example, the claim of Sikhs, gypsies, part-time workers, or homosexuals.

140 See the definitions used in Chapter 4 of the New Zealand Law Commission Paper 2006.

3 Theories and approaches to human rights

Introduction

The first chapter indicated the physical, social, economic and political environment in which human rights in the region exist. These practical considerations have considerable influence on the quotidian experience of rights. Chapter two looked at the idea of rights as human rights and indicated the legal framework which gives form to human rights in the region. Also relevant, although less immediately apparent, is the theoretical or philosophical environment which has informed contemporary discourse on human rights. This chapter considers the theoretical background to the human rights of today, drawing attention to the differing perspectives of human rights which influence the way in which rights are stated and assessed in order to examine whether human rights' theories can themselves account for some of the difficulties faced by human rights in the region.

The jurisprudence of rights

If nation states are to subscribe to values and ideals that are supra-national, then there has to be more than the articulation of government policy or the implementation of legislation to justify abandoning notions of sovereignty for a greater good. The ideas or theories behind human rights is too large a topic to be covered in any depth here, and is one which has been covered by many writers (Freeman 2002; Campbell *et al.* 1986). However, the philosophical underpinning of human rights discourse cannot be ignored because it influences contemporary views and expectations of rights. In particular, the origins of rights' ideas and their articulation are important for considering why there may be perceived shortcomings in the delivery of rights in the region or why there may be a mismatch between expectation and experience. Alternatively, consideration of some of the theories of rights may suggest that the legal form is less important than the underlying principles, so that while introduced legal institutions and frameworks may appear to be ineffective in securing or protecting fundamental rights, indigenous laws and institutions may do so, but in ways which are not immediately apparent.

The individual and the state

The early history of rights is confused by different perceptions of the relationship of individuals or groups with the state, the relationship between humans and gods, and the question of whether the individual had any claim to rights separate from those permitted by the state or adhering to the group (Freeman 2002: 14–18). Modern theories of rights were articulated to support movements aimed at re-negotiating these parameters. The earliest of these theories, which emerged in the course of the seventeenth century, was that of the natural law school. Natural law theorists such as Thomas Hobbes and John Locke advocated the view that certain rights derived from the condition of being human and therefore were inherent to all persons, regardless of class or status.[1] For this reason, such rights are often referred to as fundamental human rights because they are seen as integral to the fact of being human. Natural rights were seen as being 'rooted in the moral and rational nature of humans and their common capacity to reason' (Shorts and de Than 2001: 2). Moreover, the existence of such rights does not depend on any laws made by the state or ruler, although such laws may be made to uphold natural rights. Conversely, laws that infringed the exercise of natural rights amounted to a breach of the natural law unless the holders of those rights had voluntarily surrendered them to the ruler or state for the greater good of society as a whole. In England, the assertion of these rights supported claims made during the English civil war. To this extent therefore the rights were limited historically. However, a more universal dimension emerged through claims that God had made all men rational, equal and free. While these rights were individual, rational individuals realised that they could only be enjoyed by respecting the rights of others. The rule of law and the role of government were to protect the natural rights of mankind.

The relevance of the natural law theory is not only that subsequent theories have built on it, but also that whatever shortcomings positive law may have in giving effect to human rights, those rights which are deemed to be natural rights will still provide a rights advocacy platform. While some of the ideas of natural rights theorists may fit uneasily within the Pacific context, such as the right to private property and inequality of wealth, there are ideas which are more compatible, including rights of physical and intellectual freedom, the right to life and the obligation to respect the rights of others and exercise rights for the common good. Moreover, the basic theological principles which underpinned many of the early theories of rights were drawn from a system of beliefs which was introduced into the region by the early Christian missionaries and remains, in various forms, an important and integral feature of Pacific Island countries.

Early natural law theories were influenced by Christian theology, so that the law of nature was seen as being synonymous with higher moral and religious values – rather than the baser aspects of human nature. The established church, the jurisdiction of the ecclesiastical courts and cannon law all had an influence on the articulation of rights and the limits of powers. Gradually the idea of natural rights became more secularised and during the eighteenth century there was a gradual shift away from religious and theological theories to the more radical application of natural law as a justification for reforming or removing government which did not uphold such rights. This led to the emergence of social contract theories elaborated by thinkers such as Rousseau (1712–1778) and Thomas Paine and the notion that if governments did not respect natural rights, then those who were unjustly governed had the right to oppose and if necessary overthrow the government, as indeed happened in America (1776) and in France (1789).

The social contract theory rested on the idea that the laws of a state reflected a contract between the government and the governed. This line of reasoning also gave support to the idea that the state existed for the benefit of the individual and was therefore expected to uphold certain fundamental rights (Locke 1948). This idea is reflected in the American Declaration of Independence, which states:

> We hold these truths to be self-evident, that all men are created equal, that they are endowed by their creator with certain unalienable rights, that among these are life, liberty and the pursuit of happiness. That to secure these rights Governments are instituted among men deriving their just powers from the consent of the governed; that whenever any form of government becomes destructive of these ends, it is the right of the people to alter or abolish it.

Similarly the French Declaration of the rights of Man and of the citizen states:

> Men are born and remain free and equal in respect of rights ... These rights are liberty, property and resistance to oppression.

While the Declaration emphasised the rights of the individual, for example, to due process, to religious beliefs and to the presumption of innocence, it also acknowledged that freedoms or liberties could only be exercised in such a way as to not harm others or infringe their exercise of the same rights and freedoms.

However, the violence of the French Revolution, which sought to establish a new democratic order in which the power of government was to be harnessed to reflect the will of the people, undermined some of the theories that were used to justify it. Edmund Burke, for example, thought that the natural rights theory, with its claim to the universal nature of such rights, failed to take into account national and cultural diversity and consequently facilitated the rule of tyranny. Jeremy Bentham questioned the individualism of natural rights, advocating instead that the object of government should be to achieve the greatest good for the greatest number of people, in other words the common good.

The social contract theory of rights remains influential today, not only because it places an emphasis on individual rights but also because it presupposes a democratic form of law-making in which the citizen and the state negotiate the protection and curtailment of rights. Indeed, the nineteenth century witnessed widespread reforms to give effect to constitutional government and the protection of human rights in national legal systems in Europe. This democratic dimension is also important in considering whether it should be the elected legislative body which determines human rights issues – and which may have a clear political agenda or favour certain elites in society, or whether the unelected but non-political courts should be the bodies entrusted with determining and upholding human rights.

While many of the rights advocated and given effect in the rights' statements of the eighteenth century may be universal, such as the rights to liberty, security and freedom from oppression, others may be less so, for example, the right to property, freedom of expression and religion. There is also a tension in the social contract theory between the assertion of individual natural rights and the sacrifice of these for the preservation or enhancement of social order.

The social contract theory also supposes that the parties to the contract, being equal, negotiate in some way the terms of that contract.[2] In systems where this negotiation has not taken place then any statements of rights may not reflect a consensus between State and citizens. Further, rights which are deemed to be important to the citizens may not be reflected in the laws which govern them. So, where countries have written constitutions imposed on them with little or no debate – as happened in the majority of countries now independent in the South Pacific region – the social contract theory is undermined. Conversely, where there has been dialogue: for example, where constitutions have been amended – as in the case of Tuvalu – the social contract theory may appear more relevant.

The shift towards utilitarian theories of rights started by Bentham marked a conceptual change away from natural rights towards an assessment of law based on its value as a means of enhancing or restricting certain rights. Attention turned from natural law to economic rights, and to the universalism of rights through socialism rather than pre-industrial bourgeois capitalism. Advocacy of egalitarianism by thinkers such as Karl Marx necessitated the denial of individual rights in favour of the community and the state. Nineteenth- and twentieth-century theorists such as Marx, Weber and Durkheim were all influenced by the social changes caused by rapid industrialisation. While the historic moment was not universal, it gave rise to a number of the social and economic rights which are recognised today.

The socialist theories of rights, with the emphasis on the community or collective rather than the individual, might be expected to find a favourable response in the Pacific region. However, a number of factors probably militate against this. The first is that a socialist state needs strong government which can promote the common good of the state at the expense of individual autonomy. In many Pacific Island countries this form of government is missing. Second, the traditional social hierarchies, especially in Polynesia, present challenges to egalitarianism. Third, the countries having the greatest influence in the region as the time of initial contact and leading up to independence were those with western, capitalist economies not those with socialist governments.

Although the industrial revolution witnessed some remarkable moments in the history of human rights, for example, the abolition of slavery and the emergence of rights for women, children, and trade unions, it was not however, until the first part of the twentieth century that the rights of the individual as we know them today, were to fully emerge again. The contemporary concept of human rights is therefore relatively young historically and has undergone a number of changes in recent decades.

As information regarding the atrocities carried out under the regimes of Hitler, Lenin and Mussolini emerged in the aftermath of the Second World War, existing theories of rights seemed inadequate to provide a sufficiently strong platform on which to build a new era of respect for fundamental rights. What developed was the concept of human rights which located the individual and the state in an international arena. Although the political events which gave rise to the United Nations and its Charter in the post-war period may seem at a far remove from the Pacific region – although the region had been one of the major theatres of the war – in fact it was smaller nations, non-governmental organisations and countries from the third world that lobbied hardest for a strong human-rights commitment, while the larger powers such as the United States of America and the United Soviet Socialist Republic (USSR) were less supportive (Freeman 2002: 33).

Although initially a political statement to which the various sovereign states subscribed, increasingly human rights became a legal matter, not only because of the mechanisms and institutions put in place under the various international conventions to monitor and investigate the human rights record of nation states, but also because of the obligations incurred by those nation states to bring their domestic law in line with human rights standards advocated in those international conventions. The philosophical rationale behind the emergence of first the Universal Declaration of Human Rights and then the other United Nations instruments that followed is not express, but can be implied from the events that led up to its drafting, the players who took the greatest role and the wording of the actual Declaration, to be predominantly western liberalism, with an emphasis on civil and political rights, certain assumptions about the best constitutional environment for such rights and a focus on individualism rather than communalism. It is also based on the moral principles of egalitarianism, toleration, democracy and the rule of law.

Law and rights

While certain rights may exist according to natural law, in order to balance the competing claims of rights and to give protection to those which may be at risk, it is necessary in an increasingly complex social environment for governments to legislate to shape and maintain such rights. For legal positivists, the law is the vehicle for achieving this. The role of law in the field of human rights flows from the dual idea of rights as the entitlement of individual citizens and the role of government being directed to these ends. Law, therefore, plays a number of roles. First, in order to ensure a government which reflects the will of the people, certain constitutional laws are required to ensure a democratic framework for government. Second, national laws are required to give domestic effect to any international obligations or any obligations assumed in internal statements of rights, such as bills of rights in written constitutions. Third, the law is there to provide an adjudicative framework when a state infringes the rights of its citizens or fails to observe its obligations to its citizens. The extent to which the law is able to do this will depend on the extent to which the state and its agents can be held accountable, either through the democratic process or through the courts. Finally, the law may be used to provide a remedy for breaches of rights.

Focus on the role of law in the implementation of rights also avoided the uncertain philosophical or moral basis of human rights discourse which emerged from the United Nations. Clearly however, the idea of 'rights' preceded any international initiatives to give them effect in law. Indeed, to assert, as legal positivists might – that without law there are no human rights – undermines human rights especially where the laws which are meant to give effect to human rights are themselves weak. Moreover, the Declaration of Human Rights was just that, a declaration. There were no binding human rights treaties until the 1960s and the Human Rights Committee, the task of which was to monitor compliance with the Covenant on Civil and Political Rights, was not established until 1976. The Committee on Economic, Social and Cultural Rights was not established until 1986 and it remains the case that while these United Nations bodies do a considerable amount of work monitoring, reporting and advocating human rights, the ability to compel compliance or to intervene in human rights abuses, remains very limited and often ineffectual.

The weakness of the legal positivist view from a Pacific perspective is that if law gives effect to human rights, then a system of human rights law also presupposes an established rights-orientated legal system. In many cases in the Pacific region many aspects of the legal system were introduced for the benefit of transactions between non-indigenous people, or to facilitate the colonial administration of the country. Only on independence can it be said that the legal system was intended to provide for the indigenous people. Thus, in most cases the statement of human rights and the legal system were arrived at simultaneously and not the one before the other. Moreover, the pluralistic nature of many of the legal systems in the region has meant that only part of the extant legal system supports the human rights stated in the constitution or is perceived as supporting human rights. This has practical implications as reliance or emphasis on other legal sources within the plural whole may provide a way of avoiding, denying or defeating human rights, especially where the hierarchy of legal sources is unclear.

Increasingly, however, certainly at an international level, legal positivism has dominated rights discourse. A major influence has been the growing importance of international law in the post-cold-war period and the obligations incurred by nation states under international rights treaties to give effect to treaty obligations in domestic law. The United Nations (and its predecessor the League of Nations) has been a key player here. The preamble to the Universal Declaration of Human Rights (1948) clearly states that 'human rights should be protected by the rule of law', and it is clear from the Declaration and subsequent treaties and covenants that the making of appropriate laws is seen as being preferable to having recourse to rebellion and civil unrest to assert rights claims.

The various international institutions which have been put in place for the monitoring and enforcement of rights are of variable efficacy. While legal mechanisms are not the only way of either advocating or upholding rights the significance of a strong legal framework for successful rights advocacy can be seen in the success of certain models. In particular, the jurisdiction of the European Court of Human Rights, and increasingly the European Court of Justice, have played an important role in triggering law-making at a domestic level, where states have been found guilty of a breach of their rights' obligations under the European Convention for the Protection of Human Rights and Fundamental Freedoms.[3] Whether, in the light of the enlarged and more culturally diverse membership of the European Union, the success of the European Court will continue, remains to be seen.

Mechanisms for effective democratic participation, the lobbying of groups claiming rights' violations, and publicity surrounding rights issues are also important for influencing legislative activity. In countries where international obligations are limited or where sanctions for breach of international obligations are insignificant, or there is no independent forum for holding states liable for breaches of individual human rights, or where lobbying for legal change is suppressed or weak, legal positivists are likely to be disappointed. In the Pacific region, a number of these features may be encountered. On the other hand, law, and in particular the rule of law, may be a bridge between what are sometimes perceived of as two separate systems or sets of democratic principles: traditional values and introduced ones, especially where both are confronted by rapid change and pressures of development.

Idealism and realism

As has been indicated above, a number of different theoretical approaches to human rights have been advocated over an extended period of time. Today's discourse on rights is informed by this history of ideas and continues to reflect a number of them. In particular there is the concept of individual entitlement and state obligation, which, although not always immediately obtainable, is held out as an ideal to which governments and their citizens should aspire. The nature and scope of the entitlement and obligation is given form today primarily in internationally agreed and negotiated documents: treaties and conventions. The participation of nation states emphasises the international, political and legal nature of this process.

A consequence is that human rights have become increasingly political, rather than philosophical. There is an assumption of shared values without much analysis of the foundation on which this assumption is based. Intervention by both international institutions and other states in the human rights regimes of individual states is pragmatic, incoherent and inconsistent, as evidenced by the continuing human rights abuses in a number of countries throughout the world which appear to continue without much international outcry despite the best efforts of independent observers, non-governmental organisations and various lobby groups. The ideals as stated in the various international statements of rights continue to exist and the rhetoric of human rights is loud. The practice however is variable, with perhaps a disproportionate amount of international attention focussed on those aspects of rights which are likely to be least controversial or politically sensitive, such as reporting, observing and intervening where countries are weak, disorganised and in the eyes of the world not very important.

The lack of a theoretical underpinning of contemporary rights discourse is problematic, in so far as those countries which do not share the same history of today's rights' articulation may well ask 'why bother about human rights?' It may no longer be sufficient to state, as the American Declaration does, that the truth of human rights is 'self-evident'. If different cultures and communities have different value systems then agreement on the theoretical justification for human rights, in particular a theoretical justification which distinguishes these rights from others and holds them to be superior, will be very difficult to arrive at, with the related difficulty of reaching any consensus on the appropriate standard of implementation for any right (Maritain 1949: 9–17; MacDonald 1963: 35–55). Lack of a clear contemporary theory of human rights may, however, be a good thing for those countries which have not so far participated in the philosophical debate. It would enable, for example, a Pacific Island country or groups of countries to articulate their own normative value system and the reasons behind it and give this effect in a rights' statement. It would also enable such countries to develop their own theoretical perspective on the rights stated in international instruments. Thus, universal rights could be interpreted and given local effect through a relative philosophical understanding. Conversely, freedom from any theoretical discourse could lead to rights' abuses by a strong political power through the reinterpretation of rights supported by a particular theoretical justification – a danger illustrated by fascism or apartheid.

At the same time, however, because human rights tend to reflect ideals, the translation of these into reality requires the intervention of practices, rules and procedures. Therefore, even if there was a shared value system informing the articulation of rights, the practical implementation of such rights within different domestic spheres would be subject to variations. For example, the meaning and scope of any right has to be determined and interpreted; exceptions, limitations and justifications for breach have to be considered; the nature and extent of any corresponding duties have to be taken into account and similarly the nature and form of any remedies necessary to give effect to rights. These tasks may be primarily left to the courts, especially constitutional courts, or to the legislative body, or a combination of these. Realising human rights requires the translation of ideals into justiciable rules, which in turn requires a degree of precision and clarity which cannot be found in ideology. The reality of human rights in any one country may therefore depend on the quality of these institutions and the way in which positive effect is given to the ideals, rather than any international forums. It is important therefore that the reality of human rights as experienced in a concretised and positivised form is considered when making an assessment of human rights in any country.

In the Pacific region, the realisation of rights is found in the bills of rights in the written constitutions which both specify and limit these rights. This specification is the first stage of making rights positive (Orücü 1986: 37–59). Because this form of specification is usually rather abstract, further laws give greater clarity to these constitutional rights while case decisions provide concrete examples of the law in practice. It is here therefore, that the jurisprudence of the courts is particularly important, especially if the executive and legislative are reluctant or unable to give positive effect to the ideals of human rights.

Human rights jurisprudence and the Pacific region

The theories considered above have originated in contexts far removed from the Pacific region. This does not necessarily make them unacceptable. Indeed, by participation in the global community, Pacific Island states may, and often will, accept or endorse ideas and standards which have not been of their own making and frequently – given the size of these states and their relative youth as independent countries – in which they have played no part in formulating.

Notionally, the contemporary importance of international law and particularly the role of the human rights framework established by the United Nations, provides a greater opportunity for independent Pacific Island countries to participate in the development of human rights at a global level, and to benefit from those developments. As individual states these countries may be too small to have a voice, however, in combination with others which share similar concerns or interests, they may be more effective.

At the same time, and perhaps increasingly, countries such as those in the South Pacific region are making stronger assertions of post-colonial, national identify and uniqueness. There is a re-invigorated interest in cultural identity and a re-assertion of pre-colonial indigenous traditions which often jostle with the dynamics of development, greater access to external influences and the articulation of the aspirations of a new generation of Pacific islanders. In part, a focus on indigeneity is encouraged by the international community, for example, there is a United Nations Permanent Forum on Indigenous Issues and a Declaration on the Rights of Indigenous People was adopted by the General Assembly on 13 September 2007.[4] In part, it may be a reaction to the very process of globalisation which Pacific Island states want to engage with while retaining their own identity. Consequently, there is the dilemma of striving to achieve status and recognition internationally and resisting assimilation and loss of autonomy.

It is sometimes argued that 'human rights are seen as being against Pacific culture and identity' (Jalal 2006: 4), and that the ideology that informs human rights is alien to that which shapes Pacific values. While the 'westerness' of human rights may be refuted (Amankwah 1989: 45), opposition to theories of human rights may be partly due to the perception that these are legal theories rather than spiritual or sociological theories, whereas Pacific people see rights as integral to their place and identity. In other words, the traditional view is a holistic one in which rights are not seen as being separate from identity. The latter is composed of many dimensions. These include the spiritual – for example, links with ancestors and the larger cosmology, the physical – such as links with land, physical characteristics or attributes; and human – for example, the place of a person within and part of a wider kinship network or family (Váa 2008; Henare 1998: 25–27). The location of a person within family, place and time may explain why Pacific islanders place emphasis on collective rights and individual duties. Values such as respect, love, sharing and nurturing are part of the identity and experience of Pacific islanders, while the assertion of rights by an individual are constrained by concerns about maintaining cohesion of the social unit. Thus, while the lively debate, discussion and sometimes dispute over matters concerning land or village affairs may be expected and encouraged, total freedom of expression may be restrained by considerations of respect for seniority, rank, gender and status. 'Hot heads' if they speak out may be reprimanded or ignored. Similarly, respect for the different contributions of men and women to the welfare of families or the community will not necessarily mean that men and women are treated equally or are allowed to participate equally in the same arena. Some matters will be seen as women's affairs, others those of men. This may not be perceived as discriminatory but as necessary for ensuring continuity and stability. Restoring or maintaining the *status quo* is often used as a defence for human rights breaches that come before the courts, whether this involves returning a reluctant bride to her abusive husband, excluding by banishment the adherents of a new religion, or silencing voices raised in opposition or criticism.

An alternative argument is that if human rights are an integral part of the rule of law then adherence to the rules of customary law reflect an observation of the rule of law – depending on the status and relevance of customary law in any given legal system. The difficulty, however, arises when rights are considered to be a claim that the individual has against the state and that the state is bound to give effect to these rights in return for the individual agreeing to be bound by the laws and government of that state. This social contract theory rests on the acceptance of the state as a separate and distinct entity from the individuals which comprise it. In the South Pacific, notions of statehood are elusive, fragmented and often poorly recognised. While the centralised national legal system may officially recognise custom and customary law, it is often uncertain and unclear as to how this is to either be integrated or administered separately. At the same time, however, even if customary law is recognised as being one of several legal sources, it frequently operates within customary structures. These, while perhaps endorsed by the state, do not include the state as an entity, but may include individual leaders or identifiable groups, such as families, clans or tribes. There is therefore a difficulty in interpreting customary fundamental rights by using prevailing theories of rights.

The universal nature of human rights

These paradigms are reflected in differing approaches to human rights. At its simplest, on the one hand, there is universalism – the idea that human rights transcend national, historical and cultural boundaries and to which all players in an international arena should subscribe. On the other, there is relativism – which maintains that human rights must reflect the time and place of their implementation, and that if difference is to be respected then divergence must be allowed. These are opposite ends of a spectrum, along which there may be various modified approaches. Debate as to which approach should be accepted is relevant to the region and one in which Pacific voices have not, by and large, been heard (Corrin 2007; Farran 2005a).

The idea that human rights are universal is based on the notion that there are some fundamental principles recognised by all people that certain perceptions of what is just and right transcend national or local culture, ideology, politics and society. Universal thus means both international and transcendent in a variety of ways.

In part, the emergence of the idea of universalism is a product of the trans-national role of the United Nations, the very existence of which presupposes some form of common agenda, as well as a legacy of the jurisprudence of rights which preceded the emergence of the United Nations and the rise of international law. The United Nations unequivocally holds that human rights are universal. The Charter of the United Nations states quite simply that human rights are 'for all without distinction'.

The universal view of human rights was strengthened by the Vienna Declaration on Human Rights,[5] which stated:

> All human rights are universal, indivisible and inter-dependent and inter-related. The international community must treat human rights globally in a fair and equal manner in the same footing, and with the same emphasis. While the significance of national and regional particularities and various historical, cultural and religious backgrounds must be borne in mind, it is the duty of states, regardless of their political, economic and cultural systems, to promote and protect all human rights and fundamental freedoms.

Adherence to a universal position has the advantage that rights are seen as being beyond and outside any individual state or political context. The idea that human rights are universal – at least as goals to be aspired to – means that individual governments – which may or may not reflect the wishes of the majority and may or may not be elected democratically – are expected to meet standards which are elevated above domestic factions and preferences, and which bring the individual state into the international arena and *vice versa*. Universalism also assumes egalitarianism so that all individuals or people, whatever their status, can appeal to the same normative touchstones. An advantage of this is that human rights supported by international law may be seen as a law of persons rather than states, thereby affording the individual – whatever his or her situation – a legal framework beyond the confines of any particular state system (Beitz 1979). The disadvantage of this is that it may give rise to aspirations which are unrealistic or frustrated in the local context.

In order to arrive at a universal statement that can both encompass differences and obliterate or minimalise them, the rights enumerated may be too abstract, elusive or broad to be given practical effect at a local level. This can be a disadvantage because it may be felt that the gulf between universal and local is too great. Further, although the early human right instruments such as the Universal Declaration of Human Rights and the UN Charter were drafted to take into account the views of representatives from a range of nations, it has been argued that the end product, particularly as a result of subsequent interpretation, represents a certain cultural perspective.[6] Also it might be argued that the political model on which civil and political human rights are based denies the possibility of a strong patriarchal ruler, or the determination of the individual's place in society through the relationship with the group and the need to maintain community harmony and cohesion.

In the Pacific region, although some universal rights are either expressly or implicitly accepted, for example, the universal idea of equality between countries regardless of international status (Article 2 Universal Declaration of Human Rights), the right to self-determination (Article 1.1 International Covenant on Economic, Social and Cultural Rights), and the right to freedom from oppression, it is an oft-cited view that human rights are not compatible with Pacific values (Thaman 1998; Angelo 1992). It is, of course, true that the original inclusions of bills of rights in the written constitutions of the region were primarily not the result of a democratic exercise. In a number of countries Pacific perspectives were rarely taken on board (Corrin 2007) although in some Constitutional Conventions were used to draft independence constitutions.[7] Essentially the statements of rights reflected statements of rights articulated in a Western cultural context. This might be one reason why, while statements of rights may be called on either to condemn or justify certain actions their implementation in practical terms is more elusive than real. On the other hand, today it would be naive to suggest that western values and aspirations have no appeal for Pacific islanders although attitudes may often be ambivalent. However, there are writers who have pointed out that certain fundamental rights are so inherent to being human that it cannot be said that they are the sole product of western liberal thought (Amankwah 1989: 44, 45). Among these are the right to life, which is fundamental to the search for knowledge and understanding of the universe which humans – being the only rational creatures – seek. This search for understanding also requires freedom to enquire, to move about and to associate with others. The survival of humans requires recognition of the right to property in some form and security for the family as the basis of the community, while the enjoyment of these necessary rights and freedoms needs to be regulated so as to avoid conflict between people, thus a right to justice and dispute resolution is important. Indeed, Amankwah suggests that almost all other rights, such as the right to education, health, religion, can be subsumed under the fundamental and inherent rights of life, liberty, property, speech, association, family and justice.

The relative nature of human rights

The universalism of human rights is based on the idea that there are certain moral absolutes which are universal and invariable. Critics of this approach hold that the international human rights instruments, which purport to reflect this, are derived from a specific political and theoretical context, notably that of western liberal individualism. On two counts, therefore, it is argued that a universal approach to human rights is either inapplicable or inappropriate in many countries. First, because the focus is on the individual – not the group or community; second, because the context of their evolution is western and therefore out of touch with other cultural, philosophical or normative environments (Cobbah 1987; Civic 1995–1996; Hom 1996–1997). In former colonies, such as Pacific Island states, this last point may be taken a step further and it could be argued that not only are such ideas western but they also represent the thinking of former colonial powers and for political reasons should be rejected. In other words, not only are statements of rights a legacy of colonial rule, but the continuing advocacy of the universalism of rights and the need for sovereign states to comply with international norms is a form of neo-colonialism, whereby the more powerful states impose standards on smaller, weaker states while failing to apply or observe those same standards at home (Douzinas 2007). There is also the criticism that international instruments are insufficiently focussed on the real needs of developing countries, notably economic and social needs, because these are relegated to the bottom of the hierarchy of rights. The rights that are prioritised are therefore, in many instances, luxuries, which only the developed world can afford (Howard 1983).

The idea that human rights are relative means that local cultural, political and economic factors can be taken into account either in their formulation or their implementation. The relative approach to the formulation of human rights holds that in those societies in which the group rather than the individual is the central focus individual rights cannot exist independently of the society and culture in which the individual is situated. Ethical values are culturally dependent and therefore rights based on culture are relative. Consequently, the moral or normative underpinning of rights must take into account the particular social, cultural and historical contexts.

Cultural relativity may be relevant to the substance of rights – what rights should be protected; and the interpretation of individual rights – whether arrived at universally or relatively, and the form in which rights are implemented or protected. At its most extreme relativists might argue that all of these should be determined at a local level.

If a relativist approach is adopted, it also leads to the conclusion that human rights are not grounded in universally valid truths or moral absolutes but in ones emanating from a particular culture and time.[8] Where rights instruments are introduced or imposed on states, the relativist approach also leads to the view that such statements of human rights are rooted in imperialism – the imposition of one society's values on another.

Taken further, however, a relative approach would require consideration of different groups within a society. Culture itself is relative and in developing societies, in particular, there may be considerable difference between different generations, between urban and rural sectors and between formally and informally educated people. Culture is not static. The idea of a coherent single culture giving rise to a shared set of values is rarely found in reality. Moreover, people may belong to a number of different either overlapping or disparate cultural entities which may or may not include national or state identity. A consequence of this is that it may be difficult or impossible to arrive at a relative national determination of human rights.

The relativist implementation of rights may facilitate the practical implementation of rights, although at variable levels. However, it may also mean that standards are altered to meet domestic factions or preferences and that certain sectors of society are either treated preferentially or detrimentally by the government in power. Relativism – just as universalism – is premised on certain value judgments, but in the former case these may result in a ranking or hierarchy of values. This opens the door to manipulation of values and rights.

There is some support for adopting a relative approach to the implementation of universal human rights in the Pacific region. This would allow different cultural contexts to be accommodated and would also allow the different constitutions of the countries to maintain their different approaches to the role of custom and customary law and to the hierarchy of their sources of laws. At the same time, it would be self-evident that unequal observation of rights, for example, permitted discrimination on the grounds of gender, or race, would fall short of the universal norm. Moreover, differences in culture could be used to justify a relativist observation of human rights.

Relative universalism

As has been indicated above, there are dangers in adopting a relativistic approach to the implementation and protection of human rights. At the same time, it would be naive to imagine that the enjoyment of human rights will be the same across very different legal environments. The gulf between the two approaches may be bridged by a pragmatic compromise, which maintains that human rights are universal but that their implementation may be tailored by the means in which they are implemented at a local level. In the Pacific region, there may be considerable merit in negotiating a common ground which reconciles universal human rights principles and practices with localised core values and institutions (Vaá 2008).

At one end of a spectrum is radical universalism and at the other radical relativism. There are, however, a range of views between in which it may be possible to accommodate elements of both. For example, relativists may hold that 'rights (and other social practices, values, and moral rules) are culturally determined, but the universality of human nature and rights serves as a check on the potential excesses of relativism' (Donnelly 1984: 400). Alternatively, relativists may acknowledge that a limited number of rights are universal – for example the right to life – although the relativist approach would mean that the protection of that right or its construction may vary widely. Similarly, universalists may recognise that pragmatically human rights must be interpreted and judged taking into account cultural perceptions of moral rights and rules. They may also accept that relativism acts as a counterbalance to any potential imperialism of universalism.

As has been indicated above, cultural relativity – or indeed universalism – can operate at the substantive, interpretive or procedural level. It might, therefore, be possible to arrive at a weak cultural relativist position, which allows limited deviations from universal standards focussing on issues of interpretation and form rather than substance (Donnelly 1985). Similarly, it might be possible to move from idealism to realism in order to identify common core values in different societies. For example, Vaá indicates that obedience, love, respect and service are core values in Samoa society, and that these inform the place of every Samoan within his or her family and the wider society. Observance of these is necessary for the smooth functioning of society. He argues that these are not ideals but realities. But he also suggests that similar values are shared by other Polynesian people and their observance identifies people as true Samoans, or Tongans or Tuvaluans. Yet, a similar analysis in Micronesian countries or those of Melanesia might arrive at similar core values. What at first sight may therefore appear to be culturally unique to a particular people on closer examination of basic principle may in fact be less unique than claimed.

All too often international human rights instruments are seen as peripheral in the region because of their appeal to universalism. In fact, this often fails to acknowledge the way in which universalism may accommodate relativism. First, while the impetus for the Universal Declaration of Human Rights was the reaction to particular historic events in Europe, the United Nations and indeed international law has moved on from that point in history. Indeed, the 1993 United Nations World Conference on Human Rights attended by 180 nations was held in order to discuss differences in national perceptions of human rights and to arrive at a consensus. Increasingly the United Nations has to accommodate a broader membership and to respond to the needs of peoples from very different cultures. This is evident from the inclusion of indigenous voices and issues in initiatives such as the Permanent Forum on Indigenous Issues and its programme of activities.

Today, international lawmaking involves the participation of representatives from a wide range of developed and developing countries, representing western and non-western cultures. Indeed, the General Assembly of the United Nations might be thought to be a uniquely representative body which is well placed to represent and reflect the diverse cultures and views of many varied societies, peoples and nations and that that the statements of rights emanating from the United Nations are the result of this. Although the voices of single undeveloped nations may be weak, in combination they command attention. Therefore, identifying commonalities may be more effective than emphasising differences.

Second, universalism may recognise that universal principles require diverse interpretation and application to ensure that they are effective in varied contexts and environments. Under Article 31 of the International Covenant on Civil and Political Rights, for example, there is express provision that in the election of members to the Human Rights Committee set up under the Covenant 'consideration shall be given to equitable geographical distribution of membership and to the representation of the different forms of civilisation and of the principal legal systems', suggesting thereby the recognition of the value and necessity of diversity. Similarly, the European Court of Human Rights, in considering the rights of individuals under the European Convention on Human Rights has recognised the validity of variation and diversity in the concept of the 'margin of appreciation', especially in the context of those rights where relativism may be most significant, for example, family, religion, marriage, expression and association.

Third, states may give effect to relative values when ratifying international treaties through the use of reservations. Certainly, in the Pacific region this has been done, but other countries, including the United States of America, use reservations. Similarly, in giving effect to the provisions of these international instruments, considerable leeway is given to ratifying countries as to how they do this within their own domestic jurisdictions. Although the Universal Declaration and the Vienna Declaration both imply that human rights are indivisible, in practice states may give emphasis to civil and political rights over social and cultural rights or the converse. Pacific Island countries have the scope to do this, either through domestic legislation and internal policies or by amending their own constitutions. This latter measure permits greater relativism in the treatment of universal concepts, and indeed may defuse the perceived dichotomy between universalism and relativism because statements of rights have evolved through a democratic process. Where this has happened, for example, in Fiji and Tuvalu, the argument that statements of rights reflect foreign, western and alien concepts may not be very convincing.

There is a difficult balance to be found between the recognition of cultural difference at a national level and the danger of undermining rights which are valued at an international level. Achieving this is particularly challenging in developing countries, where victims of rights' abuse may condone or accept the *status quo* on the grounds of culture and tradition, or where those that perpetrate such abuses may be unable or unwilling to recognise these because of cultural or traditional values. At the very least, it may be necessary to understand why some rights are held to be of universal value and therefore to transcend specific localities, and to establish how and if these values are found at a local level and how they are articulated.

In the Pacific, it has been suggested that this balance may be achieved by finding common ground between customary values and international human rights. The New Zealand Law Commission Report on Custom and Human Rights in the Pacific (2006: 75–82) explored the ways in which values extolled in custom harmonised with human rights at a universal level. Its research, which was based on a wide spectrum of country reports, comment and analysis, found that there were many values in common. These included the concept of human dignity attributable to people not just by virtue of their physical being but also because of a non-physical essence, whether by virtue of links to ancestors or land or other members of the family or clan. The right of all people to both contribute and to benefit from membership of society was also identified, although it was recognised that this egalitarianism might not always result in equality of distribution, any more than religious tolerance or community participation in decision-making would mean that there were no restrictions on new religions or constraints on free speech. However, the report maintains that

> The dignity of all persons, caring concern for all persons, robust debate, respect for other beliefs and the desire to free people from fear and want point to aspirations shared by custom law and human rights law. These areas of commonality provide a basis on which custom and human rights can work together.
>
> (Para 6.9)

The Report acknowledges that there are some difficult areas, especially concerning the rights of women, children and young people. The point, however, which it stressed is that not only is custom accommodating, flexible and changing, but also that there is scope within international statements of human rights to accommodate what may be ill-conceived differences, for example the importance of duty and the rights of the group in customary societies and custom law. What clearly is important if harmonisation is to provide the way forward for human rights in the region is to identify customary values, relate these to other relevant values and then review current practices – which may be defended by claims of custom – against those values. This, as will be seen in subsequent chapters, is not always an easy task and it is not one which can be undertaken without the political will and public support of Pacific Island governments and people.

The political dimension of rights

Questions of sovereignty

The need for national action illustrates a tension between the idealism of human rights, which adheres to universal and international normative standards and the realism of human rights which relies on states, the players in the international arena, to adhere to these standards and give effect to them in their internal systems. As states are motivated primarily by self-interest, they are likely to be selective in how they do this. Consequently, many international and regional human rights initiatives remain primarily ideals with limited real impact. Perhaps this is inevitable given that a state can only sign up to an international treaty if it has sufficient sovereign status. This sovereignty not only empowers it to participate in the international domain but prevents the international domain from interfering in its domestic sphere. In countries formerly under colonial administration such sovereignty is important. It is only when a country agrees to forfeit all or some of this sovereignty that others can intervene, as has happened, for example, with the recognition by member states of the right of individuals to bring an application before the European Court of Human Rights against that member state, or the agreement of Solomon Islands to foreign intervention in the form of the Regional Assistance Mission to Solomon Islands. Sometimes, this sovereignty is unintentionally breached, for example when aid-funded consultants are placed in key positions in government offices,[9] or when decisions are made by such office holders without appropriate or required official approval.

This sovereignty is not just political but also ideological, especially among new, non-Western nations, who see their culture and history as setting them apart from the Western powers and Western philosophy. This aspect of sovereignty: of people, culture and tradition is particularly important in assertions of national identity in the Pacific region, so that it might be said that here the state and its sovereignty is no more than the sum of its parts – its people – and therefore the state has a limited separate sovereignty (Teson 1987). However, globalisation and membership of international organisations such as the United Nations implies some concessions to claims of state sovereignty, national independence and autonomy. Increasingly inter-state and trans-state relationships and transactions undermine the reality of claims to sovereignty. This is so even in the Pacific region with its widely dispersed states, where co-operation in combating anti-terrorism, drug smuggling, money laundering and even HIV/AIDS requires some sacrifices to sovereignty.

Given the importance of international law in the development and advocacy of human rights any gulf between idealism and realism is of concern. On the one hand, there is the view that human rights transcend the separate sovereignty of states, and on the other is the opposing view that under this sovereignty a state retains the right to treat its own people as it likes. The first approach would allow international intervention and restraints regardless or despite claims of national sovereignty, while the second would not – thereby rendering any international human rights law superfluous, allowing sovereign states to be only answerable to themselves as regards their human rights record.

Consequently, sovereign states, as an integral part of their membership of the global community, may be signatories to international instruments of human rights while doing little to implement rights measures or their protection in domestic legislation. Claims of sovereignty can both justify their ability to sign international instruments, and non-action in their own state. It can also be used to argue against outside intervention in the domestic affairs of a country, including its human rights record (Binder 1995). On the other hand, the desire of governments to benefit from 'good standing' in the international community, especially if they are weak economically or politically, can be an incentive for sovereign states to demonstrate their commitment to international human rights standards – although often this is more rhetoric than reality, tokenism rather than commitment. At the same time, international condemnation of poor human rights records may act as incentive to improve, although this is clearly not always the case, especially among those states which are confident in their own strength, such as China, or dismissive of such criticisms, such as Zimbabwe.

Rights discourse as a platform for international participation

Although the philosophical or theoretical underpinnings of contemporary rights discourse may be weak or obscure, the rhetoric of rights provides a platform for international political discourse. In particular, it provides a platform for non-governmental organisations and opposition parties, sometimes in exile, to express views which, because they have international support, are given validity beyond the national borders of the country in question. Indeed, the very uncertainty that lies behind modern statements of rights may in itself be a strength because it provides scope for differing views and interpretations and provides a vehicle for communication between nations with very different histories, cultures and people. Thus human rights at an international level can set the agenda for political debate while leaving it to nation states to implement (or not) any resolutions or policies which are reached. In this respect human rights can be a relatively unthreatening way of bringing nations together.

This use of human rights as a common platform for international discourse is illustrated by the United Nations Charter. The Charter imposes legally binding obligations on signatory states to respect, promote and protect 'human rights and freedoms for all without distinction as to race, sex, language or religion'.[10] However, the Charter does not specify what these human rights are. The subsequent Declaration of Human Rights, which was adopted by the United Nations General Assembly in 1948, is, as has been indicated, not legally binding, although by implication it can be argued that this should be referred to in order to enumerate the rights and freedoms referred to in the Charter.

Later Covenants, such as the International Covenants on Human Rights, including the Covenant on Civil and Political Rights and the Covenant on Economic, Social and Cultural Rights, are legally binding treaties to those who sign up to them, but the obligations imposed on signatory states rely on the exercise of state sovereignty to give effect to these.[11] The same may be said of the International Convention on the Elimination of all Forms of Racial Discrimination, which is binding on a number of Pacific Island countries, notably Fiji and Solomon Islands – by succession,[12] and Papua New Guinea and Tonga by accession.[13] However, in all these countries, with the exception of Solomon Islands, there are reservations. For example, Fiji reserves the right not to comply with its obligations in the case of laws relating to elections, in the matters of land and as regards education. Papua New Guinea made a reservation under Article 20(1) of the Convention whereby the government does not accept that the obligations of the Convention go beyond any imposed under the Papua New Guinea Constitution. In Tonga there are reservations relating to land. The scope for reservations, therefore, provides the opportunity for modifying the practical implementation of international standards. Even where countries are not signatories to these Covenants and Conventions, the pledge of member states under Article 56 of the United Nations Charter may impose obligations to take steps to achieve the aims set out in Article 55.

At the same time, the rhetoric of international human rights provides a useful and important vehicle for raising public awareness and popular consciousness of basic human needs and ideals, and a number of conventions are a consequence of this. One of the most evident examples in the region is the Convention on the Elimination of All Forms of Discrimination against Women, to which most countries in the Pacific region are signatories, with only Tonga, Nauru and Marshall Islands not being parties to this.[14] Similarly, many are signatories to the Convention on the Rights of the Child. Both these Conventions have attracted considerable publicity and lobbying in the Pacific region, and although, as will be seen in a later chapter, much remains to be done to achieve the goals which they promote, as the focus of rights' advocacy they have had a significant role in raising awareness of human rights in many Pacific Island countries.

Human rights discourse also provides a platform for international organisations which are not states and which are not non-governmental organisations to have voice. In particular, economic organisations are important players on the human rights' stage although their policies and operations may not always be conducive to all or some human rights. International financial institutions emerged as part of the re-building process in the aftermath to the Second World War. The aim was to encourage economic development and stability at a global level. These organisations, such as the World Bank, the International Monetary Fund and the World Trade Organisation, influence human rights developments because they influence economic policy both internationally and at a country-specific level. Frequently they reflect dominant but not universal economic ideologies and their intervention may be both beneficial and detrimental, especially in small under-developed countries such as those found in the Pacific region. The interplay of development, human rights and external agencies will be considered in greater detail in the following chapter.

Which rights?

Human rights theories indicate how rulers should behave in respect of those that are ruled. In particular, rulers should respect human rights. What is not always clear is whether this means that all rights should be respected equally or that some rights should be respected more than others. The evolution of human rights since the end of the Second World War has witnessed changes in the focus of rights instruments as new, previously unconsidered rights, come to the fore. The rights of women, children, the disabled, asylum seekers and migrant labourers are examples. The wrongs, which early international rights' instruments were directed at addressing, have by and large been addressed. In the Pacific region, however, where many countries are new and late arrivals to the many human rights instruments now tabled, it may be difficult to determine which rights should be given effect to first. Indeed, even if there was a communal core of universally accepted minimal rights – such as rights against murder, slavery, torture and genocide, what is meant by but these terms and what strategies should be adopted to ensure their observance are by no means universal. Each individual country must address these issues within their own jurisdiction. In many cases no action will be required. For example, if there is no apparent slavery or genocide then no positive steps need to taken to observe the duty not to permit these offences against human rights. Similarly, if the written constitution adopted at independence puts in place the civil and political rights advocated international instruments and some form of democratic government – however poorly executed – perhaps no further positive action is required. Indeed, the entrenchment of rights in the written constitutions transfers responsibility for rights to the courts and judiciary. It is only when other rights are placed on the agenda, or existing rights need to be strengthened or supplemented, that the state, via the legislature, has to do anything.

Some rights, such as those pertaining to family, social and economic rights, legal rights, may be more contested either because of conflicting interpretations or because they inherently conflict with culture, or because their importance is differently prioritised. Alternatively it is precisely these rights, of family, land, culture, language, that may be most easily recognised and therefore supported in the Pacific region.

Indeed, in some developing countries, it may be argued that until social and economic needs are met it is pointless to advocate civil and political rights. Conversely it may be argued that without civil and political rights there can be no economic or social development, or indeed that the unfettered exercise of civil and political rights help to safeguard economic security by ensuring real needs are drawn to the attention of the government. In developing countries, this dilemma can present real challenges. For instance, should certain human rights be suppressed or ignored in order to promote political stability and linked to this economic growth? For example, should trade unionism be deterred by infringing the right of freedom of association in order to avoid strike action in urgently needed services; or should freedom of movement be curtailed in order to curb urban migration, unemployment and law and order problems related to the unchecked movement of people to urban centres; or should the state interfere to control access to forests and fresh water reserves on private land in order to ensure environmental concerns are observed?

It is not unusual to find provisions in rights instruments permitting the suspension or curbing of certain human rights in specified circumstances – such as times of war or national emergency. But should the need to do this be recognised as going further than these grounds in order to achieve short term measures?

Even if it is accepted that human rights are distinct from and superior to other rights and that states have, for legal or moral reasons, a duty to give effect to these and the international community expects this, there is still the question of which rights should be elevated to this superior status, and if there are many possible candidates, how should they be ranked? There is also the question of whether all countries should accept the same ranking of rights or be permitted to make their own selection taking into account the cultural, economic, political and social context. The resource implications of giving equal effect to all rights are considerable. In the Pacific region, it is clear that the island countries do not have the resources to give equal attention to all rights.

Historically, it was civil and political rights which received attention first. These have been classified as 'first generation' rights, with economic and social rights being classified as second generation rights. The latter tended to be subsumed under 'development'. This was not simply because the first were less resource demanding, but because in the interests of respecting both sovereignty and the right of people to elect their own forms of government, civil and political rights were seen as being an essential first step and necessary for other rights. These were also fundamental rights which had been denied to a number of people in the years leading up to the Second World War and during it. They continue to be the rights which are curtailed in dictatorships and under military regimes. These rights are emphasised because the proper functioning of democratic government is seen as important for facilitating the enjoyment of a whole range of rights.

Thus, the right to vote, to be properly represented and for parliament to be accountable are seen as being essential. In part, this was an inevitable reaction against fascism, Nazism and socialism in the early period of the United Nations. For those countries which do not subscribe to western liberal philosophy, or where the right to vote is less significant than having food; or preserving a vernacular language or practising certain cultural traditions is more pressing than the right to a passport; these first generation rights may seem less important.

As more non-western and underdeveloped countries joined the United Nations, there was greater recognition of the importance of economic rights and that the influence of economic inequalities in the world could itself lead to human rights violations. If there was to be equality of social and economic rights, then underlying rights had to be recognised. These included rights to development, peace, a healthy environment and self-determination. They may also include the right to humanitarian aid in times of crisis and to benefit from global efforts on the environment. In the least developed nations of the world, these rights may be particularly important. It is these rights which are referred to as third generation rights.

The nature of this last category of rights is not entirely clear and the terminology is unhelpful. However, what is relevant, especially in the context of the Pacific region, is that this category of rights envisages not only a domestic rights framework but one that operates in the inter-state sphere, implying a solidarity between individuals and nations. In the context of environmental rights and sustainable development advocacy of these rights may in fact have some positive benefit.

These categories of rights are clearly not isolated from one and other nor do they follow chronologically as 'generations' might. Some writers suggest that social and economic rights are a necessary pre-condition for civil and political rights (Arat 1991), while others suggest the converse (Sen 1999: 88–99). Similarly both sets of rights may be found in the same instruments. They are all important in different contexts and as the membership of the United Nations has enlarged and changed, the emphasis has shifted. Today other rights have emerged, particularly rights of specific groups such as women, children and disabled people. As any individual may fall under a number of different groupings, for example because of age, gender, ethnicity, status or nationality, if all persons are to be treated equally then all rights need to be observed equally. This, of course, may not always be possible due to resource or other constraints, with the divergence between reality and idealism coming to the fore again.

Rights not duties?

One of the criticisms levelled at the early international declarations of rights is the emphasis on rights rather than duties. Where rights are understood as freedoms, however, it is axiomatic that these freedoms cannot be enjoyed or exercised if to do so infringes the freedoms of others. To that extent therefore there is always a duty correlative to the enjoyment of a freedom. Even where freedoms are expressed as rights, the exercise of these may be subject to the similar exercise of such rights by others. For example, in the Universal Declaration of Human Rights, Article 29 states that everyone 'has duties to the community in which alone the free and full development of his personality is possible' (Para 1). Further, the exercise of individual rights is frequently subject to considerations of more communal interests such as public health, public order, morality, national security and the general welfare. Rights give rise not only to claims of entitlement but also to obligations. While these obligations may rest primarily with the State and its agents, they are also owed by members of society to each other. What is less clear, however, is whether the rights-duties correlation in respect of human rights is different from other entitlement claims.

For example, it could be argued that there are other legal avenues for derelictions of duty towards others, such as through the criminal law where rights to property or bodily integrity are infringed, or the civil law, such as in the case of breaches of confidence or defamation. The problem is, however, that often rights' advocacy is perceived as carrying more weight than duty advocacy, especially when claimed by the individual. Where social organisation is strongly duty based – as in much of the South Pacific region – the transition to a rights-based society is seen as potentially destabilising and as undermining the very fabric of social organisation. There is also the concern that claims of rights, especially by individuals, would give rise to wholly unreasonable expectations of governments to deliver. Indeed, the Minister for Justice in an opening speech at the 1987 LAWASIA human rights seminar stated:

> In many Pacific cultures our human rights still rest on collective assets – our titles, our dignities, our land and our security – and every one of them must still be matched by obligations. If we are led to think of individual rights and freedoms as due to us by some wealthy government, we may unthinkingly tear out culture apart.
>
> (Hyndman 1991: 7)

There is therefore a tension between rights and obligations or duties; between the group and the individual and between the state and its people. Understanding the potential conflicts which may arise is important because if human rights are taken as reflecting certain values it is necessary to be clear what those values are. It is also important, if rights give rise to obligations or duties, that whoever bears the burden of these accepts the value system which gives rise to them. If human rights are 'socially constructed' as has been suggested by writers such as Donnelly (1985: 35–39), then, while some rights may be common to all societies, such as the right to life, the right to a family, to freedom of movement or to association, others may be more society specific, for example the right to culture, language, religion, dress. It may be necessary therefore to establish a common core of rights which both satisfies the rights entitlement of individuals while not imposing too great a burden of duty on those who must observe or give effect to these rights. The danger with this approach is that those rights which require greater effort on the part of the state or others will be neglected and those that require little effort will be upheld.

Because rights are claimable against the state – and not just other individuals – the question of the duties of the state is crucial. Here a distinction may be drawn between those rights which have correlative positive duties – which may require legislative or policy change as well as resources, and those rights or liberties which simply require the state to abstain from interference through inaction and non-intervention. Where there are resource constraints or political apathy, then duties requiring no positive action may be more successfully upheld than those that do require positive action. Thus civil and political rights may be more easily observed than economic and social rights because the former require little positive action – especially where constitutional frameworks have been put in place by departing colonial administrations. The right–duty relationship between the individual and the state is a complex one, because the duty of the State is both to be bound by human rights statements and to give effect to them. At the same time, duty advocacy can be used to defeat or deny rights, especially where the duty is advocated by the stronger power and the right claimed by the weaker one. Natural law theorists, such as Locke, held that rights could only be enjoyed if all individuals respected the rights of others. There was therefore a mutuality of rights and duties. Although the natural law theory is no longer current, the idea of mutuality persists and is reflected in most written rights' statements.

Groups not individuals?

One of the concerns which is articulated in human rights discourse in the Pacific region is that there is too much emphasis on individual rights and not enough on group or community rights. As a result, rights advocacy is sometimes seen as undermining social cohesion and stability. This is a concern that has not only been expressed in the Pacific region but by a number of theorists who advocate a more communitarian philosophy (Waldron 1987: 151; Caney 1992). In fact, there are many references to the individual within the community in international human rights instruments. Article 1 of the Universal Declaration of Human Rights, for example, states that 'All human beings ... should act towards one another in a spirit of brotherhood'; Article 27 refers to the right to 'freely participate in the cultural life of the community' and Article 29(1) states that it is only within the community that the 'free and full development of [everyone's] personality is possible'. Article 27 of the International

Covenant on Civil and Political Rights also recognises the importance of the group rights of minority cultures, religion, language or ethnic groups.

The identity of a community or group may of course vary. To refer to 'collective' rights suggests some static social entity, but affiliations of individuals to groups change. In fact collectives are fluid and changing.[15] Adherence to traditional perceptions of group rights may be as much a conservative response to a rapidly changing world as a claim to a special form of rights. There is also the danger that if 'collective' rights means the rights of the majority group then those of the minority may be at risk. Indeed, there may be reasons to consider the collective as both beneficiary of rights and bearer of duties because often it is the group, rather than the state or the individual, that perpetrates inequality of rights or the suppression of liberties. So, for example, a village council or traditional authority may make a decision which breaches certain fundamental rights of the person or persons affected by that decision.

If the 'collective' is society at large, then that would ignore the many different elements that make up that society, for example, women, children, the elderly, the disabled, adolescents, as well as able-bodied adult males, not all of whom will have the same needs or indeed the same shared values, and some of whom may be considerably more vulnerable to rights abuses than others. Moreover, one individual may belong to several 'collectives' which may have different perceptions of rights. For example, freedom of expression may be perceived differently in the home, at school or university, in church or in Parliament. Often there are cultural boundaries which cross geographical boundaries and are not necessarily coexistent with territory, and at other times there are many different cultural boundaries within a single territory. So, for example, members of the same church may have more in common even if they come from different villages or islands, than those within a village or island, or members of a clan or family or ethnic group may share values even though they are widely scattered.

Arguably, the interests of these diverse groups or collectives can be accommodated by recognising the duties which accompany the enjoyment of individual rights; through the national interpretation of rights; and through the reservations and restrictions which are frequently found in constitutional bills of rights' provisions. However, the perceptions of different collectives may also be valuable in informing an understanding of rights in a local context and of ascertaining the value systems or norms of a particular society. For example, perceptions of women's rights from the perspective of church groups, traditional leaders, women's groups and youth groups may go some way to explaining why the practical implementation of measures to give effect to obligations incurred under CEDAW face challenges in the region. Until these values and their diversities are understood it may be difficult to make progress on human rights. It is here, perhaps, that social anthropologists, sociologists and linguists need to work with lawyers to arrive at an inter-disciplinary understanding of human rights (Thaman 1998: 4).

Conclusion

In the context of the Pacific there are a number of apparent difficulties with the different theories and international statements which inform contemporary human rights discourse. However, these difficulties should not be overestimated. There are elements in many of the theoretical approaches to human rights which resonate with values and experiences in the region. It would also be a mistake to suppose that all international human rights instruments have a clear and agreed theoretical basis or that more recent instruments reflect only one culture or perspective. Human rights are dynamic and diverse. To be acceptable to many different communities across the globe they have to be adaptable as well as resilient. In many respects human rights discourse is not so different from discourses about custom or tradition. There has to be recognition and accommodation of difference, a realisation that in order to survive there has to be adaptation, and that at times there may be a gap between the expression of the ideal and the experience of the real. There are therefore many challenges to be faced in putting the theory of human rights into practice.

Notes

1 Influential were thinkers of the Natural Law School – such as Wolff (1934) and Vattel (1834). However, the natural law school dates back to some of the earliest Greek and Roman philosophers.
2 The fact that the Declaration of the Rights of Man in France was swiftly followed by a reign of terror and dictatorship highlighted the difficulty of balancing popular will with practical challenges (Freeman 2002: 25).
3 213 UNTS, 221 ETS 5, UKS 71 (1953).
4 A/RES/61/295. None of the members of the forum are Pacific islanders – there is one Australian – although the Declaration has been translated into Maori. The seventh session of the Forum held in May 2008 had a half day on the Pacific on the agenda.
5 UN GAOR, UN Doc. A/CONF.157/23, 1993.
6 Although the members of the Commission which drafted the Universal Declaration were drawn from Australia, Chile, China, France, Lebanon, the United States, the United Kingdom and the Soviet Union. The latter refused to vote on the Declaration in the General Assembly.
7 For example, in Nauru, Samoa, the Federated States of Micronesia and Marshall Islands.
8 Culture in this context is taken to include language, institutions and socially recognised groups.
9 See, for example, the rapid deportation of Australian law officers in the State Law Office in Vanuatu in September 2004, and the departure of an Australian Chief of Police in Fiji in 2006, http://news.bbc.co.uk/2/hi/asia-pacific/6123688.stm (accessed 23 June 2008)
10 Articles 55 and 56.

11 In the Pacific region Solomon Islands succeeded to the International Covenant on Economic, Social and Cultural Rights on 17 March 1982. Nauru signed the International Covenant on Civil and Political Rights on 12 November 2001, Vanuatu on 29 November 2007 and it was ratified by Samoa on 15 February 2008.
12 Fiji on 11 January 1973 and Solomon Islands on 17 March 1982.
13 Papua New Guinea on 27 January 1982 and Tonga on 16 February 1972.
14 Kiribati and the Federated States of Micronesia are the most recent countries to accede to this, the former on 17 March 2004 and FSM on 1 September 2004.
15 See comments by Sir Paul Reeves in Thomas (ed.) (1998: 11–16).

4 Fundamental rights and questions of property

Introduction

Against the background and context established in the previous chapters, this chapter considers a specific fundamental right: the right of property. Property has been chosen as the first substantive example of rights for several reasons. First, the defence of property interests was one of the early concerns of human rights theorists, who considered that property did not only include land, although this was important, but also the right to subsistence, as a natural law right, and in medieval rights discourse to life and liberty (Freeman 2002: 168). Second, and more practically, because property, especially land and related resources, is fundamental to identity, existence and survival in Pacific countries (Van Trease 1987: 3). For Pacific Island people, as for many indigenous peoples elsewhere,[1] land is more than its physical substance or exploitable potential. People and land are linked physically and spiritually. Where a person is from may be far more important than where they live; where they are buried may be far more significant than where they are born; where they are brought up may be as relevant as ties of affection. It is therefore the heritage of individuals and groups. Land is also a vehicle of national identity and has in recent years been the cause of political and racial instability, notably in Fiji and Solomon Islands.

Indeed, it is sometimes said that Pacific islanders are people of 'place'. Strong associations with particular locations can be manifested in particular customary practices, language, naming, religion and political affiliation, as well as actual rights and duties in respect of land. Vaá, describing the Samoan sense of identity and the customary concept of a human's rights, explains that from birth, and even before it, Samoans have human rights which emanate not only from being a member of a particular family but also from being born in a particular village and place. A person's place within the family is both determined by and gives rise to their relationship with others in that place, their right to titles, land and culture as well as their obligations and duties (Vaá 2008). Where people are dispossessed of land to make way for a mine, or a dam or an airport, or because of re-location by the government of the day, the disruption of sense of place is rarely compensated and can have long-term negative consequences, including leading to civil unrest.

Third, the relationship between property and human rights illustrates a number of the difficulties encountered when considering human rights in the region. In particular, claims to property demonstrate the tensions between group rights and individual rights as illustrated by changing forms and uses of property. These in turn highlight some of the challenges posed by the domestic and international pressures of development in island countries with limited resources. Property, especially the exploitation of natural resources in the region, raises questions about: the right to development and the right to a sustainable environment – and whether these two can be compatible; the internal and external forces that determine the pace of change and the issue of self-determination in deciding priorities and policies; the duty owed by national government to its citizens; and the obligations of the international community towards Pacific Island countries. Interpretations and constructions of property rights and the way in which the use of property is regulated, also highlight some of the issues confronted by plural legal systems in seeking to provide frameworks which will best promote and protect human rights. In particular customary constructions of property may be inconsistent with western or introduced ideas, while the forums for resolving property disputes may fall uneasily between the formal courts and informal traditional and more localised adjudicative bodies. Rights to property, whether land, royalties, rents or compensation payments are also significant for the peace, stability and future prosperity of the region. Finally, property, especially land and natural resources, is central to a long history of rights abuse which continues to have consequences in the region and cannot be ignored. In particular, this latter includes the deforestation of many islands by sandalwood traders, the taking and redistribution of land seen as lying idle or neglected by colonial governments,[2] the use of Pacific Islands for weapon testing,[3] and the taking of land for foreign military bases.[4] Even today, foreign governments appear to take advantage of the weak bargaining strength of Pacific Islands and the geographical remoteness of their islands.[5]

Property rights, for the purposes of this chapter, are seen as going beyond the express provisions in statements of rights which afford protection against the wrongful deprivation of property by the state through compulsory acquisition or possession, and the duty of states to observe equitable procedures and award just compensation. The protection of property rights is seen as imposing a positive obligation on states and the wider community to adopt policies and take measures which safeguard the property of Pacific Island people. Although Pacific islanders have interests in many forms of property, three have been selected for the focus of this chapter: land and some of its resources, intellectual property, and the ocean. These three forms of property are closely inter-related because they contribute to a Pacific sense of identity. For most islands, there is more sea than land, and there are many stories of creation that involve the ocean and its resources. The ocean divides islands and brings them together. The land too is a source of creation, while traditional knowledge is intimately linked with both the sea and the land. Indigenous intellectual cultural property includes that traditional knowledge and also physical manifestations of that knowledge.

Property and rights

What is at stake here is not so much the actual forms of property as the interests people have in respect of these. However, in the region, these lines cannot always be clearly drawn. For example, the relationship of people with land is more than just the use and occupation of the land, it informs their very existence. Moreover, where property is intangible, such as knowledge of genealogies, or the healing property of plants, or how to weave a particular fan or mat, it may be difficult to distinguish the property and the rights it generates. This can present challenges for arriving at adequate protection of property interests in the region.

Fundamental property rights

The protection of property rights is recognised as a fundamental right.[6] Indeed, this is acknowledged in most of the regional constitutions as a right separate from the right to privacy or security from unwarranted search and seizure. What is meant or understood by 'property' in this context may include rights to land and other property or this may be unspecified. For example, in Tonga there is no separate right to property but under section 1, Part 1 of the 'Declaration of Rights' it is stated under the 'Declaration of Freedom': 'all men may use their lives and persons and time to acquire and possess property and to dispose of their labour and the fruit of their hands and to use their own property as they will.' Only male Tongans can acquire interests in land other than by lease, so that 'all men' may or may not be intended to include women, depending on the nature of the property interest under consideration. In some cases, this right to property is included among those where discrimination is prohibited,[7] although in fact discrimination in respect of certain property rights, especially land, is a feature of the region.[8] Elsewhere, the right is stated to be a right not to be deprived of property, or a right to due process, or a right to compensation.[9] These rights are closely interrelated. A person may be deprived of their property in certain circumstances, which can be broadly divided into two categories: first, where loss or confiscation of property is a consequence of personal circumstance and occurrences such as bankruptcy, mortgage default, criminal activity, tax liability or an order of court;[10] and second, where the government appropriates such property for purposes beneficial to the public.[11] In this latter case, there are a number of elements to be satisfied if the deprivation is to be lawful. These include deprivation in accordance with the law; for a public purpose,[12] and in return for the timely payment of an agreed or just compensation determined by taking into account the criteria specified either in the Constitution or in supplementary legislation. Such compensation may include relocation or the provision of alternative land/housing as well as financial or other non-financial compensation.[13] Those deprived of their property should also have the right to due process and access to the courts to challenge any such deprivation. These types of provisions are very much modelled on western-liberal conceptions of private property and some of them, such as the administrative machinery for state acquisition of property or the compensations mechanisms, are not always appropriate or equitable in the Pacific context.[14]

The right to protection of property is therefore a restricted and not absolute right, the breach of which, even if it causes hardship, may be justified. An interesting example can be found in Papua New Guinea, where continued mining at Ok Tedi is facilitated by a raft of legislation, including the most recent Mining (Ok Tedi Mine Continuation Ninth Supplement) Agreement Act 2001. This Act opens with a preamble which among other things recognises that 'operating the Ok Tedi mine ... has resulted in adverse effects on the environment impacting landowners in the environs of (and), downstream from, the Ok Tedi mine' and 'that there are concerns that the continued operation of the Ok Tedi mine could cause additional adverse environmental impacts'. Nevertheless the Act provides for the mining to continue because, *inter alia* 'the Ok Tedi mine has generated and is generating a significant part of the gross domestic product and foreign exchange of Papua New Guinea'. Any actual or potential breaches of the fundamental rights included in the Constitution are justified on the grounds that the legislation is made for a public purpose and for 'a reason that is reasonably justified in a democratic society that has a proper regard for the rights and dignity of mankind' (1(2)(a)(iv)). In Papua New Guinea and elsewhere, the general terminology of justification grounds leaves it open to governments to interpret these as they see fit and may involve a difficult balancing act between the advantages of commercial exploitation of natural resources and the disadvantages of environmental damage, adverse social impact and related breaches to the fundamental rights of people (Filer 1999).

The nature of property rights in the Pacific

As has been previously indicated, one of the difficulties with human rights statements introduced in the region is their origins in western cultures and traditions, and, in the case of property, the legal constructions that inform the right referred to. While in some respects it is unnecessary to be precise about what rights, interests or even types of property are covered by these protections – because the focus is on procedures or mechanisms for claiming compensation for wrongful deprivation of property or wrongful interference with its use and enjoyment – at some point it becomes essential to know or to be able to ascertain who has a claim for compensation or a remedy and how the infringement is to be assessed in order to arrive at the appropriate outcome. Thus it becomes necessary to arrive at a decision on how ownership or other interests are defined and applied, what is the nature of the property and what is the relationship between the claimant and the property which gives rise to claim for a remedy. The models which inform the statements of rights in the various written constitutions of the region are grounded in notions of private property; the right of an owner to have exclusive possession and to use or exploit this property for private benefit or profit (Bhalla 1981). While this interpretation of property rights will apply to some property interests in the region, particularly in urban areas where people are acquiring more material wealth, it is not appropriate for all forms of property interests.

Land

The nature of customary interests can result in difficulties arising in respect of land, natural resources such as minerals and timber, cultural intellectual property and biological property such as marine and plant species. In particular, these forms of property may not be amenable to individual ownership. They may not even be owned – in any absolute sense – by the person or people currently benefitting from them or controlling their use. For example, in the case of land held under customary tenure – which accounts for most land in the region, custom ownership of land is rarely the right of an individual, but of a group.[15] Indeed, it has been held that '(Samoan) communal ownership of land does not confer any personal individual right of ownership'.[16] An apparent individual owner may only be the representative of a larger group. This was a point recognised in the Vanuatu case of *Noel v Toto*. [17] Here, Kent J, considering an earlier judgment of Cooke CJ, was faced with the problem that custom land was incapable of individual ownership, so that a person declared the owner of land following the resolution of a title dispute, owned it in a representative capacity only. In this case, the court also recognised that it was difficult to translate the entire concept of custom ownership into English common law principles because '(t)he nature of custom ownership is that the land cannot be actually disposed of. It is retained for the benefit of future generations'.[18] In custom, therefore, not only may interests in land vest in a number of people at the same time, but also there is a temporal dimension to customary land holding which may be less evident in common law. Land represents a continuum between ancestors, current users and occupiers and future generations. Current owners are therefore merely custodians. The significance of this, as stated in the Samoan case of *Tufele Liamatua v Mose* [1988] AHSC 1, is that '(c)ommunal lands are not freely alienable on the market'.[19] Effectively custom ownership is perpetual but not individual.[20] The consequence of this is that at the very outset an individual right to property is curtailed by custom, which in turn may be endorsed by legislation and provisions in the constitutions which may restrict the power of alienation (Farran and Paterson 2004: 189). So, for example, in Cook Islands, although there is the right to own property and not to be deprived of it, there is no constitutional limit on the power of parliament to pass legislation restricting or prohibiting the 'alienation of Native land' (Article 64(1)(c)).

A further complication is that there can be several interests over the same property, especially land, at the same time (Farran and Paterson 2004: 12–18). While these may peaceably co-exist when there is no urge to develop the land or change its use, conflict can ensue when land is taken out of traditional use and in effect rendered useless for cultivation or occupation by traditional owners. This arose in the Solomon Island case of *Zephaniah Kinisita v Orkley Ramolele and Augustine Maemarine* [1996] SBHC 52, in which primary and secondary right holders were in dispute. The primary right holders owned the land as custom owners and the secondary right holders had rights of gardening and cultivation. The primary right holders wished to grant a lease over the land for the building of a school. Clearly this would take it out of production for the secondary right holders. Muria CJ ranked the primary right holders first, holding that they alone had the right to decide whether to grant a lease or not. However, he held that the secondary right holders could not be ignored but must be taken into account because: '(i)n the Solomon Islands context nobody is landless, whether that be in terms of ownership or just usufructary right which is closely associated with the right of occupation'. In order to accommodate both sets of rights within the change of land use which the lease would bring about, the judge held that these right holders should be included as trustees of the money realised by the lease.

If each holder of these interests has a fundamental right to have it protected then there is clearly room for conflict. A further Solomon Island case illustrates this. In *Tovua v Meki* [1989] SBHC 22, there was a dispute as to entitlement to logging royalties. The difficulty was that ownership of timber rights was distinct from ownership of the land. What was unclear was whether they were sufficiently distinct so as to entitle those who held timber rights to grant logging contacts to third parties without consulting the landowners. This led to the possibility that the landowners could find themselves owners of a wasteland once all the timber was felled. The legislation put in place by the State was framed with the aim of simplifying matters for investors by identifying a limited class of people with whom agreements had to be made.[21] Clearly the Act was inspired by a desire of government to facilitate the exploitation of natural resources and generate much needed economic wealth for Solomon Islands. What the Act failed to do sufficiently clearly, was to indicate the relationship between the timber right holders and the landowners. Indeed, it has been suggested that the Act has the effect of diminishing the rights of customary landowners (Corrin 1992). Although the court found that representatives of logging-right-holders may be loosely referred to as 'trustees' by the area councils who rule on their identity, this was not stipulated in the Act. Following previous case law,[22] Ward CJ held that the logging right holders took the money (the royalties) under a 'constructive trust'. He went on to recognise, however, that there was no guidance as to how they were to carry out this fiduciary role. Moreover, it appears from his obiter statement that even the imposition of a constructive trust was doubtful – as well it might be with no legal precedent or clarification – as it would be possible:

> For one member of a tribe to enter into an agreement and take and use the royalties without consultation with, or the knowledge of, those other members of the tribe who live in isolated parts of the land and depend on the land entirely.[23]

The fundamental property rights provisions found in Solomon Islands Constitution are directed at protection from deprivation of property by compulsory possession or acquisition, but enforcement of these protective provisions is not expressly limited to the State or its agents (section 18). There is therefore potential for bringing a claim horizontally against non-State players, where the interpretation of the law or its operation effectively amounts to non-consensual taking of possession or acquisition. However, while Ward CJ acknowledged that

> Commercial logging of an area is such a devastating event that the exercise of that single right may destroy many other rights. Thus the legitimate sale of those rights may restrict or totally destroy other rights, primary and secondary, held by people living on the same lands such as harvesting rights and the right to establish gardens or use the streams.

he did not go so far as to suggest that the enabling legislation amounted to a breach of fundamental rights, indicating only that it was for Parliament to amend the legislation so as to afford greater protection to all those who had interests in the land being logged.

The existence of multiple, simultaneous or consecutive interests, is important in a number of ways. First, governments seeking to exert their powers to acquire or possess property on one of the various justified grounds, have to ensure that they deal with the correctly identified interest holders. It is also important that other interest holders, who may not be primary interest holders, are kept informed. Second, any compensation paid must be paid to those who are beneficially entitled to it. This may require payments into trusts or holding accounts for future interest holders. Alternatively it may require the possibility of renegotiating or reviewing compensation paid at regular periods into the future (Mason 1987: 23). These considerations may be perceived as impediments to development, for example where a large number of people put themselves forward as clan members deserving of compensation payment from mining companies, or where land designated for essential infrastructure is subject to lengthy title disputes. However, customary property regimes may provide security, stability and opportunity for small scale development which would otherwise be unavailable to many Pacific islanders. An example can be found in the Vanuatu case, *Noel v Toto* [1995] VUSC 3. The issue here was how the distribution of income generated by tourist visitors to a beach on the land was to be divided. The Constitution states that the rules of custom shall form the basis of ownership and use of land in the Republic of Vanuatu.[24] However, custom land law offered little assistance in this case. While other members of a custom owner's family could request custom land to use, Kent J found that this 'right' was not a 'legal right' in the common law sense because it was not enforceable. The respondent (Obed Toto) was a custom owner of land, not in his own right but as a representative of his family.[25] While he had the right to decide what areas of land each member could have for customary use, the members of the group were also owners and therefore entitled to the benefits of the land including any income generated by tourism. A further problem was that, while in custom there was evidence of discrimination in the allocation of land between male and female claimants, the Constitution of Vanuatu 1980 confers fundamental rights – including the right not to be deprived of property – free from discrimination. The right to share in the income of the land was derived from rights as custom owners but also differed in so far as, first, the income had to be able to be used and could not be kept in perpetuity for future generations – as land would be, and second, the discriminatory allocation of such income on the basis of custom could not be allowed. At the same time, however, while land might support a number of claims simultaneously or in succession, if the money were distributed too widely it would be of no practical use. The approach adopted in this case was to limit distribution to the highest level of descent and divide the money equally between them.

The underlying philosophy behind this decision was indicated by Kent J, who held:

> A person is not to be deprived of that income which they generate from their own ideas and labours. The incentive to develop must not be stifled. Family members equally ought not to be able to sit back and derive the benefits of the work and initiative of others.

While the theoretical basis of property rights may be derived from philosophies which are incompatible with Pacific Island cultures (Frame 1992), the case marks an attempt to arrive at a compromise between the recognition and protection of customary property rights and constitutional human rights. Unfortunately, the court's ruling did not end the inter-family tension between private, individual ownership of commercial enterprise and its benefits and customary ownership of the land and its benefits, and subsequent disputes have continued to come before the court.[26]

The significance of group rights or collective rights is not limited just to land and its resources, but also extends to indigenous intellectual property, or cultural property. Here, although the state may not be the direct infringer of property rights, it may enable others to do so because of a weak or ineffective protective regime. Failure by the state to take the necessary measures to protect intellectual property rights, especially those of its own people, could be seen as being in breach of its obligations to safeguard the fundamental rights of its citizens.

Intellectual property

The cultural property of indigenous people, referred to today more commonly as indigenous cultural or intellectual property, is an important property component in non-monetary economies. It encompasses many aspects of culture and identity, including: songs, music, dance, stories, costume, magic, medicine and knowledge. Sometimes this manifests itself in designs, paintings and artefacts.[27] At other times it is demonstrated by spectacle.[28] Some of this indigenous property has long been used for gifts, exchange and peace offerings.[29] For example, mats play a key role in weddings, funerals and in marking respect or apology.[30] This continues to be the case although such offerings may now be accompanied by western manufactured goods and money.

Increasing contact with outsiders has highlighted the vulnerability of such intellectual property to commercial exploitation, often without reference to the true owners or custodians.[31] Traditionally, unauthorised use of a dance, or song, or mask would breach various taboos and might result in a fine or other punishment or a curse resulting from magic, or the intervention of spiritual or ancestral powers.[32] However, where such property is taken by outsiders, especially foreigners, these sanctions are unlikely to succeed. Alternatively the matter might be brought before the courts and argued under the ordinary rules of property, or indeed the Constitution. An interesting example of this occurred in Vanuatu where custodians of the Pentecost land dive challenged a breakaway group seeking to export the jump and perform it on another island for economic gain.[33] Ultimately, the matter was heard by the Supreme Court because the thwarted exporters claimed that their constitutional rights, notably: protection of the law; freedom of expression; freedom of assembly and association; freedom of movement and equal treatment under the law had been infringed.[34] In order to determine the issue the Court focussed on procedure not substance – which meant that the Court did not have to decide if the land-dive was or was not property. Although the court found that there were no breaches of constitutional rights it did suggest that the renegade jumpers had breached the custom rights of the traditional custodians of the jump and ordered that the traditional procedures for seeking permission to use the cultural property of others should be followed (Angelo 1998).

In this case the proposed export had only been to another nearby island. However, where indigenous property is exploited outside the jurisdiction of the local courts protection may be difficult. Indeed, indigenous intellectual property is generally poorly protected in the region (Farran 2003: 81–84), and while Pacific Island governments may be under some pressure to protect western forms of intellectual property, such as patents and trade-marks,[35] limited efforts are being made to protect indigenous property rights. For example, in Tonga the Copyright Act (Cap 121) (1986) includes provisions for copyright in derivative works including, 'works inspired by folklore'.[36] Similarly, in Samoa and Papua New Guinea expressions of folklore are included within the copyright legislation.[37] However, the term 'indigenous culture' is only found in the Vanuatu Copyright Act,[38] where it is defined as 'any way in which indigenous knowledge may appear or be manifested'.[39] While Tonga will now be under pressure to reform its intellectual property law to meet WTO requirements it is unclear whether and in what way it will strengthen the protection of indigenous cultural property.

Both historically and today the prime motivation for protective intellectual property regimes appears to be to prevent intellectual property piracy operating in the region and thereby to attract inward investment which might otherwise be deterred. As has been indicated, accession to the WTO includes, amongst other requirements, complying with TRIPS. While this may enhance property rights in the region by encouraging intellectual property enterprise (Ahmadu 1998), it may also mean that access to the objects of intellectual property, including patented medicines, is denied to non-right holders. Similarly, pressure on Forum Countries to enter into Pacific–EU trade agreements (EPAs) could lead to the introduction of protective intellectual property regimes similar to TRIPS, which would bind countries in the region including those that are not members of WTO. This possibility has been highlighted by the Pacific Network on Globalisation, the Catholic Agency for Overseas Development (CAFOD) and the International Centre for Trade and Sustainable Development (ICTSD). In April 2008, Pacific civil society issued a statement expressing concerns about ongoing European Partnership Developments. In particular this highlighted as one of their four key concerns that 'The EPAs will reduce the ability of Pacific governments to meet their human rights obligations to their own people'. Specifically 'the right to the highest attainable standards of health, the right to housing, and access to essential services like water, health, and education' and that 'the stringent intellectual property clauses proposed by the EU will make some medicines more expensive for Pacific people, and an agreement on services may restrict the ability of Pacific governments to provide essential services to *all* their peoples'.[40]

Even if the Pacific Islands revise their intellectual property law to meet externally imposed standards, the models they may be encouraged to emulate are not always appropriate for the protection of indigenous intellectual property. As has been stated

> The formulation and eventual enactment of standard IPR (intellectual property) laws ... is neither difficult not problematic. What is difficult and problematic is how to accommodate and/or deal with indigenous cultural and intellectual property.
>
> (Kalinoe 2000)

There is a tension on the one hand, between preserving the heritage that is associated with the production and practice of cultural and traditional intellectual property and protecting this from the incursions of tourism, mass media, modern technology and global markets; and on the other, the economic dimensions of intellectual property which inform western models of copyright, patent and trademark law. While these latter are seen as providing incentives for economic development through the promotion of investment, innovation and creativity, employment opportunities and improved quality of products, they may be inappropriate to protect property interests in genetic and plant resources, and traditional knowledge and culture (Forsyth 2003).

There is not only externally driven concern about the scope and effectiveness of Pacific Islands' intellectual property laws. There is also domestic concern that Pacific Island governments are not doing enough to protect the intellectual property rights of their indigenous people.[41] In 2003, the South Pacific Commission noted that

> Pacific islanders traditional knowledge and expressions of culture are increasingly being appropriated and commercialised for profit by non-indigenous interests. At present there is no international or regional regime now in place that affords legal protection to traditional knowledge and expressions of culture.
>
> (Forsyth 2003)

Attempts have been made to create and put in place a regional intellectual property code. A Model Law was formulated as a result of a regional symposium held in New Caledonia in 1999. The Model Law was reviewed and finalised at a meeting jointly organised by the South Pacific Commission, Pacific Islands Forum Secretariat and UNESCO before being endorsed by the First Conference of Ministers of Culture of the Pacific Region at the South Pacific Commission in 2002. It is now gathering dust.[42]

Unless regional governments are prepared to act in concert, whatever measures are put in place by individual states are unlikely to be very effective because of problems of resources, administration and enforceability. There is also the concern that the scope of current intellectual property regimes – even if modified to include much of the cultural property indicated above, would be insufficiently broad to include other forms of property such as customary management systems of natural resources, plant and marine species, and genetic materials, which appear to be increasingly attractive to overseas consortiums.[43]

The ocean

The Pacific Ocean is the largest ocean in the world. The people of the Pacific crossed the Ocean to reach the islands they now inhabit. Even today for many islands the only access is across the sea.[44] The countries of the Pacific have extensive exclusive economic sea zones and marine resources, especially fish, are an important factor in considering economic development and Pacific perceptions of rights (Henare 1998; Senituli 1998). For the purposes of this chapter, however, it is suggested that two aspects of the Ocean in particular give rise to rights issues of particular relevance to Pacific Islands: nuclear trans-shipment and rising sea-levels.

Trans-shipment of nuclear and other waste

Pacific Islands are well aware of the dangers presented by the seas that surround them, not only in the form of natural disasters but also man-made ones (Van Dyke, Smith and Siwatibau 1984). A number of Pacific Island countries are signatories to conventions banning nuclear activity and the dumping and trans-shipment of nuclear and other hazardous waste in the region.[45] These are matters over which individual states, groups or individuals have little if any control. However, the rights issues raised by these occurrences have received some international focus. For example, the international organisation Greenpeace has been vociferous in protesting about the shipment of plutonium through Pacific Islands' exclusive economic zones. Armed nuclear freighters carry the plutonium from the United Kingdom to Japan where it is destined to be used in nuclear power plants. A number of other countries besides Japan and the United Kingdom are involved in the process, including France, where plutonium fuel from the United Kingdom is re-processed, and Belgium, where the fuel is mixed with other elements. Nuclear waste is sent back to the United Kingdom and France from Japan. Plutonium shipping appears to have first attracted media attention in the region in the early 1990s when the United States government insisted that Japan safeguard the voyage of the plutonium ship *Akatsuki Maru* with an armed warship. The *Akatsuki Maru* travelled from Japan, through the Tasman and then through the EEZs of Solomon Islands, New Caledonia, Vanuatu and the Federated States of Micronesia. Other shipments occurred in 1995, 1997 and 1998. In 1999 the Pacific Concerns

Resource Centre indicated that there were plans for up to 30 shipments in the next 15 years.[46]

In 2000, following the Japan–Pacific Island leaders' summit in Japan, Cook Islands Prime Minister, Dr Terepai Maoate and Nuie Premier, Sani Lakatani, expressed their concerns regarding the transportation not only of nuclear fuel but also of spent fuel (Hulsen 2000).

In 2002, at a summit of African, Caribbean and Pacific States held in Fiji, the 78 nations attending expressed their 'strong objection to the transport of nuclear and other hazardous materials through the waters around ACP states'. Little notice seems to have been taken as two ships, the *Pacific Pintail* and the *Pacific Teal*, carrying a cargo of faulty plutonium mixed oxide from Japan to the United Kingdom, crossed the EEZs of at least six Pacific Nations later the same year. Avoidance of the Exclusive Economic Zones of Australia and New Zealand, however, suggests that political influence may be one consideration.

The danger of such shipping lies not only in the potential environmental disaster from radio-active materials that could occur should the ships be damaged by bad weather or fire while at sea, but also the possibility that they could be hijacked or attacked. Although the freighters are armed, the opinion has been expressed that the security surrounding the shipment of this potentially dangerous fuel is 'totally inadequate'.[47] There is also concern that nuclear waste could be dumped on remote islands in the South Pacific or on the seabed. While government voices from outside the region against nuclear shipment have generally been muted, in 2000 the Pacific Islands Forum reiterated a view expressed in 1999 that 'shipments of radioactive materials and Mixed Oxide (MOX) fuel through the region posed a continuing concern'. The focus of the Forum is to arrive at a liability and compensation regime with the major powers of France, Japan and the United Kingdom, in order to provide for the possibility of economic loss caused to Pacific Island countries should there be an accident involving a shipment, rather than to articulate any protest regarding this use of Pacific Islands Exclusive Economic Zones.[48] However, there appears to be little progress on this. In a communiqué following the 2006 Pacific Forum meeting in Fiji, it was stated:

> Leaders reiterated their concerns about the risks of economic loss in an incident involving the shipment of radioactive materials through the Pacific, and restated their view that in the event of losses directly attributable to such an incident, there is an imperative on the shipping states not to leave the countries suffering those losses unsupported.[49]

Given the close relationship between Japan and the Pacific Forum, indicated in Chapter One, it is perhaps unlikely that the Pacific Forum will adopt a more vociferous condemnation of nuclear fuels shipments.

Global warming - rising sea levels

Several countries and islands in the region are threatened by rising sea levels. Tuvalu is particularly vulnerable. In Tuvalu the protection of property rights against wrongful deprivation includes 'its destruction; and ... the making of it useless or valueless for the purposes for which it was used'.[50] However, this provision does little to protect the citizens of Tuvalu from external threats of deprivation. Most of the atolls which make up Tuvalu are less than four metres above sea level. Global warming means rising sea levels and the threat of immersion of most of Tuvalu. While New Zealand has indicated that it will allow a staged migration of Tuvaluans, Australia has refused to countenance this, refuting the claims of rising sea levels or the threat to Tuvalu. At the World Summit for Sustainable Development held in South Africa in 2002, Tuvalu lobbied for international support to bring a claim against Australia and the United States of America – both of whom have not ratified the Kyoto Protocol on the reduction of greenhouse emissions.[51] In 2003, the Prime Minister of Tuvalu addressed the United Nations, stating that the threat of rising sea levels due to global warming was no different from the threat of terrorism.[52] In 2007, Tuvalu's ambassador to the United Nations raised the concerns of the country at a special session of the United Nations Security Council focussing on climate change.

There is – unsurprisingly – dispute as to the causation and whether sea levels are indeed rising as a result of climate change or whether the adversities being faced by Tuvalu are partly of their own making – overcrowding, changes in land use and pollution. Programmes investigating climate change are themselves not immune from political influence. The Pacific Islands Climate Change Assistance Programme (PICCAP) is a three-year SPREP activity funded by the Global Environment Facility (GEF). Linked to it is 'The South Pacific Sea Level and Climate Monitoring Project', funded by AusAID and managed by the National Tidal Facility (NTF), based at the Flinders University of South Australia. In Australia there have been stories that climate scientists, critical of government policy, have been gagged (Ong 2006). Whether this is the case or not it seems clear that Tuvalu and other countries with low lying islands in the regions such as Papua New Guinea, Kiribati and Niue, will be unable to save themselves without international support. Here, gradually growing international awareness of climate change and its possible consequences may put Pacific Island countries such as Tuvalu on the global map (Adams 2007; Simms 2001).[53] However, optimism for change is muted. Although the United States has indicated its support for the action-plan arising out of the 2007 Bali Conference on climate change, it has refused to commit to specific mandatory targets. Consequently, as the delegate for Tuvalu to Bali stated 'It's unlikely we're going to make lots of progress because we need strong signals from the US, and that's not going happen until the election' (Macleod 2008). It may be, therefore, that despite the example of Tuvalu and other Pacific Island countries providing useful illustrations of the impact of climate change, its fate may already be determined.

Property and the international environment

In 1986, the General Assembly of the United Nations adopted a Declaration on the Right to Development. The impetus for this was influenced by the expansion of United Nations membership to many non-Western, underdeveloped new states, formerly under colonial rule, during the 1970s and early 1980s, including most Pacific Island states. The period marked a shift in emphasis from human rights' violations in individual states to the non-state specific structural causes of human rights violations, especially the inequalities of economic wealth and opportunity. The right to development was perceived as both an individual right and a collective right. More recently the United Nations declaration of Millennium Development Goals for the world's poorest nations has placed the issue of development at the forefront of a number of initiatives, including those being put in place in the Pacific.[54]

The United Nations development agenda was stated to cover

> inter-linked issues ranging from poverty reduction, gender equality, social integration, health, population, employment and education to human rights, the environment, sustainable development, finance and governance. It includes as well systemic issues, such as the differential impact of globalization, inequalities among and within countries, and greater participation of developing countries in global economic governance. And it also addresses the question of inter-linkages between development and conflict.[55]

In advocating this agenda, it was recognised by the Department of Economic and Social Affairs of the United Nations that small island states are confronted by particular difficulties, not only in participating in world economies because of a number of economic handicaps, but also because they face a number of environmental hazards, including natural disasters and the impact of global environmental deterioration, especially rising sea levels. In order to meet development goals these countries have 'to strengthen their resilience to the economic and environmental vulnerabilities they confront' (UN Development Agenda 1990–2005: 70, 71). The agenda went on to suggest that these island countries have physical resources that they can exploit:

> For example, they can promote sustainable tourism, while protecting their culture and traditions and conserving and managing their natural

resources. Similarly, they can strive to increase the returns from fisheries by strengthening fisheries management but also ensure the sustainability of fisheries over the longer term ... These countries must be especially vigilant about the trans-shipment of hazardous wastes and materials through their jurisdictions.

(UN Agenda 1990–2005: 71)

Realistically many small islands lack the capacity or resources to confront these challenges unassisted. The United Nations Agenda recognised the need for international partnership and co-operation as well as regional initiatives, but also saw it as incumbent on island states to sign up to a range of global instruments, such as the Convention on the Conservation and Management of Highly Migratory Fish Stocks in the Western and Central Pacific Ocean, the United Nations Framework Convention on Climate Change, the FAO Code of Conduct for Respon- sible Fisheries, the United Nations Fish Stocks Agreement and the FAO High Seas Fishing Agreement and the Convention on Biological Diversity.

However, it is not the United Nations which is the economic influence in world trade but the WTO.[56] The WTO governs world trade by determining the rules of inter-country trade and providing dispute and negotiation mechanisms. Accession to WTO is intended to open up world trade and global markets to members. Some Pacific Island countries are members of WTO because they were members of its predecessor, GATT – the General Agreement on Trade and Tariffs.[57] The WTO, unlike its predecessor, deals not only in trade in goods but also services and intellectual property. Although the mission of the WTO is to support and liberalise trade across the globe by brokering negotiations and agreements between states, it has recognised that developing countries struggle to implement WTO agreements. Consequently, following the Fourth Ministerial Conference in Doha, Qatar in November 2001 a development agenda was adopted.

Under the Doha Development Agenda: Negotiations, Implementation and Development 2001 (the Doha Agenda), the WTO was hoping to encourage less developed nations to become members by getting existing members to agree on ways to integrate countries with more vulnerable economies into international trade as a way of addressing and alleviating poverty.[58] However, in 2006, the Doha Agenda was suspended following breakdowns in negotiations between current members, indicating perhaps that the world's powerful trading nations do not want to assist those who are less powerful (WTO News 2006). Despite this two Pacific Island countries, Tonga and Vanuatu, have considered joining the WTO since it was created in 1994. Vanuatu commenced accession procedures in 1995, but has not yet acceded although in May 2008 the process was resumed. There are a variety of reasons why accession negotiations broke down. In summary, it has been suggested that

> The WTO accession process was too onerous and power-based for a small, capacity-constrained country. Vanuatu officials were forced to make concessions that politicians were not prepared to sustain in the long run and which were greater than many developed and developing WTO members.
>
> (Gay 2005)

One concession that Vanuatu was not prepared to make was to revise its land laws despite strong requests from the United States to do so. This meant that concessions had to be made in other areas. Vanuatu was also prevented from taking advantage of special and differential treatment provisions in respect of transition periods for Trade-related Aspects of Intellectual Property Rights (TRIPS). This meant that new intellectual property laws would have to be in place before accession could proceed. As indicated there are a number of aspects to WTO driven intellectual property regimes which are not sympathetic or appropriate for Pacific Island countries.

The other Pacific Island country that commenced WTO accession plans soon after 1994 is Tonga. In 2007 Tonga acceded to the WTO. Hopes have been expressed that membership will reduce poverty in the country and strengthen its economy, but OXFAM has suggested that in fact membership may aggravate an already weak economy (BBC News 15 December 2005). Whether Tonga will be able to comply with the WTO requirements remains to be seen.[59] Tonga's accession has been supported by Australia, New Zealand and the United States. However, accession may lead to closer dependency on these countries not only, especially in the case of Australia, as importers of Tongan produce, but also for aid to develop the economy (Vaile 2005). Within and outside the country there has been disquiet at the lack of public consultation which has taken place leading up to accession, the lack of transparency in the process of negotiation and uncertainty about the consequences of membership, especially as Tonga has made concessions far in excess of those made by more developed countries, such as its near neighbour, New Zealand (Buchanan 2005; OXFAM 2005). This sets an unhelpful precedent for other Pacific Island countries considering joining WTO in the future, such as Samoa and Vanuatu. Indeed it has been stated that

> The terms of Tonga's accession package are appalling ... This is one of the world's smallest and most vulnerable economies, and the extortionist demands being made on it should have no place in a 'development round'. Apparently, the rhetoric of development means nothing at the WTO when pitted against the commercial interests of the world's richest countries.
>
> (OXFAM 2005)

Indeed, it is unclear whether accession to the WTO has any real benefits for small developing countries. Theoretically, greater wealth generation should place governments in a better position to enhance the human rights of all its citizens. There are, however, problems, not only in the power structures which influence the process of negotiation, compliance and dispute settlement at national and international levels but also in the resources that have to be dedicated to creating the appropriate environment for accession (Gay 2005). There is moreover a fundamental issue. The WTO is directed at global trade and commercial values. Human rights, democratic process or the specific concerns of small players are not at the top of the agenda.[60] Non-trade issues are rarely represented or heard in any of the negotiating processes, and non-government organisations in particular have difficulty in making their concerns heard. This lack of voice is aggravated where countries such as Pacific Island states have limited or more often no presence in Geneva (Kelsey 2004–2005: 261). It is also evident that there is a considerable gulf between the needs and capabilities of small developing states and large developed ones. Countries that already have economic growth may well benefit from greater access to global markets – China is an example. However, given that the economies of most Pacific Island states are already weak and heavily reliant on imports and subsidies, their ability to compete in global markets – especially when faced with the costs and logistics of reaching these – is questionable. There is also the danger that the liberalisation of services, such as telecommunications, media and utilities, will have negative consequences for local services, and that while free-trade might provide more employment opportunities it is by no means certain that it will lead to free movement of workers out of the region, or that wages within the region will necessarily improve. Even at a regional level it has been admitted that from a neighbouring perspective 'when it comes to trade there is no "special relationship" with the Pacific. Effectively, international trade strategy takes priority over the views of Pacific governments and the needs of Pacific peoples' (Kelsey 2004: 4).

In the Pacific region, whatever interpretation is given to the right to development, there is potential conflict between economic development and social and cultural rights, especially where pressure and demand to achieve the former takes place at a pace which ignores or rides rough-shod over the latter. In island countries where there may be few opportunities for outward migration, where land mass is limited, and where many people rely on natural resources and subsistence farming for survival or to provide the means for engaging with the cash economy, rights to land and other natural resources are essential At the same time, in the Pacific region, as in other parts of the least developed or under-developed world, it is a fact that rapid development is taking place and that this is impacting on both individual and collective rights. Sometimes this impact is positive, sometimes it is not. It is also evident that responsibility for both fostering development and breaching human rights is not solely that of domestic governments or single states. Indeed, the United Nations Agenda statement recognised the need for partnership between all key stakeholders and the importance of accountability of all of these in the progress of development. In setting a framework for development the Agenda highlights the importance of: national ownership of development strategies; integrating economic, social and environmental policy; securing an enabling framework characterised by good governance, peace, security and respect for human rights, all of which present challenges in the Pacific region.

Any development, whether initiated as a response to international agendas or domestic ones, has to be facilitated by an enabling framework of law, policy and practice. In maintaining a balance between competing demands the response of national governments is crucial, especially if fundamental rights are to be protected.

Regional and national property rights frameworks

At a regional and national level there are a number of initiatives in place which focus on the importance of protecting property rights, either directly or indirectly, while promoting development. The Pacific Islands Forum includes improved natural resource and environment management as a strategic objective for sustainable development in its Pacific Plan,[61] and the vision statement of its leaders.[62] The Secretariat of the Pacific Community has programmes dedicated to forestry, land, biosecurity and fisheries which benefit twenty-two Pacific Island countries and provide a link to other organisations. Its vision is 'of a secure and prosperous Pacific Community, whose people are healthy and manage their resources in an economically, environmentally and socially sustainable way',[63] and it operates by providing professional, scientific and research support technical assistance and capacity building for planning and management.

National constitutions also stress the importance of securing natural resources for future generations. For example, in Palau under Article VI the national government has the obligation to take positive action for the 'conservation of a beautiful, healthful and resourceful natural environment'. In Papua New Guinea the fourth goal of the Constitution is 'for Papua New Guinea's natural resources and environment to be conserved and used for the collective benefit of us all, and be replenished for the benefit of future generations'. To achieve this, the Constitution calls for:

(1) wise use to be made of our natural resources and the environment in and on the land or seabed, in the sea, under the land, and in the air, in the interests of our development and in trust for future generations;

(2) the conservation and replenishment, for the benefit of ourselves and posterity, of the environment and its sacred, scenic, and historical qualities; and

(3) all necessary steps to be taken to give adequate protection to our valued birds, animals, fish, insects, plants and trees.

Constitutional imperatives such as these could be taken as conferring more than merely an obligation on states not to compulsorily acquire or take possession of private property without due process and just compensation, and a more extensive property right for individuals and groups. Even where the state is responsible for natural resources, as in Palau where the Constitution of the Republic indicates that 'Each state shall have exclusive ownership of all living and non-living resources' (Article 1(2)), it is implied by virtue of the relationship between the state and its people, that these are managed for the benefit of the people. Indeed, in Kiribati the Constitution expressly indicates this partnership in declaration 3 of the Preamble, which states 'the natural resources of Kiribati are vested in the people and their Government'. In Papua New Guinea, under the third National Goal and Directive Principle, there is an obligation on the State 'to take effective measures to control and actively participate in the national economy, and in particular to control major enterprises engaged in the exploitation of natural resources' (3(6)).

That states have these positive obligations is evidenced by national legislation which is intended to regulate environmental matters, forestry and fisheries. A number of Pacific Island countries are also members of the United Nations Conventions directed at sustainable development mentioned above. For example, the Convention for the Conservation and Management of Highly Migratory Fish Stocks in the Western and Central Pacific has been signed by Cook Islands, Federated States of Micronesia, Fiji, Marshall Islands, Nauru, Niue, Palau, Samoa, Solomon Islands, Tonga, Tuvalu and Vanuatu. It has been ratified by Federated States of Micronesia, Fiji, Marshall Islands, Nauru, Papua New Guinea, Samoa and Solomon Islands and given effect in domestic legislations in Federated States of Micronesia, Papua New Guinea and Vanuatu.[64] There is therefore legislation in place which should provide a protective environment for the property rights of individuals, groups and Pacific Island people. Unfortunately it is not always very effective.

Development and human rights

The relationship between human rights and property interests has to be considered in the context of development and against the background of international goals and agendas. In the Pacific region, it may also be helpful to bear in mind the theoretical notion of 'third generation rights' mentioned in the last chapter. These rights, which include the right to development, also include the right to peace, a healthy environment and self-determination. Although the concept of 'third generation rights' is not without its critics (Donnelly 1993; Freeman 1999),[65] in under-developed countries such as many of those found in the Pacific region, this concept may serve a useful purpose, especially if these rights are interpreted in the modified universalist approach set out in the Vienna declaration, which concedes that universal human rights 'must be considered in the context of a dynamic and evolving process of international norm-setting, bearing in mind the significance of national and regional particularities and various historical, cultural and religious backgrounds',[66] and, one might add, geographical location and physical resources.

This chapter concludes with consideration of two Pacific Island countries where, despite national laws and international conventions, the nature of the development taking place may place human rights in jeopardy. These are Solomon Islands and Vanuatu.

Timber extraction in Solomon Islands

Solomon Islands is a country with little commercial development and political unrest in the 1990s, and early 2000s has thwarted the development of a tourism industry comparable to some other Pacific Islands. It has limited mineral resources and its main exports are fish, copra, palm products, cocoa and timber.[67] About 90 per cent of the land mass of 27,540 sq km is afforested.[68] Valuable woods include kuari, balsa, teak, Honduras and African mahoganies, Queensland maple, silky oak, and black bean.[69] In recent years, largely due to the shortage of any other means to earn income, hard wood logging on a massive scale has taken place. It is estimated that in 2000 the timber yield was 30.8 million cu ft of which about 24.7 million cu ft was exported as logs. Exports of forest products were valued at $51.2 million in 2000, almost all of it from logs. More recently, in 2006, it was estimated that log exports accounted for more than 60 per cent of Solomon Island government revenue.[70] Logging at current rates (15–16,000 ha/37–39,000 acres per year) exceeds the estimated maximum sustainable annual cut by three times. In 1996 the World Bank estimated that if the rate of extraction experienced in the 1990s was maintained natural forest in the Solomon Islands would be commercially exhausted before 2015. This prediction looks as if it will be realised.

While Solomon Islands is not the only Pacific Island country facing the problem of rapid forest degradation,[71] its problems are exacerbated by a combination of factors. These include problems of poor governance and corruption within central and provincial government; lack of alternative means of earning money; complex customary law systems governing land use which sit uneasily laws with laws introduced initially under colonial administration but adopted and developed since independence; and a parallel system of courts to adjudicate land claims.

Constitutional property rights

The opening declaration of the Constitution of Solomon Islands 1978 states

(*a*) all power in Solomon Islands belongs to its people and is exercised on their behalf by the legislature, the executive and the judiciary established by this Constitution;

(*b*) the natural resources of our country are vested in the people and the government of Solomon Islands.

Among the fundamental rights afforded constitutional protection is that of 'protection for the privacy of his home and other property and from deprivation of property without compensation'.[72] The deprivation of property, subject to just compensation, may be justified on a number of grounds including 'public benefit'. Economic benefit may of course be a public benefit – as has been argued in the case of mining in Papua New Guinea.

Land tenure in Solomon Islands

As is common in the region, almost all of the land in Solomon Islands (around 87 per cent) is held under customary land tenure. Although there was an initiative to encourage the voluntary registration of customary land title in the 1990s this has not met with widespread use.[73] Much land remains unregistered and unsurveyed. It is also extremely common, as has been indicated, to find that land supports a number of different interests.[74] Forms of customary land tenure and grounds of claims to land vary across the country as different areas observe different rules of succession to land rights.[75]

Use of the forests for traditional purposes such as gardens, house building materials, food, medicines and mats is part of the customary way of life in Solomon Islands. Forests also link with ancestors and the non-temporal through the location of *tabu* locations and symbols.[76] Traditionally, customary tenure provided a successful means of regulating resource use by controlling individual and communal rights, limiting access and allocating resource responsibility (Zoleveke 1979: 1–9).

Logging

Small-scale logging and milling, primarily for domestic use in house-building and related uses, such as furniture, has taken place for a number of years. The timber industry has been regulated by legislation since 1969.[77] However, the complexity of the legislation – the Forest Resources and Timber Utilisation Act, as amended – combined with abuse of the processes under it, were highly unsatisfactory. A national forest policy was formulated in late 1994 and approved by Government. This policy identified the need for sound forest management, maintaining the forests in perpetuity, improving forest industry production, increasing the level of domestic processing, enhancing employment, privatising forest plantations, and supporting research and training. In 1995, Pacific Island countries were encouraged to adopt a voluntary code of practice following the endorsement of such a code by the 26th South Pacific Forum meeting that year. A new Act was passed by the Solomon Islands Parliament in June 1999 and implemented with Regulations on 29 February 2000. This was the Forest Resources and Timber Utilisation Act (the Forest Resources Act) (Cap 40).[78]

The Forest Resources Act provides for the procedural steps to be followed in the case of the commercial felling of timber. These are intended to safeguard the relative interests of all parties, and presumably to provide a mechanism whereby the economic advantages of commercial logging and the right of custom owners of land to deal with their land as they choose, can be balanced against the possible disadvantages of commercial logging and the concerns of future custom land owners. In principle therefore the Act seeks to effect an alliance between the desirability of development with the property rights of custom owners. The operation of the legislation in practice reveals a number of problems, not the least of which is the weak protection that is afforded to a number of fundamental rights.

A failing framework

The logistics of logging agreements are complicated. Invariably a limited number of people representing or purporting to represent the customary owners of the land will enter into a logging agreement with a person or persons representing a trading company. The company in turn will employ a logger or logging company to carry out the physical work. This may be a subsidiary company incorporated in the Solomon Islands or an independent company incorporated in the Solomon Islands. In addition there may be a finance company involved which is financing the logging through the provision of plant hire, equipment, fuel, wages and road construction.[79] Sometimes these corporations will be in partnership with government or may have Solomon islanders among their shareholders. Frequently they are large overseas companies or subsidiaries of these established solely for the purpose of logging.[80] It is evident from the case-law that companies may change their names or be re-constituted to circumvent difficulties being encountered in negotiating logging agreements. Provincial authorities which collect licence fees also have a vested interest in commercial logging as these fees generate revenue for the province.[81] The local Executive Government is central to the process as it calls the initial timber hearing, sends out notices to those identified as having timber rights, and issues a 'no appeal' notice if no objections to logging are raised within the stipulated time period. All these players have a vested interest in the logging venture.

This multiplicity of potentially interested parties is complicated by the nature of customary land holding which commonly vests in a group made up of kin-groups, the membership of which may fluctuate and change over time. Custom ownership is the most common cause of dispute in the context of timber, and can involve a range of matters from challenged genealogies, disputed boundaries or maps,[82] disputed status of those purporting to be the recognised spokesperson for the clan,[83] disputed historic moments of significance which indicate who the owner of the land is, disputes as to which lineages confer land rights and disputes as to which tribal land is being logged once logging has commenced, especially where the logging company has entered into logging agreements with the customary owners of adjacent land areas. For practical purposes, land designated for logging has to be clearly delineated. Traditional land use, occupation and ownership, however, is rarely confined by clear boundaries. Cultivation practices, the granting of a variety of use and harvesting rights to non-kin or quasi-kin members and the exchange of land as bride-price or as compensation, means that customary land interests do not neatly fit within the lines drawn by a logging company's surveyor. At the same time, the economic value of claiming customary rights has clearly meant that custom has become more, not less, important, and therefore may be subject to manipulation and re-invention to capitalise on the procedures that central government might have hoped would facilitate commercial logging.

The resolution of disputes regarding customary land ownership are complex, lengthy and sometimes highly charged. Arriving at a solution takes time and in the interim temporary court orders such as injunctions will frustrate those seeking to carry out the logging. This in turn may lead to self-help measures being adopted, for example illegal logging, the use of bribes, or by-passing the safeguards put in place to protect those who may have an interest. Where logging has taken place and royalties have been paid, internal disputes may arise because of allegations that recipients or trustees have misused the trust money, rental money or royalties. Alternatively the formal agreement relating to royalties may not mirror customary agreements or practices regarding the distribution of benefits. Where there is a dispute as to royalties then the court may refuse to disrupt the continuation of logging on the grounds that the dispute is a personal one between the parties and should not affect the commercial enterprise of logging.[84] Frustration with the legal process can result in complainants taking their anger out on the investor and trying to disrupt the logging or loading operation and even sometimes seeking the demise of the investor, setting up road blocks or taking equipment. There are also allegations of logging enterprises seeking the help of police and RAMSI personnel to assist in dealing with these incidents.[85] Although, under the Forest Resources Act, there are extensive powers for enforcement officers to enter land, given the topographical nature of much of the country being logged, the remoteness of logging camps and the resource constraints, effective enforcement is a problem.

It is evident therefore that there are a number of weaknesses in the current system. Among these are the failure to devolve forestry management powers from central government to provincial government. Under section 13 and 44 of the Forest Resources Act the Minister has extensive powers to regulate the industry, including: the fees and royalties payable; the disposal of waste products and the protection of the environment; the manner and nature of reforestation; the prohibition of taking specified kinds of timber from any customary land; and the power to limit the amount of timber, removed from the land that is the subject of the agreement, required to be processed by the applicant. He can also declare certain areas to be 'Forest Reserves' where he

> is satisfied that for the purpose of conserving water resources within Solomon Islands it is necessary or desirable to protect the forest or other vegetation in any rainfall catchment area, he may, subject to the provisions of this Part, by notice declare such area or part thereof to be a forest reserve, and shall in the same notice specify what rights and the extent to which such rights may be exercised in the forest reserve.[86]

Potentially this framework could be used to support and encourage sustainable development and to protect the rights of groups, individuals and the resources of the Solomon Islands. Given the current logging crisis it can only be suggested that Ministers have been less than vigilant in exercising these management powers. To this extent, therefore, the State has failed in its obligations under the Constitution.

Responsibility lies not only with the executive but also other branches of the state. In particular, while the adjudication process is unwieldy and fragmented with some issues falling to the local courts, others to councils of chiefs, the courts have a responsibility to try and give positive effect to fundamental rights. As has been pointed out by Chief Justice Muria

> It is ... absolutely essential that the Courts must be vigilant, avoiding tabulated legalism, when dealing with cases concerning logging or similar cases on customary land in Solomon Islands. For an issue over the propriety of a logging licence over customary land impinges on the proper compliance with the law as well as custom.[87]

The present procedure under the Act appears to divorce the determination of customary ownership from approving the right to negotiate over timber. At the same time, however, it is clear that the High Court, which is denied jurisdiction to determine customary land claims, can assist the local court – which has that jurisdiction – by intervening and making interlocutory orders.[88] The High Court also has jurisdiction to consider the legality of a logging licence issued under the Act, but as has been pragmatically stated

> in all of these cases involving logging on customary land, the propriety of the logging license cannot be entirely separated from issues of ownership of customary land. As those involved in the process of administering the law on forest and timber know, sensitive issues of custom do very much affect the procedure of obtaining a logging license on customary land in this country. Thus where the issue of ownership or other rights in custom over customary land is in dispute touching on the propriety of the logging license, a party cannot simply isolate the issues of custom and come to this on the sole issue of the legality of the license.[89]

The legislature must also take responsibility because at present the structure fails to take into account the complexities of land use in Solomon Islands. For example, in the case of *Rakatau v Vanikoro Lumbers Ltd* [2007] SBHC 101, logging operations were being challenged by representatives of Tikopean descent who had resided on the land in question since the 1960s with the consent of the Vanikoro landowners. However, they had not been invited to the timber rights hearing – which had been held by the Provincial Executive at Santa Cruz, some 300 miles by water from Vanikoro. Although the courts have recognised that long-term possession *may* confer sufficient interest in land to give *locus standi*,[90] and that occupation and possession may in custom give rise to varying rights and obligations amongst the occupiers and owners, in this case it was held that 'possession in these circumstances may not afford these outsiders [the Tikopians] rights to argue the logging arrangements agreed to by those nominated to represent landowners under the Forestry Act'.[91] Custom may similarly distinguish between rights of cultivation and rights of occupation, or between land given through intermarriage with women (dowry), and land that has been reclaimed where the rights of the original landowners had been denied by the recipients of such dowry.[92] The present legal framework may therefore being denying access to justice by refusing to recognise these different interests, or by treating them unequally.

Despite the unsatisfactory state of affairs, it appears that the government is taking very little action over illegal logging.[93] This may occur either because logging is taking place without licences, or because the customary land owners had no timber rights to grant, or because licences have been granted without observing the procedures required by the Timber Resources and Utilisation Act. There is also suspicion and rumour that many people in senior positions are involved in cartels and with the wheelers and dealers of the industry and because of their vested interest are unwilling to see tighter regulation or a reduction in current logging practices.[94] Certainly there is some evidence to support these rumours both in case law and in the media.

Indeed it has been suggested that 'the Government does not really care whether operators have (an) export license or not. As long as the shipment leaves the country, the government gets its money through export duties which, over the years were in hundreds of millions of dollars ... as long as the government gets its money, the question of legality rarely comes into it'.[95]

Solomon Islanders are not satisfied with the current *status quo* and have petitioned for new forestry legislation. Their view is that the current legislation does not protect Solomon Islands' forest resources. In 2004 a new Forests Bill was proposed to better provide for sustainable management of Solomon Islands' forests. Supporters of the Bill believed that it would give local people and landowners a greater voice in decisions about forests, demand greater environmental responsibility of companies, and allow for controls to ensure that Solomon Islands' forestry industry is sustainable in the long run. To date however nothing has been done. Similarly it has been suggested that the price being paid for logs by foreign companies felling timber in Solomon Islands is well under the world market price and that often agreements between these companies and the custom land owners are not negotiated to the latter's advantage.[96]

The outlook

The prognosis for logging in Solomon Islands is very poor. It is quite clear that logging at the current rate cannot be sustained. In a report in the *Solomon Star* in September 2007 it was stated that 'The latest National Resource Assessment Update shows that the current harvest is more than three times the sustainable level and, if nothing is done to address the issue, the country's forest stocks will be gone in several years'.[97] Some efforts have been made to halt the process. For example in 1997 there was a moratorium on the issuing of new logging licences,[98] and a Timber Control Unit was set up with the assistance of AusAID. In 1998 a number of logging licences were cancelled, either because the logging had not commenced within the stipulated time period or because completion certificates had not been filed as required. More recently the export of round logs has been exempted from duties in the hope that money would be ploughed back into re-forestation and for local development, however there is little evidence that this incentive has had much success and it now appears to have been abandoned.[99] Some Provincial Councils have taken the initiative to ban logging in their areas,[100] although this may be thwarted by Ministerial approval of logging or the revival of licences granted before the ban. Non-governmental agencies are also active in the region. For example, there is a Solomon Islands Forestry Program, being implemented by the Environmental Concerns Action Network of Solomon Islands (ECANSI). The objectives of this project are not only to provide communities where there is an interest in commercial logging with information on the legal processes that need to be followed by companies or landowners who want to log, but also to develop forestry action plans with communities that decide not to pursue commercial logging. The Solomon Island Development Trust (SIDT)) is running two projects: the Eco-Forestry Unit, which concentrates on teaching chainsaw-milling and forest management, and the Conservation in Development Project, which is developing eco-tourism and Ngali nut oil production.

Despite the negative consequences of hard wood logging in Solomon Islands and elsewhere in the region, such as Papua New Guinea, external agencies continue to see timber as one of the key 'productive sectors' that will need to be exploited if Pacific Island countries are to develop their economies.[101] If the sector is to be developed to provide economic growth there are questions of how this is to be done, especially when land-tenure is seen a constraint on long term growth by some commentators.[102]

While there are, as has been indicated, a number of weaknesses in the procedures and processes under the current timber regime in Solomon Islands, the real problem lies in the policy behind natural resource extraction; the lack of accountability of decision makers who can shelter behind the complexity of the system; poor governance at central and provincial level, lack of engagement by stake-holders in the longer term effect of unsustainable logging and the need for forestry management. Changing the procedures or creating new forms may fail to address much more deeply rooted problems. Hard-wood logging provides an instant cash return for a resource that has required no labour expended on it. These are natural forests. The trees which are being felled have been there for decades. Few of them were being used for domestic use due to their inaccessibility, size and the technical problems of cutting and moving them. The removal of them may be compatible with other traditional forest resources uses provided forests can recover quickly from logging operations. Timber is however, an exhaustible resource which is rapidly being exhausted. While the short-term gain may go towards reducing Solomon Islands indebtedness (although the mismanagement of logging finances at central government level might cast doubt on this) and put ready money in the pockets of some – but not all – custom owners, it is unclear what longer-term benefits are being derived from logging. Logging ventures are fairly short-term. Machinery moves in, trees are felled and timber removed. There may be some temporary infrastructure established such as power lines to logging camps, roads and wharfs for loading logs, but unlike mining, fish farming or agricultural ventures, there are unlikely to be opportunities for longer-term local benefit. While some local labour is employed, logging companies also tend to bring in their own labour, especially for the more skilled tasks and for management of projects, and there is limited opportunity for the up-skilling of local labour. Unless there is effective use and enforcement of conditions in logging agreements, especially relating to reforestation and pollution of the environment including water resources, then it is difficult to see where the long-term benefit lies. Often royalties are not collected or poorly managed, and the fees paid for licences are used ostensibly to meet local government and administrative expenses. Money in the pockets of custom owners may be used for short term material improvement or to facilitate migration from rural areas to urban ones.

In the meantime, there is the danger that fundamental rights are being trampled on. Not only are property rights being denied or claims and interests excluded by the procedure that facilitates logging, but the government is upholding a legal framework which clearly is not guarantee to protect these rights. Abuse of power, lack of transparency and difficulties of access to justice are evident. The long-term damage to health, environment and livelihood is also not being sufficiently addressed nor are the possible consequences of land loss, migration and unequal wealth distribution being considered. Short-term economic gain may very well lead to future economic, social and political difficulties. If Solomon Islands has the right to a peaceful future, a healthy environment and development at a pace that is compatible with these then a reappraisal of timber extraction is urgently needed.

Land alienation in Vanuatu

The population of Vanuatu is not huge by international standards. In 2007 it was estimated to be around 212,000, with a growth rate of 1.46 per cent; 32 per cent of the population is under the age of 14.[103] Employment opportunities are limited and outward migration almost zero. There is increasing urban drift. Many young people are now second or third generation town dwellers. They have no inclination to return to the island homes of their parents or grandparents. Urban poverty and urban crime is on the increase, including property crime. The country's economy is based primarily on small-scale agriculture, which provides a living for 65 per cent of the population,[104] fishing, financial services (offshore) and tourism.[105] It is this last that raises concern about land alienation.

Unlike Solomon Islands, Vanuatu has virtually no timber worth felling as its sandalwood forests were cut down by traders long before independence. It has limited manufacturing activity and its off-shore financial services are constantly under scrutiny. If it wants to develop or to become a member of the World Trade Organisation, not only must it put in place the necessary facilitating legal framework but it must attract inward investment. One way of doing this is to attract foreign investment in land, either by way of tourism operators such as hotel chains, or by accommodating individuals seeking second or holiday homes.

Land alienation, even in the South Pacific, is not of course a recent phenomenon. Indeed in the region there has been a history of dispossession of land. In fact, one of the key motivating factors in the period leading up to independence in Vanuatu, then the New Hebrides, was the desire to reclaim the land from foreigners. In the decade before independence it was estimated that over half the country had been alienated, primarily as agricultural land to outsiders. As a consequence, and overnight, in 1980 all land was restored to custom owners, title to which was to be determined by diverse custom laws according to the provisions of the written constitution.[106]

As so much land had been alienated prior to independence, transition provisions had to be put in place. Foreigners who had acquired freehold titles no longer held such titles as freehold was abolished entirely. However, these settlers could remain in possession of the land they were on until either paid compensation by the custom owners, or granted a lease by the custom owners or a combination of these if the custom owners wished to reclaim some, but not all, the land.[107] Where the land was not occupied – and there were many absentee planters, then the land reverted to the custom owners. Any custom owner wishing to enter into a lease with an ex-patriate occupier had to be recognised as the appropriate person or persons to negotiate such a lease. There were however problems. After a period of over one hundred years, it was not always possible to trace the custom owners of land, most of whom had had to move elsewhere once planters took over, and who in any case may not have cultivated the land but simply used its natural resources. This led to disputed claims. The Constitution, envisaging such possibilities perhaps, provided that where title was in dispute or unclear then the land vested in the appropriate representative of the government, the Minister of Lands, until the dispute was resolved.[108]

The Minister had extensive powers to manage this land, which he enjoys and exercises to this day – although this was probably not the intention behind the provisions. In particular he has the power to grant leases over land. The fact that the Minister can give good title to a lease means that anyone seeking to lease land – especially an increasing number of land-developers – far prefer to acquire land held under the Minister's powers than to go to the trouble of dealing with custom owners, who may be difficult to ascertain, undecided and lacking unanimity. Ministers of Lands have therefore been key players in granting a high percentage of the many leases which currently exist (Farran 2003). Some of them have also been subject to adverse reports by the Ombudsman of Vanuatu in respect of the exercise of these powers.[109]

The ability to grant leases over land previously owned by foreigners met a practical need during a transitionary period. Since the 1990s, however, the leasing of land has accelerated alarmingly. Not only have an increasing number of commercial and residential leases been granted, rather than agricultural ones as previously, but sub-division has proliferated. This has been particularly noticeable on the island of Efate, where the capital Port Vila is located, but today is also occurring on other islands. As leases are registered – unless under three years – this process can be tracked. Recent survey maps suggest that almost the entire coastal belt of Efate and a number of the off-shore islands have come under leasehold. The majority of these prime sites are not held by indigenous people but by foreigners, either as private residences or as tourism destinations. In the peri-urban area of Port Vila customary land owners are finding themselves squeezed out and the general public is being denied access to beaches, the reef and former gardening land.

More recently land alienation has been facilitated by the sub-division of single plots by means of strata title, under the Strata Title Act 2000. The purported aim of the legislation was to facilitate the sub-division of urban buildings into separate lots by registering a strata title plan and thereby affording security to small businesses in shared buildings. However, it is evident that the Act has been used for sub-division of undeveloped land outside the urban areas and that this is in fact facilitated by amendments made to the original Act in 2003. As the Land Leases Act (Cap 163) already provides for sub-division it is suspected that the Strata Title Act has been used because it lacks the safeguards for lessors – the custom owners – found in the Land Leases Act.

The people of Vanuatu are not oblivious to the problems of rapid land alienation and the threat to the property interests of indigenous people. During the course of 2006, a number of provincial meetings and consultations took place to consider land issues.[110] These culminated in a National Land Summit in September 2006. The aim was to review issues of land management and development. In particular, a need to address concerns of land ownership, fair dealing, and the role of Government in the management and development of land were identified as key issues.

The National Land Summit arrived at a list of twenty resolutions, many of which sought to strengthen customary property rights. In summary, these were: the law should recognise and give effect to communal ownership of land; the central and provincial governments and the National Council of Chiefs should work together to document the custom (*kastom*) that determine ownership, land policies, boundaries and land dealings; greater awareness of the existing (plural) legal and economic framework should be undertaken; the current law of leases should be reviewed; lease agreements should be made comprehensible and inclusive in their negotiation and agreement; certificates of negotiation should be subject to increased scrutiny and publicity, especially at the local level; the Minister should cease to have the power to approve leases over disputed land; abuses of the use of strata title should cease and land owners be involved in their approval; real estate agents – most of whom are not ni-Vanuatu – should be regulated; lease rental and premium rating should be reviewed and reformed; pre-approval conditions directed at ensuring sustainable development should be put in place and effectively enforced; physical planning and zoning laws should be strengthened and a sub-divisions policy put in place at national and provincial level, and efforts should be made at all levels and to all sectors of the community to raise awareness of sustainability issues.

Following the summit aid funding was found to support a consultancy 'review' team to come up with proposals. A local Steering Committee was also formed to take matters forward. 2008 is envisaged by the Lands Steering Committee as the year in which there will be increasing public awareness of the land issues highlighted at the 2006 summit, leading to a new Land Law Act in 2009. Whether this will happen remains to be seen. However, some steps have been taken. For example, immediately following the Summit a moratorium was imposed on the granting of new sub-divisions and the surrendering of agricultural leases; detailed draft laws have been formulated to govern land use; guidelines for land sub-division have been drafted; fieldwork has been started to establish customary boundaries and case-studies have been undertaken to establish a factual understanding of customary tenure at ground level. The Review team has completed its work and produced a report which suggests that key issues are: lack of a national land policy, weaknesses in land administration and a need to reform the law. It has proposed aid-funded programmes to build capacity and good governance in the public sector and to strengthen the various institutions which facilitate land transactions. While these proposals may improve the administration of land dealings it is questionable whether they will address a more fundamental question, which is whether the continued alienation of land to predominantly foreigners is compatible with the sustainable development, peace and security of the people of Vanuatu.

Recent government changes may mean that some of the impetus of the National Land summit and its resolution will be lost. In the meantime, there is real concern among local people, especially those who are not benefiting from the economic profits of land alienation, or who have made short-term gains but see longer-term misery ahead.

As with so many areas of development, there is a tension. Although a number of the resolutions of the land summit indicate that the appropriate response lies in improved central administration, in many ways this is at odds with resolutions advocating more involvement by customary land owning groups, a greater role for chiefs, and non-governmental agencies such as the Vanuatu Cultural Centre. There is also a fundamental dilemma between the right of individuals to manage and, if they so want, lease their land for 75 years and pocket or use the money, and the need to preserve land for future generations. In part this dilemma is due to the 'western' commoditisation of land and the indigenous perception of land as heritage.

In countries such as Vanuatu, with limited usable land because of the steep volcanic interiors of islands and poor access, land is not limitless. As elsewhere in the Pacific region many of the population remain dependent on the land for subsistence, and may have nowhere else to go. The challenge is therefore how to ensure 'that traditional land tenure systems remain viable and relevant in a global economic system propelled by market forces' (Amankwah 2007). This is a question which should engage not just national Pacific governments but also the international community. If there is to be development then more effort will have to be made to ensure that it is sustainable, not just for the 'get-rich quick' present generation but for future ones. In 2006, the National Land Summit held a National Youth Essay and Poster Competition. A twelve year old prize-winner wrote this:

> By the year 2015, people might have sold out most of their lands which is not good. If they continuously sell there lands, where will their fourth or fifth generations live? Maybe they will be sitting along the streets begging for food and without any jobs. So I think that that's not a good stage for people to be at, or else Vanuatu will get worse than other Pacific Islands'.

(Laliet 2006)

Conclusion

If under-developed nations have a right to development, which is recognised universally, then it can be argued that other members of the international community have a duty to respect this, bearing in mind especially the right of these nations to, first, determine their own pace and form of development; second, to do so in a way which is conducive to a healthy environment; and third, in a way which is conducive to peace. However, the relationship between economic development and human rights is a difficult one. Internal and external pressure to attract inward investment, improve opportunities for participation in a monetary economy and achieve capital growth, may mean that individual needs are sacrificed or shelved to meet national growth plan targets, which in turn are geared to satisfying regional goals or international standards, for example to enter into an EU–ACP agreement or to comply with WTO membership criteria. Incentives for economic development and participation in its benefits can lead to widespread and sometimes gross inequalities of wealth with the gulf between the rich and poor leading to social unrest and civil disturbance. In developing countries, which are shifting from subsistence agricultural to monetary economies and are experiencing considerable urban migration, the disparity in disposable wealth between those who can participate in and benefit from a monetary economy and those who cannot may be especially great. The pressure for economic growth may also restrict certain freedoms and rights, for example by restricting freedom of movement where to allow it leads to the breakdown of law and order, or freedom of expression where adverse media coverage of corruption, fraud, crime or human rights' abuses could have a negative effect on tourism, trade negotiations or foreign investment. Of course, it may be argued by governments pursuing such policies that these negative trade-offs for economic growth are merely temporary and that ultimately equality, freedoms and needs will all be met and that civil and political rights will thrive. The truth is however that often economic development is taking place so rapidly that the victims of it are left behind and long-term consequences are conveniently ignored in favour of short-term gain. Moreover, inequalities of wealth, combined with inequalities of political power, can result in a self-perpetuating system of human rights denial, especially where those who most benefit seek to preserve the unequal *status quo*. It is rare therefore to find development matched with an enhancement of civil and political rights as well as economic and social rights.

Similarly, if the law is to be the vehicle which provides a protective framework for human rights then it is important that there is not only specific provision for the wrongful deprivation of property but also that the law which provides a facilitative framework for development does not do so in a way which itself may conspire, wittingly or unwittingly, to defeat certain rights or insufficiently protect them. For example, as illustrated by the experience of Vanuatu and Solomon Islands, legislation put in place to assist in attracting inward investment may fail to protect other interests, either because it is poorly drafted, or because it is poorly enforced, or simply because the framework bears no relationship to the reality, especially where introduced laws are used to 'shoe-horn' customary interests into concepts and institutions which are intelligible to the outside world.

In many cases, issues raised by claims to property rights will directly involve the State and its agencies – for example, where there has been State acquisition of land without adequate compensation, or continuation of mining in spite of clear evidence of adverse effects on the environment and people in the vicinity. In such circumstances the individual or group should be entitled to pursue a claim against the state. In other cases, property rights may be infringed by non-state actors, for example, private enterprise or other individuals, such as where cultural intellectual property is exploited for commercial gain by persons not entitled in custom to do so, or where a hotel corporation fences off a beach to deny public access. In these situations much will depend on whether the enforcement of rights to property operate both vertically and horizontally; whether the courts are willing to be proactive in protecting human rights; and how various constitutional provisions which permit breaches are interpreted. So, in the case of fundamental rights to property, breaches may occur not solely by direct unlawful state action, but also indirectly through the systems and laws that states put in place or fail to put in place, and the policies which governments pursue in seeking to achieve other goals.

There are also circumstances where property rights are infringed but where States are powerless to prevent the infringements and unable to provide remedies. For example where reefs are damaged by marine pollution, fish stocks are reduced by foreign fishing fleets or land is lost due to rising sea levels. It is here that the international community may also have a responsibility, for example, in taking action on climate change which threatens the right to life of Pacific islanders on low lying atolls, or by combining forces to prohibit and police the dumping or passage of toxic or nuclear waste in the region of the Pacific, or by regulating and managing the fish harvests of the world's oceans so that small Pacific Island fishing fleets are not squeezed out by the factory fleets of larger players. In these situations the advocacy of the universality of rights and the concept of third generation rights could provide an avenue of redress between the people of Pacific Island states and the wider, international community.

Clearly there is a difficulty in advocating human rights and advocating development. Rapid development is not necessarily conducive to the health of human rights. Trading-off human rights for development, however, may not necessarily lead to improved development, in fact quite the opposite may be true. Fortunately, there does appear to be a growing recognition that both human rights and development require good governance. However, the emphasis here is primarily on civil and political rights and the belief that if sound government practices can be put in place then sound economic development driven by market forces will follow. This is not necessarily so, largely because these market forces are driven by a limited number of extremely powerful corporations and wealthy states, whose influence far outweighs that of any Pacific Island state or regional conglomerate of states and whose international regime is not concerned with the social and economic rights of individuals (Held *et al*. 1999; Rodman 1998). Indeed, the very policies required by these international economic forces may make it increasingly difficult for national governments to protect the human rights of their citizens, especially social and economic rights, thereby putting these countries in breach of their human rights obligations. Unless and until non-state players are brought within the same international human rights regimes as United Nations member states, and international development is integrated with human rights' policies, this divergence of priorities is likely to persist.

Notes

1 For example, aboriginal people in Australia and Maori in New Zealand.
2 For example, in Papua New Guinea, by 1906 the Crown held around 1,000,000 acres of land, either through purchase from customary owners or by being declared waste and vacant. (Crocome and Hide 1987: 342). Similar policies were adopted in Solomon Islands (Scheffler and Larmour 1987: 312) although it was later found that about 40,000 acres of land declared waste and vacant were found to be occupied under native custom and returned to the customary owners (Kabui 1997: 124). In Marshall Islands, although the German administration did not pursue this policy, the Japanese did (McGrath and Wilson 1987: 200).
3 Notably Bikini Atoll in Marshall Islands on 1 March 1954. The repercussions of this are still being adversely experienced by Marshallese as noted by leaders at the Pacific Forum at their 2006 meeting, http://www.forumsec.org/pages.cfm/press-statments-2006/thirty-sventh-pacfiic-islands-forum.html (accessed 20 March 2007).
4 In Marshall Islands and Palau.
5 For example, the setting up of Australian refugee asylum camps on Nauru.
6 See, for example, Sections 8 and 9 Kiribati; Article IV, sections 3 and 5, Federated States of Micronesia, sections 40(1) and 64 (1)(c) Cook Islands, sections 8 and 9

Nauru, section 14 Samoa and Article 5(1)(j) Vanuatu. In Tonga property may only be taken in time of war, or to make government roads or for other works beneficial to the government (section 18). Note that in the Fiji Bill of Rights there is no express right to protection of property.

7 See, for example, Kiribati, Nauru and Solomon Islands, Tuvalu and Vanuatu.
8 For example, foreigners may not own customary land in any country of the region. In some countries non-customary land may be owned by foreigners, for example, Cook Islands, Fiji and Samoa – although in Samoa the Head of State must approve this – Alienation of Freehold Land 1972 s 6, but in others this is also prohibited. Discrimination on the grounds of gender also occurs, see Farran (2005b).
9 See, for example, Marshall Islands Constitution, Article II, section 5.
10 For example, in the case of insanity, divorce, acquisition by prescription or to effect a trust of property by vesting title in the trustees.
11 Sometimes these may overlap, for example where a person is deprived of their property because it is dangerous.
12 For example: public defence, safety, order, morality, health or planning and development.
13 See, for example, section 6 Constitution of Palau; section 5(6) Marshall Islands; section 8(1)(ci) Solomon Islands.
14 See, for example, Angelo (1995) in respect of compensation calculations used in parts of the Pacific.
15 The problem of group rather than individual land rights is addressed by Brown (2000).
16 *Tufele Liamatua v Mose* [1988] ASHC 1.
17 [1995] VUSC 3.
18 Per Kent J.
19 [1988] ASHC 1.
20 For example, the Constitution of Vanuatu Article 75 states 'Only indigenous citizens of the Republic who have acquired their land in accordance with a recognised system of land tenure shall have perpetual ownership of their land'.
21 Forest Resources and Timber Utilisation Act (Cap 40).
22 *Allardyce and Others v Attorney General and Others* [1988/89] SILR 78.
23 Problems relating to trusts and especially the accountability of trustees are discussed by Brown (2000).
24 Article 74.
25 He was also described as a 'manager', 'representative', and 'custom owner' but at no point as 'trustee'.
26 *Noel v Champagne Beach Working Committee* [2006] VUCA 18.
27 For example, fine mats from Samoa and Vanuatu, shell money from Solomon Islands, *Tapa* cloth from Tonga and Fiji.
28 Such as the *Nagol* jump or land dive in Pentecost, Vanuatu or the Beqa fire dance in Fiji.
29 See, for example, comment by Frame (1992).
30 See, for example, Kaeppler (1999); Farran (2004c).
31 An example, perhaps apocryphal, is the theft of the Pentecost land dive, and its conversion into 'bungy jumping'.
32 Serious breaches of taboos might result in stoning, banishment or death.
33 *In Re the Nagol Jump, Assal & Vatu v Council of Chiefs of Santo* [1992] VUSC 5.
34 Section 5 Constitution of Vanuatu.
35 For example, membership of the WTO requires compliance with the requirements established under the Trade-Related Aspects of Intellectual Property Rights (TRIPS), Annex 1C of the Marrakesh Agreement Establishing the World Trade Organisation, signed in Marrakesh, Morocco, 15 April 1994. This came into effect on 1 January 1995.

36 Section 6(1)(c). No definition of what this term means is given. In Fiji folklore is included within the scope of 'public performance', Fiji Copyright Act 1999.
37 Samoa Copyright Act 1998, Part 1V, Section 2; Papua New Guinea Copyright and Neighbouring Rights, Act 2000, section 2. The definition provided by the Samoan legislation is: 'group-orientated and tradition-based creation of groups or individuals reflecting the expectations of the community as an adequate expression of its cultural and social identity, its standards and values as transmitted orally, by imitation or by other means'.
38 No 42 of 2000.
39 'Indigenous knowledge' includes any knowledge that is created, acquired or inspired for traditional economic, spiritual, ritual, narrative, decorative or recreational purposes: and whose nature or use of which has been transmitted from generation to generations; and that is regarded as pertaining to a particular indigenous person or people in Vanuatu.
40 This can be found on the PANG web site, http://www.pang.org.fj/doc/290408_EU-Pacific_Seminar_Civil_Society_Joint_St.pdf
41 See, for example, *Cook Islands News*, 21 August 2001; Yombon, *The National* 11 January 1999.
42 For a review of the Model Law see Forsyth (2003).
43 See, for example, the Memorandum of Understanding between the Government of Samoa and the Regents of the University of California, Berkeley for Disposition of Future Revenue from Licensing of Prostratin Gene Sequences, an Anti-Viral Molecule [2004] PITSE 1, and other examples cited by Forsyth (2003).
44 Recently highlighted in the case of Pitcairn Islands, when Magistrates and Judges appointed in New Zealand to officiate at Pitcairn Courts had to travel by boat to the island.
45 See, for example, Convention To Ban The Importation Into Forum Island Countries Of Hazardous And Radioactive Wastes And To Control The Transboundary Movement And Management Of Hazardous Wastes Within The South Pacific Region (Waigani Convention) [1995] 1PITSE, which entered into force on 21 October 1995; Convention For The Protection Of The Natural Resources And Environment Of The South Pacific Region, And Related Protocols (Noumea Convention) [1986] PITSE 15, which entered into force 22 August 1990. A number of Pacific Island countries are also signatories to two Comprehensive Nuclear Test-Ban Treaties [1976] PITSE 1 and [1996] PITSE 7, neither of which is yet in force.
46 Pacific Concerns Resource Centre, Suva Fiji Islands, Action Alert, August 1999, http://archives.pireport.org/archive/1999/august/08-05-19.html (accessed 16 March 2007).
47 The Oxford Research Group, June 1999 and Janes Foreign Report, May 13, 1999, quoted by Greenpeace Press Release, 22 September 1999, http://archives.pireport.org/archive/1999/september/09-23-22.htm (accessed 16 March 2007).
48 Communication from the Forum Secretariat's Media Adviser, Ulafala Aiavo, Pacific Islands Report, 21 February 2001, http://archives.pireport.org/archive/2001/february/02-28-24.htm (accessed 16 March 2007).
49 http://www.forumsec.org/pages.cfm/press-statements-2006/thirty-seventh-Pacific-Islands-forum.html (accessed 20 March 2007).
50 Section 20(1) (c)–(d).
51 Saufatu Sopoanga, Prime Minister of Tuvalu, at the 58th Session of the United Nations General Assembly, New York, 24 September 2003.
52 Seneviratne, *Pacific Islands Report*, 8 September 2002. For comment on the substantive issues raised by Tuvalu's claim see Jacobs (2005).
53 See comments by Eun Jung Cahill Che, of the Honolulu-based Pacific Forum, quoted by Simms (2001).

54 See United Nations Millennium Declaration [2000] PITSE 16 and the Compact entered into between the United States of America and Vanuatu to meet millennium goals [2006] PITSE 1.
55 Department of Economic and Social Affairs of the United Nations Secretariat 'The United Nations Development Agenda: Development for All', 1990–2005, http://www.un.org/esa/devagenda/UNDA_BW5_Final.pdf (accessed 29 May 2008).
56 Newsroom Pacific Islands Forum Secretariat, 6 August 2006, 'Opening Statement By Mr Peter Forau, Acting Secretary General, Pacific Islands Forum Secretariat, At The WTO/PIFS Advanced Programme For Senior Officials On The Doha Development Agenda Negotiation Issues For Pacific Economies Trade,' 7 August 2005, Fiji, http://www.forumsec.org/pages.cfm/speeches-2006/acting-sg-forauwto-course.html (accessed 29 May 2008).
57 Fiji, Papua New Guinea and Solomon Islands were members of GATT as were Australia and New Zealand.
58 For insight into the position of Pacific Island countries during the Doha round see Levi (2003).
59 For example, it was made a condition of membership that Tonga put in place a TRIPS led patent regime. This will restrict the marketing and licencing of agricultural and pharmaceutical products within the country if there is already a patent elsewhere. Tonga has until 1 June 2008 to comply with the TRIPS requirement.
60 For example, the non-democratic processes characteristic of WTO procedures offends both CEDAW, General Recommendation 23, and the ICCPR paras 6–18, as well as the right to participation expressed in Article 1 of the Declaration on the Right to Development.
61 Pacific Islands Forum Secretariat 'Pacific Plan' available online at http://www.forumsec.org/pages.cfm/about-us/the-pacific-plan/.
62 Vision Statement, http://www.forumsec.org/pages.cfm/about-us/vision-statement/
63 SPC Vision and Mission, http://www.spc.int/corp/index.php?option=com_content&task=view&id=22&Itemid=73 (accessed 29 May 2008).
64 [1995] PITSE 10. See also Pacific Islands' commitment to the Convention on Biological Diversity [1992] PITSE 1, and the Kyoto Protocol to the United Nations Convention on Climate Change [1997] PITSE 2 via Pacific Islands Treaty Series (PacLII), http://www.paclii.org/pits/.
65 For example, Donnelly (1993); Freeman (1999: 27–47).
66 Para 5, Vienna Declaration adopted 25 June 1993 at the World Conference on Human Rights.
67 It has small deposits of gold, bauxite, phosphates, lead, zinc and nickel.
68 The total area of Solomon Islands is 28,450 sq km of which 27,540 sq km is afforested. Almost all land on which logging occurs is under customary land tenure.
69 These trees make up about 10 per cent of the total forest area but much more forest is damaged in reaching them and transporting them. Heli-logging is one alternative but this is expensive and not always feasible.
70 WWF Report (2006: 7).
71 Samoa and Tonga also have high rates of forest degradation due to overexploitation of merchantable timber resources (FAO 1997).
72 Article 3(c) and 8.
73 In 1981 Totorea (1981: 119–122) noted that about 17 per cent of land in Solomon Islands was registered. This included land leased to non-Solomon islanders.
74 Scheffler and Larmour also indicate that rights and interests can evolve and change over time, so that, for example, the mere privilege to use and cultivate

land may become a greater right, or secondary right holders may become primary right holders (1981: 310).

75 See Scheffler and Larmour (1981: 304–312).

76 In the Forest Resources Act this is referred to as 'Tambu place': 'a ... place commonly so called and considered holy, sacred or forbidden by Solomon islanders'.

77 Commercial logging commenced in 1968 with the establishment of Levers Pacific Timbers and the government soon followed with the grant of timber cutting rights over customary land. See Scheffler and Larmour (1981: 314).

78 This was amended in 2000 to reflect administrative changes to local government by the Forest and Timber Utilisation (Amendment) Act (the Amending Act).

79 See, for example, *Ado Solomons Corporation Ltd v Lagwaeano Sawmilling and Logging Company Ltd* [2000] SBHC 30.

80 *Solomons Corporation Ltd v Lagwaeano Sawmilling and Logging Company Ltd* [2000] SBHC 30. Most of the logging in Solomon Islands benefits overseas companies from Korea, Japan, New Zealand, Australia and the United Kingdom.

81 Provincial Assemblies have the power under s 26(1) and Sch 3(4) (c) of the 1997 Provincial Assembly Act to raise revenue by 'fees for services performed or licences issued' – *Premier of Isabel Province v Earthmovers Group of Companies* [2005] SBCA 17.

82 See *Mada v Viuru Forest Enterprises* [2004] SBHC 54.

83 This arose in the case of *Runimetu v Silvania Products Ltd* [2006] SBHC 13, where evidence led before the local Council of Chiefs indicated that different members of the family had been left different powers by their shared chiefly ancestor. Two of them were to look after rights and customary land ownership and one was to look after the tribe.

84 See *Runimetu v Silvania* above.

85 RAMSI is the Regional Assistance Mission to Solomon Islands by Australia, which consists of military and other personnel from Australia and other Pacific Forum countries, which was launched in 2003 to address the civil unrest and political instability in Solomon Islands.

86 Section 24.

87 *Veno v Jino* [2003] SBHC 127.

88 *Gandley Simbe v East Choiseul Area Council & Others* [1997] SBHC 67.

89 *Halu v JP Enterprise Ltd* [2003] SBHC 123.

90 *Gandley Simbe v East Choiseul Area Council & Others* [1997] SBHC 67.

91 Per Brown J.

92 *Gandley Simbe v East Choiseul Area Council & Others* [1997] SBHC 67.

93 *Solomon Star* , 27 May 2005.

94 Editorial, *Islands Business Magazine*, Fiji, 24 July 2007.

95 'Former Solomon's Minister cites Illegal Logging', *Solomon Star*, 21 December 2006.

96 Moffat Mamu 'Foreign Loggers Taking Solomons for Ride', *Solomon Star*, 10 June 2005.

97 'Solomons Timber Over-Harvest Threatens Economy' *Solomon Star*, 14 September 2007.

98 December 22, 1997 – PACNEWS, http://archives.pireport.org/archive/1997/december/12-23-03.html (accessed 3 March 2008).

99 'Solomons Revoke Logging Export Exemptions', *Solomon Star*, 20 July 2006.

100 'Temotus in Solomon Islands Ban Logging', Solomon Islands Broadcasting Corporations, June 27, 2005, http://archives.pireport.org/archive/2005/june/06-27-12.htm (accessed 3 March 2008).

101 AusAID 'Pacific Islands 2020', http://www.ausaid.gov.au/publications/pdf/pacific2020.pdf (accessed 3 March 2008).

102 See 2020 Report: 41, 45, 46. Compare however the views of Maenu'u (1994) who suggests that this is western ethno-centric view.

103 CIA World Factbook: Vanuatu, https://www.cia.gov/library/publications/the-world-factbook/geos/nh.html#People (accessed 10 May 2008).

104 Some sources claim this percentage to be as high as 80. See opening speech at the National Land Summit by the Minister of Lands.

105 For an overview see https://www.cia.gov/library/publications/the-world-factbook/geos/nh.html#Econ.

106 Articles 73–75, Constitution of the Republic of Vanuatu

107 The Land Reform Act (Cap 123) section 3. This replaced a Joint Regulation passed before independence. Joint Regulations were laws passed by the Anglo-French Condominium government – usually for indigenous people.

108 Article 87(1), Constitution of Vanuatu.

109 See, for example, report [1999] VUOM 6 and [1999] VUOM 9, accessible via PacLII.

110 Tahi (2007: 15–19).

5   Social ordering
Custom and equality

Introduction

As has been indicated in Chapter Three, some of the critique of the universalist conception of human rights is that it is based on western liberal ideas which are unacceptable in the Pacific, partly because they are associated with the imperial dictates of a colonial past and partly because they are incompatible with the cultural traditions and values of the Pacific region. However, adherence to a relativist approach to human rights, especially one based on cultural distinctiveness, can itself jeopardise human rights. While it is a universal principle that all peoples should be free from oppression and that everyone is entitled to respect for their language, beliefs, cultures and traditions, there are some cultures and traditions which do not respect and value all persons equally. Cultural relativism and claims of state sovereignty versus rights imperialism may therefore be used as a cloak to conceal human rights abuses and protect human rights violators from international scrutiny. When that happens then an appeal to universal standards of human rights may indicate that certain cultural practices or attitudes should not be sanctioned by a misplaced respect for the sanctity of all cultures. Similarly, claims of cultural relativism and state sovereignty may enable the state or other power bases to restrict, crush or obliterate certain cultures, languages or practices, while avoiding international condemnation.

The balance between claims to universal standards and acknowledgment that these must be implemented, taking into account the complexities and peculiarities of specific local situations – which will include culture, language and tradition – is a difficult one. Too strong a claim to ideas or concepts which appear to have originated outside the region can lead to negative reception, while too great a reliance on the cultural interpretation of such ideas or concepts can lead to ineffective human rights regimes. Similarly, too great an emphasis on rights may be unsuccessful if it detracts from duties, while the claim to individual rights may be seen as damaging to group or collective rights. The situation is made more challenging when the local context is diverse, changing and subject to a number of contested constructions by local people. This is the situation that faces any advocacy of the rights of women and children in the Pacific region.

This chapter examines the sometimes conflicting relationship between custom and human rights, with particular focus on the rights of women and the challenges faced by traditional social ordering in rapidly changing societies. While this chapter does not attempt to give an exhaustive account of the role of custom in the Pacific, or the role and experience of women in customary societies, it is recognised that some grasp of the meaning and scope of custom in contemporary Pacific societies is necessary as well as an awareness of some of the difficulties in pinning down this pervasive but elusive component of Pacific life. The relationship between custom and fundamental human rights is, at least at a formal level, governed by the recognition given to custom in the laws and institutions of Pacific Island countries. The way in which this relationship can have consequences for women is illustrated by considering how custom and customary institutions influence the law and its application in certain situations. Where these reach the attention of legal forums much will depend on the approaches adopted by the courts and the various tribunals which are engaged in dispute resolution. Regional jurisprudence provides some insight into the challenges presented when claims of custom are raised against claims to human rights, but is only part of the larger picture. This is illustrated by difficulties faced by women, which appear to escape the legal framework, notably domestic violence, which, as highlighted in the introduction to this book, is a major problem in the region. While there are many positive changes taking place in respect of women's rights there are still a number of obstacles which confront women in the region. First, however, it is important to recall that the human rights of women is not just a concern of Pacific Islands but of the global community.

The international arena

In the Vienna Declaration particular attention was drawn to the human rights needs of certain groups, including women and children, and it was acknowledged that 'gender-based violence and all forms of sexual harassment and exploitation' were violations of basic human rights. In 1945, the equal rights of men and women were incorporated into the United Nations Charter and a Commission on the Status of Women was established, which was eventually to successfully negotiate the adoption of the Convention on the Elimination of All Forms of Discrimination Against Women in 1979. The Universal Declaration of Human Rights also includes a prohibition of discrimination against women and imposes obligations on states, groups and persons to uphold the rights set out in the Declaration. Other international legal texts protecting the rights of women, children, disabled persons and migrant workers have followed.

In the Pacific, the decade for women in the years 1975–1985 probably had little effect. However, the fourth World Conference of Women, held in Beijing in 1995 did attract Pacific interest and delegates, suggesting that in the intervening decade women's rights had found a foothold in the region. Since Beijing and as a result of increased rights advocacy – largely by non-government organisations assisted by foreign aid funding, women's rights have been mainstreamed in the agenda of rights' discourse in the Pacific region. Today almost all Pacific Island countries are signatories to CEDAW as indicated in Chapter One.

International conventions provide important objectives for Pacific Island countries. For example, Article 2(e) of CEDAW obliges states to eliminate discrimination against women 'by any person, organisation or enterprise'. What it does not do however is impose this obligation on private persons or systems. In particular, appeals to custom, tradition and the established social ordering of communities – which is strongly patriarchal in the Pacific region, may escape the obligations of CEDAW, or be raised as justification for what might otherwise appear to be human rights violations. Indeed, some conservative traditionalists may argue that the values and concepts articulated in international conventions such as CEDAW and the CRC reflect external interference in the domestic ordering of society which is inimical to stability, social cohesion and the autonomy of Pacific Island countries. Opposition to women's rights or children's rights may be mobilised by appealing to custom, tradition, national identity or religion, while advocates of such rights may struggle to match rights claims with traditional structures and beliefs, or to embed the universal in the local, cultural and social reality.

The meaning and scope of custom

One of the features of societies in the South Pacific region is the survival and continuing influence of custom in the daily lives of many people. There is also a perception both within and beyond the region that custom is often at variance with human rights and that the two are in conflict. This is seen as being particularly relevant in the context of women and children.

Custom not only includes the observance of certain cultural practices, but also the retention of certain institutions, such as the status of chief or assemblies of traditional leaders. It also determines procedures, for example rituals at birth, death and marriage, but also in dispute resolution. Many of these impact on the status of women and their fundamental rights. For example, the custom of arranged marriage may appear to conflict with the exercise of individual autonomy, while the practice of 'bride price' which is common in Melanesian societies, may be interpreted by its critics as the buying and selling of women and therefore demeaning. The institution of chief or 'Big Man' may be seen as being a way of keeping women out of positions of power, as these roles are invariably taken by men, while membership of traditional assemblies such as the Great Council of Chiefs in Fiji, the Council of Chiefs in Vanuatu, or the *Iroij* in Marshall Islands are predominantly if not solely male. Even where women have a voice in decision making, for example at local or village level, their opinion may be ranked lower than that of men. For example, in Samoan villages men and women meet separately to consider village matters, as do young adults. The women's voice is taken into account but is inferior to that of the men's house, while that of the young adults is even less important. Even more modern 'western' institutions such as the legislative assemblies are predominantly male, thereby excluding women from central and generally provincial government.

While custom and tradition may be asserted to maintain stability and social cohesion, they may also stand in the way of development and particularly the empowerment or emancipation of women and children. Alternatively, custom may be seen as being a positive influence in the enhancement of human rights, particularly if introduced human rights can be interpreted and viewed through the customary lens and if common ground can be found between customary values and those inherent in human rights. Before considering both these perspectives it is necessary to understand the meaning and scope of custom in the Pacific region.

What is custom?

While the term custom is used frequently its meaning is not always clear. This is partly a problem of translation, not just of language and terms, but of concepts and systems. For many Pacific islanders custom is a way of doing something or conducting oneself, rather than substantive rules. Consequently, trying to interpret custom within a common law framework can be challenging, for custom is as much about procedure as substance. So, for example, in Samoa, adherence to the *'fa'a Samoa'* is a claim to do things in the traditional Samoan way. The main features of this system were stated in *King v Andrus* [1977] ASHC 1 as 'the "aiga" or extended family, the "matai" or chieftal system, the land tenure system under which nearly all land is communally owned, and the custom of "foga" whereby one family renders formal apology to another for a serious offense committed by one of its members'. While women have their place in this scheme of things it may not be very prominent. For example, the head of the extended family is usually male, *matai* titles tend to be held by men (although women are not prohibited from holding chiefly titles), land tenure is predominantly managed by men or determined by the Land and Titles Court, and the system of *ifoga* – which is considered further in Chapter Seven – while it may take into account factors such as a victim's status and age, is negotiated between heads or representatives of families and the views of the victim may carry little weight. The composite elements of custom may, therefore, either taken separately or together, present their own challenges to the equitable experience of human rights.

But interpretations of custom are not homogenous. Custom may also be used to refer to those systems or institutions which are perceived as belonging to or originating from indigenous people (Bolton 1998: 179), as opposed to the ways of doing things which have been introduced into the region by missionaries, colonial administrators and others. Doing things in a traditional way does not necessarily mean that these traditions have remained rigid or firmly rooted in ancient history. In some cases, however, custom does seem to be frozen in time, for example, in Cook Islands custom is defined as 'the ancient custom and usages of the Natives of the Cook Islands'.[1] Ntumy suggests this precludes recognition of 'new or changed custom' (Ntumy 1993: 5). So, for example, chiefly titles can only be conferred on a person in accordance with custom. However, it has also been held that in the Cook Islands 'custom was never immutable in all its aspects',[2] suggesting that the 'ancientness' of the custom might be a flexible measure. Nevertheless, if custom pointed to a particular outcome then on those matters to be determined by custom the role of the court was to 'follow the appropriate native custom, not to impose what we ourselves might think was a more fair result than the custom produces'.[3]

Definitions from elsewhere in the region are of limited assistance. For example, Schedule One of the Papua New Guinea Constitution states that custom is defined to mean: 'the customs and usages of indigenous inhabitants of the country existing in relation to the matter in question at the time when and the place in relation to which the matter arises, regardless of whether or not the custom or usage has existed from time immemorial', thereby suggesting that modern forms of custom may be pleaded as well as those the origins of which are uncertain. Similar temporal flexibility is found in Tuvalu where the Laws of Tuvalu state that 'Customary law comprises the customs and usages, existing from time to time, of the natives of Tuvalu',[4] while the Constitution of Solomon Islands states that customary law consists of 'rules of customary law prevailing in an area of Solomon Islands' (section 114), which, while not indicating any temporal dimension, does suggest that the rules are variable geographically, so that the application of customary rules may have inconsistent outcomes depending on the area of their origin. In Samoa it would appear that only customs or usages which have 'acquired the force of law' are to be taken into account.[5] This force of law can be acquired through the confirmation of custom by legislation or by way of a court ruling. This begs the question, which courts? This is particularly important in Samoa where, under the Village Fono Act 1990, village councils wield considerable power but it is not expressly stated that they are courts. Their powers are defined as those that accord 'with the custom and usage of that village'[6] and the punishments which a *fono* may impose are to be 'in accordance with the custom and usage of its village'.[7] Again this suggests a degree of inconsistency and variability is likely to be encountered.

In the Federated States of Micronesia there is no provision for customary law in the Constitution but there is scope for separate legislative intervention to protect 'the traditions of the people of the Federated States of Micronesia'.[8] 'Traditions', however, may not amount to customary law or customs having the force of law. An example can be found in Kiribati. Here, the Medical and Dental Practitioners (Amendment) Act 1981 states 'Nothing in this ordinance shall affect the right of i-Kiribati to practice in a responsible manner Kiribati traditional healing by means of herbal therapy, bone-setting and massage, and to demand and recover reasonable charges in respect of such practice'.[9] Clearly this reference is not to custom as law but custom as traditional practice. Less straightforward however is the Native Lands Ordinance (Cap 61), which recognises wills made and attested in accordance with native custom and customary adoption.[10] Here, where the will is a document from which a number of legal consequences will flow, customary practice has the force of law.

This confusion between custom as law and custom as practice or tradition has consequences, particularly for women. For example, it is not a law that women are not permitted inside the meeting place of men, but various sanctions may follow if they breach the 'taboo' or custom of exclusion.[11] Similarly, it may be custom that only women attend childbirth, so that male doctors may be unwelcome; or that female adolescents are strictly chaperoned while their brothers have much greater freedom of movement, so that if they are assaulted or raped they get the blame and not the attacker or rapist.

The New Zealand Law Commission, aware of the difficulties in defining custom, stated in its report

> There is no settled definition of custom law. Some consider that the search for a definition is unhelpful and that custom, being fluid, cannot be defined but only described. Several have warned against defining custom law in terms of Western law, because the concepts involved are substantially different.
>
> (2006: para 4.23)

The Report went on to adopt the term 'custom law' to encompass references to 'custom' and 'customary law' and to describe 'the values, principles and norms that members of a cultural community accept as establishing standards for appropriate conduct' (para 4.26).

This is not entirely helpful as it may be crucial to distinguish whether a value, principle or practice is indeed law, not least to determine whether an infringement of a fundamental right is one that is permitted by law. For example, in the case of *Tanavalu v Tanavalu* [1998] SBHC 4, the widow of the deceased challenged the right of her father in law to collect and distribute the deceased's entitlement under the Solomon Islands National Provident Fund. The distribution which had occurred had excluded the widow entirely. The problem was that the deceased had not nominated his widow as recipient of the fund and the legislation governing the fund stated that, in such circumstances 'the amount or the portion shall, notwithstanding any law to the contrary, be distributed in accordance with the custom of the member, to the children, spouse and other persons entitled thereto in accordance with that custom'.[12] The issue was whether the customary patrilineal distribution of the fund was discriminatory as provided for under section 3 and 15 of the Constitution.[13] The court held that: these provisions only referred to a law that is 'made' which excluded customary law because customary law 'is not made; it evolves or was already pertaining at the time of the adoption of the Constitution'; it excludes customary law because customary law is not written; and that sections 15(5)(c) and (d) of the Constitution permit discrimination in the case of devolution of property at death and in circumstances where there is a law which makes provision for matters to be determined by reference to customary law, as was the case here. The court concluded that 'a person acting "by virtue of" customary law may treat another in discriminatory manner if that is in accordance with the applicable rule of customary law'. It found that

> The rules of customary law ... entitles the father in law to exercise his discretion to refuse to distribute any part of the estate to the widow ... on account of her having left the home without compliance with custom or by permission or agreement of the deceased's parents.

The judge cited with approval the reasoning of an earlier case concerned with the system of electing members of a provincial government. It had been argued that the system was unconstitutional because traditional chiefs were usually men, therefore including elected traditional chiefs would discriminate against women. This argument had been unsuccessful. The court had held that 'the Constitution recognises that the "traditional chiefs" should play a role in government at the provincial level. The Constitution itself therefore recognises this imbalance or discrimination and it will remain until the role of "traditional chiefs" under the Constitution is re-evaluated'.[14]

In both these cases, the recognition of customary law as part of the legal system, together with provisions that allowed customary practices to evade the fundamental rights provisions of the Constitution, meant that women were adversely affected. The potential for similar outcomes is not limited to the Solomon Islands. Where constitutions give formal recognition to custom or customary law, and fail to adequately ensure that the application or observation of custom is not discriminatory, then similar outcomes can be anticipated unless the courts step in and address the issue; as they did, for example, in the case of *In the Matter of an Application under Section 57 of the Constitution; Application by Individual and Community Rights Advocacy Forum Inc (ICRAF); In re Miriam Willingal* [1997] PGNC 7. In this case, Miriam had been offered as a compensation payment along with some pigs to settle an inter-tribal dispute. The likelihood was that she would be compelled into a customary marriage against her will. The court accepted that 'head pay' was a recognised custom and also that it took the form of compensation payments of money, pigs and other valuable personal items. What the court was less clear about was whether the custom also included the payment of young single women. Proof of such a custom had to comply with the requirements of the Customs Recognition Act (Cap 19). Having heard expert witnesses the court came to the conclusion that while there was no evidence in custom of young women forcefully being included in compensation 'head pay', there was clear evidence of a

> general custom of deceased's mother's tribesmen requesting the dece-ased's tribe to return a young unmarried woman from deceased's tribe, preferably the grand-daughter or great-grand daughter of the deceased's tribe, to marry a man from the deceased's mother's tribe. This request is made as part of 'head pay' at the time 'head pay' in the form of material goods is requested or demanded. Depending on how it is put, it may be a request or a demand.

The court noted that 'Everyone in the tribe including the women are aware and co-partakers in this commitment. But the women are passive co-partakers and the decision is made by the men. Women have no right to make customary commitments on behalf of the tribe'.

The court also found that Miriam had been identified as a suitable potential candidate for this marriage and had consequently come under pressure to enter such a marriage. She feared that if she did not comply with the requests of male members of both tribes she would be forced to do so. In Papua New Guinea the Constitution provides that custom shall be adopted and applied as part of the underlying law of the country provided it is not 'inconsistent with a Constitutional Law or a statute, or repugnant to the general principles of humanity' (Schedule 2.1). This includes any inconsistency with the fundamental rights provisions. In this case, Miriam was perhaps fortunate that the Marriage Act (Cap 28) expressly prohibited forced marriages, so that to compel Miriam to marry against her will or to put her under pressure to do so was contrary to the Act. It was also held that to put her under this obligation was contrary to her right to freedom (section 32) and equality of citizens (section 55), contrary to provisions in the Customs Recognition Act, which provides that 'a custom which is not in the public interest or would create injustice' should not be recognised (Section 3(1)) and repugnant to 'general principles of humanity'.

The judge however acknowledged the challenges faced by the courts, not just in this case, but in any case where customary practices had to be weighed against other laws. He observed

> It is not easy for any outsider to fully understand the customs and the underlying values and purposes they serve. Any outsider including the modern courts must not be quick to extract those customs and their values and pass judgements on their soundness or otherwise ... To one ethnic society, the custom 'head pay' which includes women may sound offensive to women, discriminatory of women, oppressive or inhuman whereas it may not be so to the ethnic group that practices it ... Courts must be careful not to pass quick judgements on the legality and soundness of traditional customs and customary practices and their underlying values.

The formal recognition given to custom

As is suggested by the above case, custom may be formally incorporated into the legal system, either in general or by specific reference to certain topics, or both.[15] For example, in Cook Islands there is a general clause in the Constitution Act 1964 which provides that 'custom and usage shall have effect as part of the law of the Cook Islands',[16] and a specific provision that 'every title to an interest in customary land shall be determined according to the ancient custom and usage of the natives of the Cook Islands' in the Cook Islands Act 1915.[17] These provisions are balanced by two others. First, the scope of the general principles can be restricted or curtailed by legislation. Second, the general provision cannot be taken to apply to 'any custom, tradition, usage or value that is, and to the extent that it is, inconsistent with a provision of this Constitution or any enactment.' This can be compared with the provisions found in the Constitution of Tuvalu, where not only does the Preamble state that the laws of Tuvalu include customary law but the Laws of Tuvalu Act (Cap 1B) confirm that customary law is part of the laws of Tuvalu.[18] Although customary law cannot be applied if it is inconsistent with any legislation, the Constitution makes a number of references to Tuvaluan values and culture. In particular, the enjoyment and exercise of the fundamental rights and freedoms are subject to 'acceptance of Tuvaluan values and culture, and with respect for them.'[19] The right to be free from discrimination is excluded in a number of circumstances which could have an adverse impact on women, in particular in respect of: adoption, marriage, divorce, burial, land, or 'any other such matter, in accordance with the personal law, beliefs or customs of any person or group'.[20] So, in the case of *Tepulo v Pou* [2005] TVHC 1, an unmarried mother unsuccessfully contested the claim of her young boy's father to take and raise the child. His right to do so not only rested on Tuvaluan values and customs but also the Native Lands Ordinance

(Cap 22) which permitted the court to make an order for the father to have custody

> If the father being a native accepts the child as being his, such child shall after reaching the age of 2 reside with the father or his relations and shall in accordance with native customary law inherit land and property from his father in the same way as the father's legitimate children.[21]

That the law was discriminatory, conflicted with established welfare principles for the custody of young children and was contrary to Tuvalu's obligations under international law, made little impression on the court (Farran 2005c).

In some countries, there is no reference to customs and traditions as a source of law but other legislation may make provision for custom to be considered. So, for example, in Nauru the Constitution does not expressly provide for recognition of customs and traditions as a source of law but the Customs and Adopted Law Act 1971 directs the courts to give effect to the customs and usages of Naruans – unless such customs and usages are repealed, restricted or changed by statute. However, the Supreme Court has held that customary law only has effect to the extent that it is applied by ordinance or statute. So, for example, land disputes can be decided according to custom because the customary authority of chiefs has been placed on a statutory footing under legislation.[22]

In Fiji, under the 1970 Constitution, custom appears to have had no formal legal status,[23] although provision was made that Parliament could enact legislation for the recognition of custom. However, the short-lived 1990 Constitution established custom as a primary source of law so that cognisance of Fijian customary law would apply unless either an Act of the Fiji parliament provided otherwise or that custom, usage or tradition was found to be inconsistent with a statute, the Constitution or 'repugnant to the general principles of humanity'. In making new laws Parliament was to have 'particular regard to the customs, traditions, usages, values and aspirations of the Fijian people'.[24] The Constitution also provided that decisions of the Native Lands Commission regarding the customary ownership of land or any matters relating to Fijian custom usage and tradition were not reviewable by any court of law. These provisions of the 1990 Constitution marked a u-turn in the status of custom in Fiji returning it to a pre-independence position. However, the 1997 Constitution did not include any provision similar to that found in the 1990 Constitution, with the consequence that customary law is no longer an express source of law. What the 1997 Constitution does do is to continue in force all those laws which were previously in force unless expressly repealed. This would include customary law along with existing statutes and the principles of common law. The new Constitution also provides that Parliament must 'make provision for the application of customary laws and for dispute resolution in accordance with Fijian processes' and in doing so 'have regard to the customs, traditions, usages, values and aspirations of the Fijian and Rotuman people'.[25] As will be indicated in Chapter Seven, the recognition of customary dispute processes does not always serve either the public interest or take into consideration the rights of the victim. It has been suggested that one of the reasons why the 1997 Constitution may omit customary law as a formal source of law is the problematic nature of its potential conflict with human rights, particularly as regards discrimination against women (Corrin 2000). Indeed, the Fiji Women's Rights Movement and the Fiji Crisis Centre had previously made representations to the Beattie Commission expressing concerns about the re-introduction of the Fijian Courts 'on the grounds that traditional courts worked against women' (Corrin 2000).[26] Although the apparently weaker position of customary law in 1997 Constitution might be cause for optimism for gender equality and respect for fundamental rights, there are still many concerns regarding the stereotyping of women in society, the endorsement of patriarchal ordering of society by a public service that reflects this, and the impact of poverty, tourism and the break-down of law and order on the lives of women (Kotoisuva 2004; Shameen 2004).

Some countries incorporate customary law into their systems but with very little indication of its scope or limitations. For example, in Vanuatu the Constitution states that 'customary law shall continue to have effect as part of the law of the Republic',[27] and that the courts should determine matters 'whenever possible in conformity with custom' where there is no rule of law applicable to the matter before the court.[28] An example of the application of this principle can be found in the case of *Waiwo v Waiwo* [1996] VUMC 1, in which the court resorted to custom in arriving at the quantum of damages payable for adultery. An out-of-court settlement had been decided by a council of local chiefs. Although the aggrieved wife had been awarded a small sum this had in effect been cancelled out because she had also been fined for insulting the co-respondent. Regarding the damages for adultery as punitive in nature because of the gravity attached in custom to adultery and finding no guidance in the applicable legislation, the Magistrate's court awarded her a considerably larger sum on the basis that 'the rules of "custom" allowed for punitive damages to be awarded for adultery against named correspondents'.[29]

In this case, custom appeared to favour the wronged wife but all too often custom adopts differential standards for men and women, some of which find their way into legislation, others into the attitudes of society and from there into the courts, often exacerbated by the introduction of legislation and procedures which are themselves based on sexist and patriarchal ideas. Examples can be found in the law of evidence, the law of trusts, criminal law and procedure, property law and family law. These last two will be considered here.

Land

As has been suggested in Chapter Four, the systems of land tenure, and the determination of interests in land is extremely complex in the Pacific region, owing to the plurality of laws which govern such interests. While women in the region may experience the same disadvantages as women elsewhere in respect of raising mortgage finance, asserting interests based on non-financial contribution or establishing sufficient degrees of dependency or reliance, coupled with detriment to support claims to property, they also experience the disadvantages of customary land tenure systems which favour males, even in matrilineal societies where land rights may be inherited through the female side of the family. This is because the management of land and decisions relating to it are invariably the preserve of men. For example, the *taupulega* in Tokelau consists solely of elderly men who decide on the allocation of rights to village lands and their produce, the use of kin group lands and related rights such as the right to water (Hooper and Huntsman 1997: 127–131). In Fiji, land rights are often linked to male rituals and ceremonies in which women are marginalised (Bolobola 1986: 2–5). Similarly, where land matters are decided by institutionalised forums these tend to be predominantly male, for example, the *aiga* in Samoa or the *mataqali* in Fiji. Even at a national level, male-dominated institutions may govern customary land interests. For example, in Marshall Islands, the *Iroj-Laplap* – which is a council of high-ranking chiefs, has to consent to the alienation of any land, while in Cook Islands the House of Ariki may be called on to approve to any changes in laws affecting native land, just as the *Malvatumauri* in Vanuatu may be consulted by Parliament on such matters. These councils are predominantly or solely male.

It is not just in the management of land or in respect of decision-making affecting land that women are disadvantaged. In custom, in patrilineal societies it is presumed that a woman on marriage will acquire the right to use the land of her husband and that therefore it is unnecessary for her to retain land use rights in the land of her own parents.[30] This is fine provided, first, that her husband's family has land rights and sufficient land, and second, that she remains married to him. Problems can arise, however, where women move to urban areas with their husbands and lose land rights or where a woman divorces her husband or he leaves her, or she becomes a widow. In these circumstances, her right to remain on the land of her husband's family may become precarious and difficult. She may find herself compelled to marry a member of the same clan or village, or she may find that she has to return to her own family although her children may be claimed by her husband's family – especially if bride price has been paid. Urban widows in particular may find themselves in a difficult position as they may have lost the right to use lands in their birth place and not acquired them in the island village of their husband.

Unmarried women may also encounter disadvantages. In custom, an unmarried girl is usually supported by her family until such time as she marries and becomes the responsibility of her husband and his family. Unmarried girls and married girls seldom have full customary rights to land held under customary tenure. Even in matrilineal societies, although land title may pass through the female line, decisions and day to day management is usually the preserve of brothers or uncles. Where land is not held under customary tenure women may be no better off. For example, in Tonga, women have virtually no land rights as land is only allocated to males.[31] Elsewhere, single mothers who are earning a salary may be able to acquire leases, but the greater probability is that they will either be dependent on their own parents or hold precarious licences over land owned by others, as in squatter settlements.

Where a marriage breaks down there may also be adverse property consequences for women. In part, these will be determined by the law that is applicable to the distribution of property on divorce, but here two problems can arise: either there is no relevant legislation and so the courts must consider what to do, or the legislation is not applicable because the marriage, and therefore the divorce, is governed by custom. An example of the first is illustrated by the case of *Halapua v Tonga* [2004] TOCA 5, in which a wife was opposing the divorce. Here the Court of Appeal discovered that 'there is now no matrimonial property legislation in the Kingdom (of Tonga)' and that 'Without any such provisions there remains the distinct possibility that one party to the marriage, usually the wife, may be unfairly disadvantaged'. The cause of this legal lacuna was the Civil Law (Amendment) Act 2003 which removed recourse to English statutes of general application.[32] Consequently, the court held that it could not make any order regarding the matrimonial property, recommending instead that 'the legislature should consider whether there should be legislative provisions relating to the division of matrimonial property on the breakdown of marriage'.[33]

An example of the second can be found in countries where the payment of 'bride price' remains an important aspect of customary marriage. If the marriage breaks down there is the question of who owns the bride price. In the Solomon Island case of *To'ofilu v Oimae* [1997] SBHC 33, the plaintiff successfully claimed a refund of the bride price once it was discovered that the bride was pregnant by another man at the time of the wedding. Similarly, in the Papua New Guinea case of *Kere v Timon* [1990] PGNC 103, it was claimed that the bride price should be returned on the breakdown of the marriage. The issue then arises as to who must repay what and how the quantum is to be calculated. For example, in the Solomon Island case, it was suggested that where a bride runs away from her husband then full bride price must be repaid, whereas if the husband rejects his wife only half should be repaid. In the Papua New Guinea case it was suggested that 'if parents of man pay bride price for a girl and the girl leaves husband without good reason the girl's family must return the bride price. Second, if the girl does not like the husband and leaves the husband and the husband asks her to return and she does not, then the parents of the man have to repay the bride price'. These considerations lead to considerable pressure by families on both sides, either for the continuation of the marriage or because of the bad feelings generated between the families due to the breakdown of the marriage. The individual wife and husband may be relatively insignificant players in this situation – especially the wife.

The involvement of the extended family in the affairs of its members can mean that unravelling property rights is a complex challenge for the courts. This is illustrated by the case of *Kofe v Kofe* [1999] TOSC 45. Here, the parties were married but separated. He had gone to live in New Zealand but she remained in Tonga. Contesting the wife's claim were members of the husband's family as well as the husband. The difficult issue of establishing who owned what reflects the complications of family relationships, where obligations, exchange and reciprocity all combine to obscure clear claims of ownership. Here the house had been built with family labour on land held by the husband and his family; some contributions had come from the husband's mother; other finance had been contributed by family members and further loans had been secured against a variety of property without any clear investigation of title. In trying to sort out the matter the court held that all the property in dispute was to be treated as if it was jointly owned. However, it was recognised that the husband's family might have claims against him for the various loans and assistance they had given him. It was also recognised that it would be impossible to allocate the house to the wife, taking into account its location on land held by the husband's side of the family, especially now that he had new partner. The wife, therefore, would have to be housed elsewhere and the total sum of joint property reduced by honouring the various loans. As is the case in other countries, where the wife has very little financial autonomy either before or during the marriage, her material position on divorce may be considerably worse than during the marriage. While the extended family may ameliorate some of these consequences it can also aggravate them.

It may also be difficult for a divorcing wife to establish any personal claim to custom property other than land. This is illustrated by the Solomon Island case of *Sasango v Beliga* [1987] SBMC 5. Here, a widow with seven children was seeking the return of custom property, including pigs, shell money and porpoise teeth, from her late husband's brothers. The plaintiff claimed that some of the shell money and the porpoise teeth were her own personal property and others had been held on trust by her husband for the children. The defendant, the deceased husband's brother, claimed the right to the property and as successor to his brother in custom. The court did not deny this custom but on the facts of this case held that it could not extend to the personal property of the wife or to the property held on trust for the children where the wife was awarded custody of the children.

It is also the case that succession to land does not always favour women. First, because in a number of Pacific Island countries land held under customary land tenure cannot be alienated by will so must devolve according to custom,[34] which does not always favour the widow; and second, because in some countries there is clear discrimination against women when it comes to succession to land.[35] Even if a deceased makes a will, this may be challenged on the grounds that it goes against custom or that it makes insufficient provisions for certain members of the family.[36]

There are various ways in which greater equality to land could be ensured. First, all express discrimination in legislation could be removed. Where this no longer reflects actual practice, as may be the case in Kiribati, then this should not present any great problems. Where however, this would mark a radical shift in land allocation then this could be more difficult. For example, in Tonga, there is already insufficient land to meet the entitlement of all male Tongans, so that to remove the present discriminatory practices would have significant resource constraints. An alternative, and perhaps a compromise in such circumstances, is to ensure that other rights and interests which may be held by women are better secured and understood by women. So, second, interests in land which are facilitated by an introduced regulatory framework, especially leases, could be in a way that ensures that women's interests are safeguarded. This is as much a matter of education as of ensuring that there are practice guidelines in place in respect of those who deal with women and married clients, for example banks and lenders, land officers and land courts. This may require positive discrimination in favour of women.

However, even if these measures were adopted there is still the issue of land held under customary tenure. In Fiji all Fijians who are appropriately registered are able to benefit from the land managed by the Native Land Trust Board, even if the management at all levels is predominantly male. The same is true in some other countries where trusts are used to manage native or custom land.[37] Elsewhere, however, the management of customary land is governed by prevailing social structures which are seen as being essential to the preservation of social stability. Perhaps what is needed here is recognition that the social fabric is changing and that custom needs to be clear about how this is to be accommodated. For example, what customary practices are in place to accommodate urban migration, or those who return after a long absence to their village of birth, or where customary land owners are permanently absent from the day to day management of land? In particular, consideration needs to be given to whether current customary land tenure practices are compatible with women's right to equality and how that is to be interpreted.

Family

The disadvantages that women may suffer in the family context is not solely the experience of Pacific women, they are experienced by women in many parts of the world. Often these disadvantages are related to the disempowerment of women and the patriarchal ordering of society, both of which are supported or reflected in legal institutions, laws and structures. The consequence is that women are disadvantaged in both the public domain and in the private domain including the family. Here, where women traditionally make the greatest contribution, they may still be undervalued and discriminated against. Some examples from the region illustrate this.[38]

Article 16 of CEDAW emphasises the equal rights and obligations of men and women with regard to choice of spouse, parenthood, personal rights and command over property. CEDAW also makes a number of references to women's reproductive rights,[39] including the right to choose whether to have children or when to have them, and therefore the right to family planning advice and assistance.[40]

The Preamble to the Convention states:

> Bearing in mind the great contribution of women to the welfare of the family and to the development of society, so far not fully recognized, the social significance of maternity and the role of both parents in the family and in the upbringing of children, and aware that the role of women in procreation should not be the basis for discrimination but that the upbringing of children requires a sharing of responsibility between men and women and society as a whole

and recognises that traditional perceptions of women within the family and society may result in unequal treatment of women. It therefore imposes on party states the obligation to modify social and cultural patterns which perpetuate inequalities between men and women or stereotypes which either expressly or impliedly place women in an inferior position to men. Member states are also expected to put in place measures which give effect to the equal responsibility of parents to their children and to family life.

In the Pacific family, law is governed by a chaotic mixture of introduced law, domestic legislation, principles of common law and equity and customary law. The nature of the latter has been modified by missionary influence, particularly on practices of sister exchange, infanticide, polygamy, the putting to death of widows and polyandry. Some customary practices however remain, including that of 'bride price' and arranged marriages. Moreover, Christian influence on family life has not always had positive benefits for women. For example, Pulea mentions male distrust of wives who use contraceptives, believing that this will encourage their female partners to be permissive or unfaithful without being caught out, concern that the availability of contraception will encourage pre-marital promiscuity in societies where virginity is still valued, or that contraception interferes with the 'will of God' (Pulea 1986: 66). Similar sentiment continues to criminalise the procurement of a miscarriage, abortion and the concealment of a newly born child; crimes which are usually committed by women, often in deeply unhappy circumstances. An illustration is found in the Samoa case of *Police v Rosa Loi* [2005] WSSC 33, where the accused was a 26 years old, a working mother of five children all under the age of nine. Her *de facto* husband was unfaithful, abusive and neglectful. Shortly before the baby's birth he had run off with another woman. When the child was born she abandoned it and was charged with 'failing to provide necessaries of life'.[41] In this case she was fortunate in so far as the court placed her on probation for two years on condition that a report, funded by legal aid, was made on her psychiatric health.[42] Not all countries have these resources.[43]

Understandably, for most newly independent countries, private law matters were not high on the political agenda – and indeed have remained a fairly low priority – so that it is not unusual to find dated statutes introduced from England, New Zealand or Australia, still in force. Even where national legislation is in place much of this dates back to the early days of independence and often represents no more than a nationalised version of an introduced Act. For example, in a number of countries discriminatory provisions apply in respect of the age of marriage, so that in Papua New Guinea, Vanuatu and Samoa males must be 18 years or over before they can marry, whereas the age for females is 16 years old.

International concern has been expressed about the age at which young people may marry, as evidenced by the Convention on Consent to Marriage, Minimum Age for Marriage and Registration of Marriages.[44] However, only two Pacific Island countries are parties to this Convention: Fiji and Samoa,[45] and throughout the region the law tends to permit marriage at a relatively young age; for example, in Solomon Islands and Tonga the parties to a marriage need be no more than 15 years old, and in Cook Islands, Tuvalu and Kiribati the parties can be as young as 16.[46] It is also the case that where customary marriage is permitted, children younger than this may be married and certainly their marriages may be arranged when they are still infants.[47] This is not just a problem for young Pacific islanders but also for female members of the Indian community in the region and there have been a number of cases where the court has had to consider whether a marriage is void on the grounds of duress or mistake.[48]

Where customary marriage is recognised, as in Vanuatu, Solomon Islands, Papua New Guinea, parts of the Federated States of Micronesia and in principle at least, in Marshall Islands,[49] it is often accompanied by the payment of 'bride-price'. Bride price is a term used to describe the transfer of valued moveable property, usually from the family of a groom to the family of the bride, often with reciprocal exchanges, which may or may not be of the same value. Typical property which may be exchanged are garden foodstuffs, pigs, mats, calico, manufactured household goods and garden implements, cash, and in the Solomon Islands shell money. Indeed bride price may be paid even where the marriage is not a customary marriage, as noted by the court in the Vanuatu case of *Waiwo v Waiwo* [1996] VUMC 1, where it was stated that

> (I)t is common ground in Vanuatu communities that customary and/or local usages (practices) play an important role ... An example of common element of custom to be taken into account in relation to civil, religious and custom marriages is the bride price (bearing in mind that in Vanuatu society, bride price is commonly known as '*the payment of the spouse-wife*' and it is the man who *pays* the wife).

Criticism of the custom of bride price is that it reduces women to the level of commodities, encourages domestic violence, fosters male chauvinism and patriarchal dominance, and infringes women's rights. While some of these claims may be well founded others are less so. For example, in the Vanuatu case of *In the Matter of the Constitution of the Republic of Vanuatu and the Infant Priscilla Vorongo* [1986] VUSC 4, it was argued in evidence that 'after the bride price is paid, the girl, belongs to the man in custom'. The court does not appear to have accepted this. Similarly, in Papua New Guinea it has been held 'that bride price payment does not entitle a husband to do whatever he likes with his wife' and that custom must be understood and applied in the context of constitutional principles.[50] However, in some countries where bride price is found it is not clear that this practice infringes any constitutional rights because the Constitution upholds custom and customary law as part of the legal system. Among traditionalists, including women, there are many who support the role of bride-price in building strong kinship and inter-clan links, in valuing women, and in securing the stability of family life. It is not therefore a custom that can easily be abolished.

For many Pacific islanders, especially in rural areas, customary practices govern much of family life although these practices may not amount to law. So, for example, the residence of a young married couple may be determined by custom, which usually, but not always, sees the bride going to live with her husband's family or in the same village as her husband's family, while married sons tend to stay in their birth place or the village of their father. Custom may also determine matters surrounding the birth of children, from practices on confinement, to naming or nursing.[51] Child rearing practices may also be governed by customs, including the residence of children, whether they visit and stay with members of the extended family and whether they are subject to various initiation or grade taking ceremonies. Even where the law intervenes this may be against a background of cultural practices. So, for example, in the case of a divorce there may be considerable negotiation and arbitration both before and after a divorce involving the local church minister, village elders and chiefs and various members of the family.

An example of where custom and introduced ideas have come into conflict is in the case of disputes over custody of children. Where the parents are married in custom and bride price has been paid it has been argued that once bride price is paid the children belong to the family of the husband.[52] Similarly, it has been acknowledged in case law that in custom a father may have automatic rights of custody over his children, a view expressed by Chief Justice Edward C. King in the case of *Pernet v Aflague* [1990] FMSC 8, who said, 'under historical Pohnpeian customary law only the husband had rights over the children of the marriage'. Similarly, in the Papua New Guinea case of *Enakali v Enakali* [1992] PGNC 7, where the parents had been married in custom and divorced in custom the court rejected the claim by the wife for custody of the child on the grounds that 'the customary obligations and rights created by the payment of brideprice give the man's line, by virtue of having passed some wealth to the woman's line, the right of custody of any children of the marriage.'[53]

In fact, this latter argument has generally been rejected. For example, in the Vanuatu case of *Molu v Molu* [1998] VUSC 15, attention was drawn to the (mis)conception held by members of society that, on the basis of social and cultural beliefs, 'parents and in the majority of cases husbands/ fathers based their application on the mistaken belief that they have some property right to "own" the children'. Instead, the courts have increasingly been prepared to prioritise the 'welfare principle', which tends to favour women, although once children are considered old enough to make their views known there may be different outcomes.[54] Sometimes the application of the welfare principle will coincide with customary approaches to custody, sometimes it will run contrary to customary approaches (Brown 1997). An example can be found in the Solomon Island case of *K v T and KU, In re Custody Application* [1985/86] SILR 49. Here it was argued that the welfare principle was an alien concept which should give way to customary law, which would have automatically awarded custody of the child to the father.[55] While it was accepted that customary law was part of the law of the Solomon Islands, the court held that until such time as Parliament ruled that custody questions were to be governed by customary law the welfare principle would prevail, even if, as in this case, bride price had been paid. Although this approach gives preference to an introduced notion – 'the welfare principle' – over custom, it is important that its interpretation accommodates the local context (Farran 2003). The long-term welfare of a child may be better secured if rights and entitlements under custom are also taken into account as well as considerations of more western matters such as education and health care.

In most countries of the region, balancing the equities in family law has fallen to the courts because of the reluctance of legislative bodies to engage in the personal law of citizens. However, Fiji Islands has been the one country which has embarked on a programme of reform and, following an extensive consultation exercise, enacted the Family Law Act in 2003.[56] While this initiative commenced in the 1990s, adverse feedback to Fiji's CEDAW report in 2002 provided added impetus from the perspective of gender inequalities experienced under the existing system. In the final stages consultants were seconded under the Australian/Fiji Law and Justice Sector Programme and under arrangements with the Family Court of Western Australia to provide in-country training. The result is an Act which closely follows that of Australia.[57]

The Fiji initiative was funded by Australia and New Zealand. It introduces far reaching changes in both procedural and substantive family law.[58] It includes new rules of procedure for dedicated Family Courts, the establishment of a counselling service and the acquisition of a range of sophisticated technology – such as audio visual facilities and computerised case management systems, appropriate physical infrastructure and staff with specialist skills. Law reform of this magnitude cannot occur in the region without external funding and expert assistance. Indeed, in opening the new Family Court the (then) Vice-President Ratu Joni thanked the Australian and New Zealand governments, saying that 'without their advice and technical assistance, particularly in relation to how things are done, would not have made this day possible'.[59] Therein, however, lies the question. Knowledge and advice of how things are 'done' in New Zealand or Australia is not necessarily an infallible recipe for success in Fiji. As pointed out by Imrana Jalal,

> Whether the Act lives up to its promise now ultimately depends on the political will of those who have the power to make the Act a living instrument; and how the civil service responds to it. This in turn depends on the financial and human resources that are allocated to the new law to implement it. Most importantly the civil service needs to understand clearly the regime proposed by the Act.[60]

Moreover the family law model, particularly procedures, is not without its critics in the parent legal system,[61] where it has been pointed out that alternative dispute resolution may operate against the interests of vulnerable women and children, and that emphasis on out-of-court procedures such as counselling, negotiating and welfare or social reports can cause delays which have negative consequences.[62]

The Fiji Family Law Act is ambitious in its aims. Its passage has attracted considerable controversy and debate.[63] It is not universally popular and still has its detractors.[64] Certainly there is a danger that the machinery and resources introduced to support the new law will prove costly to implement and maintain, a situation which may now be aggravated by the current political situation in Fiji and the deteriorating relationship between the governments of Fiji Islands, Australia and New Zealand.[65] It remains to be seen therefore whether this new approach to family law in the Pacific region will really 'allow women and children, especially the poor and marginalised, better access to justice'.[66]

The pervasive influence of custom

If custom is understood to be the way things have been traditionally done, then the influence of custom is not simply attributable to its place in the legal system but also to the way in which it informs social organisation, power structures, and accepted normative standards. As has been experienced elsewhere, including in the developed world, customs relating to or based on gender are deeply entrenched. They inform the language of the law, the way in which courts and deliberative bodies operate, the way in which women are viewed as litigants, witnesses and defendants, and the way in which justice is administered. Outside the courts these attitudes inform gender role expectations, the evaluation of contributions to the family and society and the allocation of resources and responsibilities. This is no different in the Pacific region, but here it is perhaps exacerbated by the combination of several factors.

First, the pervasive and prevailing influence of Christianity, introduced by missionaries and today deeply rooted in Pacific Island culture, was essentially patriarchal and advocated a model of social organisation in which the monogamous family was central, and the husband was the head of it. Wives and daughters were expected to be modest, obedient and subservient. Today the leadership of the church in the region is ambivalent about gender equality. Some churches are strong advocates of the need for gender equality, others are more reserved. This is evident in area of domestic violence which will be considered below. Churches are often torn between condemning violence and advocating obedience and commitment to the institution of marriage regardless of the personal cost.

Second, the employment opportunities offered by colonialism, either on plantations or later in the colonial administration, reflected the gender inequalities experienced in the country of the metropolitan power. Consequently, those who were employed were predominantly male, and where local male labour could not be found, indentured male workers were brought in. Women, if they were employed at all, tended to be employed in domestic roles or menial labour, or later for poor wages, as in the textile and clothing industry in Fiji. Moreover, in their transactions with custom leaders colonial administrators dealt with men, not women, thereby strengthening male dominance (New Zealand Law Commission Report 2006 para 7.18–7.21). Colonial administration also tended to focus its attention on matters of public law rather than private law so that those areas in which women were most involved, the family, subsistence agriculture, indigenous cultural property, were largely ignored (Brown and Corrin 1998).

Third, the reassertion of the role of custom, customary law, traditional values and cultures at independence did not create an environment which was necessarily conducive to the gender equality provisions of the new constitutions, while the political structures put in place effectively removed women from the realm of politics because the foundations on which they were built, such as political parties, public speaking, lobbying supporters, providing favours in return for votes, were outside the experience of most women. This was aggravated in a number of countries by the constitutional inclusion of male strongholds such as the *Bose Levu Vakaturaga* (Great Council of Chiefs) in Fiji, the *Malvatumauri* in Vanuatu, the House of Ariki in Cook Islands and the Council of Iroij in Marshall Islands. Although, as indicated in Chapter One, these institutions are of variable influence, nevertheless they can prove an obstacle when legislation which threatens the customary ordering of society is proposed.

Finally, the systems of adjudication, both in the formal courts introduced into the region and in the informal traditional courts, may fail to adequately address the needs of women. For example, adversarial procedures which see the court room as a modern battle ground is more suitable for male adversaries rather than intimidated and subservient women and children. Men predominate on the bench and – although this is less so – in the court room (Shameen 2004). In cases which may adversely impact on women corroborative evidence is often required, for example, in claims of adultery, in rape and in aggravated sexual assault. In traditional forums of dispute resolution the dominant voices may be male and the expected demeanour of women may prevent them from being heard or being sufficiently taken into account. Even where efforts have been made to improve the gender balance on of customary tribunals – as in Vanuatu with customary land tribunals, this has been unsuccessful in achieving anything like equitable representation.

These various factors combine to create an environment in which women face particular challenges in asserting their fundamental human rights. This chapter concludes by looking at an area of national and international concern, as highlighted in the Introduction to this book: domestic violence.

Domestic violence

One of the grounds for divorce which is recognised in the region is that of cruelty. Usually, but not always, the petitioner is the wife. However, in the legal systems of some Pacific Island countries the cruelty complained of has to be 'persistent' or 'habitual', thus one incidence of cruelty will not usually suffice.[67] This means that the victim spouse may have to endure a number of acts of cruelty over an extended period of time. For example, in *Garae v Garae* [2000] VUSC 72, the victim claimed to have been assaulted seventeen times in the course of eight months. While corroboration is not essential for claiming divorce on the grounds of cruelty, often medical evidence will be presented to support the claim and the court is unlikely to be persuaded without some form of corroborative evidence. There is also the problem of persuading the judge that the incidents amount to more than 'the ups and downs of married life'.[68] There may also be the need to persuade the judge that this is not a matter which can be remedied by custom payments or expressions of remorse on the part of the aggressor. Habitual cruelty has been defined to describe a situation where

> a person has a propensity to cruel conduct, which propensity it can be seen will be exercised and is in fact exercised whenever there be obstruction to that person's wishes, views or desires, and its exercise or apprehension of its exercise results in a deterioration in health of the party against whom it is directed ... albeit it is not of daily or weekly or even monthly occurrence.[69]

This situation may be aggravated in those systems where cruelty by itself is not a sufficient ground for divorce but must be coupled with intoxication. This is the case in Cook Islands, Niue and Samoa, where the law requires that the respondent be not only habitually cruel but a 'habitual drunkard' as well. Consequently, the victim of matrimonial cruelty may have to endure a number of attacks over an extended period of time.

It may also be the case that the victim does not wish to seek a divorce or is in a relationship in which the possibility of divorce does not exist, for example, a *de facto* union, or where the victim is not a spouse but a parent or child. There is, of course, the criminal law but unless the police are willing to become involved in domestic matters the criminal law is unlikely to be an effective deterrent of the phenomenon widely known as domestic violence. Moreover, some acts of domestic violence, notably marital rape, fall outside the criminal law of Pacific Island countries.

This is not to suggest that the issue of domestic violence is ignored, for it is not. In fact, there have been a number of reports on domestic violence in the region. In 1982 the Law Reform Commission in Papua New Guinea was mandated to enquire and report on:

1. the nature and extent of domestic violence as a social problem; and
2. the legal remedies available for complaints of domestic violence; and
3. any changes to the law which may be necessary or desirable to achieve the protection of women from domestic violence; and
4. the steps which should be taken to bring the problem of domestic violence to the public notice.[70]

This produced an interim report in 1987 and a final report in 1992. It found that over two-thirds of families were affected by domestic violence, which predominantly took the form of wife-beating, and that the problem was so extensive that it was a matter of public concern and not just a private matter. The final report recommended an approach which combined strengthening the legal framework as well as raising awareness. It saw a role for improved counselling as well as broader education on the adverse effects of domestic violence and the avenues of redress available to victims. In its summary the report states

> Priority is given initially to legal measures. The law is a powerful tool in motivating behaviour change, both in terms of its practical value through punishing offenders and in terms of its wider educational and preventive value as a statement of what society will not tolerate. The success of the other educational and social measures recommended by the Commission also depends on the effectiveness of the legal measures.

While some legal measures may have been adopted, for example better police training and campaigns to improve public awareness, there is little evidence to suggest that Papua New Guinea has put a strong legal framework in place to deal with domestic violence. In fact in 2006 Amnesty International published a critical report on the failure of Papua New Guinea to address escalating domestic violence in the country. The report found that

> women face gender-based discrimination and violence. Traditional patriarchal customs, often distorted by changed circumstances, are invoked to justify gender discrimination and subordination. Meanwhile, the protections which at least sometimes used to accompany those customs have been eroded. ... The formal justice system offers the promise of equality, protection and redress but in practice is remote, inaccessible and ineffective. Women are as at risk of gender-based discrimination and violence as ever.[71]

Similar investigations into domestic violence have taken place elsewhere in the region. For example, in 1994, a community survey of Domestic Violence in Solomon Islands was undertaken following the identification of domestic violence as a major concern by the National Council of Women in 1988. Of the 1,000 women surveyed 30.3 per cent were victims of domestic violence (Poerio 1995: vi). The report suggests that although rural dwellers may be more conservative in many ways, victims of domestic violence are likely to be less isolated there than in urban areas. While in rural and urban areas views of domestic violence were informed by a woman's religious obligation to her marriage and that a women was the property of her husband, communities in general did not think that accepting violence was part of the woman's role as a homemaker and that violence in the home was not acceptable. Although reporting domestic violence to the police was not a favoured option, police training in domestic violence took place in all provinces in 1995. A Victim Support Group was also set up and a Family

Support Centre established in Honiara. Unfortunately, civil unrest since then, has probably frustrated some of these initiatives.

In Vanuatu, it has been recognised that domestic violence is a development issue in so far as good governance should include the sound management of human and financial resources and that gender equality and respect is integral to that (SR International and Associates 2003). In 2004, research into domestic violence was undertaken under the auspices of the Department of Women's Affairs (Tor and Toka 2004). In particular, the report looked at the impact of *kastom* on domestic violence and especially whether modern justifications for domestic violence on the grounds of *kastom* had any historic basis. The report found that, prior to contact with missionaries and western culture, women probably had greater freedom, more power and more respect. They were less marginalised and able to do more within their own small communities. Although both the various chiefs and church ministers who were interviewed for the report indicated that domestic violence was not acceptable in *kastom*, the experience of women in the community is that contemporary *kastoms* and beliefs are more discriminatory; women are more marginalised and less valued. The report concluded that while many felt that stopping domestic violence was the responsibility of the couple involved, others felt that the chiefs and the church had a role to play. Pre-marital counselling was required, either by the chiefs who were involved in custom marriages or the priests who conducted church marriages. Men, too needed to be involved so that domestic violence was not seen as just being about women, and indeed in 2001 the Vanuatu Women's Centre launched a 'Men Against Violence ' programme, which, if only for its novelty, attracted media attention. Although lobbyists against domestic violence in Vanuatu have tried to get a bill for the Family Protection Act passed for several years, this has been continually frustrated. Consequently, in 2001 the Chief Justice's working party for the reform of Civil Procedure in consultation with stakeholders decided to offer a civil procedure solution.[72]

In 2001, Domestic Violence Protection orders became available for victims of domestic violence, enabling them to approach the court without first having to seek the intervention of the police, and without needing the assistance of a lawyer. However, police co-operation was still required for serving any court order on the perpetrator of the violence and while interim relief could be ordered in the long run the domestic situation might not be resolved. The Vanuatu Women's Centre has also been very active in raising awareness about domestic violence, lobbying for change, and providing a safe-house for victims of such violence. Staff from the Centre also assist victims to get Domestic Violence Protection Orders and in the period 2001–2003 took 99 cases to the courts.

In Fiji, the Law Reform Commission has published a report on Domestic Violence and in 2005 drafted a Domestic Violence Bill. In approaching the issue of domestic violence the Commission recognised the need to take a holistic view of both the problem and any solution. It acknowledged that in addressing issues of domestic violence Fiji would also be addressing concerns about social development, the well-being of families and children, women's rights and issues of gender equality, and 'human rights including: due process, equality before the law, and the right to security of the person'.[73] This has not yet been given legal effect.

Generally, however, the legal response appears either to have been limited or ineffective. For example, in Samoa, there have been a number of initiatives targeting domestic violence. In 1993 the NGO *Mapusaga o Alga Inc* was formed and, in collaboration with the Ministry of Women's Affairs, which had been established in 1991, published a report in 1996 seeking to correct the various common myths about domestic violence. In 2004 a national plan of action to implement CEDAW was adopted (Peteru 2004) and District Courts adopted a procedural policy of not allowing complaints to be withdrawn, on the grounds that the wider public interest needed to be taken into account (Kotoisuva 2004). Despite these efforts, however, as indicated in the Introduction, in a report in which Samoa was the only Pacific Island country (discounting Japan for the purposes of this book) included in the survey, it was suggested that there could be a 'hidden epidemic' of domestic violence in the country (WHO 2006: 5). As reported cases only represent a fraction of the occurrences of domestic violence and as a high proportion of these tend to be withdraw or dropped, it might be questioned whether recourse to the courts or legal process is an effective way of dealing with domestic violence. Reasons for domestic violence include anger on the part of the husband, sometimes fuelled by alcohol; disobedience on the part of the wife, including 'answering back'; a culture in which it is accepted that violence in the home is a 'man's "right" in marriage'; and that violence in the home is a "normal" and "private" matter (Peteru 2004: 27). Reluctance of victims to have recourse to legal authorities, reluctance of police to become involved in cases of domestic violence, and the nature of legal procedures suggest that, while a legal response is often advocated, it can only be of limited help in dealing with what is a complex issue which has consequences for the whole of society.

The problem of domestic violence has been recognised within the region and internationally and yet Pacific Island governments appear to be remarkably reluctant to act, leaving much of the burden to NGOs and civic society. Yet, it is recognised that domestic violence not only amounts to a threat to the right to life but also subjects its victims – primarily women but also indirectly frequently children who witness such violence – to inhuman and degrading treatment. Governments who do nothing therefore are not only permitting the abuse of these fundamental rights but conniving in that abuse. It is therefore incumbent on governments, which are overwhelmingly male, to act and to realise that taking steps against domestic violence is not a sign of weakness but of strength. That domestic violence is not simply a women's issue but one that affects the whole of society, and that cultural assertions that justify domestic violence not only misconstrue cultural values but may damage claims to *kastom*.

Taking gender equity forward

Women, in Pacific Islands as elsewhere in the developing world and in parts of the more developed world, face a number of challenges in gaining equality and in achieving the full enjoyment and protection of all their fundamental human rights. Much of this may be due to the continuing patriarchal ordering of society and the ways in which contemporary custom supports this. However, customary institutions and practices are not the only factors which impact on the rights of women in the region. Nor should it be thought that this state of affairs goes unchallenged. It does not. There is a slow but steady empowerment of women as a result of a number of developments.

Particularly important is the contribution of women in civic society, especially in the non-government sector. In part this may be attributable to the marginalisation of women from positions of power and decision-making at the formal level, as well as their more traditional networking through church and social groups. Some of these organisations have emerged as champions of women's rights and are increasingly being identified as important stake-holders and key players in the developing Pacific, as will be evident in Chapter Seven.

Improved provision for and access to education is also empowering young women, with many more now going on to university and further training. Educated and articulate women are being employed in the public and private sector, including in the courts and legal profession and although senior positions are still predominantly staffed by men, there are women magistrates, women judges and many more female lawyers today than ten years ago. There are also more women in the police force with some countries providing specially trained units to deal with cases involving women and children. There are also strong women's voices in civic society, in the public service and in education and health care services. Together these women are making a difference.

There is moreover increasing recognition that some aspects of custom and customary law can be harnessed for the positive good in developing human rights in the region. If custom plays a significant part in the lives of a great number of Pacific Island people then one way of bridging a real or imagined gulf between custom and human rights is to seek common ground. Another approach would be to consider avenues available for negotiating and reaching compromise or change. One of the approaches advocated by the New Zealand Law Commission Report on Custom and Human Rights in the South Pacific is to seek values or aspirations which are found in both custom and human rights instruments. The Report draws attention to traditional values such as respect for all members of the family, clan, or group regardless of age or sex; the emphasis placed on care, sharing and mutual support (2006). It recognises women's rights as being one of the 'hard issues' which needs to be confronted if human rights are to prosper in the region and makes three suggestions as to how progress might be achieved. First, to improve access to justice for women and to enhance their participation in the adjudicative process, especially at the local or community level, by recognising them as experts in their own right and by taking into account women's dispute resolution processes. Second, to allow women to choose the forum in which crimes of violence against them are proceeded with. Third, to ensure that women's construction of custom is taken into account and to reassess customary practices to ensure that the customary value of respect across genders is given effect (New Zealand Law Commission 2006: 102,103).

Certainly enlisting custom on the side of human rights development may be one way to overcome antagonism or antipathy to human rights as the 'introduced other'. Alternatively, providing a greater focus for custom may be perceived as giving it greater significance than it actually has at present, either because it is formally limited to specific matters; or because the Constitution or applicable legislation does not recognise custom when it is in conflict with rights provisions; or because the courts are prepared to take a pro-active role in upholding human rights claims when they conflict with those of custom, as is evident in some of the case-law of the region; or because an increasing number of people do not feel bound to respect custom anymore, for example, urban dwellers and youth. There is also the danger that any elevation of custom will strengthen already entrenched stereotypes or values, such as those used to justify domestic violence.

To accommodate the international perspective of human rights within the customary perspective of fundamental duties and *vice versa* is no easy task. While, the fluidity of custom is recognised (New Zealand Law Commission 2006: paras 4.23 and 4.63) and it has the ability to respond to or absorb new elements, there is a danger that from the perspective of any universal and equitable application of human rights, custom may be perceived as an obstacle to change, modernisation and development. A relative claim to human rights on the basis of respect for custom or traditional values may ignore the fact that these, like any system, can operate unequally. Nor should it be presumed that the situation of all women is the same. High ranking, educated or financially independent women may experience and perceive custom and tradition very differently from less educated, unranked and unpaid women. Those in urban areas with greater freedom of movement, greater access to information and a variety of forums with which to associate, may be very differently placed from rural women with very limited opportunities for association other than the local church, and neighbouring villages, with no access to newspapers, limited radio broadcasting and probably no television. On the other hand, these women may have stronger support networks through kin groups than women who are isolated in towns, especially those women who are widows, unmarried mothers or divorced wives.

In this context it is relevant to consider and weigh the advantages and disadvantages of advocating group rights over individual rights. The conferment and recognition of individual rights enables the individual to claim and exercise his or her rights in a variety of contexts, so for example, gender equality can be claimed in the work place, in school and in the language of the law. Group rights however may benefit individuals who by themselves feel powerless, inarticulate and marginalised. Thus advocacy of 'women's rights' in general may be seen as a positive development even if there are individuals or sub-groups of women who do not support the claims being put forward. The danger with such advocacy is that it may be perceived as an inter-group conflict – women's rights versus men's rights. Moreover, confronted with rapid change and development the restriction of human rights to communal rights may result in the exclusion of certain individuals who have left the group – either permanently or temporarily or who cannot establish sufficient membership of the group. These dichotomies need to be addressed, not just at a national level but also internationally.

Conclusion

There is a danger that in adopting a liberal approach to the diverse cultures and peoples of the world international human rights discourse will be 'soft' on cultures and practices which fail to meet universal standards. In part, this could be due to a fear of accusations of racism or imperialism or a desire to be perceived as 'politically correct' and therefore tolerant of cultural relativism in the belief that this demonstrates respect for difference. There is, however, a distinction between being culturally sensitive and being aware of the dangers of cultural arrogance, and wilfully shutting ones eyes to human rights abuses which are perpetuated in the name of culture, custom or tradition. To do so could amount to 'collaboration with oppressive cultures' (Freeman, 2002). If all human beings are to be afforded dignity then it is important that dominant groups or elites are not given a free rein to ignore the fundamental rights of other groups or individuals and in particular that those most vulnerable or subject to rights abuses do not remain marginalised or dismissed as being of no account within the local context. It is therefore essential to establish how local cultures give expression to respect and dignity. In doing this it is important that the voices of all are heard – not just the politically or socially powerful. Indeed it is usually the case that those who have least rights have the least voice and so continue to be treated without the same respect and dignity which is afforded to those who already enjoy that right (Falk 1992: 48). Respect for any set of cultural norms or for cultural diversity requires that the claimed cultures or values are truly representative of all who are subject to these values or cultures. If this internal cultural dialogue is achieved then there is the possibility of identifying the human rights which are already present and respected within those cultures; identifying those areas where there is quite clearly an unacceptable conflict between customary or cultural practices and fundamental rights; and identifying those gaps where there is no customary practice so that other rights can be incorporated in an acceptable and workable way

Notes

1 Section 422, Cook Islands Act 1915.
2 *In re Vaine Nooroa O Taratangi Pauarii (No2)* [1985] CKCA 1.
3 As above.
4 Section 5(1) Cap 1B.
5 Samoa Constitution 1962, article 3(1).
6 Section 3(2).
7 Section 6.
8 Article V. An example can be found in the National Criminal Code Public Law No. 1–134.
9 Section 37.
10 Section 2.
11 For example, on the Island of Tanna in Vanuatu certain *nakamals* or *nasaras* are prohibited to women. In Samoa women of the village attend their own meetings separate from the men's meeting and those of the younger women and men of the village. In Fiji women may attend village meetings but must position themselves behind the men or in a particular area.
12 Section 36(c) Solomon Islands National Provident Fund Act (Cap 109).
13 Section 15 (1) 'Subject to the provisions of subsections (5), (6) and (9) of this section, no law shall make any provision that is discriminatory either of itself or in its effect.
    (2) Subject to the provisions of subsections (7), (8) and (9) of this section, no person shall be treated in a discriminatory manner by any person acting by virtue of any written law or in the performance of the functions of any public office or any public authority.'
14 Per Williams JA, *The Premier of Guadalcanal v The Attorney General*, Civil Appeal Case No. 3 of 1997.
15 For an overview of the region see the table in Corrin (2000).
16 Section 66(A)(3).
17 Section 422.
18 Sections 4 and 5.
19 Section 11(2)(b).
20 Section 27(2).
21 Section 20(2)(i).
22 Under the Nauru Lands Committee Ordinance 1956–1963.
23 *Timoci Bavadra v Native Land Trust Board*, Civil Action No. 421 of 1986 unreported Rooney J, Supreme Court, 11 February 1986.
24 Section 100.
25 Section 186.

26 The Beattie Commission was a Commission of Inquiry on the Courts, Fiji 1994.
27 Article 93(3). This is as a separate and distinct source of law: *Qualao v Government of the Republic of Vanuatu* [2004] VUSC 133.
28 Article 47(1).
29 *Banga v Waiwo* [1996] VUSC 5. On appeal this sum was reduced but on different grounds.
30 This is illustrated by the reasoning in *Noel v Toto* [1995] VUSC 3.
31 Land Act Cap 132 s 43. Women may enter into leases, but if they are married this is likely to be in her husband's name.
32 Sections 3–4, Civil Law Act Cap 25 as amended by the Civil Law (Amendment) Act No 9 of 2003 section 2 and 3.
33 Para 26, 27.
34 For example, in Cook Islands – section 445 Cook Islands Act 1915 (NZ) and in Niue – section 489 Niue Act 1966 (NZ).
35 For example, in Tonga where succession is to the eldest legitimate male heir and in Kiribati, where under the Lands Code (Cap 61), where a person dies intestate then succession is determined by a hierarchy which favours male heirs over female heirs. Similar discriminatory provision is found in Tuvalu under the Native Lands Ordinance (Cap 22) section 9(ii).
36 For example, in Fiji under the Inheritance (Family Provisions) Act (Cap 61); Papua New Guinea, Part VI, Wills, Probate and Administration Act (Cap 291).
37 As in Vanuatu, where there are a number of small trusts such as the Ifira Trust or the Mele Trust, which manages land for the benefit of a village or clan.
38 For more comprehensive coverage refer to Jalal (1998).
39 For example, in the Preamble of the Convention, Article 4, 5, 10h and 16e.
40 See, for example, Article 12(1).
41 See, for example, sections 77(1) and (2), Crimes Ordinance 1961, Samoa.
42 See also in Samoa *Police v Sipaia* [2007] WSSC 16 and *Police v Toga Pe'e Fuimaono* [2001] WSSC 37.
43 Lack of resources can be significant not only for establishing medical causes, which may cause a mother to kill or reject her newborn baby, but also for establishing paternity in order to claim child maintenance where DNA is unavailable.
44 Opened for signature on December 1962 in New York and came into force on 9 December 1964.
45 Fiji succeeded to membership on 19 July 1971 and Samoa acceded to the Convention on 24 August 1964.
46 See sections 5 and 7, Marriage Act (Cap 54) (Kiribati) and the Marriage Act (Cap 29) (Tuvalu).
47 See, for comment, Luluaki J, 'Sexual Crimes Against and Exploitation of Children and the Law in Papua New Guinea' (2003–4) 29 *Melanesian Law Journal* 35.
48 See, for example, *Singh v Kumar* [2005] FJHC 315 where a decree of nullity was granted on affidavit evidence that the consent to a marriage arranged by the girl's parents had been obtained by duress.
49 The Islanders Marriage Act (Solomon Islands) (Cap 171), section 4, recognises marriage celebrated in accordance with the custom of islanders as a valid marriage. While the Marriage Act (Cap 60) (Vanuatu) recognises a civil marriage which is celebrated before a District Registrar (s. 1 (a)); religious marriage which is celebrated before a minister for celebrating marriages (s. 1 (b)); or custom marriage which is celebrated in accordance with custom (s.1 (c)).
50 *Kere v Timon* [1990] PNGLR 103 per Los J.
51 So, for example, Duckworth 2002) indicates that in Tuvalu it is customary for the expectant mother to return to her own village for the confinement so that

her mother can assist her. Elsewhere it may be aunts or other female collaterals who are called in.

52 *Molu v Molu* [1998] VUSC 15; *In re the Constitution of the Republic of Vanuatu, The infant Vorongo* [1986] VUSC 4; *In Re B* [1983] SILR 223 and *Sasango v Belinga* [1987] SILR 103.

53 Per Woods J.

54 As was done in the case of *Re B* [1983] SILR 223. For comment see Brown (1997).

55 A custom which was confirmed in the case of *Re B* [1983] SILR 223.

56 For further detail on the stages leading up to the law reform see Jalal, 'A woman's quest for equality', *The Fiji Times*, 25 November 2003, http://rrrt.org/page.asp?active_page_id=14 (accessed 20 September 2007).

57 See the address to the Fiji Law Society by Justice Stephen Thackray, July 2006, in which he states 'your new Act adopts the most important provisions of the Australian *Family Law Act* 1975 ... One thing that is very similar to our law is the method Fiji has adopted to deal with division of property following marriage breakdown'. Author's copy.

58 Including new rules for the division of matrimonial property on divorce which incorporate more guidelines for the exercise of court discretion and the possibility of taking into account non-financial contribution.

59 'Vice President Ratu Joni opens new Family Law Court', 2 November 2005, http://www.fiji.gov.fj/publish/printer_5678.shtml (accessed 20 September 2007).

60 Jalal, 'State on Track with new Act', *The Fiji Times*, 27 July 2004, <http://rrrt.org/page.asp?active_page_id=172> (accessed 20 September 2007). See also Jalal's personal mission statement in 'Why Fiji needs a Family Law Bill', *The Fiji Times*, 18 November 2003.

61 See, for example, Graycar (2000).

62 See, for example, Field (2005).

63 Especially from church representatives but also from the more conservative sectors of Fiji society.

64 As ascertained by the author in conversation with Justice Mere Pulea, Judge of the Family Court, Fiji, July 2007.

65 Fiji has a history of political coups, the most recent being in late 2006. The physical location of the family court in the capital Suva, is currently shared with military personnel and vehicles. It is perhaps pertinent to recall the words of C. E. McGuire (1932) 'the easy migration of ideas and the borrowed refinement of legal processes thrive best in the calmer years'.

66 Buadromo 'FWRM Congratulates Government on Establishment of Family Court', Press Release, 2 November 2005, Fiji Government, <http://www.fiji.gov.fj/publish/page_5681.shtml> (accessed 27 July 2007).

67 *Garae v Garae* [2000]VUSC 72. Matrimonial Causes Act (Cap 192) s 5 (a)(iii) (Vanuatu).

68 This phrase was used in the *Garae* case where the judge suggested that 'Usual argument or just slapping on the face in marriage life could be referred to as usual ups and down in marriage life and cannot satisfy the elements of cruelty under section 5 of the Matrimonial Act.'

69 *Brennan v Brennan* [1973] PGSC 7 relying on common law authorities; *Cole v Cole* (1970) 15 F.L.R. 297, at p. 298 and *Dahlitz v. Dahlitz* [1945] S.A.S.R. 47.

70 Constitutional and Law Reform Commission of Papua New Guinea 'Final Report on Domestic Violence', Report No 14, 1992, http://www.paclii.org/cgi-bin/disp.pl/pg/LRC/REP_14.htm?query=domestic%20violence (accessed 1 July 2008).

71 Amnesty International (2006) 'Papua New Guinea: Violence Against Women: Not Inevitable, Never Acceptable', ASA 34/002/2006, http://www.amnesty.

org/en/library/asset/ASA34/002/2006/en/dom-ASA340022006en.html accessed 18 October 2006).

72 The author was a member of this working party with responsibility for matters affecting women and children.

73 Fiji Law Reform Commission: Domestic Violence Review 2005 http://www. lawreform.gov.fj/common/Default.aspx?page=domesticRev (accessed 30 June 2008).

6 Freedom from discrimination

Introduction

The recognition of the rights of women in the face of customs and structures which may frustrate or oppose these is essentially a claim to the universal equality of people. This, as has been indicated in the previous chapter, may require a reappraisal of certain traditions, systems and institutions. However, it is not only the rights of women which face challenges in the region. This chapter considers the experience of human rights where identities are being redrawn and freshly examined as a result of international influences. In particular this chapter looks at discrimination and notions of freedom. All individuals belong to a range of groupings which taken together will make up a person's identity, which in turn will determine the extent of his or her fundamental rights. Although the rights may be expressed as being individual rights in many cases they are derived from group rights and if the individual is part of that group then those rights will apply. As has been indicated previously in this book, the relationship of individual and group is of considerable importance in Pacific societies. In some cases, a person may change status and group membership either at will – for example, by joining a church or leaving a church; by change of circumstance – for example, by ceasing to be a child and becoming a woman; or involuntarily, for example by becoming a refugee or prisoner. There may also be circumstances in which a person's status is changed where individual consent to the change of circumstances may be less important than other considerations, for example, initiation and circumcision for boys or arranged marriage for girls. In some cases, however, a person cannot change identity – or at least not easily, for example, the ethnic group to which he or she belongs, the colour of his or her skin or the place in which he or she was born.

This chapter looks at some of those labels which can determine the human rights regime which is applicable to an individual by virtue of his or her membership of a certain group, and considers the relevant legislation, the case law and comment which relates to this and where the challenges to human rights lies. In particular, this chapter considers those aspects of an individual's identity which may attract discriminatory treatment and possibly – but not always – abuses of human rights, by considering some of the situations and frameworks within Pacific Island countries which facilitate or address inconsistencies in the experience of human rights on the basis of personal attributes, notably sexual orientation, religion and ethnicity.

Protected positions and human rights

Constitutions can entrench certain positions in such a way that either certain rights are denied to certain people or that certain people have rights which are not enjoyed by all. This apparent inequality of rights might be justified on the grounds that if the constitutions of newly independent Pacific Island countries were to work at all then those constitutions had to reflect – at least partially – some of the main features of the society to which they applied. So, in Tonga the rights and powers of the monarch are ensured by a number of provisions in the Constitution,[1] as is the elevated position of nobles.[2] Similarly, in Samoa the elevated status of *matia* title holders is reflected in their sole right to be elected to parliament.[3] In Fiji, only those of Fijian descent can benefit from native land managed by the Native Lands Trust Board on their behalf, and throughout the region only indigenous people can own land held under customary tenure.[4]

In some cases, the significance of traditional structures and social ordering has been strengthened since independence especially where constitutions have been amended to better reflect the values and aspirations of the people they govern. Events in Tuvalu and Fiji illustrate this. In Tuvalu the constitution granted at independence in 1978 was amended in 1986 to give greater effect to Tuvaluan values and customs. The present Constitution is to be interpreted in the light of the Principles set out in its opening paragraphs. These include 'the maintenance of Tuvaluan values, culture and tradition, including the vitality and the sense of identity of island communities and attitudes of co-operation, self-help and unity within and amongst those communities' (Principle 3) and 'the acceptance of Tuvaluan values and culture, and ... respect for them' (Principle 6). Under the Bill of Rights a justification of a breach based on 'national interest' includes therein 'the protection and development of Tuvaluan values and culture' (9(2) (f)). The impact of this on the enjoyment of fundamental rights is evident in the exceptions to a number of rights. For example, although at the outset apparently everyone has equal freedom under the law (section 11(1)) the right to freedom from slavery and forced labour may be lawfully infringed by reference to traditional or cultural obligations (18(2) (b) (vii); as may the right to freedom of expression (section 24(1) (b)) and the right to freedom of assembly and association (section 25(1) (b). Indeed, an entire section, section 29, is dedicated to justifying restrictions of these rights on the grounds of consideration of Tuvaluan values and culture. In particular the right to freedom from discrimination does not include the right to be free from discrimination on the grounds of sex, sexual orientation, age or status (section 27). Even where there is discrimination on a prohibited ground, as has been previously indicated, this may be justified or exempted in a range of situations, including adoption, marriage, divorce, burial or any other matters which are 'in accordance with the personal law, beliefs or customs of any person or group' (section 27(3)(d)). Discrimination is also permitted in the case of land, thereby endorsing the discriminatory provisions found in the Native Lands Ordinance (Cap 22) which includes the Tuvalu Lands Code L.N. 27/62.

While traditional values and cultures are not static, as is recognised in the Tuvalu Constitution, which, having asserted its claim to Tuvaluan values, states

> Nevertheless, the people of Tuvalu recognize that in a changing world, and with changing needs, these principles and values, and the manner and form of their expression (especially in legal and administrative matters), will gradually change, and the Constitution not only must recognize their fundamental importance to the life of Tuvalu but also must not unnecessarily hamper their expression and their development.
>
> (Principle 7)

there is the danger that the claim to relative 'traditional' values may 'trump' or undermine universal ones. This possibility is illustrated by events which took place in Fiji Islands.

In Fiji Islands, following a coup in 1987, the 1970 independence constitution was revoked by the military government.[5] In 1990, a new constitution was brought into effect by decree. Not only did this elevate the status of customary law – which was to be applied by all courts,[6] but it also included a number of measures specifically designed to afford stronger protection to indigenous interests.[7] In particular, it strengthened the position of Fijians by reserving the positions of Prime Minister, any acting Prime Minister and the Chairman of the Police Service Commission to Fijians; and reserved 25 of a total of 34 senator positions for Fijians or Rotumans.[8] The distribution of Parliamentary seats was adjusted to ensure an imbalance in favour of ethnic Fijians and the existing national roll of electors was abolished in order to create the likelihood of a Fijian majority in the House of Representatives. These measures were intentionally discriminatory but were proposed as means of redressing perceived weaknesses of the 1970 Constitution (Corrin *et al.* 1999: 18).

Although the 1990 Constitution was eventually replaced by a new one in 1997, which emerged as a result of a much more inclusive consultative process and was endorsed by Parliament, the Fiji experience, especially subsequent challenges to the 1997 Constitution,[9] illustrates the potential danger that adherence to conservative values and ways can disadvantage certain groups and that a culturally relative approach to human rights can operate to frustrate or oppress the fundamental rights of certain people in certain circumstances. Indeed there is still some concern that the existing constitutional structure in Fiji remains ethnically biased (Mori 2006).

Discrimination

First, it is necessary to be clear about what is meant by discrimination in the provisions and protections of rights. While there may be a universal principle that all people have the right to certain basic liberties and rights, it is clearly not the case that all people are equally able to take advantage of these rights and liberties or that all of these are absolute. In many cases, a person's own ability, age or comprehension may limit or restrict the exercise of a right or a liberty. For example, a child may not be able to express a view on religious belief and his or her parents may protect the child from total freedom of movement or association. In other cases, circumstances will justifiably impinge on the enjoyment of certain rights, for example, a prisoner does not have freedom of movement or association, but there may be a range of other rights that prisoners should be entitled to enjoy such as freedom of religion, freedom from torture and inhuman and degrading treatment and a right to life. It has to be recognised therefore that the exercise of certain liberties and rights take place on an uneven playing field. Nevertheless, because the state and its agents have a duty to secure these rights and liberties to all its citizens, and in most cases to non-citizens in the territory which the state has control over, it should in principle and as a starting point afford equal rights to all, regardless of certain individual characteristics and should only derogate from that equality of treatment on clearly specified grounds which also apply equally to all persons in the same circumstances, regardless of their individual characteristics. Discrimination is where laws and practices are in place, which treat people differently on the grounds of characteristics which they have and which they may not be able to change, such as race, colour, disability or sex, or which they have acquired, such as marital status. That discrimination can be direct, as for example where only men are eligible for land under the scheme of tax and town allotments – as in Tonga; or indirect, where the effect of unequal treatment leads to inequalities of opportunity and experience, for example, a franchise based on property holding, wealth or rank, or preferences for educating boys rather than girls.

Discrimination and its consequences are not a phenomenon limited to the South Pacific region and throughout history there have been examples of human rights abuses caused by discrimination based on race, language, religion, sex, disability and sexual orientation. In line with the international human rights movement as well as national initiatives – sometimes achieved through the ballot box and sometimes by civil uprising – many of these forms of discrimination have been addressed, at least in principle, some only fairly recently, for example, discrimination against indigenous minorities, discrimination against people with disability and discrimination based on ageist attitudes. The consequences of discrimination however have long-term effects and take decades to address and eradicate. Removing discrimination is not simply a matter of making legal provision. Discrimination is often deeply rooted in attitudes, language, institutions and normative frameworks.

Pacific Island countries are party to the various international shifts in attitudes towards discrimination but also have their own particular challenges to address. The starting point is the provision found in most of the constitutions of the region, supported by international human rights instruments to which countries are signatory, such as CEDAW. The grounds on which discrimination is unlawful are not exactly the same in every country although there are many similarities, as indicated by Table 6.1.

Discrimination by itself may not be unlawful unless it results in some disadvantage, restriction or disability. It is therefore often permitted to discriminate or to offer unequal treatment under a law or by way of administrative action if the consequence is a benefit. Indeed some of the constitutions in the region provide for this 'positive' or 'affirmative' discrimination. For example, in Vanuatu it is stated that

> The Republic of Vanuatu recognises, that, subject to any restrictions imposed by law on non-citizens, all persons are entitled to the following fundamental rights and freedoms of the individual without discrimination on the grounds of race, place of origin, religious or traditional beliefs, political opinions, language or sex but subject to respect for the rights and freedoms of others and to the legitimate public interest in defence, safety, public order, welfare and health.
>
> (Article 5(1))

However, the Constitution also indicates that ' no law shall be inconsistent with this sub-paragraph (providing for equal treatment under the law) insofar as it makes provision for the special benefit, welfare, protection or advancement of females, children and young persons, members of underprivileged groups or inhabitants of less developed areas'.[10] Similarly, in Papua New Guinea laws may be made which discriminate in favour of children and those with disabilities or the development of disadvantaged or underdeveloped groups or areas.[11]

Non-discrimination is therefore premised on the idea that there should be equality of respect and treatment across or in spite of differences, so that the consequences of those differences are minimalised as far as possible, and that 'difference should not be the basis for exclusion, marginalisation, stigma and punishment' (*The National Coalition for Gay and Lesbian Equality and the South African Human Rights Commission v The Minister for Justice, The Minister of Safety and Security and the Attorney General of The Witwatersrand* [1998] (12) PCLR 1517, para. 132).

Table 6.1 Grounds on which discrimination is prohibited

Country	Sex	Sexual orientation	Age	Religion or non-observance	Colour or ethnicity	Marital or other status
Cook Islands	Yes	No	No	Yes	Colour, race, national origin	No
Federated States of Micronesia	Yes	No	No	No	National Origin, race	Ancestry, language or social status
Fiji	Yes (gender)	Yes	Yes	Yes	Yes, including place of origin	Birth, primary language, economic status, disability
Kiribati	Yes	No	No	Yes	Yes, including place of origin	Political opinions
Marshall Islands	Yes (gender)	No	No	Yes	Yes, including national or social origin and place of birth	Family status or descent, political or other opinion
Nauru	Yes	No	No	Yes	Yes	Political opinions
Niue[a]	NA	NA	NA	NA	NA	NA
Palau	Yes	No	No	Yes	Yes	Language, social status or clan affiliation
Papua New Guinea						
Pitcairn Samoa	Yes	No	No	Yes	No, unless included under social origin	Descent, language, political or other opinion, social origin, place of birth, family status
Solomon Islands	Yes	No	No	Yes	Yes, including place of origin	Political opinions
Tonga	No	No	No	Yes	No	Same law for all classes – chiefs and commoners, non-Tongans and Tongans
Tokelau[b]	NA	NA	NA	NA	NA	NA
Tuvalu	Yes	No	No	Yes	Yes including place of origin	Political opinions
Vanuatu	Yes	No	No	Yes including traditional beliefs	Yes including place of origin	Political opinions, language

a. Niue has no bill of rights.

Invariably, the right to equality of treatment and equality of rights can be curtailed or circumscribed on a number of grounds. Often these are vague. For example, in Solomon Islands the protection from discrimination in the Constitution is 'subject to such limitations ... designed to ensure that the enjoyment of the said rights and freedoms by an individual does not prejudice the rights and freedoms of others or the public interest'.[12] This suggests that there are two different but often overlapping competing claims: those of other individuals and those of the state representing the public interest. The extent to which these are distinct will vary depending on where the power lies to determine what is in the public interest, and whether that public interest is being claimed at a national level, for example, in the case of national emergency, or a local level, for example at the village or community level. Here, as in other rights areas, the experience of rights will depend on who wields power, what their agenda is, and whether those whose rights are being oppressed have a voice or grievance procedure available to them. Here too, the question of horizontal and vertical application of rights may be relevant, as is the issue of what laws apply, especially as discriminatory treatment may be grounded not in laws but in moral or cultural attitudes, and practiced not by representatives of the state but by private individuals.[13]

These dilemmas can be best understood by considering some specific areas in which discrimination occurs in Pacific Island countries.

Sexual and gender orientation

Discrimination on the grounds of sex, particularly with disadvantages to women, is, as has been intimated in the previous chapter, pervasive throughout the region. Sometimes this is entrenched in legislation, for example, the discriminatory land rights of men and women in Tonga, or the rules that determine custody of male children in Tuvalu, or the rules that determine inheritance in Kiribati. Often it is entrenched in attitudes such as the restrictions of movement and association imposed on girls in some rural areas, the priority given to boys in access to education, or the acceptance that husbands have a right to chastise their wives. Sometimes discriminatory and patriarchal attitudes are reflected in the language of the law and the way in which it is administered. As has been indicated in the previous chapter, women suffer a number of disadvantages, but there is also progress and change occurring in a most Pacific Island countries which seek to address and ameliorate the adverse effects of discrimination based on sex. However, other forms of discrimination remain.

Homosexuality

Apart from Fiji, none of the countries of the region prohibit discrimination on the grounds of sexual orientation. This means that homosexuals are vulnerable to discrimination and indeed the criminalisation of homosexuality continues to apply throughout the region. Even in Fiji homosexuals run the risk of prosecution, as illustrated by the case of *Nadan v The State* [2005] FJHC 1; *McCoskar v the State* [2005] FJHC 500. The criminal law section 175(a) and (c) and section 177 of the Fijian Penal Code (Cap 17) prohibit homosexual acts even if they take place in private between consenting adults – as was the case here. Nadan and McCoskar were charged with offences under these provisions. On appeal against conviction and sentence of two years' imprisonment it was argued that the law breached fundamental rights of rights of privacy, equality and freedom from degrading treatment provided for in the 1997 Constitution, as well as public international law which had to be taken into account in interpreting the Constitution and evaluating the compliance of national laws with the constitution.[14] The State argued that prosecution was warranted on the grounds of public interest and morality, taking into account the Christian preamble to the Constitution and the conservative and religious nature of Fijian society, and that the criminalisation of such conduct was proportional to the offence it caused. The prosecution also argued that the criminal law was gender neutral and therefore non-discriminatory. The court accepted this interpretation of the law as expressed in section 175, but found that its application was discriminatory in so far as no cases involving female homosexuality (lesbianism) had been brought to the attention of the Fiji courts, so that for all practical purposes it was a law against homosexuals. Section 177 on the other hand was clearly discriminatory insofar as it could only apply to males because of the way it was worded. The court held that the Constitution proceeds on the basis that all laws made to prior to it are consistent with it but if they are found not to be then the Constitution must prevail (Article 195 and Article 2(2)). To the extent that they are inconsistent with the Constitution they are invalid, taking into account not only Fiji's own Constitution but also Fiji's commitments under public international law including specifically section 17 of the ICCPR.[15]

In this case, the court had to weigh the fundamental rights provisions of the Constitution and principles of international treaties with the considerations of the moral values of Fijians. This is a dilemma which has had to be faced by courts in many jurisdictions of the world in addressing the rights of homosexuals, and the decision refers to difficult cases faced in South Africa, Tasmania and Northern Ireland among others. In the end, the Court of Appeal found the law to be inconsistent with the fundamental rights provisions and consequently invalid. In reaching its conclusion the court recognised that:

> while members of the public who regard homosexuality as amoral may be shocked, offended or disturbed by private homosexual acts, this cannot on its own validate unconstitutional law. The present case concerns the most intimate aspect of private life. Accordingly, there

must exist particularly serious reasons before the State or community can interfere with an individual's right to privacy.

Limitations may, therefore, validly restrict such rights provided they are prescribed by law, and reasonable and justifiable in a free and democratic society. Here, however Winter J held that

> this right to privacy is so important in an open and democratic society that the morals argument cannot be allowed to trump the Constitutional invalidity. Criminalizing private consensual adult sex acts against the course of nature and sexual intimacy between consenting adult males is not a proportionate or necessary limitation.

The decision concludes with a wise, but perhaps optimistic observation:

> What the Constitution requires is that the Law acknowledges difference, affirms dignity and allows equal respect to every citizen as they are. The acceptance of difference celebrates diversity. The affirmation of individual dignity offers respect to the whole of society. The promotion of equality can be a source of interactive vitality. The State that embraces difference, dignity and equality does not encourage citizens without a sense of good or evil but rather creates a strong society built on tolerant relationships with a healthy regard for the rule of law.
> A country so founded will put sexual expression in private relationships into its proper perspective and allow citizens to define their own good moral sensibilities leaving the law to its necessary duties of keeping sexual expression in check by protecting the vulnerable and penalizing the predator.

The law, however, does not change people's attitudes – at least not overnight. It is widely recognised that homophobia in the Pacific is an obstacle to the type of tolerance advocated above (McIntosh 1999; Jowitt 2005; George 2007). After the decision in the *McCosker* and *Nadan* cases an increase in attacks on gays was reported,[16] and Fiji Methodist clergy called for the Constitution to be amended.[17] Although overt homophobia may be suppressed, press coverage highlights anti-homosexual attitudes.[18] These attitudes are not solely limited to religious spokespersons. Following this Fiji case the *Fiji Times* reported that 'Attorney-General Qoriniasi Bale disagrees with the High Court's interpretation of the Constitution's sexual orientation clause which it defined when it ruled in the Thomas McCosker case last week.'[19] It was also reported that following the original conviction of Nadan and McCoskar the Fiji Director of Public Prosecutions, Josaia Naigulevu, had sent an email calling on his church friends to take 'a stand for righteousness – and boldly declare and uphold God's precepts, values and principles against homosexuality.'[20] Elsewhere, in Papua New Guinea the Deputy Prime Minister, who was also Minister for Trade and Industry, was reported as saying that the gay and feminist lobby had an agenda 'to create division and hatred between the sexes'.[21]

Anti-homosexual attitudes have repercussions beyond the immediate islands of the region. In New Zealand Tongans have opposed the appointment of gay clergy,[22] and in France an illegal immigrant from Fiji successfully resisted deportation on the grounds that as a homosexual he would face abuse and possible imprisonment.[23]

Clearly this is a topic which gives rise to conflicting views. Sometimes these are informed by strong religious convictions and sometimes by ignorance. The decision in Fiji did not legalise homosexuality, nor did it remove the power of the courts to impose fairly severe punishments in cases of homosexual assault, especially on children and non-consenting adults. There are also, it should be pointed out, advocates of greater tolerance. For example, the non-government group Women's Action for Change (WAC) has spoken out against homophobia in Fiji, urging people to 'to remain true to the democratic principles that separate church and State' and pointing out that

> If we attack any minorities on religious principles, we are getting dangerously close to fundamentalist statehood and this has implications for all of us in Fiji who believe in democracy, human rights and rule of law.[24]

While attitudes towards homosexuality appear to be increasingly being voiced, those towards transgender groups found in the Pacific region seem to be rather more muted and perhaps more ambivalent. Yet these groups too experience forms of discrimination.

Trans-gender people in the Pacific

Throughout the South Pacific region, but particularly in Polynesian countries, there are people, who, while of one sex, might regard themselves or be regarded as being of the opposite gender. Although the phenomenon is not unknown among women, these people are predominantly of the male sex. These are the *fa'afafine* of Samoa,[25] the *fakaleiti* of Tonga,[26] the *pinapinaaine* of Tuvalu and Kiribati, and the *vakasalewalewa* of Fiji (Besnier 1994; Mageo 1992; Schmidt 2003).[27] These men, who may or may not be cross-dressers, and may or may not be homosexual, perform roles in both genders and across genders. They contribute to society in many ways, are often valued members of communities and churches and by and large are accepted for what they are by their families, their friends and their colleagues.[28] Nevertheless, they may be the victims of discrimination because the laws which exist have differential consequences for them compared to others.

At the most fundamental level laws tend to be premised on a clear binary divide: people are male or female, men or women. There is little scope within the law to provide for groups of people who are gender-liminal, bi-gendered or trans-gendered. More specifically there are laws which are directed at proscribing certain activities based on a person's sex which can have a discriminatory impact on *fa'afafine, fakaleiti* or any of the other groups indicated above. For example, in Samoa, the Crimes Ordinance 1962, section 58N makes it an offence for a male person to have 'on or about his person any article intended by him to represent that he is a female or in any other way is impersonating or representing himself to be a female'. The offence must be committed in a public place and there must be the intention to deceive another person as to his 'true sex'. The purpose of the section was to criminalise transvestite prostitution, and may have been incorporated as a result of foreigners being tricked into having sex with attractive Samoan girls, who turned out to be boys.[29] In Tonga, a similar provision is found in section 81(5) which was added to the Criminal Offences Act (Cap 18) in 1978. As elsewhere in the region, homosexual acts are also criminalised.[30] Although prosecution under the cross-dressing criminal provisions appears to be rare, the retention of these in the criminal law under offences connected with prostitution not only imply that this is the primary purpose of cross-dressing but also potentially have adverse consequences for trans-gender people in Samoa and Tonga (Farran and Su'a 2005). At the very least these provisions could be scrapped as offences relating to prostitution are already sufficiently broadly framed.

It may also be the case that increased publicity surrounding homosexuality and conservative reaction to this may have adverse consequences for *fa'afafine* and *fakaleiti*, who are not a recent product of western sexual influences but have a long history within the region (James 1994; Schmidt 2001). This possibility is demonstrated by a comment made in 1996 by a Pentecostal church leader in Samoa:

> We must take a firm stand on this issue (*fa'afafine* as cross dressers and homosexuals) now or we've got big problems on our hands. It's hard enough trying to keep our people from these negative influences ... the bible condemns homosexuality, we need good role models and they (*fa'afafine*) don't fit the bill.
>
> (Peteru 1996: 43)

Categorising all Pacific trans-gender people as homosexual would be to seriously underestimate the complexity of their sexuality and could result in a failure to appreciate that they too can be victims of homosexual assault, domestic violence and gendered abuse (Besnier 1994: 299–302; Poasa 1992). Aligning trans-gendered Pacific islanders with homosexuals also creates obstacles to appreciating that these individuals, as much as any others, deserve respect for their private and family life and the right to enter into voluntary, consensual intimate relationships. Unlike developments taking place in other parts of the world, trans-gender Pacific islanders do not have the opportunity to lawfully enter into relationships with partners of their choice, either by entering into recognised same sex partnerships, or *de facto* relationships, or by having their choice of gender recognised (Farran 2004b). Indeed, many may lead double lives as married men who are also *fa'afafine* or *fakaleiti*. These people have yet to benefit from the liberalisation of family laws or gender recognition laws which have taken place elsewhere, including in Australia and New Zealand.[31] Given the presence of Pacific Island people in these locations, especially in New Zealand but also in the United States of America, and the pervasiveness of global media, it might be wondered how long Pacific Islands can resist addressing these issues. On the other hand, developments abroad could equally trigger a conservative backlash supported by claims to customary values, religion and the traditional ordering of society.

Although Pacific trans-gender people live in a form of legal limbo – because they are not specifically acknowledged, and may be adversely affected by laws which are not primarily directed at them but have a discriminatory impact on them, they are in some respects better provided for than homosexuals, because, unlike other minority groups, they are visible in the public domain. *Fa'afafine* and *fakaleiti* enjoy freedom of association and movement and form active social and sports groups. Their pageants and beauty contests in New Zealand, Tonga and Samoa are popular events, which attract considerable publicity and their unique identity is represented in Pacific Arts Festivals, as well as more recently in film and theatre.[32] At the same time, however, there is the danger that this publicity may exoticise *fa'afafine, fakaleiti* or their counterparts elsewhere in the Pacific and that the voyeur's fascination could obscure or ignore the complexities of their lives and the human rights abuses which they may suffer.

Religion

It has been stated that 'In the Pacific the primacy of religion in all aspects of life is the dominant feature, irrespective of whether it is our traditional religion or Christianity or a mix of both' (Henare 1998: 25). The importance of the influence of religious attitudes is evident in the examples above. Religious intolerance and religious persecution may also give rise to other forms of human rights abuses, not only historically but contemporaneously. The inclusion of rights to freedom of religion within the Constitutions of Pacific Island countries is therefore an important touchstone on which to build religious tolerance in the region. It may also, however, provide the foundation for intolerance, prejudice and repression if used by extremists or ultra-conservatives, or if religious tolerance is perceived as threatening the *status quo*.

Religion, especially Christianity, has played and continues to play an important role in the Pacific region (Paterson 2003). In many cases it was one of the earliest manifestations of western contact – along with traders and beachcombers – and from the start religion and politics interacted, with missionaries recognising that the support and conversion of chiefs and traditional leaders was essential for the success of their missions. Indeed, in many instances the colonial administrators relied on the early overtures of missionaries to pave the way for colonial administration or used missionaries to broker colonial policies. Early missionaries also acquired considerable tracts of land in the region.[33] In some countries this land-holding dimension of the various established churches has been placed on a statutory footing – for example, in Papua New Guinea, where a raft of legislation has been passed vesting church property in property trusts. Elsewhere unpicking early grants of land to churches and mission settlements has been a cause of considerable litigation.[34]

This religious influence continued in the years leading to independence, informing, in a number of countries, the drafting of the national constitution. Although some of the constitutions of the region make no reference to God or religion in their opening preambles,[35] the overwhelming majority call on God to variously bless, witness, guide or generally oversee the transition to independence, the operation of the constitution and the running of the country. For example, the Fiji Constitution opens with the words 'We, the people of the Fiji Islands, seeking the blessing of God who has always watched over these islands' while the people of Kiribati acknowledge 'God as the almighty Father in whom we put our trust' and those of Nauru 'acknowledge God as the almighty and everlasting Lord and the giver of all good things'.

There is, moreover, direct reference to Christianity in the preambles to the constitutions of Fiji, Papua New Guinea, Samoa, Tuvalu and Vanuatu. This does not necessarily mean that Christianity is the official religion of the state. Indeed in Fiji – and only Fiji – there is constitutional recognition of 'other faiths' in the context of 'forbears of subsequent settlers,'[36] but elsewhere there is no such recognition in the opening words of the Constitutions. It would be true therefore to state that the Pacific Island states are predominantly Christian states.

What is interesting about these preambles is the close association between monotheism and Christianity with tradition and historic values. For example, the Vanuatu Constitution opens with the words (*inter alia*) 'We the people of Vanuatu ... (H)ereby proclaim the establishment of the united and free Republic of Vanuatu founded on traditional Melanesian values, faith in God, and Christian principles ...'; while that of Samoa states '(W)hereas the Leaders of Western Samoa have declared that Western Samoa should be an Independent State based on Christian principles and Samoan custom and tradition'; and that of Kiribati opens with the words 'acknowledging God as the Almighty Father in whom we put our trust, and with faith in the enduring value of our traditions and heritage ...' and closes with 'we shall continue to cherish and uphold the customs and traditions of Kiribati'. The cynic might think that these statements are contradictory. How can the pre-Christian, heathen past be cherished and maintained alongside post-contact, monotheistic Christian principles? The answer may lie in the modification of custom by Christianity – so that today the two may be claimed in the same breath, and the accommodation of custom by Christianity. For freedom of religion this dualism is significant for two reasons; first, it permits the survival – albeit of a small percentage – of traditional systems of beliefs and spiritual observation; second, it brings into sharp relief the question of what happens when Christian principles or values collide with customary ones?

Table 6.2 indicates the major religious beliefs of the region.

In the light of the strong Christian sentiments expressed in many of the Constitutions it might be wondered if Pacific Island States are indeed

Table 6.2 The contemporary religious picture

Country	Major religions	Constitutional provisions
Cook Islands	Christian (Cook Islands Christian Church)	Article 64(1)(d)
Fiji	Christian 52%	Section 35(1)
	Methodist 37%	
	Roman Catholic 9%	
	Hindu 38%	
	Muslim 8%	
	Other 2%	
Federated States of Micronesia	Roman Catholic 50%	Article IV Section 2
	Protestant 47%	
Kiribati	Roman Catholic 52%	Section 11
	Protestant (Congregational) 40%	
	Other (Seventh Day Adventist, Muslim, Baha'i, Latter Day Saints and Church of God)	
Marshall Islands	Christian (mostly Protestant)	Section 1
Nauru	Protestant 67%	Section 11
	Roman Catholic 33%	
Niue	Ekalesia Niue 75%[a]	
	Latter Day Saints 10%	
	Roman Catholic, Jehovah's witnesses, Seventh Day Adventist 15%	
Palau	Roman Catholic 41.6%	Section 1
	Protestant 23.3%	
	Modekngei 8.8%[b]	
	Seventh Day Adventist 5.3%	
	Jehovah's Witness 0.9%	
	Latter Day Saints 0.6%	
	Other 3.1%	

Continued

Table 6.2 Cont'd

Country	Major religions	Constitutional provisions
Papua New Guinea	Roman Catholic 22% Lutheran 16% Presbyterian/ 　Methodist/London 　Missionary Society 8% Anglican 5% Evangelical Alliance 4% Seventh Day Adventist 1% Other Protestant 10% Indigenous beliefs 34%	
Pitcairn Islands		
Samoa	Christian 99.7%[c]	Section 11
Solomon Islands	Anglican 45% Roman Catholic 18% United 　(Methodist/Presbyterian) 　12% Baptist 9% Seventh Day Adventist 7% Other Protestant 5% Indigenous beliefs 4%	Section 11
Tonga	Christian (primarily the Free 　Wesleyan Church)	Article 5
Tokelau	Congregational Christian 　Church 70% Roman Catholic 28% Other 2%	Cross reference to the 　Universal Declaration of 　Human Rights and the 　International Covenant on 　Civil and Political Rights
Tuvalu	Church of Tuvalu 　(Congregationalist) 97% Seventh Day Adventist 1.4% Baha'i 1% Other 0.6%	Section 11(e) and section 23
Vanuatu	Presbyterian 36.7% Anglican 15% Roman Catholic 　15%Indigenous Beliefs 7.6% Seventh Day Adventist 6.2% Church of Christ 3.8% Other 15.7%[d]	Section 5(f)

Source: These statistics are taken from the World Factbook unless otherwise indicated, https://www.cia.gov/library/publications/the-world-factbook/

a. This is a Protestant church closely related to the London Missionary Society.
b. Indigenous to Palau.
c. This includes London Missionary society – about half the population; Congregational, Roman Catholic, Methodist, Latter Day Saints and Seventh Day Adventist.
d. This includes Baha'i, Muslim and Jon Frum Cargo Cult.

secular or not. A good example is Fiji where the Constitution states quite clearly 'Although religion and the State are separate, the people of the Fiji Islands acknowledge that worship and reverence of God are the source of good government and leadership' (section 5, Act No 13, 1997).

While church and state are officially separate in the region, in practice religion and politics may be closely related. This manifests itself in a number of ways. Sometimes these are extreme. For example, in 1987, following the coup in Fiji, religion and politics became inseparable. Writing in 2000 Tessa MacKenzie, the Honorary Secretary to the Council Interfaith Search Fiji, stated

> When the Fijian nationalist-led Coup d'Etat ruptured what had appeared to be a harmonious multi-cultural, multi-religious nation, which boasted that it was 'the way the world should be', underlying resentments and prejudices leapt out as from a Pandora's Box. Politics and religion became inextricably mixed as the new governing regime justified itself as acting according to God's will and direction, and sought to impose Christianity with the expressed intention of making Fiji a Christian state. For some months a Decree forbade any activity on Sunday which was not strictly religious. There were sporadic outbreaks of anti-Hindu activities with desecration and even destruction of Hindu temples and idols, and religious books by Christians. Fortunately the last ten years has seen efforts to restore calm and re-create a harmonious society, including the adoption of a new Constitution suitable for a multi-ethnic country.
>
> (MacKenzie 2000)

Less extreme is the relationship of religion and politics on a daily level. This manifests itself in a number of ways. First, there are political parties which are closely aligned with the church, for example the Christian Democratic Party in Papua New Guinea and Samoa, and the merged Fiji Democratic Party, which incorporated the former Christian Democratic Alliance as well as a number of other parties. Second, respect and status may depend on a person's standing in the church, measured for example by commitment to church activities, contributions to church funds, or the assumption of lay roles. It is not at all unusual to find village elders holding positions of influence in the local church, nor is it unusual to find church leaders holding positions of status equivalent to chiefs (Duckworth 2002; Kepa 1998: 105). While in some countries of the region a person may not be a candidate for election to Parliament in a number of circumstances, being a priest or pastor is not usually one of these,[37] consequently it is not unusual to find church gatherings the focus of political lobbying, as demonstrated in the case of opposition to any liberalisation of laws affecting homosexuality. At the level of local politics, and even in the context of national elections therefore, churches can have a significant influence. Third, church groups may also be important influences in either lobbying for or opposing legal change. For example, in Tonga leading church figures have been instrumental in founding and continuing the work of the Human Rights and Democracy Movement and in Fiji the Fijian Ecumenical Centre for Research, Education and Advocacy engages with a number of projects relating to human rights, development and empowerment.

It should also be borne in mind that the churches of the Pacific region are members of wider regional and global organisations such as the Pacific Ecumenical Regional Group and the World Council of Churches. These organisations offer networks across the Pacific with secular and non-secular associations, and provide programmes of action on important issues such as environment, sustainable development, poverty, women, youth and violence. Often they offer alternatives to government programmes or aid-funded initiatives. For example, in 2002 Pacific churches met in Fiji and produced an alternative approach to economic globalisation.[38]

Rights provisions for religion

Besides being a constitutional ground on which prohibited discrimination is based,[39] the right to observe a religion exists as a separate right in many of the Constitutions. This may be expressed as a right to: 'freedom of thought, conscience, and religion',[40] 'freedom of conscience and worship,'[41] 'freedom of belief',[42] or 'freedom of worship'.[43] Whatever the terminology, this freedom includes the right to give expression to beliefs in a variety of forms, to assemble with others to do so, and to live according to those beliefs.

Some Constitutions go much further though. For example, the law in the Federated States of Micronesia states that 'No law may be passed respecting an establishment of religion or impairing the free exercise of religion, except that assistance may be provided to parochial schools for non-religious purposes' (Article 1V Section 2). Similarly, in Palau the Constitution states that 'The government shall not recognise or establish a national religion, but may provide assistance to private or parochial schools on a fair and equitable basis for nonreligious purposes'.[44]

In Fiji, where many Indo-Fijians are not Christian, besides conferring the right to 'freedom of conscience, religion and belief' and the right to manifest that religion or belief in 'worship, observance, practice or teaching' the Constitution also extends the right to 'religious communities or denominations to provide religious instruction as part of any education provided by them, whether or not they are in receipt of any financial assistance from the State'.[45] Freedom of religion is also taken to include the right to change religion or to have no religion at all. There are also usually safeguards in place to protect compulsory religious observance for children of religions other than their own in schools and places of education.[46]

Not all Pacific Island countries expressly provide for freedom of religion or list it as one of the grounds where it is prohibited to discriminate. For example, the Constitutions of Vanuatu, Tonga and Cook Island make no express provisions for freedom of religion. Some such as Kiribati provide that there should be no discrimination on account of 'creed',[47] and include religion under freedom of conscience, which includes 'freedom of thought and of religion, freedom to change his religion or belief, and freedom, either alone or in community with others, and both in public and in private, to manifest and propagate his religion or belief in worship, teaching, practice and observance' (section 11). In Palau by contrast this freedom includes philosophical beliefs, while in Papua New Guinea it is expressly stated that 'religion includes a reference to the traditional religious beliefs and customs of the peoples of Papua New Guinea'.[48]

The issue of freedom of thought, conscience, belief or religion rarely presents a problem as an internalised process. The problem tends to come when these freedoms are outwardly manifested. In liberal societies, the outward manifestation of beliefs is generally tolerated provided such manifestations do not harm any one or interfere with the rights of others to hold different beliefs or follow different religions. However, this is not an absolute right and it is usual to find permitted grounds for restricting the exercise of such freedoms. Usually these are worded very generally. So, for example, the freedoms established in Fiji may be subject to limitations prescribed by law which are necessary 'to protect ... the rights or freedoms of other persons or ... public safety, public order, public morality or public health: or ... to prevent a public nuisance' (section 35(4)). In Papua New Guinea the exercise of any freedom is subject to consideration of 'the rights and freedoms of others' and must not be prohibited by law.[49] However, the right to freedom of conscience, thought and religion is a qualified right and may be limited or restricted by any of the considerations which apply to qualified rights listed in section 38 of the Papua New Guinea Constitution. This provides for laws to be made which restrict or regulate the exercise of a right or freedom on the grounds that the public interest makes this necessary, for example because of considerations of defence, public safety, order, welfare or health, taking into account the general goals and principles of the Constitution.

Provided these restrictions are 'prescribed by law' and are 'necessary' then the balance between rights and freedoms should be maintained. There are however two issues which can arise. First, whether the measures taken are really necessary. In other words are they proportionate to the anticipated or actual harm? Second, are the measures taken lawful? In other words do those who take such measures have the authority to do so? Some of the cases in the region illustrate the problem.

In Samoa there have been a number of cases where the power of the village authority to restrict the number of churches in a village has been challenged. The village authority, which is a council predominated by *matai*, has extensive powers both in custom and under the Village Fono Act 1990. Effectively local law and order is devolved to this authority. Its powers may be reinforced by recourse to the Lands and Titles Court, established under the Land and Titles Act 1981, which has jurisdiction to determine matters concerning titles and customary land. The combined effect of these two authorities may be to restrict freedom of religion and worship. This was the situation in the case of *Sefo v Attorney-General* [2000] WSSC 18, in which the court was asked to consider:

> whether the Alii and Faipule (village authorities) ... or the Land and Titles Court have the power and/or authority to restrict freedom of worship and/or religious instruction or activity upon customary village lands under their authority, and whether they have jurisdiction and/or authority to prevent or restrict a particular religion or religious instruction within their village, and whether they have jurisdiction to prevent or restrict religious instruction, worship, and/or belief being conducted upon freehold lands within their village.

The answer was no. Indeed it has been held in *Su'a Rimoni Ah Chong v Mulitalo Siafausa Vui*, an unreported decision dated 16th August 2006:[50]

> the power of the village and matai is important and ought to be respected by this court. But their power is not greater than the power of the Constitution, the Legislative Assembly, the Supreme Court of Samoa or the rule of law. The matai must understand and respect this statement. In turn this court ought to respect their title. But it is the law which governs us all.

Addressing the question of whether it was a reasonable or necessary restriction on the right to freedom of religion to restrict the number of permitted churches to three in the village, the court held that

> Limiting the number of churches in a village is neither a restriction imposed by existing law nor does it impose 'reasonable' restrictions on the exercise of the right to freedom of religion ... It is a form of religious intolerance or discrimination on the ground of religion.

Defeated on this front, village councils may still interfere with religious freedom by using banishment orders to either exclude villagers on other grounds, thus preventing them from attending their usual place of worship,[51] or to punish them for not attending church,[52] or to curtail the activities of those seeking to establish churches or attract new converts.[53] The power to impose orders of banishment is claimed to emanate from custom and usage and therefore to be included within the ambit of powers conferred on the village council by the Village Fono Act 1990.

The justification of such banishment is to preserve the peace and harmony of a village and to prevent matters escalating into violence or property damage.[54] Its use may be justified in the public interest or on the grounds of preserving law and order. The Land and Titles Court also has the power to make a banishment order pursuant to the interpretation of sections 34 and 37 of the Land and Titles Act 1981, given in the case of *Taamale v Attorney General* [1995] WSCA 12 – although there is no express reference to the power to banish in the Act. However, it has been held that the scope of the village *Fono*'s powers of punishment, as set out in the Village Fono Act, do not include banishment. Despite this, the punishment continues to be used,[55] and village councils continue to exert considerable power over the inhabitants of the village. Because central government has effectively devolved the regulation of local law and order, dispute settlement and the allocation and management of resources to these councils, it can be argued that the *fono* are agents of the state and ought to be brought within the constitutional framework, including that of human rights. However, to date, it would seem that no attempts have been made to revise the Village Fono Act in order to ensure that it complies with the rights obligations of the state and that this task is being left to the courts.

Elsewhere, however, similar problems are encountered. In Tuvalu in the case of *Teonea v Kaupule* [2005] TVHC 2, the applicant, a church pastor of the Brethren Church, held bible classes on the island of Nanumaga. Prior to his arrival, the local council, the Nanumaga *Falekaupule*, had resolved that no new religions other than the Ekalesia Kelisiano Tuvalu (EKT) should be allowed on the island. Like the Samoan *fono*, the *Falekaupule* exercises its powers under traditional authority and statutory authority in the form of the Falekaupule Act 1997. The justification for this resolution was to preserve the 'the spirit of togetherness of the community as a whole', although it was admitted that there were already four different religions on the island. Refusing to abide by the ruling of the *Falekaupule* the applicant was effectively driven off the island following incidents of stoning and threats of violence. He challenged the right of the *Falekaupule* to make such a ruling in contravention of the fundamental rights of freedom of belief, expression, assembly and association, and the right not to be discriminated against on the ground of religious belief. The breaches of these rights were not in fact denied, but their breach was claimed to be justified by the need to protect the rights and freedoms of others, including the right to impose restrictions on rights the exercise of which may be divisive, unsettling or offensive to the people, and to protect Tuvaluan values or culture as set out in sections 23–25 and 29 of the Constitution. The court referred to the jurisprudence of the region, noting

Consideration of cases from other jurisdictions, including some from Tuvalu's near neighbours in the Pacific, support the applicant's claim that the attempt by the Falekaupule to restrict new religions and, in particular, the applicant's church, was a denial or restriction of the applicant's rights under the Constitution.

However, a distinction was drawn between the development of the law in a country such as Samoa and the situation in Tuvalu, where 'the emphasis in our Constitution on the importance of traditional values as an over-riding condition for the exercise of some rights finds no parallel in the Samoan Constitution'. The rights subject to section 29, which makes express provisions for consideration of Tuvaluan values and customs, include the right to freedom of belief, but excludes the right to be free from discrimination. If the court was satisfied that the *Falekaupule* had the traditional right to decide on such matters according to Tuvaluan values and customs, and had done so in order to preserve local Tuvaluan Nanumagan traditional values, then the applicant's breach of rights would be justified. Although the court was satisfied on these grounds it extended this reasoning to the applicant's claim relating to discriminatory treatment. While the court found that there clearly had been less favourable treatment shown towards the applicant on the grounds of religious belief and despite the recognition that the right to freedom from discrimination does not include the preservation of Tuvaluan values in the provisions to which the right is specifically subject, the court held it would be inconsistent to find that those same actions were unconstitutional because they were discriminatory. This decision has been subject to some critical comment (Oluwu 2005). In particular, it might be argued that had the framers of the Constitution wished to allow justification of religious discrimination on the grounds of Tuvaluan values, express provision could have been made. It was not.

One of the aspects these cases demonstrates is the power of traditional leaders to influence the application and protection of fundamental rights. In this case it was accepted that 'in Tuvalu the *matais* necessarily and legitimately exert great influence and their decisions carry great weight'. In the Samoan case of *Asiata v Asiata* [2007] WSSC 4, it was apparent that individual *matais*, who may bear ill-will towards an individual, his family, or group, can shield behind the anonymity of the village council against whom any action must be brought. Where the victim of these rights abuses is not a *matia*, or is an outsider, they may be considerably disadvantaged. In Tuvalu, it is clearly stated that fundamental rights are enforceable against private individuals as well as the state and its agents, in other words horizontally.[56] In Samoa the limits to the enforceability of rights is not expressly stated, so much will depend on how the courts approach the question.[57]

Religious intolerance on the grounds of custom has also been experienced in Solomon Islands. In the case of *Lobo v Limanilove* [2002] SBHC 110, a Christian Outreach Centre (COC) challenged the power of the local Catholic parish council in a predominantly Roman Catholic area to determine whether or not it could carry out its activities. The policy of the

Council was that 'any religious group or denomination that intends to do or undertake any activity in the zones within its jurisdiction must first of all seek the permission of the Council.' In effect, therefore, the Catholic council was seeking to exercise religious jurisdiction over a specific geographical area. The factors which the council would take into account were

> whether the steering committee in the zone being affected directly does consent to the proposed activity or undertaking taking place in its area of jurisdiction. Furthermore, the Council would look at whether or not such activity or undertaking would cause ill-feeling and division within the community or breach of custom and acceptable standard of good behaviour or bad effect on the community or the religious group or denomination would co-operate with the leaders of the community into which such religious group or denomination would wish to come.

The Solomon Islands' Constitution protects freedom of thought, conscience and religion (Section 11) and Section 3 of the Constitution lays down the fundamental rights and freedoms of every person in Solomon Islands, irrespective of his or her race, place of origin, political opinions, colour, creed, or sex. The State may intervene by legislation under 11 (6) (a) of the Constitution in the interest of defence, public safety, public order, public morality, or public health to restrict rights and freedoms. It is also a criminal offence, under section 131 of the Penal Code Act (Cap 26), for any person to destroy or defile any place of worship or any object which is held sacred by any class of persons with the intention of insulting the religion of any class of persons or with the knowledge that any class of persons is likely to consider such destruction, damage or defilement as an insult to their religion, and under section 135 of the Penal Code Act it is a criminal offence for any person to deliberately hurt the religious feelings of any other person in Solomon Islands. The law appears, therefore, to strongly endorse religious tolerance.

Although the case acknowledged the many different churches already established in Solomon Islands and the fact that the customary owners of land used by both the Catholic church and the COC had equal rights to freedom of religion, it recognised the difficult balancing exercise that had to be achieved in allowing freedom while maintaining respect and tolerance for differences of belief, including the observation of customary religious rituals such as funeral feasts, the payment of customary compensation for immoral or irreligious conduct and the institution of bride-price – which the COC had been critical of. The judge, in upholding the constitutional right to freedom of belief, noted

> this right and freedom of religion under the Constitution when exercised by individuals has the tendency of creating division between families and close relatives. It runs counter to the Melanesian concept

of a family unit in terms of togetherness in doing things and meeting custom obligations. Division within the family context can be devastating in terms of compromising the Melanesian concept of the family acting together in a common cause.

Nevertheless, the court went on to hold that freedom of belief or religion was a personal thing, which each individual had the right to observe – subject only to the limitations permitted by the Constitution, and could not be constrained by group or collective pressure. The council therefore had no right or power to make laws which contravened this individual constitutional right. The lawful powers of the Catholic parish council in this case are therefore distinct from the powers of the village *fono* in Samoa or the *Falekaupule* in Tuvalu. Whether a locally influential authority is placed on a statutory footing or not, however, it seems highly probable that its decisions and policies can have a considerable impact on the human rights experience of individuals brought within its exercise of power.

What is interesting about these cases is that most of them have come before the courts in the last decade. Whether this means that there were cases prior to this that were unreported, or that people were not so aware of their fundamental religious rights, or that there were fewer competing religions is uncertain – although the latter seems less likely as the battle for hearts and souls has been an integral part of the history of missionary influence in the region. What emerges, however, is that individuals are prepared to challenge the decisions and policies, not so much of the state but of other institutions, where these rights are under threat and that courts are having to address issues of what religious tolerance and freedom means in practice and how the balance between individual and group rights, spiritual and custom rights can be achieved.

As in the case of discrimination on the grounds of sex or sexual orientation, however, the law or a legal approach is not the only consideration. In the case of freedom of religion there may be a number of practical obstacles to overcome (Paterson 2003: 593–622). Small rural villages may be unable to support more than one church, either in terms of congregation, land or other resources. Difficulties of travel and transport may prevent worshippers from attending their preferred church. The religion available may be very much on a 'first come' basis, so that more recently arrived religions may struggle to find a foothold in rural areas. Moreover, family traditions, the example of village elders or chiefs, and perhaps the form of education available, will tend to foster adherence to a particular church. Communal decision-making and the conservative nature of custom may thwart or frustrate individual choice of religion by preventing new churches from being established in the locality. On the other hand, limitations to the diversity of religions and religious practices mean that there is less rivalry between churches for converts and resources and that village harmony and stability is maintained. As in other areas of human rights, the interests of the collective and the rights of the individual have to be carefully weighed, compromises may have to be reached and pragmatic solutions sought.

Colour or ethnicity

As indicated in the opening chapter, the islands of the Pacific are populated by people of different origins and different colours. While the predominant groups are Melanesian, Polynesian and Micronesian there are others such as Chinese, Malay, Indian, European, Filipino, Japanese, Vietnamese and other Asian. In some cases these groups have intermarried. In a number of countries there are sizeable communities of other Pacific islanders. For example, in Nauru 26 per cent of the population is other Pacific Islander,[58] many of them i-Kiribati. In Samoa 7 per cent of the population is 'Euronesian', while in Fiji approximately 40 per cent of the population is Indian or Indo-Fijian.

Although discrimination of the grounds of colour or ethnicity may be unlawful in most countries of the region, as indicated in Table 6.1, constitutional exceptions, supported by further legislation, means that in certain circumstances, notably in the case of land, citizenship and in some cases family matters, the ethnic or national group to which a person belongs can be relevant for determining rights.

Land

It was evident from the earliest Western contact with the Pacific Islands that land was held under various forms of customary land tenure. As a consequence, and in contrast to the experience of Aboriginal people in Australia, colonial government generally left customary land tenure in place, although it frequently misinterpreted its structure and in some countries reinterpreted it to accommodate colonial administration (Corrin *et al.* 1999: 235,236). Alienation of land to non-indigenous people was restricted by colonial administration in some countries of the region, for example, Cook Islands, Fiji, Niue, Samoa and Tokelau, probably due to a fear of large sectors of the population becoming landless. The independence constitutions and subsequent legislation retained land for indigenous people,[59] and maintained restrictions on sales of land to foreigners.[60] In some cases land which had been alienated was restored to custom owners – as in Vanuatu, or the form of tenure of alienated land was modified. For example, in Solomon Islands freehold estates were abolished in 1977 by the Land and Titles (Amendment) Act. However, perpetual estates, which were introduced in 1959 by the Land and Titles Act (Cap 133) permit Solomon islanders to hold an interest in land which is very similar to a freehold except that it is encumbered with a number of conditions and obligations. As from the end of 1977 all perpetual estates which were held by non-Solomon islanders were converted into fixed term leases of 75 years.[61] Elsewhere foreigners may acquire freehold, for example in Samoa and Fiji, but the percentage of land held under freehold is very small indeed. More usually, as has been indicated in Chapter Four, foreigners hold land under leaseholds which will be of fixed duration.

These discriminatory land holding provisions can be justified on the grounds that they ensure that land can be passed on to future generations and that forms of customary land tenure are respected. However, the exclusion of large sectors of society from security of land tenure can operate unequally. This is illustrated by the situation of Indo-Fijian farmers in Fiji at the turn of the millennium.

Indo-Fijians

About 80 per cent of land in Fiji is vested in the Native Lands Trust Board to be managed for the benefit of native Fijians, as provided for under the Native Land Trust Act (Cap 134) (Sharma 1999). As from 1940 the Board has administered that land. Within the Board's powers is the right to grant leases over Native Land. Revenues generated from the Board's management of the land are paid to the beneficiaries of the trust, whose right to receive these is governed by their registration as eligible Fijian natives.[62] Their shares are determined by the Native Land (Leases and Licences) Regulations 1985. The Board retained 25 per cent to meet costs and the rest is divided among Fijians according to rank.[63] The leasing of land for agricultural purposes is regulated under the Agricultural Landlord and Tenant Act (Cap 270) (ALTA). While this Act, which came into effect in 1977, applies non-discriminately, in practice it has had considerable impact on Indians farming sugar cane in Fiji. Indentured Indian labour was brought to Fiji by the British administration at the end of the nineteenth century to work in the sugar industry, since when Indians have played a significant role in the Fijian economy. When their indentures ended a number of Indians used their experience to farm their own, usually small, sugar holdings, harvesting and milling it co-operatively to support the Fiji sugar industry.[64] They leased their land either directly from the Native Land Trust Board or from Fijian landowners. When ALTA was legislated the Act was retrospective and made every lease which had come into effect between 1967 and 1977 a ten-year lease, with the possibility of renewal of two further periods of ten years. Leases entered into for agricultural purposes after the Act were for a maximum period of 30 years. Some protection was afforded to existing tenants, in so far as where a tenant had been in occupation of land for at least three years prior to 1967 – the date at which the previous ALTA Act has come into effect, a lease of 30 years was presumed to exist unless the landlord had taken steps to evict the tenant. This provision was directed at addressing the uncertain status of a number of casual and poorly document leasehold and licence arrangements which had been between Indian sugar farmers and Fijian landowners. Provision was also made for any disputes arising under the Act to be referred to an Agricultural Tribunal,[65] with a right of appeal to the Central Agricultural Tribunal.[66] There was no further right of appeal to the ordinary courts except by way of judicial review. In particular, the Tribunal had the power to determine compensation payable when a lease terminated. However, compensation was only payable for improvements if the landlord had approved of these.[67] In a number of cases, Fijian landlords had entered into arrangement with Indian tenants by-passing the Native Land Trust Board in order to get a better financial deal.[68] Often Indian tenants had farmed and developed the land with very little interest or participation on the part of Fijian landlords. The cumulative effect of ALTA provisions was that a number of leases determined during the 1990s.

The ending of agricultural leases coincided with political upheaval, notably the coup of 1987, the new constitution of 1990 and the events leading up to the coup in 2000. As has been indicated, the political climate was one in which ethnicity played a key role. Many native Fijian landowners refused to renew the agricultural leases of Indian sugar farmers, indicating instead that they would farm the land themselves and participate in what was then a lucrative sugar industry accounting for about one third of Fiji's exports in 2000. While the refusal to renew leases and a desire to derive greater benefit from their land may be understandable (Sharma 1999), a consequence was that many Indians were left homeless as they were driven off the land they had farmed for decades, either because the lease was not renewed or because they could not afford to pay the new higher rents. Although compensation mechanisms for the unimproved value of the land were put in place, many claimed that these were woefully inadequate to meet the years of labour and resources invested in the land. In 2003 the Asian Development Bank estimated that 'The next 5 years will see nearly 5,000 farms disappear, forcing some 14,500 families to look for other sources of income' (ADB 2003). While the Fiji Sugar Corporation offered training to Fijian landowners now wanting to farm the land themselves – many of whom had shown no interest in doing so previously,[69] the retraining of Indian sugar farmers – many of whom knew no other form of employment, was left to aid donors such as the Asian Development Bank. Some compensation packages were promised, and a few were paid out, enabling enterprising Indian farmers to transfer their agricultural skills to other forms of farming. For others, however, the future remains uncertain and impoverished.

The final tranche of leases granted under ALTA are likely to expire by the end of 2009. Most of these are held by Indo-Fijians. Under the current military rule it is unclear what lies ahead for the sugar industry or the Indian farmers. In 2004 the government was proposing 50-year leases, on 'fair and reasonable terms' (Field 2004).[70] That government, however, is no longer in power. It remains to be seen, therefore, whether ethnicity will stand in the way of agricultural development, which is essential to the Fijian economy, or whether compromises and co-operation can be achieved. In the interim, however, many Indo-Fijians have left the land and left Fiji.

Citizenship

Some of the constitutions of the region indicate at the outset that non-citizens may be denied certain fundamental rights or may have restricted enjoyment of these. For example, in Papua New Guinea the opening statement to the provisions on Basic Rights states 'subject to any restrictions imposed by law on non-citizens, all persons in our country are entitled to the fundamental rights and freedoms of the individual'. Similar provision is found in Vanuatu. In Palau this denial is not express but implied by the inclusion of the term 'citizen' in a number of the rights listed. So, for example, only a citizen is permitted to enjoy freedom of movement or to exercise the right to access to government information. However, non-citizens appear to be entitled to the other rights listed. Other Pacific Island countries do not discriminate on the grounds of citizenship. For example, in Nauru 'every person in Nauru is entitled to the fundamental rights and freedoms of the individual'.[71] Similarly, in Tuvalu every person in the country is entitled to the rights and freedoms enumerated, although the frequent reference to the Tuvalu people, and the values and customs of Tuvalu, may imply that the views and practices of non-Tuvaluans may be ignored. In Tonga, the law expressly states that 'There shall be but one law in Tonga for chiefs and commoners for non-Tongans and Tongans.'[72]

Citizenship is conferred on a person by virtue of birth, descent, marriage, naturalisation or honorifically. In the latter two cases the conferral of citizenship is discretionary and in the case of citizenship by naturalisation, conditional on a number of factors being satisfied, including understanding the obligations and duties of being a citizen of a particular country. These may include being familiar with the language or languages of the country and appreciating the culture and traditions of that country.[73] Usually citizenship is regulated by a combination of constitutional provisions and legislation. Citizenship confers various benefits, such as the right to vote, the right to hold a passport of the country and the right to live in the country indefinitely. Citizenship may also give rise to certain obligations and duties. Some countries permit a person to be a citizen of more than one country (dual-citizenship), others, such as Vanuatu, do not. In the Pacific, as has been indicated in Chapter One, some Pacific Island citizens are automatically citizens of other states. This is the case for Cook Islands and people from Niue. For these Pacific islanders it is very easy to travel to and from New Zealand. For other Pacific islanders it is considerably more difficult except for tourist visits. For example, following the division of Samoa into American Samoa and Western Samoa (now Samoa), Samoans are now restricted in how often and for how long they can visit family and friends in American Samoa. Freedom of movement may therefore be directly affected by questions of citizenship.

A child born in a Pacific Island country, whose parents are not citizens of that country, will not always automatically become a citizen by birth. This was made very clear by the Citizenship Act (Amendment) Decree of 2000 made by the interim military government in Fiji. This Decree also excluded the possibility of acquiring citizenship by marriage. Where a married person wished to acquire Fijian citizenship he or she had to do so by application for registration and to have been resident in Fiji for a total of three of the preceding five years. Quite what the purpose of this amending legislation was is unclear. It may operate to exclude Indians living in Fiji who have retained Indian citizenship, or other races who have come to Fiji and married into the community from becoming citizens if discretion is not exercised in their favour or conditions are imposed which are not met.

One of the discriminatory features of the region is the way in which acquisition of citizenship operates. In a number of countries, a married woman may, if she wishes, acquire her husband's citizenship on marriage. If dual-citizenship is not permitted she will loose her former citizenship. She may in some circumstances apply to regain it, for example on the dissolution of her marriage.[74] The same may not be true of a married man unless the law is framed in gender-neutral or gender-inclusive terms.[75] This can have adverse consequences for married women, as they may be compelled to choose between remaining in their homeland or accompanying their husband to a country where he is a citizen, and has an unfettered right to reside and work (Jalal 1998: 38). In Vanuatu the office of the Ombudsman has published a report on the illegal and unconstitutional discrimination which is promoted by the Citizenship Act (Cap 121). In its report it stated

> The Citizenship Act is illegal and unconstitutionally discriminates on the basis of sex by providing unequal entitlements to women and men. This is a violation of the fundamental right to equality under Article 5 of the Constitution. This is also contrary to the Convention on the Elimination of all Forms of Discrimination against Women (Ratification) Act, which is binding in Vanuatu.
>
> (Vanuatu Ombudsman 8809/9/08 1999: 2)

It recommended that the Act be amended and that in the interim the Citizenship Commission should advise applicants that they are aware of the problem and that they will not oppose any legal applications to the court on constitutional grounds. Whether the latter has done so is not known. Certainly, the Act has not yet been amended.

Rights to citizenship can also operate in a discriminatory fashion where a person is born overseas. For example, in Fiji, Kiribati and Tonga a child whose mother is a Pacific Islander but whose father is not, and who is born overseas is denied the citizenship of his or her mother. By contrast, in Samoa, the Citizenship Act makes express provision for citizenship by descent where at least one parent of a person born outside Samoa, is Samoan.[76] As children have no say in who their parents are, discrimination against the parent leads to discrimination against the child.

Citizenship is not simply a matter of individual status, it is also relevant to the enjoyment of fundamental rights such as freedom of movement, participation in the electoral process, questions of jurisdiction and the determination of certain rights which are dependent on national identity, such as the right to work without a permit, to reside indefinitely in a country, or to claim rights to land. Citizenship also links the individual with a wider group which may also be important for claiming rights. However citizenship is only one aspect of an individual's identity.

Family

Discrimination in the context of family law tends to focus on status. So, for example, a widow may be treated differently from a married woman in terms of land rights or rights of support, or an unmarried father differently from a married father when it comes to questions of custody or access to children. Occasionally, however, a person's ethnicity or race is relevant, for example, a country may have a policy that abandoned or orphaned children are only adopted by adoptive parents of the same race or ethnic group, or in custom this may be important in order to ensure rights of inheritance. In the Pacific region, where many family matters are still governed by the personal, customary law of individuals, there are circumstances where racial or ethnic identity may cause some difficulties. One of these is marriage.

Generally Pacific islanders are free to marry anyone, although they may require parental consent if they are below a certain age. In Nauru, however, it is still the law under section 23 of the Births, Deaths and Marriages Ordinance 1957–1967, that the Nauru Local Government Council and Head Chief has to give its consent to a marriage if one of the parties is a Nauruan. In the case of *In re the Constitution, Jeremiah v Nauru Local Government Council* [1971] NRSC 5, in which a Nauruan wished to marry a non-Nauruan, this consent was refused. As a result the requirement was challenged as being contrary to the fundamental rights set out in the Constitution, notably the right to private and family life. However, it was held by the court that as there was no express right to marry included within the statement of rights, this claim could not be upheld. The right to private and family life did not expressly include the right to marry and the court could not allow a claim to fundamental right to marry which applied outside the express provisions of the Constitution. While the primary purpose of the legislation appears to have been to prevent marriages between people who are too closely related, or where there is a suspicion of duress, quite clearly, as in this case, the law could be used to prevent mixed marriages. Although the law may no longer be observed in practice it nevertheless remains on the statute books.

Elsewhere, mixed marriages are not uncommon, although the plurality of laws which may govern them can create difficulties. For example, in Solomon Islands, as a result of common colonial practice, there are three different laws regulating marriage: the Islanders Marriage Act (Cap 47), the Pacific Order 1893 and the Pacific Islands (Civil Marriages) Order 1970. The first was intended to be limited to the marriages of Solomon islanders, while the others related to religious and civil marriages of non-Solomon islanders. As the term 'islander' has been held to cover anyone resident in Solomon Islands, rather than a native of the Solomon Islands, potentially both indigenous and non-indigenous persons are covered by all three. Similarly, in Kiribati and Solomon Islands the divorce of non-indigenous persons is differently regulated from the divorce of indigenous persons, while in Fiji there is still provision for the marriage of British subjects to be regulated by the Foreign Marriages Act 1892 (UK), although in practice this is not resorted to.

In plural legal systems an additional question which can arise is whether, because of one of the spouse's race or ethnic group, they are brought within or excluded from the ambit of customary law.[77] This can be an issue where customary as well as civil or religious marriages are permitted, as in Vanuatu, Solomon Islands and Papua New Guinea. Here there may be uncertainty regarding the validity of the marriage and therefore the legitimacy of any children, as well as uncertainty regarding the appropriate divorce procedures to follow should the marriage break down. These considerations in turn can influence issues such as rights to support and questions of matrimonial relief, for which different rules may apply, depending on whether the marriage is governed by custom or not. For example, the invalidity of a marriage stigmatises a child as illegitimate, which may place the child and the mother in a disadvantaged position as regards maintenance and often entitlement to inheritance.[78] Valid customary marriages must be dissolved according to customary laws and these too have discriminatory consequences (Corrin and Brown 2004). For example, in custom the grounds for divorce may be more limited (Hicks 1997), claims for support – especially of an abandoned wife – may be more difficult to pursue, rights to custody of children may be challenged, and the wishes of the individual spouse may be suppressed in the interests of the collective, especially the two families or kin groups linked by marriage.

The above examples illustrate that instances of discrimination can occur. Some of these remain clearly justifiable, for example, the protection of indigenous rights to land. Others are more controversial, such as the laws relating to citizenship. Some are simply unacceptable, for example, the inconsistencies in the realm of family law, many of which are the consequence of retaining outdated, pre-independence legislation, most of which have long been abandoned or reformed in their country of origin.

These examples also demonstrate that there are circumstances in which discrimination on the grounds of race or ethnic group is clearly permitted according to law. However, there are situations where race or ethnicity remains an unresolved issue. In some countries there is a long history of inter-tribal tension, where, although people may all be from the same ethnic group they identify themselves with discrete sub-groups. This has occurred in Solomon Islands and continues to occur in Papua New Guinea. Sometimes these groups identify strongly with a particular island, as in Vanuatu, where urban dwelling representatives from one island may clash with those from another island. In other cases, however, individuals from entire ethnic groups may be adversely affected. Indo-Fijians in Fiji are the most obvious example (Mori 2006), but there is another much smaller group whose existence and contribution to the Pacific is often ignored: the Chinese.

The Chinese in the Pacific

Chinese communities are found throughout the region, primarily in retail, restaurant and servicing businesses but also in small scale manufacturing enterprises. In many countries the Chinese have been a presence since well before independence, for example, in Fiji the Chinese community celebrated 150 years of Chinese presence in Fiji in 2005. Chinese, however, have been the subject of sporadic human rights abuses for a number of years. While attacks on their properties and lives may not be purely attributable to racism, but may also be motivated by greed, pure criminality, trade rivalry or as part of much more widespread Chinese gang activity, incidents against individual Chinese are regularly reported in the regional press. Crimes against Chinese include murder, brutal attacks, arson and looting. Sometimes these are isolated attacks, as in the case of the murder in Fiji in May 2005 of Yin Keen Chan, and that of Fang Xiao Wen in Port Vila, Vanuatu in June 2005,[79] or they may be more widespread, as in the Solomon Islands, with the torching of Honiara's Chinatown in April 2006,[80] or the looting of Chinese stores in Nukualofa, the capital of Tonga, in November 2006.[81] In Papua New Guinea, where it was reported that at least four Chinese business operators had been killed by employees in the period 2000–2004, the Crimes Director Assistant Commissioner suggested that the murders might be due to cultural clashes and misunderstandings regarding the resolution of conflicts arising during business operations.[82] While this cultural claim does not excuse criminal behaviour, it may in part explain the uneasy relationship Pacific islanders have with their Chinese communities. Although some Chinese become citizens of Pacific Islands,[83] many Chinese retain Chinese citizenship and their own language. Their degree of integration into the local community varies considerably from place to place. In rural areas they may be relatively few in numbers and fairly isolated. Fear of victimisation, reprisals or attacks may deter them from registering complaints with the police, while cultural constraints may deter them from taking cases to court.

In some cases, the victims of abuses have attracted formal or informal condemnation because they are illegal immigrants, or because they are suspected of being involved in criminal activity themselves. For example, in the Marshall Islands, where immigration and police officers have been pro-active in locating and reporting Chinese over-stayers, a government lawyer claimed that detainees had been arrested without a warrant, held without being charged and mistreated in jail. The response of the Attorney General to such claims was that his office would 'continue to combat illegal immigration with or without criticism. It was inevitable that when we finally get proactive, that these civil issues will be raised'.[84] Similarly, in Fiji investigations into illegal immigration activities by the police have in turn led to claims of police harassment of members of the Chinese community there.[85]

The advocacy of Chinese human rights in the region appears to be muted. In a number of cases police seem slow to investigate attacks or complaints. However, in Fiji some positive measures have been deployed to protect Chinese farmers who were being attacked and robbed through the involvement of the Community Policing Unit in an area where Chinese lease agricultural land from Fijians.[86] Elsewhere, however, police protection has been markedly missing. For example, during the riots in Tonga media coverage noted the absence of police presence – this despite undertakings by the Police Minister Clive Edwards in 1999 that a protection plan for the Chinese community would be worked out.[87] It appears therefore that the Chinese inhabitants of the region may be a silent minority whose rights are simply being ignored.

The rights of Pacific islanders

Colour, ethnicity, age, sex, nationality and status are all important factors in determining identity and rights in the south Pacific region. Despite the widespread constitutional provisions regarding equality, discrimination is a fact of life in the Pacific and inequalities of treatment and experience are pervasive. Issues such as legitimacy, disability, sexual orientation, status and ethnicity remain key concerns for those who are discriminated against and those seeking to achieve better rights for these groups.

A broader question, however, presents itself. Are Pacific islanders or the people of the Pacific, victims of discrimination and should they be afforded special protection in some way? In other words, should third generation rights be afforded to Pacific communities by the international community?

There are two dimensions to this. First, should minorities within the region be afforded special measures, either by the state within which they live or by the international community or a combination of these, so that their rights are sufficiently protected – for example, groups which are small numerically or which are in the minority within a larger group?

Second, should Pacific islanders, as indigenous people, be afforded special rights in the international arena?

There are two related international responses which are relevant to these questions: the rights of minorities, and the rights of indigenous people. In his Millennium statement Kofi Anan (then Secretary-General of the United Nations) said:

> Most conflicts happen in ... countries, especially those which are badly governed or where power and wealth are very unfairly distributed between ethnic or religious groups. So the best way to prevent conflict is to promote political arrangements in which all groups are fairly represented, combined with human rights, minority rights and broad-based economic development.[88]

Minorities

Article 27 of the International Covenant on Civil and Political Rights provides some scope for special measures to be adopted in respect of minorities. It states:

> In those States in which ethnic, religious or linguistic minorities exist, persons belonging to such minorities shall not be denied the right, in community with other members of their group, to enjoy their own culture, to profess and practice their own religion or to use their own language.

Although the scope of this provision is flawed, in so far as it imposes no positive duties on states and it is not clear if it applies to groups or only to individuals, it marks at least recognition that membership of a minority group can present particular problems for the full enjoyment of human rights. In December 1992, the United Nations resolved to adopt the Declaration on the Rights of Persons Belonging to National or Ethnic, Religious and Linguistic Minorities.[89] This Declaration takes minority rights a step further than Article 27 by indicating that 'persons' may be collectives as well as individuals. However, the grounds on which a minority might be identified are limited. While these grounds would cover, for example, i-Kiribati in Solomon Islands, or Chinese in Tonga, or perhaps today French speaking ni-Vanuatu in Vanuatu, they probably would not include gays, prisoners, refugees, political prisoners or the mentally ill – all of whom are minorities numerically but not ethnically.

In 1995, a United Nations Working Group on Minorities was established. This group, which is a subsidiary of the Sub-Commission on the Promotion and Protection of Human Rights, meets once a year for a week in Geneva. Its role is to encourage dialogue and to act as a focus for minority issues, which can then be considered in the wider context of human rights.

To date a number of regional reports have been considered by the Group, although none yet from the Pacific region. Within the ambit of the focus of the Minorities Group are many issues of relevance to the Pacific region, including issues of cultural diversity, language, religion, women and children belonging to minority groups, non-citizens and indigenous people.

Given its limited activity and subsidiary status it is unclear how much impact this United Nations initiative can have. However, in combination with other lobby and research groups, its role may be of some significance to Pacific Island states and the minorities within them.

Indigenous issues

The topic of indigenous people, which is one of the issues addressed by the Minorities Group, has attracted specific United Nations attention. In 2000, the United Nations established a Permanent Forum on Indigenous Issues (UNPFII) as an advisory body to the Economic and Social Council of the United Nations. The Permanent Forum is mandated to 'discuss indigenous issues related to economic and social development, culture, the environment, education, health and human rights.'[90] In 2004, the General Assembly of the United Nations adopted a resolution establishing a second decade on indigenous people to run from 2004–2014,[91] which includes within its programme of action human rights for indigenous people.

In September 2007, United Nations adopted the Declaration on the Rights of Indigenous Peoples.[92] The seventh session of the UNPFII was held in April–May 2008. A notably feature of this session was that half a day was dedicated to Pacific people and that the agenda was of particular relevance to the region was because it addressed issues of: climate-change, migration, urbanisation and development and human rights. Among the latter those of concern to Pacific Island people – especially Maori and Aboriginal people – included loss of ancestral and customary land and prejudicial and discriminatory attitudes towards indigenous rights.[93] Following the half-day meeting the Permanent Forum recommended that Pacific States endorse and implement the Declaration on the Rights of Indigenous Peoples.[94] Whether this special focus on the Pacific will now be a regular feature of UNPFII meetings and whether the voices of the smaller and more remote indigenous island people will be heard remains to be seen, but it is an auspicious start.

Conclusion

While Pacific Islands may be currently at the periphery of these developments within the United Nations, there does appear to be more interest at an international level for considering the specific needs of particular people within the international and global context. It is too early to speculate on the extent to which, if at all, focus on minority issues and indigenous issues will benefit individuals or groups within the Pacific region. Arguably, the recognition of minorities on any grounds could be counter-productive to human rights. First, to allow for difference may undermine the notion that all people have equal rights and that differences should take second place to the good of the whole of society (Locke 1689; Rousseau 1762). Second, the emphasis may shift from individual rights, regardless of status, to group rights, in which the individual is obliterated – although, as has been previously mooted, in the Pacific region this may have its supporters. Third, the admission of multi-culturism in societies which seek to advocate a distinct national cultural identity which justifies the relative implementation of human rights may undermine this claim by presenting a fragmented national identity.

Fourth, the singling out of minority groups for special human rights treatment could result in a tendency by states to deny the existence of such minorities if to acknowledge them requires a special rights regime. An example in the Pacific is the denial, which persisted for a long time, of the existence of people with HIV/Aids. Fifth, a claim to special protection of minority rights could be divisive, especially where one group among many may claim special status. This may happen where small groups of island people living traditional life styles claim special indigenous status.[95] Not only can this have fragmentary consequences, especially if certain (financial or other) advantages are perceived as flowing from this declaration of special status, but that same status may be used to conceal certain human right abuses within the minority group, for example: women may be denied modern child birth medical assistance in favour of traditional child birth practices, children may be denied the opportunity to attend schools other than '*kastom*' schools, or members of the group may be denied freedom of religion, movement or association. Finally, attributing special status to certain groups or members of such groups may aggravate the opprobrium already experienced by these groups or its members. For example, to advocate special rights for homosexuals in the region may aggravate not ameliorate homophobia. Similarly, to suggest that the transgender orientation of *fa'afafine* or *fakaleiti* should attract some kind of special regime may create greater opposition to ideas which are seen as western liberal agnostic values and create greater not fewer barriers to external interference.

This is not to suggest that positive measures to advance the human rights of the most vulnerable should not be adopted by states and indeed in some Pacific Island constitutions there is scope to do so. However, a better way forward might be to recognise the fundamental rights of all individuals without discrimination and to make a start by removing those provisions proscribed by law which expressly adopt discriminatory language and which directly or indirectly discriminate against particular classes of people, and to ensure that those agencies and institutions which have the power to influence the daily experience of rights are mindful of their duty to do so within the wider human rights framework.

Notes

1 See, for example, sections 7, 9, 32, 36–40.
2 See, for example, section 60 of the Constitution, which gives nobles as many seats in the legislative assembly as representatives elected by the people and the grant of hereditary estates under the Land Act (Cap 132) and section 104 of the Constitution.
3 Electoral Act 1963.
4 The importance of ethnicity in this regard will be considered further later in this chapter.
5 Fiji Constitution Revocation Decree 1987.
6 Section 100(3). See Corrin (2000).
7 For example, Chapter II dealt exclusively with the protection of Fijian and Rotuman interests 'by promoting and safeguarding (their) economic, social, educational, cultural, traditional and other interests' and required the Cabinet to act on such matters in consultation with the Great Council of Chiefs or the Council of Rotuma.
8 Rotumans are a recognised minority group within Fiji. Although politically part of Fiji Islands, the people of Rotuma, an island to the north of Fiji Islands, have their own language, culture and identity. They also benefit from a number of special legislative provisions.
9 As occurred following the 2000 coup. See *Republic of Fiji Islands v Prasad* [2001] FJCA 2.
10 Article 5(1) (k).
11 Section 38 (1) (F) and (G). This had been relied on to permit the continuation of mining in certain areas on the grounds that it brings benefits to that area.
12 Para 3 Protection of Fundamental Rights and Freedoms of the Individual, Constitution of the Solomon Islands.
13 See, for example, the case of *Family Kalontano v Duraki Council of Chiefs* [VUSC] 32 and comment by Forsyth (2005).
14 *State v Mutch* [1999] FJHC 149; *State v Pickering* [2001] FJHC 51; *State v Silatolu and Attorney General* [intervena] *and Fijian Human Rights Commission* [intervena, by leave] [2002] FJHC 69.
15 Article 17(1) provides that 'No one shall be subjected to arbitrary or unlawful interference with his privacy, family, home or correspondence, nor to unlawful attacks on his honour and reputation'.
16 'Violence Against Gays On Rise In Fiji', 4 May 2005, *Fijilive*, http://www.fijilive. com, http://archives.pireport.org/archive/2005/may/05-04-06.htm (accessed 10 June 2008).
17 'Fiji Methodists Seek Reversal Of Gay Rights', 30 May 2006, *Fiji Times* Online, http://www.fijitimes.com, http://archives.pireport.org/archive/2006/may/05-31-04. htm (accessed 10 June 2008).
18 See, for example, 'Samoa Church Leader Calls For Ban On Gays', 14 July 2006, *Radio New Zealand International*, www.rnzi.com *Pacific Islands Report*, http://archives.pireport.org/archive/2006/july/07-14-18.htm; 'Fiji Pastor Condemns Homosexuality', 25 April 2005, Fiji Sun, http://www.sun.com.fj/ Pacific Islands Report, http://archives.pireport.org/archive/2005/april/04-25-14.htm; 'Png Deputy Prime Minister Denounces Gays', 28 August 2003, *Papua New Guinea Post-Courier,* www.postcourier.com.pg/ Pacific Islands Report,

http://archives.pireport.org/archive/2003/august/08-28-06.htm (accessed 11 June 2008).

19 'Fiji Ag Disagrees With Court's View On Homosexuality', 30 August 2005, *Fiji Times*, http://www.fijitimes.com/ (accessed 10 June 2008).

20 'Fiji's Top Prosecutor Exhorts Against Homosexuality', 4 May 2005, *Radio Fiji News*, http://www.radiofiji.org/news/current/currnews.htm (accessed 10 June 2008).

21 Reported in the Post-Courier and quoted in *Pacific Magazine*, 28 August 2003, in an article entitled 'PNG: Demonic gays promote sex hatred', http://www.pacificmagazine.net/news/2003/08/28/png-demonic-gays-promoting-sex-hatred.

22 'Tongans Challenge Gay Minister In New Zealand', 6 March 2003, *Pacific Islands News Association*, http://www.ifex.org/members/pina/ Pacific Islands Report, http://archives.pireport.org/archive/2003/march/03-06-19.htm (accessed 11 June 2008).

23 'Homosexual Fears Harsh Treatment in Fiji', 25 January 2005, Oceania Flash, http://newspad-pacific.info/ Pacific Islands Report, http://archives.pireport.org/archive/2005/january/01-25-16.htm (accessed 10 June 2008).

24 WAC co-ordinator Noelene Nabulivou, 30 August 2005, *Fiji Times*, http://www.fijitimes.com/ (accessed 11 June 2008).

25 A term which means, effeminate man or youth.

26 Literally 'like a lady'.

27 In Tahiti and Hawaii these are *mahu* or *rae rae*. Besnier comments 'these terms can function as nouns to refer to a person, as verbs to refer to demeanour or action and often as adverbs to specify the manner in which an action is being performed' (in Herdt 1994: 286).

28 Schmidt (2001) suggests differently.

29 This has historical origins and is recorded in the writings of Besnier 1994: 288–292 and James 1994: 39–40.

30 Section 58D Crimes Ordinance 1962, Samoa and sections 136–140 Criminal Offences Act, Tonga.

31 See, for example, the Gender Recognition Act (UK) 2004 and the Civil Partnership Act 2004(UK); the cases of *Attorney-General v Otahuhu Family Court* [1995] 1 NZLR 603 in New Zealand and *The Attorney General for the Commonwealth and 'Kevin and Jennifer' and Human rights and Equal Opportunities Commission* [2003] Fam CA 94, in Australia and state legislation giving effect to *de facto* relationships such as the De Facto Relationships Acts of Tasmania (1999), New South Wales (1984), South Australia (1996) and Northern Territory (2004).

32 For example, the Miss Galaxy Beauty pageant in Tonga referred to by Besnier (2002), the Auckland Pasifika Festival referred to by Schmidt (2001). Plays and film include Croall's 'Paradise Bent: Boys will be Girls in Samoa' (1999) and Kightley and Fane 'A Frigate Bird sings' (1996).

33 See, for example, the land dispute in *Board of Trustees of the Congregational Church of Samoa v Pouvi* [2003] WSSC 4, in Tonga *Saafi v Veikoso - Judgment* [2000] TOSC 14 and in the Federated States of Micronesia *Wito Clan v United Church of Christ* [1993] FMSC 24.

34 See, for example, *Harrington v Board of Trustees of the Congregational Christian Church in Samoa* [2003] WSSC 44, *Wito Clan v United Church of Christ* [1993] FMSC 24 and *Unikannara v Catholic Beterin Ambo* [2007] KICA 9.

35 For example, that of the Federated States of Micronesia.

36 Specifically Pacific islanders – other than the ancestors of indigenous Fijian and Rotuman people –Europeans, Indians and Chinese.

37 See, for example, in Vanuatu, Representation of the People Act (Cap 146), section 23 and the Constitution of Tuvalu, section 95.

38 'The Island of Hope: an alternative to economic globalisation', Dossier No 7, 2001, http://www.oikoumene.org/fileadmin/files/wcc-main/documents/p3/dossier-7.pdf (accessed 10 June 2008)

39 As found for example in Cook Islands, section 64(1); Article II, section 1(1) and 12(2) Marshall Islands; and Article 5(1) Vanuatu.

40 As in Cook Islands s.64(1)(d), Article IV section 5 Palau.

41 Article 5(1)(f) Vanuatu.

42 Section 23 Tuvalu.

43 Section 5 Tonga.

44 Article IV, section 1.

45 Section 35.

46 See, for example, the provision in Nauru section 11(3) and section 45 of the Papua New Guinea Constitution.

47 Section 3. See also the Constitution of Nauru, section 3. Arguably this is broad enough to cover any form of belief or philosophy.

48 Section 45(5).

49 Section 32(2).

50 Referred to in *Asiata v Asiata* [2007] WSSC 4.

51 *Leituala v Mauga* [2004] WSSC 9.

52 *Tuivaiti v Faamalaga* [1980] WSSC 2.

53 *Lafaialii v Attorney-General* [2003] WSSC 8.

54 Sapolu CJ in *Italia Ta'amale and Ta'amale Toelau v The Attorney General* (unreported 8/5/95) quoted in *Leituala v Mauga* [2004] WSSC 9.

55 *Leituala v Mauga* [2004] WSSC 9. This seems to be the case, especially in criminal cases; see *Police v Luka* [2008] WSSC 28, *Police v Vui* [2008] WSSC 27 and *Police v Vaa* [2006] WSSC 5.

56 Section 12(1)(a).

57 As in *Tuivaiti v Faamalaga* [1980] WSSC 2. Compare however the Kiribati case of *Teitinnang v Ariong* [1986] KIHC 1.

58 CIA The World Factbook – Nauru http://www.cia.gov/cia/publications/factbook/print/nr/html (accessed 21 February 2005).

59 In Cook Islands, Fiji, Kiribati, Nauru, Niue, Samoa, Solomon Islands, Tokelau, Tuvalu and Vanuatu there is provision for land to be held according to the customs, usages and traditions of the indigenous people.

60 See, for example, Cook Islands, Fiji, Kiribati, Nauru, Niue, Samoa, Solomon Islands, Tonga, Tuvalu and Vanuatu.

61 Land and Titles (Amendment) Act 1977, section 6.

62 This is the *Vola ni Kawa Bula*, registration which entitles a person of Fijian or part-Fijian descent to benefit from Native Land rights.

63 Head of tribes get 3.75%, the Head or Chief of the *Yavusa* gets 7.75%, the Head of the *Mataqali* gets 11.25% and non-titled Fijians receive the remaining 52.5%, as the number of members of this last class is not fixed but can expand; as new Fijians are registered their individual shares can be diminished over time.

64 Indentures of Indian labourers on the sugar plantations started to end in the 1920s and they were enfranchised in 1929. For background to the Fijian/Indo-Fijian situation see Gatty (1953).

65 Section 42.

66 Section 48.

67 Section 40.

68 These cash deals are known as '*vakavanua*' arrangements.

69 See *Wansolwara News* online, Vol. 6, No. 2, June 2001, 'Ethnic dilemmas', http://www.usp.ac.fj/journ/docs/wansol/62ethnic.html (accessed 14 June 2008) and the report of the Fiji Government, 15 August 2005, 'Extensions

services offered in sugar mills'. http://www.fiji.gov.fj/publish/page_5226.shtml (accessed 14 June 2008).

70 Field, M 'Fiji sugar turns sour', *Pacific Magazine*, 1 March 2004, http://www. pacificmagazine.net/issue/2004/03/01/fiji-sugar-turns-sour (accessed 14 June 2008).

71 Article 3.

72 Article 4.

73 See, for example, the requirements to become a citizen in the Marshall Islands Citizenship Act, section 403, MIRC, Ch 4.

74 See, for example, section 18, Citizenship Act (Cap 112), Vanuatu.

75 As is the case with the 2004 Citizenship Act in Samoa. See also Cook Islands and Tuvalu.

76 Section 7, Citizenship Act 2004, Samoa.

77 See, for example, the Solomon Island cases of *Mahlon v Mahlon*; *Reid v Reid* [1984] SBHC 1, where non-Solomon islanders married Solomon islanders and then sought, unsuccessfully, to have the marriage set aside on the grounds that there could not be a customary marriage in such circumstances.

78 *Moeaki v Fakafanua* (1927) II Tonga LR 26.

79 'Chinese in Vanuatu frightened by killing', *The Independent*, 6 June 2005, http://www.news.vu/en/ Pacific Islands Report, http://archives.pireport.org/ archive/2005/june/06-07-04.htm (accessed 16 March 2007)

80 Sean Dorney 'China Evacuates Honiara Riot Victims', *ABC News* Online, 23 April 2006, www.abc.net.au/ra; *Pacific Islands Report*, http://archives.pireport. org/archive/2006/april/04-24-04.htm (accessed 16 March 2007).

81 'Tongan Capitol a "Town Gone Wild"', *Tonga Now*, http://www.tonga-now.to/; *Pacific Islands Report*, http://archives.pireport.org/archive/2006/november/ 11-16-up2.htm (accessed 16 March 2007).

82 Clifford Faiparik 'Culture Clash seen in PNG Killings of Chinese', *The National*, 2 September 2004, www.thenational.com.pg/. Pacific Islands Report, http://archives.pireport.org/archive/2004/september/09-03-16.htm (accessed 16 March 2007).

83 For example, in Solomon Islands Chinese made up the largest num- ber of new citizens approved in the ten years up to 2002. 'Chinese Dominate New Solomon Islands Citizens', *Solomon Star*, 23 April 2002. Pacific Islands News Association (PINA), http://www.pinanius.org Pacific Islands Report http://archives.pireport.org/archive/2002/april/04-24-20.htm (accessed 16 March 2007).

84 Giff Johnson 'Lawyer alleges abuse of Marshall Islands Chinese', *Marianas Variety*, 11 May 2006, www.mvariety.com *Pacific Islands Report* http://archives. pireport.org/archive/2006/may/05-12-14.htm (accessed 16 March 2007).

85 'Fiji's Chinese Community concerned by Police Action', *Fiji Times*, 1 April 1999. *Pacific Islands Report*, http://archives.pireport.org/archive/1999/april/04-02- 14.html (accessed 16 March 2007).

86 'Chinese farmers targeted in Fiji Attacks', *Fiji Times*, 18 December 2005, http:// www.fijitimes.com/ *Pacific Islands Report*, http://archives.pireport.org/archive/ 2005/december/12-19-06.htm (accessed 16 March 2007).

87 'Concern over rise in crime against Chinese in Tonga', *Radio Australia*, 11 January 1999, http://archives.pireport.org/archive/1999/january/01-12- 04.html (accessed 16 March 2007).

88 Kofi Annan, Secretary-General of the United Nations Statement on presenting his Millennium Report, 3 April 2000, http://www.unhchr.ch/minorities/ (accessed 19 June 2008).

89 A/Res/47/135, 18 December 1992.

90 UNPFII http://www.un.org/esa/socdev/unpfii/ (accessed 19 June 2008).
91 Resolution 59/174 December 2004.
92 Australia and New Zealand were among the four countries that voted against the declaration.
93 'Indigenous Peoples in the Pacific Region Fact Sheet http://www.un.org/esa/socdev/unpfii/documents/factsheet_Pacfic_FINAL.pdf (accessed 19 June 2008).
94 Press release 15th and 16th meetings http://www.un.org/News/Press/docs/2008/hr4953.doc.htm (accessed 19 June 2008). The resolutions of the session were presented to the Permanent Forum in document E/C.19/2008/L.3, available (in French) online at http://daccessdds.un.org/doc/UNDOC/LTD/N08/320/51/PDF/N0832051.pdf?OpenElement (accessed 19 June 2008).
95 Lini-Gamali, L 'Indigenous communities more secured economically: Motarilavoa' *Vanuatu Daily Post*, 25 June 2005: 5.

7   Rights advocacy and enforcement

Introduction

If the human rights of individuals and groups are to be protected and advanced then there needs to be an effective facilitating framework and mechanism which can do this. Merely giving expression to fundamental rights in written laws is not enough. These can be ignored or circumvented or at best given weak acknowledgment. Nor can the advocacy, monitoring and reporting of human rights in the region be left solely to one institution or system. This is not simply because of the resources which would be required to carry out the task, but also because the experience of human rights operates at many different levels and, in a region where people are scattered geographically, may be denied access to information or various institutions, such as the formal courts, the office of the Ombudsman or central offices of government, a more diversified approach is needed.

This chapter looks at various players in the rights' arena, taking into account both the legal and formal structures and the non-legal or informal institutions which play a role in shaping human rights in the region. Here it is not intended to draw a clear line between the State and civil society but to suggest that there are many institutions and organisations – some of which overlap and many of which interact – which can and do have a role to play in the protection, promotion and enhancement of human rights in the region.[1]

Parliament

At the top of the rights' machinery should of course be the legislative assemblies of the Pacific Island countries whose task it is to give effect to the country's obligations incurred under international conventions, to commit to others and to ensure that domestic legislation is compatible with the supreme law, the Constitution. In all the countries of the region there is an elected legislative body which is empowered to make laws (Corrin *et al.* 1999: 96–98). At independence provisions were made in the constitution, or in separate legislation, to establish what laws from the former colonial era remained applicable (Corrin 1997). Although it may have been envisaged that these transitionary provisions would only be required for a relatively short period of time before these introduced laws were replaced by domestic or national laws, in fact many have remained in force and continue to be applied. Frequently, these laws are outdated, and in many cases pre-date concerns with human rights in their country of origin – usually the United Kingdom, New Zealand or Australia. Given the many pressures and resource restraints on Pacific legislative bodies this state of affairs is perhaps understandable. Nevertheless, the consequence is that regional parliaments have a disappointing record on human rights law reform and development. This is not only evidenced in the poor record of Pacific Island countries in signing up to international conventions, as has previously been indicated (Baird 2007; Jalal 2006), but also in giving effect to those to which they are signatories in domestic law. There are of course exceptions. For example, in Vanuatu the CRC and CEDAW have been given effect in domestic law, the former in the Convention on the Rights of the Child (Ratification) Act 1992, and the latter in the Convention on the Elimination of all Forms of Discrimination Against Women (Ratification) Act 1995.

Leaving aside international conventions, the picture that emerges in the region is at best patchy. Some progress has been made. For example, the Fiji Family Law Act 2003 represents an enormous step forward in integrating into domestic law many of Fiji's obligations under the CRC and CEDAW. On the other hand, rule by military decree and the imposition of martial law in the aftermath of the coups in 2006 are less positive features of legislative activity in Fiji. In Samoa, following court challenges on the grounds of fundamental rights,[2] the enlargement of the franchise to non-*matai* in the 1990 Electoral Amendment Act marked a break-through in political rights, but the retention of status-based eligibility criteria for standing for Parliament has yet to be addressed. Elsewhere, as indicated throughout this book, legislative measures to address human rights issues are variable and, although a number of laws which have been put in place to facilitate development may also assist human rights, this is often incidental. In none of the countries of the region has there been a thorough review of existing legislation to determine its compatibility with human rights obligations.[3] Similarly, it is evident from case-law that courts are often confronted by national legislation which frustrates human rights claims and where the court may feel unable to do more that hope that Parliament will address the issue.

Consequently, other avenues of human rights advocacy and protection have to be considered.

The role of the courts

The entrenchment of bills of rights in written constitutions is neither a guarantee of their observation nor the only way of securing such rights for citizens. As has been indicated previously, fundamental rights flow from a number of sources, including unwritten laws. Moreover, the obligation to give effect to such rights may be express or implied. While the law is not the only source of human rights it remains an important one. Similarly, although recourse to the courts is not the only way in which remedies might be sought, the constitutions of the region indicate that it is an option open to those whose rights have been infringed.[4] The courts to which claims of human rights abuses should be referred are generally the upper level of courts, for example the Supreme or High Court, because they raise matters of constitutional importance. From these courts there is appeal to the Court of Appeal of the country, which is rarely a permanent court, and often consists of a number of visiting judges. Where lower courts are confronted by human rights issues they may refer them to the higher courts, or their decisions may be reviewed by higher courts. Sometimes, however, they may make rulings on human rights issues, which may then be appealed. The danger with some lower courts is that either they are not aware of the human rights considerations, because these are not brought to the attention of the court, or they fail to deal adequately with these. Increasingly and incrementally, however, the law officers of the region are becoming aware of human rights and their obligations in respect of these.

For example, in 1997 Pacific Island judges met to consider gender equality in Fiji. Chief Justices and judges from throughout the region attended. The meeting gave rise to what became known as the 'Denaru Declaration.' In effect this was that 'Every judge in his or her own court should strive to meet a high and consistent standard of fair and equal treatment of all members of the community', and that each and every judge 'should recognise and where appropriate take steps to implement the principles of gender equality'.[5] Achieving these goals requires positive steps on the part of the judiciary and support by way of continuing training, access to relevant information and awareness on the part of every judge of his or her obligations in meeting these goals. Judges also need to appreciate that the way in which courts interpret and apply the law when confronted by issues of human rights not only determines the outcome for individual claimants but, because of the publicity attached to court decisions and the legacy of the operation of the common law rule of precedent, will influence the effective enjoyment of rights and their protection for other members of society. It is the decisions of the courts which give life to the law.

This was expressed by the Privy Council in *Lennox Ricardo Boyce and Jeffrey Joseph v The Queen* (Barbados) [2004] UKPC 32, in which the Barbados Constitution was referred to as a 'living instrument' in respect of fundamental rights. Explaining what this meant the Privy Council said:

Parts of the Constitution, and in particular the fundamental rights provisions ... are expressed in general and abstract terms which invite the participation of the judiciary in giving them sufficient flesh to answer concrete questions. The framers of the Constitution would have been aware that they were invoking concepts of liberty such as free speech, fair trials and freedom from cruel punishments which went back to the Enlightenment and beyond. And they would have been aware that sometimes the practical expression of these concepts ... had been different in the past and might again be different in the future. But whether they entertained these thoughts or not, the terms in which these provisions of the Constitution are expressed necessarily co-opts future generations of judges to the enterprise of giving life to the abstract constitutional text and the messy detail of their application to concrete problems. And the judges, in giving body and substance to fundamental rights, will naturally be guided by what are thought to be the requirements of a just society in their own time. In so doing, they are not performing a legislative function. They are not doing the work of repair by bringing an obsolete text up to date. On the contrary, they are applying the language of these provisions of the Constitution according to their true meaning. The text is a 'living instrument' when the terms in which it is expressed, in their constitutional context, invite and require periodic re-examination of its application to contemporary life.[6]

Judges, therefore, can make a significant difference to the protection of human rights. This is as true of the Pacific region as elsewhere, and in fact it may be argued that the role of judges is even more crucial here, where legislative bodies are slow or reluctant to actively promote human rights. Indeed, the case-law of the region, examples of which are cited throughout this book, highlights this.

Ascertaining a complete picture of the region's human rights' jurisprudence is impossible because most of the decisions of the lower courts are unpublished. Unless decisions are appealed to the higher courts, or are referred to the higher courts for the very reason that they raise matters concerning human rights, it is rare to discover what local, village and customary courts are ruling or to ascertain the extent to which, if at all, human rights are being either observed or ignored. At the higher court and appeal court level the problem of information and knowledge has in recent years been address by the exponential increase in the output of the Pacific Islands Legal Information Institute (PacLII), based in Vanuatu.[7] This has been complemented by a digest of human rights case-law collated by the Regional Rights Resource Team (RRRT) based in Fiji.[8] These developments have compensated for the lack of official or sporadic law reports from the individual countries. These sources provide valuable insight into the experience of human rights as seen through the courts of the region and highlight the importance of judicial activism in protecting human rights. The following human rights cases involving young people illustrate this.

In the Papua New Guinea case of *State v Noimbik* [2007] PGDC 63, the accused, having abandoned his wife and small son for a period of six months, eventually returned late one night. He was drunk and proceeded to beat up his wife. He then turned on his son who was less than two years old and proceeded to try and suffocate him. During the assault he squeezed the child so hard that he broke one of the child's ribs. The applicable law was Section 95(2)(a) Child Welfare Act (Cap 276) which provided a maximum sentence of one year. The court found that the district courts provide no guidelines on how the court was to exercise its discretion under the Act in circumstances where the victim was a child. Indeed, the judge found that

> The lack of judgment writing coupled with the possibility of the lack of desire to pursue complaints under this provision of the law has, by and large, contributed to no sentencing trend before the District Courts of such an offence. Such may often than not result in inconsistent decisions ... and individual courts would therefore be left to their own devices to judge appropriate sentences based solely on internal assessment than help from elsewhere.

In the circumstances, the judge could give no greater sentence than 12 months, which he did, noting that the accused had not only breached domestic law but also international law in the form of Convention on the Rights of the Child, to which Papua New Guinea is a signatory to. He also observed that

> If PNG is serious about its international commitment to give a high priority to the rights of children, to their survival, their protection and development, and still remembers its obligation under Article 19 of the Convention ... then it must act now to make appropriate legislative changes.[9]

In the Tonga case of *Tone v Police* [2004] TOSC 36, four teenagers aged between thirteen and sixteen had been charged with housebreaking and theft. While in police detention, their parents had been denied access to them and they received no legal advice regarding their pleas or rights. In all respects the young offenders were treated by the police as adult offenders. The court was confronted by the problem that, although Tonga is a signatory to the CRC, it has not given it any effect in domestic law. The judge noted that

> despite an apparent time limit of two years for compliance imposed by the convention, Tonga appears to have taken no steps to enact any of the provisions. It can only be hoped that Government will recognise its obligations and enact legislation to bring Tonga into line with international standards of fair and humane treatment of young persons ... In the absence of any such legislation, the police were acting

within the law albeit a law which allows harsh and, I would venture to suggest, unconscionable conduct. The result was that these young people arrived at court to face serious charges without the opportunity to consult even with their parents.

Undaunted, the judge noted that the court could allow 'an appeal against conviction following a guilty plea if there is some evidence of equivocation in the guilty pleas entered'. There was nothing on the record to support this possibility but the court had discretion to allow an appeal 'if there are circumstances which leave the court with a serious doubt that the appellant understood the procedures under which he was to be tried'. Weighed in the light of the provisions of the CRC the court held that not only was the conduct of the police towards these youngsters unacceptable, but procedures had not been correctly followed and the sentences imposed were disproportionate. Appeal against conviction was upheld.

Where judges have discretionary powers, they may exercise these to send a human rights message. For example, in the Fiji case of *Seniloli v Voliti* [2000] FJHC 28, the High Court judge upheld an award for punitive damages awarded by a magistrate where a child of fourteen had been wrongfully arrested by police. The child had been handcuffed to a post inside the police station for four hours. At no time had reasons his arrest or detention been explained to him, he had not been given access to a lawyer nor been allowed to contact his next of kin. He was eventually released without charge. The trial magistrate found that the plaintiff's constitutional rights, his rights under the Convention on the Rights of the Child and his rights under the Judges Rules had been breached and that 'the conduct of the police officers ... was outrageous, a gross abuse of powers and an absolute disregard to the fact that (the accused) is a child.' Similarly, aggravated damages in the case of police brutality towards a child have been awarded in Tonga,[10] where the court had no difficulty in giving effect to obligations under the CRC despite Tonga's failure to fully ratify the Convention, on the grounds that 'accession indicates a willingness by the nation to be bound by its terms'.[11]

However, the courts are not always willing to take a pro-active role in ensuring that fundamental rights are safeguarded especially if there is legislation in place which should address such matters. For example, in the Solomon Island case of *Regina v K* [2005] SBHC 80, a juvenile, whose age was fourteen or fifteen, had been charged with murder under section 200 of the Penal Code (Cap 26). If he was found guilty he faced a mandatory life sentence. Since his arrest in October 2003 he had been detained in an adult prison until the date of the hearing in May 2005. Counsel for the accused raised the question of whether, given his age and maturity, the trial procedure would be fair. In particular because he would not

> be able to participate in the trial given his age, his maturity and intellectual and emotional capacities ... he will ... be tried in a secure

court with armed guards of the Australian Protective Services and be faced with the court in which the only indigenous actors are the interpreters.

Attention was drawn to Solomon Islands' obligations under the Universal Declaration of Human Rights; the International Convention on Economic, Social and Cultural Rights; the International Convention on the Elimination of all Forms of Racial Discrimination; the Convention on the Rights of a Child; and the Convention Against Torture, and other Cruel and Inhuman or Degrading Treatment or Punishment. However, there was also in place domestic legislation which was meant to deal with juvenile criminals: the Juvenile Act (Cap 14). This and provisions in the Penal Code which allowed for the criminal prosecution of children as young as eight, and the provisions in the CRC which allow for the criminal prosecution of children,[12] led to the judge holding that there was 'adequate protection in conformity with the provisions of the Constitution of the Solomon Islands and the Juvenile Act and indeed the relevant legislation'. Noting the lack of detention facilities for children and Solomon Islands' failure to give proper domestic effect to its international obligations under the above conventions, the court stated

> The Government of the Solomon Islands has the responsibility indeed the obligation to enact legislation that will give effect to these conventions. The court notwithstanding will ensure in the absence of legislations to do all within its powers to protect juveniles within the safeguard provided by the Constitution the supreme law of the land and the Juvenile Act ... The court consider the lack of proper detention facilities for juvenile offenders as of serious concern, but ultimately it is the responsibility of the Executive and the Parliament to ensure adequate facilities for the lawful treatment and containment of juveniles are provided.

Similar distancing from human rights deficiencies is seen in cases from Tuvalu. For example, in *Anderson v R* [2003] TVHC 27, the court noted the danger that although there was a process for review of sentences of imprisonment, this was not automatic. Consequently, a young offender who was sixteen when he committed the crime and who was sentenced to life imprisonment might not in practice be considered for release, contrary to the provisions of Article 37 of the CRC, which states that no person under eighteen years of age shall be sentenced to life imprisonment without possibility of release. Noting 'that courts and legislatures around the world are recognising the need to make special provision for the treatment and punishment of young offenders' and that Tuvalu was a signatory to the CRC, the court nevertheless refused to review the decision of the sentencing court, on the grounds that 'the law in Tuvalu makes no such provision'.

All the judge felt able to do in the circumstances was to respectfully suggest that the legislature 'should consider legislation to ensure that all cases of imprisonment for life or very long terms must be submitted with all necessary information to Cabinet and thence to the Governor General', who had the power to review sentence.

The fact that reported cases probably only represent a fraction of the number of circumstances giving rise to human rights issues is itself a matter of concern, because it may be indicative of other fundamental rights challenges, such as access to justice, impartial and fair treatment and access to effective remedies. While the topic of due process is too wide to consider in great depth here, there are practical elements which can frustrate the protection and promotion of human rights in the region.

Access to justice

None of the countries of the region have a forum specialising in human rights claims. There are no dedicated constitutional courts and there is no regional equivalent to the European Court and Commission of Human Rights. Consequently, human rights issues come before the ordinary courts. The structure of the courts varies considerably from country to country (Powles and Pulea 1988; Corrin *et al.* 1999: 279–324). Depending on the status of customary law within the hierarchy of the sources of law, a number of countries have parallel or separate systems of courts which adjudicate on matters governed either wholly or partially by customary law (Powles 1997). So, for example, in Solomon Islands there are local courts, the jurisdiction of which are constituted according to the custom of the area in which they are located;[13] in Vanuatu and Tuvalu, there are island courts,[14] and in Papua New Guinea there are village courts.[15] Elsewhere dedicated courts dealing with land matters may be governed by a mixture of legislation and customary law, for example, the Land and Titles Courts in Samoa established under the Land and Titles Act 1981 and the Customary Land Tribunals in Vanuatu.[16] There are also Pacific Island countries where many disputes are resolved outside the formal court structure, for example, in Samoa where the village *fono* has extensive powers under the Village Fono Act 1990 and the *Taupulega* in Tokelau.[17]

Before an individual or group can call on the law to give positive effect to human rights in specific cases there has to be recognition of the human rights at stake and access to the legal machinery; that is the courts, lawyers and arbitrators. Several factors may prevent this. First, ignorance: about human rights in general, about the legal avenues available, and about how to pursue human rights through the legal process. Second, even if a person or group is aware of such matters they may not be able to access the whole machinery of justice. For example, there may be access to informal or local courts but it may be almost impossible to access higher courts or more formal courts at the lower level. This may be for reasons of geography, finance, knowledge or status. Third, even if these forums are accessible there may be procedural obstacles. For example, it may be the case that local courts are predominantly staffed by men of a certain age or rank, which makes it difficult for women's voices to be heard, or the experts or adjudicators of custom may be drawn from a limited class, so that while they may include women, they are unlikely to include young people. Alternatively, different rules of procedure may be applied in different courts, or different burdens of proof be imposed (Corrin and Zorn 2001). Different rules of evidence may also be applied, particularly in the case of establishing custom. Dispute resolution mechanisms may vary, with the more formal courts which follow an adversarial process ruling on a winner and loser, while lower or customary courts may adopt a more conciliatory approach, in which they are prepared to arbitrate and negotiate for a compromise solution which may be primarily directed at restoring the peace and harmony of a community rather than compensating a victim whose rights have been breached.

Legal aid and access to courts

It is, of course, possible for any person to appear in court without legal representation, and indeed many Pacific islanders do so. However, this may leave them at a disadvantage, not only because of the complexity of court procedures and legal language, but because they may lack the knowledge or skill to present their own case to the best advantage. On the other hand, many people simply cannot afford to pay a lawyer, so the issue is whether access to justice and the right to a fair trial require the state to provide legal assistance. In some countries of the region, the right to a lawyer or to legal representation is a constitutional right. For example, in Cook Islands everyone who is arrested or detained has the right not only to be informed of the reason for their arrest or detention but also to be informed of the right 'wherever practicable to retain and instruct a barrister or solicitor without delay'.[18] Similarly, in the Federated States of Micronesia the defendant in a criminal trial has the right 'to a speedy public trial, to be informed of the nature of the accusation, to have counsel for his defense, to be confronted with the witnesses against him, and to compel attendance of witnesses on his behalf'.[19] Of course, the right to legal representation does not necessarily mean free legal counsel. This is made clear in the Constitution of Nauru which provides that a person charged with a criminal offence 'shall be permitted to defend himself before the court in person or, at his own expense, by a legal representative of his own choice or to have a legal representative assigned to him in a case where the interests of justice so require and without payment by him in any such case if he does not, in the opinion of the court, have sufficient means to pay the costs incurred'.[20] In Fiji the options are in the alternative: either a person may represent him or herself, or 'be represented, at his or her own expense, by a legal practitioner of his or her choice' or, if he or she declines either of these options, be given the services of a legal practitioner under a scheme for legal aid, if the interests of justice require it.[21]

There is also provision in most countries of the region for a person charged with an offence to have access to an interpreter. Given that there are many languages and dialects throughout the region and that a number of judges, especially at Supreme Court or Court of Appeal level, may not speak or understand the local language, especially where they are brought in from outside, this facility is essential.

There are a number of issues here. First, the right to legal representation tends to be limited to criminal trials. An exception is Fiji where the Legal Aid Act (Cap 15) permits the granting of legal aid in cases of divorce where there is an appeal to the Court of Appeal from the Supreme Court, or where there is an appeal to the Supreme Court against an order made under the Maintenance and Affiliation Act (Cap 52). However, it is clear that the granting of legal aid, either in the case of criminal trials or a limited range of family matters, is discretionary and means tested. This was considered in the case of *State v Silatolu* [2002] FJHC 69. Here it was clearly stated that the right to legal aid was not an absolute right but conditional on such aid being required in the 'interests of justice'. The accused was facing charges of treason. If found guilty he faced the possibility of the death penalty. He had been refused legal aid, although the Legal Aid Commission had offered him a lump sum towards payment of legal representation, an offer which was within its powers under the Act. There was evidence that the accused was probably bankrupt as his liabilities exceeded his assets. The question was what did 'in the interests of justice' mean? Reference was made to the case of *Artico v Italy* (1980) 3 EHRR 1, in which it was suggested that the test was whether it appears to be 'plausible in the particular circumstances' that a lawyer would be of assistance on the facts. After reviewing the law of a number of different common law jurisdictions the court held that

> In applying the law to the facts of this case, it is readily concluded that it is plausible, in the special circumstances of this extraordinary and unusual case in Fiji, that 'the interests of justice require' that the applicant succeed in his application, particularly bearing in mind the seriousness of the offence with which he stands charged, the length and complexity of the case, the potential sentence involved, and the inability of the applicant, as a non-legal person, being able to contribute effectively to his defence if he was forced to defend himself in person.[22]

Second, does legal representation mean representation by a qualified lawyer, or is it a role which can be performed by anyone. Usually, this will depend on the domestic law governing the right of appearance before a court. Some legal systems permit unqualified persons to appear on behalf of another before the court. For example, in Tuvalu an accused is allowed a 'representative of his own choice',[23] while in Cook Islands in criminal trials the accused may be represented by a person who is not legally qualified with the leave of the court.[24]

Third, even if a person is entitled to legal representation, what will the quality of this be? If a person has funds then they will be able to obtain the legal counsel they can afford. A wealthy defendant may therefore be able to command the services of a highly qualified lawyer while a person who earns a modest wage may be insufficiently poor to qualify for legal aid where that is available, but insufficiently well off to be able to afford more that a moderately skilled or experienced lawyer. Even where a person charged with a criminal offence is entitled to legal representation, for example, in Vanuatu where every person charged with a serious offence is entitled to a lawyer,[25] resource constraints may mean that young or inexperienced lawyers have to fulfill these roles. So, for example, it is not unusual in the region to find the offices of the Public Solicitor in Vanuatu or the Peoples' Lawyer in Kiribati or Tuvalu staffed by recent graduates. While lawyers in private practice may take on indigent clients, unless there is a professional requirement that they undertake *pro bono* work, this commitment depends very much of their good will weighed against the attractions and demands of their commercial clients. Further, even where there is a legal aid fund, as in Fiji, it is not limitless. Indeed, in recent years it has had to increasingly rely on aid donors to fund it. This means that in exercising discretion whether or not to grant legal aid the Legal Aid Commission has drawn up its own set of guidelines. The application of these was challenged in *Lyndon v Legal Aid Commission* [2003] FJHC 323, in which a non-Fijian facing deportation to America was denied legal aid. The justification of the denial was partly on the grounds that there was barely enough legal aid funding to provide for impoverished Fijian citizens and so the denial of legal aid to a non-Fijian was justified as necessary, reasonable and proportional in the circumstances. The court held that the guidelines which reserved legal aid to Fijian citizens was unconstitutional as it offended equality of treatment. However, it also found that the facts of the case did not amount to circumstances in which the interest of justice required legal aid to be provided.

In the course of the judgement, the judge, Justice Singh, reflected on the situation where there was no legal aid – in Fiji the situation prior to 1996. He said

> The objective of (legal aid) is to serve the interest of a disadvantaged group of persons that is those who are impoverished and who are brought before the courts of this country for one reason or another. Prior to 1996 even those who were charged with serious offences often appeared unrepresented in trials because they could not afford a counsel .... Equally in matrimonial matters even where children were involved, parties were unrepresented and the welfare of children was sacrificed in the process. The scheme of legal aid greatly assisted deserted wives and children to seek remedies through the courts.

However, Fiji is one of the few Pacific countries with a Legal Aid Act.[26] So what happens to the disadvantaged, the indigent, women and children in other countries, or indeed in Fiji when the funds run dry? In some countries such as Tonga there is no provision at all for a public defender or legal aid scheme. If the extended family cannot provide sufficient finance then an accused must defend him or herself. Elsewhere the accused must rely on the overstretched services of the Peoples Lawyer, the Public Solicitor Office or in Nauru a system of semi-qualified pleaders (Powles and Pulea 1988: 321). These may be supplemented by other support services. For example, in Fiji the Human Rights Commission may intervene – as happened in the case of *State v Silatolu* [2002] FJHC 69. In Vanuatu those living in or near Port Vila may be able to use the services of the Community Legal Clinic, established by the Law School of the University of the South Pacific, which works in close association with the office of the Public Solicitor,[27] while in Papua New Guinea the Individual and Community Rights Advocacy Forum has taken a leading role in assisting access to justice in a number of cases.[28] The challenge for those who do not automatically have a right of audience before the court – such as solicitors or barristers – is to establish that they have *locus standi* to represent a litigant. In Papua New Guinea this is facilitated by the provisions of the Constitution, which allows *locus standi* to 'any person, be it corporate or natural, who has an interest in the protection and enforcement of Constitutional rights or in the maintenance of the principles of rule of law to apply to the National Court for the protection and enforcement of a person's Constitutional rights.'[29] This includes non-government associations incorporated under the Associations Incorporation Act (Cap 142). Elsewhere it is not clear if 'persons' who may bring a case involving human rights includes such organisations.[30]

Not only may there be no legal aid for those charged with criminal offences in some countries, and more generally limited legal assistance for civil litigation, but in some courts lawyers are not allowed. For example, in Vanuatu, in both the Island Courts and the Customary Land Tribunals litigants or the accused are not permitted to be represented by a lawyer.[31] In practice, it is likely that there is little or no legal representation in many local courts, such as the Village Courts in Papua New Guinea or the Local Courts in Solomon Islands, with the consequence that prevalent social structures and attitudes are likely to be reflected in the administration of justice at this level.

Laws and legal procedures

The prevalence of legal pluralism in the region means that some matters will be decided by some courts and others by different courts, or that a matter may start in one system of courts and then transfer to the other system. It also means that one person may be subject to one set of laws while another may be subject to different laws, for example, customary laws may not apply to non-indigenous litigants. It may also mean that some legal matters may be subject to one set of laws while others will be subject to a different set of laws. Thus land matters may be governed by customary laws if the land is held under customary tenure but where the interest is a lease or freehold then non-customary laws will apply; customary adoption will be governed by custom while formal adoption will be governed by written laws. This legal pluralism may be an obstacle not only to the coherent development of law (Weisbrot 1989) but also to the promotion of human rights (Farran 2006).

First, there may not always be clear boundaries between those issues which are decided under customary law and those which are decided under introduced or non-customary law (Powles 1997). As society evolves and people move from rural customary communities to more urban westernised communities these boundaries become increasingly nebulous. For example, the customary adoption of children is not unusual, but disputes as to custody or land rights flowing from adoptive status may fall to be decided by legislation and the ordinary courts. Moreover, people may interact in ways which do not bring them within the jurisdiction of traditional dispute resolution mechanisms. For example, while the heads or representatives of families or clans may mediate inter-familial of inter-clan disputes, when disputes arise in the course of other interpersonal relations, for example, sports clubs, work environments or night clubs, the protagonists may have no associations which provide the basis of traditional dispute resolution. Similarly, if disputes arise between local and non-local people or between indigenous and foreign groups customary dispute resolution may be inapplicable.

Second, even where matters are reserved to customary or specialised courts, the incorporation of such courts into the formal legal system may mean that the procedures adopted in them are not entirely customary. As Ntumy has pointed out 'the separation of substantive customary rules from procedural customary norms will alter the meaning and impact of the customary law'.[32] On the other hand, if certain procedural safeguards are not in place there is the danger that rights to due process or a fair trial will be undermined or breached. In particular, there may be concerns that women's voices will not be heard or that the concerns of victims will be ignored in favour of restoring inter-familial or community relationships. An example of the former occurred in the Vanuatu case of *Public Prosecutor v Walter Kota and Ten Others* [1992] VUSC 8,[33] where male chiefs, together with other male members of the family, decided to deal with the behaviour of a female member of the family, by first forcing her to attend their meeting by enlisting the help of the police and then kidnapping her and taking her back to her home island. An example is found in the Samoan *ifoga*,[34] which may be taken into account in considering sentencing in Samoa. For example, in the case of *Police v Taueu* [2007] WSSC 93, a husband had stabbed his wife following various domestic difficulties. Because he had made an *ifoga* to the family of the victim the matter was regarded as 'reconciled and settled'. Although the accused received a custodial sentence, the court took into account the *ifoga*, along with other matters, to give him a reduced sentence. Similarly, in *Police v Filipo* [2007] WSSC 69, where the accused, a married man twelve years older than his victim, had had sexual intercourse with an underage girl, the payment of *ifoga* by his family to the child's family was accepted by them as settling the matter in accordance with Samoan custom. Another example is the Fijian *bulubulu* which is offered as an apology by the family of the offender to the family of the aggrieved claimant or victim. For example, in the case of *Seruitata v the State* [2004] FJHC 20, the appellant had been charged with indecent assault. His victim was his seven-year-old niece. The victim's father and family had accepted his offering of *bulubulu*. However, on appeal against sentence of three years the judge pointed out that this customary offering operates in favour of the perpetrator, not the victim or the public interest. He stated:

> many offences, while committed against an individual, remain in the public domain. They are offences that are deemed injurious to the public at large offending society's sense and standard of morality. For such offences, it is not enough to show that reconciliation even in the traditional Fijian way, has been achieved. The State must be free to impose its own sanction on behalf of the society as a whole. Without it our standard of human decency becomes meaningless.[35]

Third, there is the question of whether litigants or aggrieved parties should be allowed the choice of forums for their disputes. One of the features of traditional dispute resolution mechanisms is that these tend to be collective, with less focus on the individual's rights or remedies and more on the group of which that individual is a member or representative. While there may be distinct advantages in encouraging parties to resolve their disputes by traditional means – including resource advantages to overburdened court systems – and indeed most modern systems of law are now increasingly advocating alternative dispute resolution or mediation, there may also be drawbacks. One of these is the lack of public record of disputes resolved outside the formal court system. This does not mean that there will be no publicity. In fact, one of the strengths of many forms of traditional dispute resolution is the publicity which surrounds it and which can become incorporated into local history and oral traditions. However, the absence of a written record may be disadvantageous when matters are taken to a higher level or into a more formal legal system, as might occur on appeal. If adjudication is to rest solely with customary procedures then it may be much more difficult to ensure parity of justice for all citizens, or to hold adjudicators to account. Similarly, it may be easier for abuses of due process to occur without being detected – at least by outside agencies.

Fourth there is the question of an appeals procedure. Unless a separate and parallel system is to prevail at all levels then inevitably at some point there may be a cross-over from the more informal customary dispute forum to the more formal introduced forum, where, as indicated, rules of procedure, burdens of proof and rules of evidence may be different and less familiar to the litigant.

The systems themselves, the procedures adopted within them as well as the laws which are applied, may alone or in combination be experienced as obstacles to equal access to justice. The search for solutions is a continuing one. In some countries there has been a compromise between recognition of customary laws and processes and those introduced in the legal system by incorporating the use of assessors knowledgeable in custom to sit alongside formally appointed judges, as occurs for example, in the Land Court of Tonga and the Land and Titles Court of Samoa. Alternatively, those courts which deal with matters which fall to be determined by customary law are staffed with those knowledgeable in such matters, such as the Customary Land Tribunals of Vanuatu. In some cases, customary or traditional ways of resolving matters will be considered, either by way of evidence, or in sentencing, or both – as indicated by the role of *ifoga* in Samoa. Even if it is decided that the matter before the court is one governed by customary law or one in which considerations of custom may be relevant there may still be a need to determine: first, has the custom been proved to exist to the satisfaction of the court, and second, even if it has what weight should be attributed to this in reaching a decision. In a rapidly changing legal environment these are shifting sands. One of the factors that contributes to this is the evolving professionalism of the judiciary.

The judiciary

In 1988 when Powles and Pulea edited *Pacific Courts and Legal Systems*, it was still the case that a number of judges, magistrates and court personnel had little or no legal training. For example, the judges of the High Court of Cook Islands were 'laymen with local on-the-job training' (1988: 301); while in Tonga magistrates had no formal training and 'sometimes also have administrative duties on behalf of central government' (1988: 350,351) and in the Federated States of Micronesia no State Court Justices had law degrees (1988: 304). In virtually all countries except Papua New Guinea, where judges or magistrates were legally qualified, they had obtained their degrees from outside the region, many judges were ex-patriate and a number did not even live in the country where they were sitting.[36] This situation has changed considerably since 1988, not only because of the development of legal studies programmes at the University of the South Pacific (Paterson 1988: 286) but also because of country initiatives and regionally co-ordinated training projects.

These have been significant for improving the administration of justice in the region because one of the greatest challenges faced by the advocacy of human rights through the courts is the issue of resources and training of court staff, the judiciary and lawyers. Even today, many courts are understaffed and housed in poor facilities and often there are insufficient senior judicial officers, either to fill public law posts or the judiciary, with the result that ex-patriates continue to be called on to do so, that aid-funding is required and that existing staff are over-stretched.

While the number of judges, magistrates and other court personnel who have received no or very little legal training has diminished since 1988, even as recently as 2005 it was evident that there are still judges and magistrates in the region who lack a formal legal training.[37] This is even more of an issue in those adjudicative forums staffed by assessors and non-judges, such as island courts, native land courts and councils of chiefs, as are found in Vanuatu, Solomon Islands and Papua New Guinea. There is moreover a need for those judges and magistrates who are legally trained to be kept up-to-date with legal developments and techniques, in particular the way in which human rights relates to their work. There are however, various opportunities available to judges and magistrates in the region.

Senior judges may have the advantage either of being based outside the Pacific Islands – as in the case of a number of Court of Appeal judges who are drawn from New Zealand and Australia, and be able to benefit from continuing professional development overseas – or they may have the opportunity to participate in training organised under the auspices of international bodies such as the Commonwealth Magistrates and Judges Association, which has a Pacific region section, or the Conference of Chief Justices of Asia and the Pacific, which is organised biennially under the auspices of LAWASIA. Other legal personnel may be able to benefit from a number of aid-funded programmes which are run in the region, for example, the recently established Pacific Judicial Development Programme. The aim of this programme is to 'strengthen governance and the rule of law' in the various nations of the region covered by the programme.[38] Besides enhancing the skills and competencies of judicial and court officers especially those of the lower courts, the programme aims to encourage judicial independence and to educate judiciaries on the national and regional social context in which justice should operate, including the rights of women and children. A number of current and proposed initiatives focus on court and case management, but some proposed workshops have a human rights dimension. More importantly the workshops and programmes are targeting some of the smaller Pacific Islands and legal officers at the level of the lower courts. Already model 'bench' books are appearing on PacLII.[39] Complementary projects are also being initiated by the Asia Pacific Regional Centre of the International Development Law Institute, which to date has had relatively little input in the Pacific Islands.[40] Other programmes have been run by Interights, an international organisation which focuses on strengthening the ability of the legal sector to protect, defend and advance human rights. The organisation connects to the Pacific region through partnership with the Commonwealth. In collaboration with the Fiji Human Rights Commission it has been involved in a number of programmes directed at strengthening the skills required for successful litigation and building a regional human rights jurisprudence, which in turn both draws on and contributes to the Commonwealth jurisprudence of human rights.[41]

In 2004 Interights co-hosted a regional colloquium on 'Access to justice in a changing world'.[42] The aim of the meeting was to address issues of: the independence of the judiciary and the primacy of the rule of law; the role of the judiciary in the fight against terrorism; the role of the judiciary in safeguarding and protecting human rights in a world where terrorism is a reality; the role of international laws in asserting human rights under domestic laws; and how to guarantee effective access to justice for all people, both citizens and non-citizens. In the same year it also organized a two-day session, in conjunction with the Fiji Human Rights Commission, in order to encourage practitioners to use comparative and international human rights jurisprudence before the courts and become stronger and more effective human rights advocates in litigation.

The increased emphasis on the importance of developing and strengthening an impartial and effective judiciary through regional initiatives is not the recent 'brainchild' of aid donors.[43] One of the earliest of these was the formation of the Pacific Islands Legal Officers Network (PILON). This was formed in 1982 as an informal association of regional legal officers, with the aim of meeting to discuss how the administration of justice in the region might be improved and enhanced. Since then the Pacific Islands Legal Officers Network has convened a meeting (PILOM) regularly to bring together legal officers from the region for a week of intensive skills development assisted by judicial officers and senior practitioners from outside the region.[44] While PILOM agendas are skills-based rather than issues-based, improvement in legal services, the effective administration of the court systems, better trained judges and better trained legal personnel at all levels are all important for the citizens of Pacific Island countries. While these measures may not directly enhance human rights they do mean that where rights issues are raised in court they may be properly considered. Moreover, PILON provides an opportunity for senior law officers, including police and prosecutors, to meet with others from within and beyond the region and to enhance their understanding of the wider context in which the administration of justice operates. This can act as a valuable counterweight to some of the limitations experienced at a local level, especially where senior law officers may be quite isolated.

Complementing but separate from PILON is the Chief Justices Conference (CJC) which meets every two years in one of the countries of the region. This is an informal organisation which brings together representatives from a wide Pacific region, including French Polynesia, Guam and Hawaii. In the period 1999–2004 the CJC, in collaboration with funding partners such as ADB and AusAID, ran a judicial training programme.[45] The CJC has always operated completely separately from the Pacific Islands Forum, although as with PILON, meetings are normally attended by representatives of all Forum member countries. PILON, on the other hand has until recently had tenuous links with the Forum.[46] This is in some respects unfortunate as greater integration might lead to positive initiatives in the field of access to justice and equality before the law being advocated at a regional level. On the other hand, there might also be the danger that PILON would be hi-jacked by the Forum to focus on its priorities,[47] with a consequent confusion between the legal role of PILON members and the policy and law-making role of Forum members.[48] However, it has been recognised that the current annual gathering of PILON is insufficient to address the needs of the region. In a review undertaken at the request of PILON the Pacific Islands Forum Secretariat published a report in January 2007.[49] The report highlights the challenges faced by the legal profession in the region, noting *inter alia*.

> The relatively recent and accelerated opening up of Pacific states to the world has brought with it a raft of international obligations in areas covering economics, trade, human rights, security and more. Most new treaties require new or amended legislation, increasing the already high demand on limited legal drafting resources. ... Beyond ratification and legislative implementation of various treaties, international regimes in areas such as counterterrorism; maritime security and human rights also have ongoing reporting requirements which put an onerous burden on the small bureaucracies of island states.
>
> (para 11)

One of the issues that is evident from the report is that, while the Pacific Plan developed by the Forum has a number of objectives in its agenda which will need legal input and co-operation, this has been formulated without PILON input. PILON has its own list of priorities, which include addressing the increasing demands for legal drafting in the region; maintaining and improving ethical and professional standards; improving access to legal training; addressing the relationship between different systems of law in the region; dealing with land, electoral and constitutional issues.

The report envisages PILON retaining its autonomy but co-operating more closely on three key areas: regional security, progressing shared areas of concern, such as the production of model legislation and the sharing and dissemination of resources through an established secretariat – to be located either at USP, or the Forum or one of the member countries (Australia or New Zealand were proposed). Whether PILON will buy into the recommendations of the report remains to be seen. If it does there is a danger that it will loose its autonomy and jeopardize the separation of powers envisaged by the Constitutions of the region. On the other hand, many senior law officers are already government appointees especially in the public law offices. More fundamentally, however, judges and law officers may see their priorities differently. This is reflected in the Suva Declaration.[50]

The Suva declaration

In June 2006, judges from a number of countries of the region attended a workshop and colloquium on the theme of 'The Justiciability of Economic, Social and Cultural Rights in the Pacific Region'.[51] The event was convened in the context of the United Nations Framework on Regional Cooperation for the Promotion and Protection of Human Rights in the Asian-Pacific Region, and facilitated by the Office of the United Nations High Commissioner for Human Rights, in collaboration with the Fiji Human Rights Commission, Interights and the Commonwealth Secretariat. The outcome was a statement of recommendations entitled the Suva Declaration. This included the following points: the importance of promoting a domestic legal framework which provides effective remedies for those persons whose human rights, including economic, social and cultural rights, have been violated; the need to encourage academic institutions, professional bodies and judicial education programmes to include the study of international human rights standards and the relevant jurisprudence of regional and international human rights bodies, as well as comparative national jurisprudence in their curricula and training programmes; the importance of promoting human rights capacity building for judges and lawyers; support for existing efforts to collect the decisions of national courts which refer to international human rights, and encourage regional or international bodies to support the collation of the full text of these decisions and ensure their dissemination, including through websites and databases. In particular the participants recognised 'the key role of an independent, impartial, informed and adequately resourced judiciary, which is essential for the interpretation and enforcement of all rights' (Conclusion 8). The participants also acknowledged the role of non-government organisations or civic society in protecting and promoting human rights, as well as the importance of a free and independent media in raising public awareness of human rights and remedies available for breach of these.

It is clear, therefore, that combined efforts are required to create the best environment for human rights advocacy and protection. The role of players other than the courts also needs to be noted.

Legal literacy

The issue of legal literacy or overcoming ignorance about rights is not solely a matter for lawyers and the courts, although they clearly have a role to play, but is increasingly a challenge being taken up by civic society, non-government organisations and the media. Freedom of association, of expression and freedom of information are all, therefore, important, not only as rights themselves, but in facilitating access to justice to fight for human rights by improving rights awareness among the public.

Non-government organisations

The role of non-governmental organisations in human rights activism has long been recognised as crucial to the development of human rights. Early NGOs formed in the eighteenth century advocated the abolition of slavery and humanitarian intervention in times of armed conflict.[52] NGOs were also active in lobbying for the inclusion of human rights in the United Nations statement of aims and the United Nations Charter made provisions for the Economic and Social Council to consult with NGOs.[53] Today there are thousands of NGOs which have that status; some are national but many are international with branch organisations operating at a national or regional level.

Within the Pacific region, where links between self-identity and national identity, or group-identity with state identity may be weak, and the political will to give effect to human rights obligations may be lacking, non-governmental organisations play a vital role and often provide a way of crossing group, ethnic or status boundaries. The strength of NGOs is that they are often independent of government and represent associations of ordinary citizens, although not all NGOs operate at 'grass-roots' level. Sometimes they are unpopular with government because they represent liberal democratic views. Sometimes they are unpopular with ordinary citizens because they are perceived as representing an elite – members of whom often have had the benefits of a liberal western education, foreign travel and comfortable life-styles. Occasionally, international or regional organisations are resented because they are perceived as seeking to impose foreign standards and ideas which fail to appreciate the local context or culture. Nevertheless, NGOs in the Pacific and elsewhere publicise human rights violations, campaign for greater awareness of human rights, lobby government for change and advocate international standards at a local level. Increasingly they are represented at international human rights conferences and submit alternative reports when countries are required to submit national reports on compliance with certain human rights instruments such as CEDAW.[54] This dimension of NGO influence is important as often NGOs will present information which is quite different from the official line of government and therefore expose human rights issues which government may prefer to gloss over. An example is found in the 2002 'NGO Report on the Status of Women in the Republic of Fiji' compiled by Fiji Women's Rights Movement (FWRM), Fiji Women's Crisis Centre (FWCC) and the Ecumenical Centre for Research Education and Advocacy

(ECREA) as a counter report to Fiji's official CEDAW report.[55] This NGO report was highly critical of Fiji's post-2000 coup, human rights record and drew attention especially to the adverse effects political instability had on women's rights.

NGOs are also able to give a different perspective on human rights issues to media, academics, the international community and to the general public. As a voice for human rights therefore their role is important. Suppression of NGOs tends to reflect the denial of human rights by states and suppression of human rights' violations.

The weakness of NGOs is that they are often under resourced and have a limited number of members. They may have limited access to media, to government or to similar groups, or they may be poor at pooling or managing resources or co-operating with other groups. Although NGOs often seek to appeal to international law, for example, international human rights instruments, to criticise government and highlight human rights' concerns, they often have very limited opportunity to make their voice heard. This is particularly so in small Pacific Island countries where the cost of sending delegations to the United Nations or international human rights conferences is prohibitive and often if a delegation does attend it is carefully selected and may not be truly representative. A consequence is that sometimes the concerns of the Pacific are seen as being homogenous or as represented by one of the larger Pacific Island countries such as Fiji Islands or Papua New Guinea, which ignores national distinctions. The picture is even more inaccurate if countries such as New Zealand or Australia are taken to represent the Pacific region. Similarly, the western-orientated origins of some NGOs may be seen as undermining their Pacific credibility or relevance especially when the standards they advocate are not generally supported in the region.

Dependency on the non-governmental sector as a prime advocate for human rights has drawbacks. First, it may absolve government from taking responsibility for human rights initiatives, especially human rights awareness education. Second, it may skew the agenda depending on which NGOs are most active in advocating rights issues. For example, women, because they tend to be marginalised in the political arena, are very active in NGOs in the region. This means that human rights issues raised by CEDAW and CRC have greater prominence than perhaps those raised by other conventions. Third, because government funding of NGOs is very limited, if it exists at all, NGOs are dependent on fund-raising activities or outside aid. While the former can be time and resource consuming, the latter can be controversial. The major aid donors have their own agendas. Aid is often linked to broader initiatives to encourage civil and political rights – especially good governance, democracy and accountability. It might be argued that these are necessary pre-requisites for the enjoyment of other human rights. However, governments may resent what is sometimes perceived as interference by the back door.

The extent to which NGOs have been successful in the human rights arena is difficult to measure. While they may succeed in getting human rights on the political agenda this does not always mean that any positive consequences will flow from this, in the form of legislation or policy change.[56] NGOs may be poor political lobbyists and be reluctant to engage in the political arena directly, especially if it means adopting party politics. However, sometimes representatives of NGOs are included in government consultations or government delegations and can add their voice without compromising their independence and principles. There are also clearly NGOs and other representatives of civil society – some of which are mentioned in the course of this book, which have been, and continue to be, very effective advocates of human rights and whose views are respected and called on to inform the review or reform of law.

Whatever the drawbacks or weaknesses of NGOs, a vigorous non-governmental sector in the region is vital for developing and enhancing human rights awareness, especially in those countries where either violations of human rights are incorporated into legislation, or where parallel provisions within the constitution allow custom and customary law to prevail in a way which is inconsistent with human rights, or where governments are unable or unwilling to support human rights reforms and initiatives.

Local NGOs can also provide a valuable contribution to the relative interpretation of human rights taking into account local culture, social organisation and concerns. In this way NGOs can provide a number of bridges, between diverse communities, between international ideas and their national implementation and between rural and urban dwellers. Increasingly NGOs are organising themselves into national umbrella associations such as VANGO (Vanuatu Association of Non-government Organisations),[57] which in turn link together under the Pacific Islands Association of NGOs (PIANGO). While the efficacy of these national organisations waxes and wanes and is sometimes debilitated either by lack of resources or internal divisive politics, potentially these collectives could play an even greater role in the advancement of human rights in the region, by providing local focus groups for regional initiatives such as those of the United Nations agencies, the Pacific Forum or the Commonwealth Secretariat.[58]

Although there are far too many NGOs to do justice to all of them, the scope and significance of what they can achieve is illustrated by a few examples. In Fiji, one of the most notable non-governmental forums for advocating multi-ethnic constitutional development has been the Citizens Constitutional Forum (Lal 2003: 345). The Forum was formed in the mid-1990s with the aim of enhancing public awareness of human and constitutional rights. In 2001 it successfully challenged the appropriateness of Justice Fatiaki sitting to hear a case brought against the President of Fiji on the grounds of bias.[59] In late 2001 the government de-registered the organisation and threatened to do the same to other NGOs which did not 'tow the line'.[60] However, this does not seem to have silenced the work of the Forum which, in 2004, drafted a Freedom of Information Bill for Fiji (Rigamoto 2005).

Also significant in the region is the Regional Rights Resources Team (RRT). Described in a report to the United Nations as 'a Pacific grown organisation that provides technical and policy advice, capacity building and training on human rights at macro, meso and micro levels' (Jalal 2005), RRRT is the first regional human rights advocacy and training organisation. Although based in Fiji it recruits staff from most of the Pacific Island countries and focuses on raising awareness through workshops, human rights literacy programmes and lobbying. It works closely with other non-governmental organisations, with governments and with international agencies and for a number of years has benefitted from UNDP support. It has in recent years published several human rights reports and documents and has done much to raise awareness of human rights issues, especially the concerns of women and children. Its regional nature has the advantage of giving it Pacific credibility as well as sufficient objectivity, although its location in Fiji has been cause at times for some scepticism and its sometimes outspoken liberal approach has not always had positive effects. However, the establishment of nationally based legal rights training officers has provided a bridge between the local and the regional level of human rights advocacy, especially as these officers have been deployed to build the capacity of national partners to promote and protect human rights. The challenges faced by the organisation and its officers are, first, sustainability and the need for sufficient financial support independent of governments and, second, managing the many and various demands on these resources to address the different human rights issues which arise.

A third organisation which is worthy of mention is the Pacific Concerns Resource Centre. This is an organisation which brings together a wide range of non-government and other groups with the aim of lobbying for five key areas of relevance to the Pacific region: demilitarisation, decolonisation, environment, human rights and good governance and sustainable human development.[61] Among other things it campaigns for a nuclear-free Pacific and has advocated caution on commitment to regional initiatives such as PICTA and PACER, membership of the WTO, and ACP–EU agreements. Its concern is to find avenues of sustainable development for the Pacific in the face of global pressures.

The role of the press and the media

The media, too, at local and international level has an important role to play in strengthening rights awareness, not only in publicising breaches of human rights, but also in educating the public on human rights issues. However, in the Pacific region the media operates in a challenging environment.

Besides the fact that Pacific Island populations are scattered over a vast area, with the majority resident in rural areas, there are major logistical problems in communicating information about human rights.

Table 7.1 gives some idea of the communications environment.

While literacy rates throughout the region improve year on year, access to printed material is a different matter, especially in rural areas where the very limited number of newspapers published in any country, may be unavailable. It should also be borne in mind that power supplies may be disrupted due to adverse weather – cyclones and earthquakes, industrial action, or civil unrest. Moreover, telecommunications are expensive owing

Table 7.1 Media coverage in the region

Country	Radios	Televisions	Internet service providers	Internet users
Cook Islands	14,000 (1997)	4,000 (1997)	3 (2000)	3,6000 (2002)
Federated States of Micronesia	9,400 (1996)	2,800 (1999)	1 (2000)	6,000 (2002)
Fiji	541,476 (1999)	88,110 (1999)	2 (2000)	55,000 (2003)
Kiribati	17,000 (1997)	1,000 (1997)	1 (2000)	2,000 (2002)
Marshall Islands	NA	NA	1 (2002)	1,400 (2003)
Nauru	7,000 (1997)	500 (1997)	(1, 2000)	300 (2002)
Niue	1,000 (1997)	NA	1 (2000)	NA
Palau	NA	NA	NA	NA
Papua New Guinea	410,000 (1997)	59,841 (1999)	3 (2000)	75,000 (2002)
Pitcairn				
Samoa	174,849 (1997)	8,634 (1999)	2 (2000)	4,000 (2002)
Solomon Islands	57,000 (1997)	3,000 (1997)	1 (2000)	2,200 (2002)
Tonga	61,000 (1997)	2,000 (1997)	2 (2000)	2,900 (2002)
Tokelau	1,000 (1997)	NA	1 (2000)	NA
Tuvalu	4,000 (1997)	800	1 (2000)	1,3000 (2002)
Vanuatu	67,000 (1997)	2,300 (1999)	1 (2000)	7,500 (2003)

Source: Information taken from CIA World Factbook unless otherwise indicated (accessed 21 February 2005).
Figure in brackets indicates the year of survey; NA = not available.

to lack of market competition and therefore prolonged access to the internet or telephones is unlikely to be available outside the workplace or educational establishments. Also telecommunications are frequently non-existent or very rare in rural areas, and the range and availability of radio broadcast bands may be poor or limited. There are therefore physical and economic obstacles to communication. This makes it all the more important for human resources to be deployed effectively in raising human rights awareness and indeed a number of programmes and projects endeavour to do this. However, distance, poor infrastructure infrequent flights or boats and financial constraints all combine to make this difficult. The consequence is that while people in urban and peri-urban areas may have reasonably good access to information, workshops and publications, the opposite is true of those in the rural areas.

Together with these physical and technological challenges the media is subject to restrictions on freedom of information and freedom of expression.

Article 19(2) of the ICCPR provides that

> Everyone shall have the right to freedom of expression; this right shall include freedom to seek, receive and impart information and ideas of all kinds, regardless of frontiers, either orally, in writing or in print, in the form of art, or through any other media of his choice.

While it is envisaged that there may be restrictions on this right, such restrictions should only be as provided by law and so far as is necessary 'for respect of the rights and reputations of others' or 'for the protection of national security or public order, or of public health or morals' (Article 19(3)).

Most of the constitutions of the region give effect to this freedom, although the possible restrictions vary. In Federated States of Micronesia, for example, it is clear that 'no law may deny or impair freedom of expression (Section 1, Article IV),[62] while in Fiji there is an extensive list of when such restrictions may be imposed (Section 30(2)(a)–(g) although these are meant to be limited by considerations of reasonableness in a 'free and democratic society'. In Marshall Islands restrictions must not be imposed which 'penalise conduct on the basis of disagreement with the ideas or beliefs expressed' (Section 1(2)(c)). In Samoa only citizens appear to be entitled to freedom of speech and expression, while in Tonga the freedom of the press is upheld but 'nothing in this clause (clause 7) shall be held to outweigh the law of slander or the laws for the protection of the King and the Royal Family'. In Tuvalu there is freedom of expression but it is curtailed by a range of considerations, including the protection of Tuvaluan values, culture and tradition.[63] A number of common law limitations are also found throughout the region, such as the right to bring proceedings for defamation or contempt of court and the concept of freedom of speech in Parliament, or the equivalent legislative assembly, protected by parliamentary privilege. There is also domestic legislation in force which regulates the media, for example, the Newspaper (Restriction on Publication) Act, Vanuatu (Cap 156) under which a non-citizen may not own or publish a newspaper in Vanuatu without ministerial permission; the Newspaper Registration Act 1988 of Kiribati, which requires all newspapers or other printed publications to be registered. There are also cultural constraints of respect which may limit freedom of expression in the daily lives of Pacific islanders, for example the accepted order of speaking in village assemblies, the dedicated role of orators in some Polynesian societies, or the exclusion of women's views from male deliberative bodies.

In a number of Pacific Island countries the media, especially the press, has a constant battle to maintain a voice.[64] This has been particularly true in Tonga where attempts to restrict freedom of expression by legislation have been challenged on the grounds of human rights. These matters came to a head in the case of *Taione v Kingdom of Tonga* [2004] TOSC 47, in which the court was being asked to consider the constitutional validity of legislation which had been passed by Legislative Assembly, the Cabinet, the Privy Council and His Majesty the King.[65] The legislation in question was the Media Operators Act 2003, the Newspaper Act 2003 and a 2003 amendment to the Constitution itself, which enlarged the permitted restrictions on freedom of the press by amending clause 7 so as to provide

(1) It shall be lawful for all people to speak write and print their opinions and no law shall ever be enacted to restrict this liberty. There shall be freedom of speech and of the press for ever but nothing in this clause shall be held to outweigh the law of defamation, official secrets or the laws for the protection of the King and the Royal Family.

(2) It shall be lawful, in addition to the exceptions set out in sub-clause (1), to enact such laws as are considered necessary or expedient in the public interest, national security, public order, morality, cultural traditions of the Kingdom, privileges of the Legislative Assembly and to provide for contempt of Court and the commission of any offence.

(3) It shall be lawful to enact laws to regulate the operation of any media.

It was suspected that the measures had been put in place to gag the media after publication of stories alleging corruption by government officials and the royal family.[66] The court found that both the Media Operators Act 2003 and the Newspaper Act 2003 were unconstitutional and therefore invalid and that parts of the amended clause 7 were also unconstitutional. It held that while 7(3) remained valid, 7(2) should be amended so as to read 'It shall be lawful, in addition to the exceptions set out in sub-clause (1), to enact such laws as are considered necessary in national security, public order, morality, privileges of the Legislative Assembly and to provide for contempt of Court'. What the court did not strike out was the Protection from Abuse of Press Freedom Ordinance 2003, which made it an offence to bring into Tonga either the *Taimi 'o Tonga* newspaper or any Lali Media Limited publications, an omission which meant that possession of such publications could attract criminal sanctions.

Freedom of the press or media may be easier where the media is independent of government. This has been an issue in Samoa where the leader of opposition successfully challenged the government's manipulation of the state owned radio, television and the newspaper *Savali*.[67] Even where the media is not state owned, the state may frustrate freedom of expression by withholding or cancelling work permits, deporting journalists or preventing the distribution of newspapers or the broadcasting of radio.[68] For example, in February 2008, Russell Hunter, the publisher of the *Fiji Sun*, was detained overnight and then put on a flight to Australia, allegedly on the grounds that he had breached the Immigration Act.[69] David Robie, formerly Head of the University of the South Pacific Journalism programme, has indicated that the media is facing suppression in a number of countries of the region, including Kiribati and Papua New Guinea, as well as Tonga (Robie 2003).[70] The situation in Papua New Guinea has recently been confirmed by comments of Sir Arnold Amet,[71] and in 2007, following the escape of the Solomon Islands Attorney General from Papua New Guinea, the government was called on to demonstrate its commitment to democracy and transparency.[72] In Cook Islands, too, there have been concerns over the suppression of freedom of the media by government in order to silence criticism of government policy.[73] Here, as in Fiji, there have been proposals to set up a Media Bill with a government-controlled media commission. However, in Cook Islands there are now proposals to adopt a self-regulating approach through a media council, which appears to be supported by the major media players in the country.[74]

Freedom of the press, radio and television exercised responsibly within the confines of the law remains central to the enjoyment of human rights. In *Taione v Kingdom of Tonga*, reviewing previous decisions, Chief Justice Webster quoted his predecessor in the case of *'Utoikamanu v Lali Media Group Ltd* [2003] TOCA 6, who stated 'freedom of the press is not so much conferred on the press as on the people whom it sets at liberty to receive knowledge and opinions, and to debate matters concerning them freely. This has always been regarded as the hallmark of a free society'. The freedom to know, and to be informed, through the dissemination of information is therefore crucial, not only in order to ensure that government is transparent and accountable but also that other organisations which impact on the lives of ordinary people cannot hide behind a veil of secrecy. So, for example, it has been held by the High Court in Fiji in 2007 that the public had a right to know what the auditors said about the Fiji National Provident Fund, not only because ordinary people had a considerable amount of money invested in the fund but also because 'in the current circumstances in Fiji the freedom of the press assumes an even greater significance in matters of public interest'.[75]

In some respects, civil society, whether in the form of non-governmental organisations, the press or other groups such as churches, youth groups or labour unions, provide a fourth strand to the sectors that influence human rights in the region, alongside those of the judiciary, the executive and the legislative. A fifth, but often less effective strand, is those institutions which are established either under the constitution or legislation or a combination of these and are quasi-governmental, but at the same time are meant to be independent from government. Examples are the office of the Ombudsman and the establishment of human rights institutions such as commissions.

The Ombudsman

The office of the Ombudsman is found in six Pacific Island countries: Cook Islands, Fiji, Samoa, Solomon Islands, Papua New Guinea and Vanuatu.[76] In four of these – Fiji, Papua New Guinea, Solomon Islands and Vanuatu, the office of the Ombudsman derives its authority from the Constitution, with the result that the office has constitutional status and is not merely a creature of statute, making it much more difficult to abolish (de Jonge 1998). In all but Papua New Guinea the post is vested in an individual. In Papua New Guinea a commission is appointed. This has advantages in so far as the task of the Ombudsman is to 'expose injustice, incompetence and maladministration'[77] which can be unpopular and lead to attacks on the office holder. Even in Papua New Guinea however this may happen. For example, in April 2006 the Chief Ombudsmen faced allegations of misconduct in public office which were not declared to be unfounded until December 2006. The allegations were made by a member of parliament who had been investigated by the Commission.[78] In Fiji the office of the Ombudsman appears to be protected from this type of action under section 9 of the Ombudsman Act which provides that

> Neither the Ombudsman not any officer is liable to an action, suit or proceeding for or in relation to an act done or omitted to be done in good faith in exercise or purported exercise of a power or authority conferred by the Constitution or this Act.

The extent to which the various ombudsmen can make these enquiries is limited by their mandate. For example, in Solomon Islands the Constitutional provisions relating to the Ombudsman are rather constrained. While he or she may 'enquire into the conduct of any person to whom this section applies in the exercise of his office or authority, or abuse thereof; ... assist in the improvement of the practices and procedures of public bodies; and ... ensure the elimination of arbitrary and unfair decisions'[79] such enquiries may not extend to 'the Governor-General or his personal staff or to the Director of Public Prosecutions or any person acting in accordance with his instructions' or 'any decision of any judge, magistrate or registrar in the exercise of his judicial functions'.[80] Under the Ombudsman (Further Provisions) Act 1988, it would appear that the Ombudsman may not make an enquiry into the action of a Minister if the Prime Minister indicates in writing that the Minster was exercising his deliberative judgment.[81] However, an Ombudsman may investigate a complaint notwithstanding that there may be a remedy before the courts if the complaint refers to any fundamental right listed in Chapter two of the Constitution. The office of the Ombudsman may either initiate an investigation on its own initiative or as a result of a complaint by an individual or group. In addition Ombudsmen may have specific duties, for example in Vanuatu the Ombudsman has to table an annual report on the state of the country's three official languages in order to highlight whether parity is being maintained (Annandale 1997).

As maladministration in office and poor governance in public office undermines the political health of Pacific Island states and place at risk the civil, political and economic rights of Pacific Island people, the institution of the Ombudsman can play a key role in ensuring an enabling environment for the protection of fundamental rights. For example, speaking at the Australasian and Pacific Region Ombudsmen conference in New Zealand in 2005, the Ombudsman of Fiji urged fellow Ombudsmen to promote the right to freedom of information as being central to the effective scrutiny of government and public administration (Rigamoto 2005).[82] Where the office of the Ombudsman is specifically mandated to enquire into compliance with the Leadership Code of the country, as in Vanuatu[83] and Papua New Guinea, then the consequent reports can provide an insight into governance in public office.

However, there have been suggestions that the office of the Ombudsman is not always immune from political influence, that there may be pressure exerted not to proceed with certain investigations, or that the results of certain investigations are not made public or there is an attempt to 'gag' the Ombudsman. Where the Ombudsmen can initiate their own enquiries there is a danger that the office-holder may elect and pursue their own agenda, which may or may not be beneficial to the public at large, for example, a preference for avoiding enquiries into race or the process of granting government tenders may mean that these issues are not examined[84] while engaging with them may mean that the Ombudsman makes more enemies than friends (Lal 1997). Moreover, office holders are in a difficult situation. The post is meant to be totally independent of government but is usually financed and staffed from government funds. Unpopular office holders may find that their contracts are not renewed or they may be starved of resources to undertake enquiries or to deal with the number of complaints they receive.[85] Where the post is created by statute the powers can be curtailed by amending the statute.

It is also the case that while the publication of reports serves a useful role in highlighting matters of concern and making recommendations, in some cases there is a need to take matters further. In Vanuatu the Ombudsman can refer a matter to the public prosecutor, the police or the Attorney-General for further investigation or prosecution. Exceptionally the Ombudsman can take a matter to court in order to enforce compliance with recommendations.[86] In Samoa this possibility does not exist. Here the report is sent to the head of the relevant department or authority, with the possibility of a copy going to the Prime Minister, who may raise the matter in Parliament. In either case there may be no further action. By contrast, in Papua New Guinea, because the Ombudsman Commission is supported by its own Organic Law – which has a higher status than other laws (other than the Constitution) – it has been suggested that it is one of 'the most powerful in the world' (de Jonge 1999: 7). This is because not only is its function and status shielded by virtue of the way in which it has been created, but also because it has extensive powers to carry out its mandate.

The success of any 'watchdog' body, such as the Ombudsman, ultimately depends not only on the framework which establishes it but also on the integrity and often courage of the individuals in post, the willingness of government departments or public bodies to assist with enquiries and to respond positively to findings and recommendations. Where the Ombudsman has no enforcement powers and is dependent on others to put recommendations into effect, as is usually the case, then it is important that this is done. It is also vital that the work of the Ombudsman is made public, because in many cases publicity is the major weapon of the Ombudsman, so, as indicated above, a free and informed media is essential.

The office of the Ombudsman is only one of several types of watchdog bodies that can be found. Others include electoral commissions, public service commissions, the office of the Attorney-General and in some countries, Human Rights commissions.

Human Rights commissions

In 1998, Mary Robinson, then the United Nations High Commissioner for Human Rights, suggested that states could enhance human rights by adopting a four-stage approach. The first stage would be to establish a 'National Action Plan for Human Rights'; second, to establish a 'National Plan for Human Rights Education'; third, to establish or strengthen a national human rights institution, and fourth to focus on the delivery of economic, social, cultural and developmental rights (Jefferies 1997: 889). Pacific Island countries do not appear to have proceeded

in this way. Although national plans of action frequently focus on economic development there is little evidence to suggest that states have
national human rights plans of action or that governments are investing
large resources in human rights education. More usually, as indicated
above, this task falls to non-government organisations, or non-government
organisations in partnership with government and other agencies. An
exception is Fiji, which has set up a Human Rights Commission.[87] The
Fiji Human Rights Commission has two main functions: to educate the
public about the nature and content of the Bill of Rights in the Constitution, together with the international conventions and instruments
which inform it and the Committees and bodies of the United Nations
involved in the overseeing of human rights in the international arena;
and to make recommendations to government regarding compliance with
human rights obligations.[88] The Commission is also empowered under
this same section to recommend that the opinion of the Supreme Court
be sought about the legal effect of any provision in the Bill of Rights. It
has a residual power to perform any other functions conferred on it by
Parliament.

In the short time that it has been in existence the work of the Fiji Human
Rights Commission has been impressive. It has produced a national digest
of human rights case-law,[89] a number of training brochures and leaflets and
organised several colloquia. For example, in June 2004 it organised a round
table consultation 'on the human rights issues affecting the region including
the mechanisms required to respect, promote, protect and fulfill Human
Rights'. This was attended by a wide range of representatives from civil
society, representatives from government and from international offices.[90]
It has also intervened on behalf of those whose rights have been infringed
in some way, sometimes successfully as in the case of age discrimination,[91]
sometimes not.[92]

However, since the coup in 2006, the Fiji Human Rights Commission
has come under increasing pressure, on the one hand to speak out
about racism and human rights abuses, and on the other to support the
current military regime.[93] For example, the chairman of Fiji's branch of
Transparency International has criticised the Commission for not doing
enough to highlight or challenge pre-2006 Fiji 'apartheid', while the ex-
Prime Minister has dismissed such claims as 'laughable'.[94] The extent to
which the Commission is able to remain apolitical is difficult to assess.
In its report on the 2006 crisis it makes some interesting observations on
Australia's aggressive response to the political events leading to the coup,
and concludes

> This FHRC Special Investigation Report raises some very serious
> concerns about the presence of the Australian SAS forces, warships and
> Black Hawks in Fiji in 2006. Clearly there needs to be some meaningful
> discussion in forthcoming Pacific Island Forum meetings about the

obligations of sovereign States to each other and the rights and duties of members of this sub-regional body under international law pursuant to the UN Charter and relevant Declarations noted in this Report.[95]

Its lack of political distance, however, appears from the summary of its recommendations made in its 2008 report on Freedom and Independence of the Media, which while reflecting the difficult political climate of Fiji, makes a number of recommendations which would appear to shore up the military regime. These include controlling ownership of Fijian media – to prevent outside interests owning media in Fiji; the introduction of legislation to regulate the industry and in particular to provide restraints for any publication which offends public order or incites sedition; the non-renewal of all work permits relating to those employed in the media industry; taxation of the industry; and the establishment of a Media Tribunal and Media Development Agency. The purpose of the tribunal would be to remove complaints against or by the media from the ambit of the ordinary courts and the use of lawyers. The role of the Media Development Agency would be to monitor the industry along the lines of a similar agency found in Singapore. Why the model of what some might consider to be a police state should have been chosen is not made clear. What does emerge from the report however and the subsequent communications relating to it, is that relations between the Fiji media and the Fiji Human Rights Commission have deteriorated.

Regrettably, in late 2007, the Fiji Human Rights Commission indicated that if would no longer be part of the International Coordination Committee of National Institutions for the Promotion and Protection of Human Rights (ICC) of the OCHRC. This self-ostracism is unfortunate as it could leave the Commission in Fiji isolated, vulnerable to political manipulation or pressure, and unable to carry out its mandate in an effective and objective way. The recent experience of the Fiji Human Rights Commission might also make other Pacific Island countries, which have yet to take this step, wary of doing so.

Regional organisations

There are a number of regional organisations which play a part in the articulation of human rights and the promotion of human rights policies, if not directly, then indirectly through their various programmes and strategies.

Pacific Islands Forum

The Pacific Islands Forum is both a regional and international organisation. The founding members of the Forum were Australia, Cook Islands,

Fiji Islands, Nauru, New Zealand, Samoa and Tonga but today membership includes FSM, Kiribati, Niue, Palau, Papua New Guinea, the Republic of Marshall Islands, Solomon Islands, Tuvalu and Vanuatu. Its purpose is 'to strengthen regional cooperation and integration' (Article 11).

The main decision-making body of the Forum is the Forum Leaders Summit which meets annually. This is assisted by the Pacific Islands Secretariat. The constitutive treaty for the Pacific Islands Forum Secretariat was the Agreement Establishing the Pacific Islands Forum Secretariat, of 30 October 2000. In 2004, as part of a range of recommendations to reform the Forum, leaders directed that its constitutive agreement be reviewed to reflect the new purposes and functions of the Forum. The resulting new agreement was opened for signature on 27 October 2005 in Port Moresby, and has since been signed by all Forum members.[96]

There are a number of legal dimensions to the Forum's agenda and the Plan and in recent years the Secretariat has undertaken a large amount of legal assistance work in the areas of security, transnational crime and anti-terrorism, in accordance with the Honiara Declaration 1994 on law enforcement,[97] and the Nasonini Declaration 2002 on regional security, in respect of anti-terrorism measures.

The purpose of these declarations is to create regional consensus on matters of concern, not only to Pacific Island countries but also to their immediate neighbours, especially Australia and New Zealand – whose interests in these matters has no doubt provided the impetus for the direction taken by the Forum. As a consequence, the Forum seeks to encourage Pacific Island governments to implement regional policy in national action, for example, by enacting domestic anti-terrorism or drug-trafficking legislation. While these do not directly refer to human rights, the Biketawa Declaration 2000, which is essentially a regional security framework declaration, does include a commitment to upholding democratic processes and good governance, recognition of indigenous rights and cultural values and a process for addressing crises in the region. To date, however, it seems to have been invoked largely to justify Australian intervention in the region: in Solomon Islands (RAMSI) and in Nauru (PRAN).[98] It was also very nearly used to justify interference in the 2006 Fiji coup. This dimension of the Forum's activities illustrates the challenges confronting human rights advocates globally, a matter which will be taken up in the final pages of this book. More positive however is the recent articulation of the Pacific Plan.

The Pacific Plan represents the Forum agenda, which is viewed as a 'living document' which is updated and revised from time to time. It was last updated in 2007. In its statement on governance it

> Agreed that greater attention be given to encouraging participatory democracy (Pacific Plan Initiative 12.6) and implementing international

conventions on human rights (Pacific Plan Initiative 12.5) as essential
tools to underpin improvements in institutional governance

This statement suggests that the Forum is now proposing to engage more
directly with human rights issues, the possibilities of which will be explored
more fully in Chapter Eight.

The Forum is also a significant player in the region because of its links
and partnerships with various other regional organisations. One of these is
the Secretariat of the Pacific Community.[99]

Secretariat of the Pacific Community

The Secretariat of the Pacific Community is based in Noumea,
New Caledonia.[100] Unlike the Pacific Islands Forum the Secretariat focuses
on providing practical technical assistance, policy advice, and training
and research services to twenty-two Pacific Island countries in areas such
as health, human development, agriculture, forestry and fisheries. It has
dedicated sections and programmes focusing on land resources, marine
resources and social resources. Although not directly engaged with human
rights issues, its work on encouraging sustainable development of forestries,
fisheries and land has significant social and economic rights consequences
for Pacific Island people. In particular it focuses on using traditional
or customary methods of resource management of natural resources to
promote sustainable development. For example, within the region the
Secretariat's Forests and Timber focus group encourages the sustainable
management of forests, which is seen as one of the key objectives of
the Land and Development Policy of the region. Various initiatives and
projects have been launched in Pacific Island countries, for example in
Tonga, Niue, Samoa, Vanuatu and Fiji. In recent years it would appear that
the Pacific Forum and the Secretariat of the Pacific Community share a
number of overlapping concerns. For example, the Pacific Plan lists both
economic growth and sustainable development as two of its key pillars and
its 2007 Report states that it will continue to support 'National Sustainable
Development Strategies ... around the region ... work to develop innovative
financing models to support conservation efforts and work in areas of ...
forestry'.[101] It is to be hoped that ways can be found to capitalize and build on
the long-established practical experience of the SPC while avoiding wasteful
and unnecessary duplication.

Although not previously an express advocate of human rights, this aspect
of SPC may be changing. In July 2008 RRRT, which had previously been
a United Nations Development Programme partner within the 'Poverty
Reduction with Access to Justice for All' programme, joined the SPC. It
will be interesting to see how this new relationship works out, especially as
links with the Secretariat provide a clear connection between development
and human rights.

International reporting

In today's global environment human rights in Pacific Island countries are subject to international scrutiny, either through official channels such as the reporting obligations under the various conventions, or through international organisations such as UNICEF or Human Rights Watch,[102] or reporting mechanisms such as the American country reports on human rights.[103] The extent to which these international reports have any impact at a national level within Pacific Island countries is difficult to gauge.[104] In particular, it is questionable whether the reporting mechanisms under intentional conventions are a very effective means of bringing about changes to human rights at a national level. In part this is due to the generally weak enforcement mechanisms in place under international conventions but also to the lack of local publicity that surrounds the reporting process. In the case of most Pacific Island countries compliance with reporting requirements is poor. Reports are frequently late or a number of reports are combined together or no reports have yet been submitted. Indeed, throughout the region the reporting record is poor. For example, while Cook Islands have recently submitted a report on CEDAW (2007) it does not appear to have done so in respect of the CRC, Federated States of Micronesia have submitted a report on the CRC but the second and third reports are already overdue, which is also the case of Fiji for both CRC and CEDAW. Nauru is overdue on three reports on the CRC, as is Papua New Guinea in respect of CEDAW. Vanuatu and Samoa have submitted reports on CEDAW but these were the combined reports of the first, second and third reports which were due (Baird 2007). Where reports have been submitted and recommendations made by the United Nations Committee little may be done to give these effect. For example, following the submission of the Vanuatu combined report on CEDAW which was considered in 2007, the United Nations Committee made a number of recommendations. Included among these was that

> the State party (Vanuatu) ... clarify the primacy of the principle of equality of women and men and the prohibition of discrimination, over customary law ... the State party ... include in domestic law a definition of discrimination against women that encompasses both direct and indirect discrimination in line with article 1 of the Convention ... the State party (is encouraged) to sensitize the judiciary, lawyers and prosecutors to the provisions of the Convention and to the Optional Protocol[105]

and that

> to complete without delay its legislative reform so as to ensure that all discriminatory legislation is amended or repealed to bring it into

compliance with the Convention and the Committee's general recommendations. It encourages the State party to set a clear timetable for such reforms, in particular for the passage of the family protection bill and the revision of the Citizenship Act, and to raise awareness of legislators on the need to achieve de jure and *de facto* equality for women.[106]

There is no evidence however that these recommendations attracted great publicity in Vanuatu or that anything has been done about them. In time they may be recalled and used as a lobbying point, but in the meantime the *status quo* persists.

However, the requirements to report on human rights performance as a result of obligations incurred under international treaties does provide a public forum, albeit of limited effect, for Pacific Island countries to 'show-case' their human rights record and to come under the scrutiny of the international community. While this may bring the human rights of individual Pacific Island countries to the attention of a limited international community, any publicity regarding the recommendations made as a result of the report is soon forgotten. The reporting burden is moreover onerous and resource intensive, and may be one reason why Pacific Islands countries are reluctant to take on more international conventions. The significance of this is considered further in Chapter Eight.

Conclusion

While the enforcement of rights is primarily the role of the courts, many players have a role in rights advocacy. Although there may be some overlap between these roles, this environment is essential if rights awareness and rights protection is to improve in the region. Clearly there is scope for strengthening certain aspects of the organisations and institutions mentioned above. Notably, the role of the Ombudsmen in most countries where this exists could be enhanced and perhaps lessons learnt from the Papua New Guinea model. The lack of national Human Rights' commissions, apart from Fiji, means that there is a lack of central focus both for governments seeking to improve the rights provisions of legislation and for individuals or groups seeking assistance in pursuing rights claims. However, the current crisis confronting the Fiji Human Rights Commission needs to be considered and lessons learnt from it. It is also clear that legal pluralism can act as an obstacle to the pursuit of rights claims and it is important that increasing the human rights awareness of the judiciary does not omit to include those who adjudicate at lower and more local levels, especially in rural and remote areas and that practical solutions to the better observation of human rights are considered and implemented. Increasing awareness on the part of magistrates, assessors, court and tribunal personnel, as well as lawyers and judges, of the ways in which each element of the administration of law can contribute to enhancing human rights requires integrated training programmes, which need to be sustained in order to provided continuing professional development at all levels. At the same time the role of a free media is essential, not only to act as a human rights watchdog but also to educate the public at large about human rights developments in the Pacific Island countries of the region and the wider international community. A free media also provides an outlet for local, regional and international NGOs to reach a wider audience, for greater publicity to be given to the reports of internal and external agencies and to link scattered Pacific Islands with the global community as well as with each other.

The various roles of these players in the region contribute to the protection of human rights and their advocacy. As will be considered in the next chapter, some of these players could play an even greater role; others could co-ordinate their efforts more effectively, while others clearly need to be strengthened or have better resourced if they are to fulfill their potential as champions of human rights.

Notes

1 For comment on the concept of civil society in the region, see Larmour (1992: 107).
2 Notably *In re the Constitution, Attorney-General v Olomalu* [1982] WSCA 1.
3 In Vanuatu a thorough review of discrimination in legislation was undertaken in 1999 as part of a VANWIP (Vanuatu women in politics) project and published at a workshop in 2000. Various legislative amendments were proposed but nothing came of this.
4 See, for example, section 41 of the Fiji Islands Constitution (Amendment) Act; section 17 of the Constitution of Kiribati; section 14 of the Constitution of Nauru; and section 4 of Part II of the Constitution of Samoa.
5 RRRT (2005) 'The Big Seven: Human Rights Conventions and Judicial Declarations', Fiji: United Nations Development Programme 130,131.
6 Cited with approval in the Solomon Island case of *Nori v Attorney-General* [2006] SBHC 134.
7 PacLII can be found online at http://www.paclii.org.
8 See http://www.rrrt.org/. A second volume is due to be completed in mid-2008. For an earlier review of the role of the courts see Tamata (2000).
9 Article 19(1) states 'State Parties (member states) shall take all appropriate legislative, administrative, social and educational measures to protect the child from all forms of physical or mental violence, injury or abuse, neglect or negligent treatment, maltreatment or exploitation, including sexual abuse, while in the care of parents, legal guardian(s) or any other person who has the care of the child.'
10 *Fa'aosa v Paongo* [2006] TOSC 37.
11 Chief Justice Ford, para 24.
12 Article 37.
13 Local Courts Act (Cap 19).
14 Island courts Act (Cap 167) Vanuatu; Island Courts Ordinance (Cap 3) Tuvalu.
15 Village Courts Act 1973.

16 Established under the Customary Land Tribunal Act 2001.
17 Village councils of elders.
18 Article 65 (1)(c)(ii), Constitution of the Cook Islands.
19 Section 6, Article IV, Constitution of the Federated States of Micronesia.
20 Section 10(3)(e).
21 Section 28(1)(d), Constitution (Amendment) Act.
22 Per Wilson J.
23 Section 22(3)(d), Constitution of Tuvalu.
24 Section 53(3), Criminal Procedure Act 1980–1981.
25 Article 5(2)(a).
26 Marshall Islands has a Legal Aid Office established under the Republic of the Marshall Islands Legal Aid Office Act 1984 but in 1987 it appeared to be under investigation for financial mismanagement: *In the Matter of the Audit of the RMI Legal Aid Office* [1997] MHSC 1.
27 See http://legalcentre.vanuatu.usp.ac.fj/
28 Most notably in the case of *In the Matter of an Application under Section 57 of the Constitution; Application by Individual and Community Rights Advocacy Forum Inc (ICRAF); In re Miriam Willingal* [1997] PGNC 7.
29 Section 57 (1) and (2). This was applied in the *Willingal* case cited above.
30 See, for example, section 17, Constitution of Kiribati and section 4(1) of the Constitution of Samoa.
31 Section 27, Island Courts Act (Cap 167) and section 27(4) Customary Land Tribunal Act 2001.
32 Ntumy (1993: xxii).
33 With the help of an NGO the matter was brought to the attention of the formal court system and the accused were charged and convicted under the Penal Code ss 35 and 105(b).
34 The term *ifoga* means a ceremonial request for forgiveness made by the offender and his *aiga* (family) to those injured. It is performed by public act of self-humiliation, accompanied by the gift of fine mats, speeches and food *Attorney General v Matalavea* [2007] WSCA 8, referring to Cluny and La'avasa MacPherson (2005) 'The *Ifoga*: the Exchange Value of Social Honour in Samoa' 114(2) *Journal of the Polynesian Society*, page 109.
35 Per Justice Jitoko.
36 For example, the Chief Justice and Associate Justice of the Supreme Court in Marshall Islands resided in Hawaii, while the Chief Justice of Nauru's Supreme Court resided in New Zealand.
37 *Pacific Magazine* 'Marshall Islands: Training for Pacific judges', 10 February 2005, http://www.pacificmagazine.net/news/2005/02/10/marshall-islands-training-for-pacific-judges (accessed 19 June 2008).
38 Pacific Judicial Development Program (PJDP) Newsletter, March 2007, Issue 1.
39 See http://www.paclii.org/PJDP/ (accessed 19 June 2008).
40 In 1996 it ran some workshops on development law and assisted with the drafting of anti corruption action plans for Papua new Guinea 1999–2000 with financial assistance from the Asian Development Bank. http://www.idlo.int/Documents/WHERE_Asia.pdf.
41 Notably the Commonwealth Human Rights Digest and Bulletin and the Commonwealth and International Human Rights Case Law Databases.
42 With the Fiji Judiciary and the Fiji Human Rights Commission.
43 Indeed there are a number of examples given by contributors in Powles and Pulea (1988).
44 For an example of the activities of the annual conference see Hughes (2004).
45 This has now been replaced by a Pacific Judicial Development programme funded by AusAID and NZAid which commenced in 2007.

46 Other separate entities exists, such as the Pacific Islands Chiefs of Police, the Oceania Customs Organisations and the Pacific Immigration Director's Conference.

47 A number of which are driven by the Forum's dominant members and external forces and included, for example, extradition, proceeds of crime, trans-national organised crime, terrorism, money laundering, drug-smuggling, customs and electronic crime.

48 There have been proposals that a Secretariat of PILON be located within the Forum Secretariat and that appointment of its staff be controlled by the Forum Secretariat. Pacific Islands Law Officers Meeting Review by the Pacific Islands Forum Secretariat 2005 – discussion paper.

49 Pacific Islands Law Officers' Meeting (PILOM) Review, http://www.pilonsec. org/www/pilon/rwpattach.nsf/PublicbySrc/Pacific+Islands+Law+Officers+ Meeting+(PILOM)+Review.pdf / $file / Pacific+Islands+Law+Officers+ Meeting+(PILOM)+Review.pdf (accessed 19 June 2008).

50 The conclusions and recommendations of the Colloquium and Workshop for Judges and Lawyers on the Justiciability of Economic, Social and Cultural Rights in the Pacific Region, 2006.

51 Interights 'Pacific judges affirm justiciability of Economic, Social and Cultural Rights', http://www.interights.org/suva (accessed 19 June 2008).

52 See, for example, the British and Foreign Anti-slavery Society which was formed in 1839, the International Labour Organisation which was formed at the end of the First World War, and the International Red Cross which was formed in 1959.

53 Article 71.

54 For example, the Vanuatu 'Combined initial, first and second report on the Convention on the Elimination of all forms of Discrimination Against Women' (2004) was complied by a committee representing men and women from government and non-government organisations and followed wide consultation with civil society.

55 The report drew on the contributions of other representatives from civic society, notably: Women's Action for Change; Fiji Nursing Association; Fem'Link Pacific; Fiji Women's Catholic League and the Girl Guides Association.

56 Advocacy to address the issue of domestic violence is an example. While the Fiji Women's Rights Movement has been successful in lobbying for change in legislation the Vanuatu Women's Centre has been less so.

57 Similarly SANGO in Samoa and FANGO in Federated States of Micronesia.

58 See Chapter Eight.

59 *Citizens' Constitutional Forum v President* [2001] FJHC 28.

60 NGO Report on the status of women in the Republic of Fiji 2002.

61 The Pacific Concerns Resource Centre is a partner of the ACP People's Forum. See http://www.mwengo.org/acp/partners/pacific_concerns.htm (accessed 21 June 2008).

62 Although the individual states may be more restrictive. For example in Kosrae it seems permissible to bring in laws which protect tradition while restricting freedom of expression – *Kosrae v Waguk* [2003] FMKSC 3.

63 Section 24 read with section 29.

64 See, for example, the Vanuatu Ombudsman report on 'Deportation of the Publisher of the Trading Post Marc-Neil Jones from Vanuatu' [2001] VUOM 5; 2001.08 (31 October 2001).

65 This case followed others in which the law had been found to be unconstitutional. See *Lali Media Group Ltd & 'Akau'ola v 'Utoikamanu & The*

Kingdom of Tonga [2003] TOSC 14; *Lali Media & Others v Prince_'Ulukalala Lavaka Ata & Others & The Kingdom of Tonga* [2003] TOSC 30; *'Utoikamanu v Lali Media Group Ltd* [2003] TOCA 6 (CA).

66 'Banned Tongan newspaper plans return', 14 October 2004, *Pacific Islands Report*, http://archives.pireport.org/archive/2004/october/10-14-01.htm (accessed 20 June 2008).

67 *Efi v Attorney-General of Samoa* [2000] WSSC 22.

68 See, for example, complaints by the pro-democracy candidate in Tonga in the run up to the Tongan elections in 2008, 'Tonga candidate protests broadcast blackout', *Radio New Zealand International*, 7 April 2008, http://archives. pireport.org/archive/2008/april/04-08-07.htm (accessed 20 June 2008).

69 Reported as a postscript in the Fiji Human Rights Commission Report on Freedom and Independence of the Media'. See also 'Bainimarama warns against "irresponsible reporting"', *Fijilive*, 27 February 2008, http://archives. pireport.org/archive/2008/february/02-27-fj2.htm (accessed 20 June 2008)

70 Robie, D, 'Censoring Pacific Media', 16 April 2003, *Mediawatch*, http:// archives.pireport.org/archive/2003/april/04-16-comm.htm (accessed 20 June 2008). For a useful review of the media, especially in Fiji, see Tupeni L. Baba, 'Reflections on the role of Pacific media', 9 March 2004, *Pacific Islands Report*, http://archives.pireport.org/archive/2004/march/ pjr_baba.htm (accessed 20 June 2008).

71 'PNG Governor criticizes Somare over media threats', *The National*, 20 June 2008, http://pidp.eastwestcenter.org/pireport/2008/June/06-20-20.htm (accessed 21 June 2008).

72 'PNG slams door on public's right to know', 9 January 2007, *PNG Post-Courier*, http://archives.pireport.org/archive/2007/january/01-09-ed2.htm (accessed 20 June 2008).

73 'PINA alert over threats to Cook Islands News Media', 24 September 2004, *PINA Nius online*, http://archives.pireport.org/archive/2002/september/09-24-20.htm (accessed 20 June 2008).

74 'Cook Islands lawmakers laud new Media Council', 7 December 2007, *Cook Islands News*, accessed through Pacific Islands Report, http://archives.pireport. org/archive/2007/december/12-07-09.htm (accessed 20 June 2008).

75 Justice Coventry, reported by *Radio New Zealand International: www.rnzi.com*, accessed via Pacific Islands Report 'Landmark Fiji ruling: media free to publish', 22 October 2007.

76 Established under the Ombudsman Act 1984 (amended in 1991) Cook Islands; Ombudsman Act 1998 Fiji – which developed constitutional provisions in the 1970 Constitution; Ombudsman(Further Provisions) Act (Cap 88) Solomon Islands which developed provisions in the 1978 Constitution; Ombudsman Act 1988 Samoa; Ombudsman Act 1998 Vanuatu. In Papua New Guinea the Ombudsman Commission is established under Division VIII.2 of the 1975 Constitution and the Organic Law on the Ombudsman Commission 1998.

77 Charles Manio, former Papua New Guinea Chief Ombudsman, quoted by de Jonge (1999).

78 December 2006 Newsletter of the Papua New Guinea Ombudsman Commission, http://www.paclii.org/pg/OC/Newsletter/2006Dec_Wasdok.pdf (accessed 1 July 2008).

79 Section 97(1).

80 Section 97 (3) and (4).

81 Section 7(3). The need for such enquiries has been highlighted in Vanuatu, see for example *Ombudsman v Batick; Ombudsman v Jimmy* [2001] VUSC 45.

82 The need for freedom of information legislation or transparent government information disclosure polices has been identified and supported by the Pacific

Centre for Public Integrity which sees it as essential for counteracting human rights violations, weak rule of law, lack of democratic elections, poverty, unemployment and corruption – Commonwealth Human Rights Initiative Newsletter 2006 (accessed 13 November 2007).

83 Section 11, Ombudsman Act 1998.

84 De Jonge (1999: 17) suggests that this is the approach in Fiji, while the second is perhaps illustrated by the experience of the first Ombudsman in Vanuatu and the continuing approach in Papua New Guinea.

85 See First Annual Report 1995 to Parliament by the Ombudsman of the Republic of Vanuatu (1995: 6). In Papua New Guinea there is some safeguard against this in section 225.

86 *Korman v Ombudsman of the Republic of Vanuatu* [2001] VUCA 13.

87 Established under the 1997 Constitution Amendment Act, section 42. The Human Rights Commission is regulated by the 1999 Human Rights Commission Act.

88 The work of the Commission can be accessed via PacLII http://www.paclii. org/databases.html#FJ or at http://www.humanrights.org.fj/.

89 Fiji Human Rights Commission Digest 2004, http://www.paclii.org/fj/ indices/cases/Human%20Rights%20Digest%202004.htm (accessed 21 June 2008).

90 Pacific Islands Human Rights Consultation, Suva, Fiji Islands, 1–3 June, 2004, 'Concluding Statement And Recommendations', http://www.humanrights. org.fj/pdf/ConcludingStatement.pdf (accessed 21 June 2008).

91 *Fiji Human Rights Commission v Suva City Council* [2006] FJHC 44.

92 As in *Fiji Human Rights Commission v Commissioner of Police* [2003] FJHC 49 where it was found that the Commission lacked *locus standi* to bring an action outside the already wide scope of the 1999 Act. However, the Commission did successfully appeal the quantum of damages awarded in the case of non-consensual police medical inspection of a woman suspected of concealing the birth of a child. *Proceedings Commission, Fiji Human Rights Commission v Commissioner of Police* [2006] FJCA 75.

93 The current commissioner has been accused of being a 'coup apologist', Fiji Human Rights Commission report on 'Freedom and independence of the media in Fiji', February 2008, http://www.humanrights.org.fj/pdf/ fhrcmediarpt2007.pdf (accessed 21 June 2008).

94 'What was the FHRC doing about apartheid', *Fiji Live*, 25 April 2008, http://www.humanrights.org.fj/pdf/tifijilive.jpg (accessed 22 June 2008).

95 Fiji Human Rights Commission 'Special Investigations Report Australian intervention in Fiji in October–November 2006 – an issue of international law', 31 March 2008, http://www.humanrights.org.fj/pdf/SIRAI.pdf (accessed 21 June 2008).

96 Tonga was the last party to sign in October 2006.

97 In particular, extradition, mutual assistance in criminal matters, reciprocal enforcement of foreign judgments and prohibition of illicit drugs.

98 It has also been used to warrant election observations in Bougainville, Solomon Islands and Fiji.

99 Others include the FAO, UNDP, USP, SPREP, PILON, PIPSO, SOPAC, PIFFA, PIDP and SPTO.

100 http://www.spc.int/corp/index.php?option=com_frontpage&Itemid=1.

101 Annual Progress Report 2007, p.16, http://www.forumsec.org/pages.cfm/ about-us/the-pacific-plan/ (accessed 10 March 2008).

102 http://www.hrw.org/.

103 http://www.state.gov/g/drl/rls/hrrpt/2007/.

104 As Binder (1999: 217) states: 'international human rights law is not part of an effectively functioning legal system that delivers on the promise of stability, social peace, humane living conditions and democratic responsiveness'.
105 Para 11, Committee on the Elimination of Discrimination against Women, Thirty-eighth session, 14 May–1 June 2007, Concluding comments of the Committee on the Elimination of Discrimination against Women: Vanuatu. www.un.org/womenwatch/daw/cedaw/cdrom_cedaw/EN/files/cedaw25years/content/english/CONCLUDING_COMMENTS_ENGLISH/Vanuatu/Vanuatu%20CO-3.pdf - 2008-01-10 (accessed 26 June 2008).
106 Para 13.

8   Taking rights forward

Introduction

There are a variety of pressures on Pacific Island states to give effective protection to human rights. These include obligations under international conventions to which they are parties, pressure from non-governmental groups which may lobby both internally and externally, economic and political pressure from within and without, and the opinion of other members of the international community. Many Pacific Island countries 'talk the talk' of human rights without 'walking the walk' of human rights (Freeman 2002: 135). It has been suggested that there are various phases of human rights development (Risse, Ropp and Sikink 1999). The first is where states seek to repress any news or publicity of human rights violations, often by gagging the press or disbanding groups which are critical of the regime's human right's record. Without this publicity it is difficult for non-governmental organisations, both within and outside a state, to bring these matters to the attention of the international community or, often, even to the attention of the country's own citizens. In repressing any news of human rights violations national sentiment may be manipulated and harnessed to criticise any outside view or interference. Incidents of this repressive response occur from time to time in the Pacific region – most recently in Tonga following disturbances in the capital in 2006, and in Fiji following the military coup of 2006. Denial of any human rights' infringements or concerns is the natural consequence of such repression. Once there is some awareness of human rights concerns or violations then denial can lead to both internal pressure and external influence, for example, by way of trade sanctions, foreign policy and diplomatic initiatives, and economic sanctions may be used to persuade a state to change its tactics. This has occurred in respect of Fiji. At the most extreme this external response may involve foreign intervention by armed forces, as has occurred historically in Papua New Guinea and currently in Solomon Islands. These pressures may or may not be successful. The offending state may eventually make some tactical concessions, for example, by allowing some freedom of the press, or providing for an ombudsman, or by allowing international organisations to monitor human rights within the country – such as Transparency International, the International Red Cross or United Nations missions. Tactical concessions may include signing various international conventions on human rights or responding to the obligations already incurred under such instruments, for example, by submitting reports or reforming domestic legislation. Governments in such states may make human rights concessions or 'trade-offs' in return for economic aid, or accept that various aid-funded programmes are required for improving rights. Thus both internal pressure groups in the form of non-governmental organisations and civic society and external players, including foreign states intervening in the form of aid, acquire greater scope to engage in human rights dialogue. Tactical concessions may be sufficient to maintain a passive human rights environment for some time. In the Pacific, a number of states appear to make such tactical concessions, mixed occasionally with regression to denial or repression. Some also progress to the next stage, in which governments accept human rights as legitimate, not only through the ratification of human rights instruments – which may only be tactical – but by giving them positive effect in national legislation. This can include incorporating bills of rights into constitutional statements. In the Pacific, of course, this latter phenomenon is widespread, but not, it might be argued, because national governments have elected to do so but because these were integral to the movement to independence from colonial rule. What are much less common are domestic laws giving effect to human rights, especially the obligations of Pacific Island countries under international human rights instruments. In this phase of human rights development it is accepted that human rights violations occur and that citizens have recourse to the courts to seek remedies for such violations. In other words, there is ongoing dialogue of human rights internally and externally. The final stage of human rights development is where compliance with human rights standards is an every day matter and the rule of law is effectively upheld as a means on ensuring compliance with internal and external obligations. This model of human rights is helpful in understanding the evolution of human rights within societies, although the various indicated stages of development will not meet all situations or accurately reflect the internal dynamics of each and every country. Also, elements of each phase may be found at any one time.

At present, it is suggested that very few if any Pacific Island countries have achieved this final ideal and that many still have some way to go in progressing through these various stages. The foregoing chapters have suggested that the experience and protection of human and fundamental rights in the region is, at best, patchy, not only as regards the different Pacific Island states but also in respect of the different rights provided for. Many factors may influence the future of human rights in the region, for example the extent to which national governments feel compelled to heed international pressures, or internal lobbyists; whether the international community has any interest in the region and in particular whether foreign policy towards Pacific Island states will be linked to human rights regimes; the extent to which internal dynamics, influenced by ethnicity, land pressure, poverty, or religion affect the environment of human rights; the strength or weakness of territorial integrity and cohesive government; the effectiveness of domestic and international non-governmental organisations in keeping human rights to the fore and the overall acceptance or rejection of the normative framework on which human rights are based.

This concluding chapter speculates on the way ahead, the function and impact of regional and international agencies and the possibilities that present themselves when considering the development or demise of human rights in the region.

National governments and related institutions

Pacific Island states are in a state of rapid change and development. There is an understandable desire to cling to what is known rather than embrace that which is unknown and foreign. Global cultural and normative structures threaten to engulf the values and traditions of small nations and international discourse on human rights may be perceived as part of this phenomenon. If human rights are to become rooted in the fabric of island states, the focus of human rights law may have to shift towards greater emphasis on the democratic involvement of all sectors of society, and towards concentrating on those needs which are most important in developing countries. Greater sensitivity towards difference in trying to accommodate universally held values and more attention to the practical challenges of giving effect to human rights may achieve more than emphasis on the ideological goals. This may require a reconsideration of rights priorities for two related reasons. First, human rights need to be higher up the political agenda of governments, because essentially national governments bear the responsibility of not only ensuring that the rights enumerated in their own constitutions are given effect, but also that domestic legislation is passed to put into effect international conventions to which their countries are signatories. By and large Pacific Island governments are slow to do this although there are some initiatives in the region. If this antipathy is to be addressed then human rights have to attract the same level of concern as legislation being passed through the various legislative assemblies to give effect to commercial interests, international concerns such as international terrorism, money-laundering and international criminal activity. In other words, a focus on human rights has to be seen as necessary and desirable, both internally and by external agencies, which influence the parliamentary agendas of Pacific Island governments. Second, human rights have to resonate with the everyday concerns of voters so that in democratic systems these concerns are channeled through representatives in the legislative body. The fact that many members of parliament, or its equivalent, are not very concerned with constituency matters once elected is a problem of poor governance, lack of accountability and corruption in public office. However, there are ways in which human rights concerns can be channeled through parliament by effective and tactical lobbying. An example can be found in Papua New Guinea, where focus on the vulnerability of children to sexual abuse facilitated the adoption of new legislation which affords more protection to young women as well as children.[1] Similarly, in Fiji, the Family Law Act 2003, which addresses a number of inequalities formerly experienced by women in the area of divorce and matters of concern regarding children affected by family breakdown, and which gives practical effect to many of the commitments incurred under the CRC, was launched as a means whereby marriage would be strengthened and traditional forms of disputes settlement enhanced and incorporated within the family law framework rather than on the grounds that divorce would be made easier or greater gender equality achieved.

There are many opportunities for strengthening the human rights régime of Pacific Island countries though amendments to existing legislation, sometimes of quite a minor nature. For example, amendments to Interpretation Acts to ensure that the male always includes the female would be a simple first step. Ensuring that citizenship can be passed through both male and female lines would be another simple step. Removing provisions across a range of existing legislation that at present is expressly discriminatory would be a move in the right direction. A little more controversial might be strengthening the role of the Ombudsman for those countries which already have legislation in place, by ensuring that the role is not only passive but also pro-active and that human rights are included within the mandate of the office of the Ombudsman. In Vanuatu, Papua New Guinea, Fiji and Samoa, where the Ombudsman may provide a watchdog function over the worst abuses of government power, this position could be strengthened by giving the Ombudsman the power to bring cases to the courts, to compel the attendance of witnesses or to instigate enquiries into suspected cases of human rights abuses.

A further initiative which could be put in place by national legislative assemblies is the establishment of a human rights commission or commissioner. As has been indicated in the previous chapter, this has been done in Fiji, where, despite the dangers posed to human rights as a result of political turmoil, coups and constitutional change, national legislation in the form of the Human Rights Law Commission Act 1999 is in place. This empowers a Commission to investigate allegations of human rights violations and to investigate unfair discrimination in employment. The establishment of a national commission or commissioner marks a positive step in implementing measures to give effect not only to the country's own constitutional rights but also its international treaty obligations.

Similarly, the establishment of Law Reform Commissions or Commissioners to review the compliance of domestic law with human rights obligations could be effective, especially in making recommendations for amending domestic law to give effect to measures such as equality of treatment and non-discrimination. At present only Fiji and Papua New Guinea have Law Reform Commissions – although there are proposals to set one up in Vanuatu. Certainly any body or agency considering law reform should be expected to keep fundamental rights clearly in mind and not to draft laws that derogate from the international obligations of states.

The difficulty with relying on national legislative assemblies to effect these types of change is, as indicated at the outset of this book, that these institutions do not always function very effectively. Moreover, one of the problems encountered in the Pacific region is the disengagement of people and groups with the state and its role in the international arena. In part, this may be due to a post-independence rejection of structures put in place under colonialism. It may also be attributable to the persistence of cultural institutions and traditions at a local level and to disenchantment and disillusion with the central government for a variety of reasons. Political unrest, lack of party allegiance, reliance on coalition governments, poor and often unaccountable leadership and self-interest, combine to undermine the integrity of many legislative bodies. Lack of resources in terms of drafting skill and often lack of legislative time set aside for human rights issues, present practical challenges. The role and influence of traditional second houses, or the refusal of the head of state to approve of legislation where this is required, may also prove to be an obstacle to human rights legislation. Similarly, unless there is a strong sense of national identity in which people have sense of civic involvement beyond the local level, there is unlikely to be much progress through the formal law-making process.

Two alternatives present themselves. The first is to concentrate on developing the nation-state through the integration of local institutions and other structures within the framework of government. The second is to consider other non-state-specific avenues of human rights advocacy, including those that take the remit for human rights beyond national boundaries.

Re-configuring rights players

The commitment of national governments to human rights is important. At the very least it places human rights on the political agenda. If governments prioritise human rights as a matter of policy then legislation and other programmes to give effect to human rights can follow. However, it is evident in the region that there are a number of other players in the human rights arena who may be more effective in promoting human rights, or who, at the very least should be involved in any initiatives to do so.

The courts are the most obvious ones, and certainly the judgments of the courts and the development of a regional human rights jurisprudence is an important element in the advocacy and practice of human rights. It is clear also that there is room for improving access to justice and for further strengthening of the legal process. Often, however, the formal court system is an anathema to many Pacific Islanders, whose experience is more likely to be with the informal and local dispute resolution mechanisms. It is important therefore that these too are brought 'on board'. This may be through increasing human rights awareness at this level, though the integration of practices and procedures across the different adjudicative systems, or by combining personnel or officers from both systems, for example, through the use of assessors in formal courts or the deployment of visiting magistrates or circuit courts to more remote areas. The consequences of a parallel system of courts found in some of the countries of the region for the egalitarian application of human rights law needs to be examined and addressed. Legal pluralism, especially in procedures, may leave some litigants disadvantaged in the context of their human rights.

Civil society at all levels also has a role to play, including non-government organisations, youth groups and church groups. Whether these organisations and groups are primarily concerned with human rights or not they bring together people who not only have human rights but also have a range of skills, knowledge and experience. Members of civil society, therefore, can be both protagonists and beneficiaries of human rights. Thus civil society – which may be much more relevant to the lives of ordinary citizens than the state – could lead the way in respecting and giving positive effect to human rights within its various organisations and groupings. It is also important that government and the courts work with civil society in ascertaining and addressing the rights, needs and perceptions of Pacific islanders. Increasingly, this is being done, whether it is through the representations of non-government organisations to the reporting bodies of United Nations conventions, in representations to constitutional reform commissions or other law reforms working parties or committees. If the energies of civil society can be harnessed to support human rights then this could balance deficiencies in government-led initiatives and be a positive force in taking rights forward.

It is suggested therefore that while it is to be hoped that national governments will do something about human rights, there are other players who can make a difference, either in lieu of government initiatives, or to support these or to prompt or pressurise governments into action.

The other alternative is to approach the development of human rights from 'off-shore' through encouraging regional initiatives. There are, as has been previously indicated, several regional programmes and organisations which seek to encourage co-operation, mutuality and standard setting among Pacific Island states. While a number of these are directed at trade, this is by no means solely the case. The University of the South Pacific, which provides tertiary education for the Pacific islanders of its twelve member countries and beyond, is an example. There are a number of possible regional approaches which might advance human rights.

A regional charter

Although there have been various Asia-Pacific initiatives (Muntarbhorn 2005), the vastness of the region and the diversity of its people and situations has led to calls for a more localized approach. Consequently, there have been calls to develop a regional mechanism to advance human rights (Deklin 1992). These were first made at a conference in Sri Lanka in 1980, organized by the human rights committee of LAWASIA (Law Association for Asia and the Pacific), a non-governmental organisation which has been active in the field of human rights in the region since its inception in 1966. In 1985, LAWASIA held a further conference entitled 'Prospects for the Establishment of an Intergovernmental Human Rights Commission in the South Pacific'. The following year, LAWASIA organised a working party seminar in Apia, Samoa to consider the draft of a Pacific Charter. This led to two committees being set up: a drafting committee and a working committee. The former made four recommendations: to consider the African Charter as a model, with modifications, for the Pacific; to set up a Pacific Human Rights Commission modelled on the African Commission; to define the Pacific region which was to be included in a regional initiative;[2] to establish a human rights office attached to an existing Pacific organisation, the SPEC – the forerunner to what is now the Pacific Forum. Three of these recommendations were accepted by the working committee at a subsequent meeting in 1986, the second recommendation being rejected. The final report 'Report of the working party on a Proposed Pacific Charter of Human Rights' was published in December 1986. The proposed Charter included individual legal, economic, social and cultural rights and collective rights of people. Provision was also made for limitations of rights on specified grounds and for derogation of rights in times of national emergency. These provisions marked a departure from the African Charter model and drew on European and American models. The proposed Pacific charter also included three specific duties to be observed: the duty (of the state) to guarantee the independence of the courts and any other institutions that protect rights; the duty of individuals towards family, societies and communities; and the duty of individuals to respect each other without discrimination (Deklin 1992: 103). The report also recommended the establishment of a seven-member Commission with the broad mandate of promoting respect for human and people's rights and defending these. While it was not envisaged that the Commission would have coercive power it was envisaged that it could hear complaints by states against other states, or by individuals or groups against states or other organisations which were not party to the Charter, and could both investigate and mediate between these disputing parties, including using naming and shaming techniques familiar to Pacific islanders, whereby the Commission's reported findings or conclusions would be notified not only to the parties to the complaint but to other members of the Charter. The 1986 meeting was followed by a further seminar in 1989 at which delegates from a number of Pacific Island countries were invited to comment on the draft charter and its preamble. The proposal was that the draft would then be sent back to governments for in-country consideration and comment, which would be taken into account at a further meeting in 1990 where the Charter would form the basis for the development of a regional treaty and human rights mechanism (Hyndman 1992). It was identified as crucial that some form of human rights body be established in each country in order to advance discussion of the proposals, act as a focus for discussion and awareness raising, and as a lobbying agency to persuade national governments, not only to respond to the report but to sign up to the ultimate Charter and Commission, and then to given effect to its provisions in domestic legislation and positive action.

The proposed Charter had many strengths. It not only brought together a number of existing human rights provisions found in the written bills of rights in the constitutions of the region as well as in international conventions but it also sought to combine an emphasis on rights, freedoms and duties, both of the individual and of the collective, including the government. The Charter also sought to bring conformity to discrepancies found in national rights statements, for example, in the grounds on which discrimination would be unlawful, and to eradicate gender-biased language. Some of the innovations of the Charter are worth revisiting. For example, suggestions included that there are separate provisions for access to justice and the right to a fair trial, and that the right to a person's honour and reputation is incorporated either as a separate right or as part of the right to family and private life. Similarly, the right of property and the right to dispose of own resources is treated separately, with care being taken to avoid limiting interests in these to individual rights.

Although the model of the African Commission on Human Rights was rejected, the Pacific model suggests a compromise between the more robust one of the European Commission and that of the Inter-American Human Rights Commission. Some of the Commission's proposed activities were very practical, for example: to assist governments in the region to promote rights awareness, to review existing legislation for rights compliance, to advocate the ratification of international treaties and to assist in the report obligations which arose from these. Its intervention in human rights disputes however was perhaps more controversial, and less acceptable to sovereign states, although its role here might in fact have been relatively weak, with its main functions being educative and facilitative rather than adjudicative.

The final report recognised the need to sell the idea of the Charter and the regional protection and promotion of human rights to Pacific peoples and national governments. It also realised the need to get Pacific Islands with good human rights records 'on side' in order to take the proposals forward. Interestingly it noted that New Zealand and Australia were unlikely to champion human rights in the region owing to their own difficulties with minority and indigenous issues. Finding role models with sufficient persuasive powers and enlisting the political will of other Pacific countries was, therefore, a challenge. There were also fundamental weaknesses in the proposals. For example, the sources from which the Charter drew inspiration were themselves charters of rights which were foreign to the Pacific, although a number were integrated into national constitutions. There was little sense of Pacific ownership of the project either to inform its development and content or to take it forward. It was also unclear how the Commission and its work were to be resourced and whether inequality of funding would have any influence on its composition or location. Another concern on the part of Pacific Island countries may have been that 'their cultural identity would be in jeopardy should a Human Rights Charter for the Pacific come into force' (Butler 2005: 112; Angelo 1992: 47). A further reason may have been that the idea emanated predominantly from 'outsiders' by albeit knowledgeable in the region and may have been driven more by the impetus for a bill of rights in New Zealand than a desire for one by Pacific leaders. It may also have been simply that the time was not ripe for this development because of a general and widespread lack of human rights awareness in the region and because of the other concerns of Pacific Island governments.

Although nothing came of the Charter, the Pacific Plan articulated by the Pacific Islands Forum in 2005 and updated in 2006 included among its provisions commitment to the 'ratification and implementation of international and regional human rights Conventions' (Pacific Plan 2006). Whether this envisages a revival of the Pacific Charter is not stated. What does seem clear, at least from an international perspective, is that any regional Charter would have to meet as a minimum the universal standards set out in existing United Nations statements. However, a regional charter might have the scope to prioritise rights in a different way and to place more emphasis on those aspects which are deemed to be of greater relevance in the Pacific region, for example, the environment, food resources, family, duties and collective rights. Alternatively, a regional convention might be used to draw up a structural framework for human rights in the region building on a number of existing initiatives and perhaps integrating new ones, for example, a regional human rights commissioner or human rights commission or agency. Thus its focus would be less on substantive rights than on creating an operating framework to advance the relationship and interaction of national, regional and international mechanisms for the protection and enhancement of human rights already stated in other instruments, including national constitutions as well as international treaties.

The possibility of a regional mechanism was revived at a conference held in Apia, Samoa in April 2008. This was organised by the New Zealand

Centre for Public Law, Victoria University of Wellington, New Zealand, the Attorney-General's office of Samoa and the organisation Interights, with funding from the Commonwealth Secretariat, the New Zealand International Aid and Development Agency and the Foreign Office of the Federal Republic of Germany. The theme was 'Strategies for the future: Protecting Rights in the Pacific'. The aim of the symposium was to identify key human rights challenges and to consider strategies for strengthening existing mechanisms and enhancing the protection of human rights. This symposium brought together a wide range of representatives from civil society, international organisations, academia, legal practice, inter-governmental agencies such as the Commonwealth Secretariat, the Pacific Island Forum Secretariat and public sector representatives. A number of countries of the region were represented and national reports were submitted for several of these. While there may have been hopes that the Pacific Charter would have been revived or a new one emerge, this did not happen. Nevertheless there appears to be substantial support for taking human rights to a new level in the region, although whether this is shared by smaller island countries or those that were not represented at the symposium or those in government or at grass roots level is less clear. Certainly, there is considerably more rights awareness and rights debate today than in 1986, due no doubt to the many initiatives which have occurred in the interim. The climate of human rights, therefore, may be right for a change of pace and focus. Mechanisms or strategies for taking rights forward which are acceptable to and supported by Pacific Island people, however, remain unclear.

A Human Rights Commission

The 2008 symposium provided a useful opportunity for considering possibilities and bringing to a wider audience the many initiatives currently taking place in the region. Among these it appears that there may be some support for a regional mechanism such as a Human Rights Commission for the Pacific. Whether this would provide merely an advisory role or also an adjudicative one – similar to the former European Human Rights Commission, would have to be resolved, as would the relationship between a regional commission and national commissions should more countries in the Pacific create these. There is also the question of whether those countries which cannot resource a national commission would be willing to recognise a regional one, especially if this was perceived as reflecting the views of the larger more dominant Pacific Island countries. There would also be issues as to where such a commission should be based and how it should be staffed. The most obvious location is within the Pacific Forum Secretariat which has its administrative centre in Fiji. Fiji's own human rights record, however, may make this problematical. Locating a possible Human Rights Commission within the Forum would give concrete effect to the articulation of concern about human rights in the current Pacific Plan which lists as its priorities under 'Good Governance' the 'establishment of a regional ombudsman and human rights mechanisms to support implementation of Forum Principles of Good Leadership and Accountability' (Pacific Plan 2006). This is listed under strategic objective 12 within the Forum's Implementation Strategy: Initiatives for the First Three Years (2006–2008), and marked up as 'Implement' and 'Further analysis required', reflecting perhaps the willingness to engage with human rights at a regional level but the difficulties of doing so. The Forum seeks to encourage and facilitate regional strategies and co-operation, but it is mindful of the need to respect the sovereignty of its member states, as well as the cultural differences between them. Human rights issues present tricky dilemmas as often the worst offenders of human rights are the governments whose leaders attend the Forum, the focus of which is essentially political and economic. It is also clear from the Pacific Plan that the Forum does not perceive human rights to be integral to all forms of development in the region. There is for instance no mention of human rights in the leading priorities of the Forum Plan, which are economic growth and sustainable development. Any regional mechanism integrated within the Forum might therefore find itself not only limited in its mandate but also proscribed in its ability to effect changes.

A Commission could however be independent of the Forum but linked to it, as is the case with various other Pacific organisations such as the Pacific Islands Forum Fisheries Agency, which is based in Honiara in Solomon Islands; the Secretariat of the Pacific Regional Environment Programme (SPREP), which is based in Apia, Samoa; and the Pacific Islands Development Programme which is based in the East-West Centre in Hawaii. An independent regional human rights mechanism would have the advantage of being involved in the implementation of Forum strategies and of providing advice and information on human rights issues in the region, without being curtailed or restricted by considerations of political tact or diplomacy. Such a mechanism would however require independent resourcing to maintain a distinct identity from that of the Forum.

Alternatively, a regional mechanism might not be a Human Rights Commission but a Human Rights Desk or information point for the region. This is not a new idea. The possibility of a Human Rights Officer attached to a regional organisation (then the South Pacific Bureau of Economic Co-operation) was mooted in the 1980s (Hyndman 1992: 106). Certainly today there is a need to bring together the considerable body of expertise and experience both within the region and beyond on human rights. This could be done by utilising existing structures. For example, there could be such a 'desk' linked to the Pacific Legal Information Institute (PacLII) which, funded by donors and located in Vanuatu, provides an electronic data base for a wide range of legal materials to the region and is freely accessible globally to anyone with internet access. The viability of such a resource would be dependent not only on dedicated funding and staffing, but also the willingness of national governments and the public law sector to provide information to be published. The advantage would be that PacLII is apolitical, it is accessible to anyone – including those in countries which are not members of the Forum or any other Pacific regional organisations; those people who have not yet achieved independence, for example the *Kanaks* in New Caledonia or the people of Tokelau; or those who are often regarded as peripheral to the region, such as indigenous people in Hawaii, in American Samoa, in Palau and in French Polynesia.

A further alternative which appears to be mooted in the Pacific Plan is the creation of a regional ombudsman. Such a mechanism could provide not only information on human rights but also act as a focal point for various non-governmental organisations which wanted to report on human rights abuses and concerns. In part, this function might duplicate that which is already provided by the Pacific Islands Association of Non-Government Organisations (PIANGO), although this umbrella organisation includes a number of non-governmental organisations which are not directed primarily at human rights. It might be envisaged that a regional ombudsman would do more than function as a point of collection and dissemination of human rights information and be able to initiate enquiries into suspected human rights abuses as well as compile national reports for public dissemination. Whether such a mechanism would be able to take the further step of acting upon adverse human rights reports would be debatable. Historically, ombudsmen in the region have been generally 'toothless' and their reports which recommend prosecution have fallen on 'deaf ears', especially when those at fault have been government ministers or those in public office. Conceivably, however, a regional ombudsman might be able to bring diplomatic pressure to bear through the Forum, which is after all a meeting of Pacific leaders. Whether the Forum would be willing or able to exert any meaningful pressure on members who had abused human rights is questionable. To date there has been little evidence of this.

Whether a regional mechanism will emerge, and the form that if might take if it does so, seems to be some way off. If it does then its success will depend on the extent to which it is recognised and accepted as being a Pacific creation which reflects the concerns, views and aspirations of Pacific islanders. To enhance the recognition and protection of human rights in a practical way will therefore require a clearer understanding of how human rights are perceived, constructed and experienced in the different island countries of the region so that common ground can be established and used as the foundation for further initiatives.

A model for rights development

Some work on recognising the importance of bridging what is often perceived of as a gulf between universal declarations of human rights and local perceptions of rights has already been undertaken. In particular, the New Zealand Law Commission's 2006 'Converging Currents' report reflects this realisation. This report suggests that as a first step there needs to be an 'operational alignment between custom and human rights in the legal systems of the Pacific region' (2006: 240). This it suggests would require the involvement of governments, legislative bodies, courts and communities in working together to explore ways in which custom and human rights can be harmonised in such a way that, on the one hand custom can be developed and sustained equitably, without having to give way to human rights or be threatened by them, and on the other hand human rights can be recognised and realised in culturally relevant terms. In other words human rights are used 'to enhance custom, just as customary values enable communities to internalise human rights' (2006: 80 para 6.26). Its second suggestion is that legal systems are developed to incorporate traditional dispute settlement mechanisms while at the same time promoting the observation of human rights standards and values within these community justice institutions. The third suggestion is that the courts develop an 'indigenous jurisprudence that draws upon both custom and human rights' (2006: 240).

In addressing the practicalities of achieving these aims, the Report has a number of recommendations for strategies which could be adopted by courts, community justice bodies and the state. In particular, the Report suggests that the state should provide a framework to direct how courts should harmonise custom and human rights; should ensure that legislation or amendment to constitutions allows for the horizontal as well as vertically application of human rights; and that there should be clearer state recognition of social, cultural and economic rights as well as group rights and duties. In respect of community justice institutions and systems the Report suggests that there is greater scope for these to be recognised in legislation and for their human rights role to be enhanced through appropriate training. It is also suggested that closer links be forged between the formal courts and these community justice systems. The bulk of the Report's suggestions apply to the administration of justice and the courts. In particular, the need is recognised that courts need to be made more accessible to women and more responsive to the views and rights of women. Courts are also seen as having a significant role in addressing hard cases in human rights, for example where freedom of speech, movement and religion appear to conflict with customary practices. Indeed, the Report seems to envisage the courts as arbiters between custom and human rights, tasked with the responsibility of examining customary practices to establish customary values and considering whether in the light of those values, practices could not be modified to reflect both customary and human rights values. It is this role of the courts which would generate an indigenous common law for Pacific Island countries. This is a considerable task for judges and magistrates. One practical suggestion is that each country develops custom law commentaries for judges. This might work where custom is relatively homogeneous, for example in Samoa and Tonga, but where it is not, as in Papua New Guinea, Solomon Islands, Vanuatu and the Federated States of Micronesia, the exercise could result in a number of commentaries and associated differences in statements of values and practices. There is also the question of whether the courts have the resources and skills to embark on such enquiries and whether it will be possible for judges and magistrates to exclude their own subjective opinions and views on custom. The Report does, however, make a number of possible procedural suggestions, for example greater involvement of assessors, a move away from the adversarial approach towards an inquisitorial approach where issues of custom are raised, less stringent observation of the rule of precedent in cases involving custom and human rights so that changes and developments can be accommodated, less strict requirements of evidence, and greater capacity building and training for judges. The Report also considers how the role of public review bodies might be enhanced to benefit human rights, for example, by enlarging the scope of the ombudsman or monitoring bodies established under leadership codes, to include consideration of how custom and human rights might be harmonised, as well as extending their powers of investigation to the exercise of statutory functions by customary authorities.

A number of suggestions of the Report are already given effect in some Pacific Island countries, so there are regional models which comparative law reformers might consider. The Report realistically appreciates that there are hard areas where accommodating customary values and fundamental human rights may be difficult, for example gender equality, women and children, migrant and minority groups, young people, freedom of religion, expression, and movement. It also recognises the need for in-country empirical studies to establish and record customary practices and the need to bring together representatives from all sectors to arrive at consensus on underlying customary values. By focussing on the role of the administration of justice, both through the courts and through community justice forums, there is, perhaps implicitly, recognition of the difficulties of getting the state to act through legislation. The major challenge, however, which is presented by the suggestions of the Report, is to ensure that consideration and accommodation of cultural values does not derogate from the human rights values established in international instruments under which Pacific Island states have obligations.

Arriving at a consensus between the traditional and the modern, what is customary and what is universal, especially in legally plural systems where each unit may wish to assert its own cultural identity, is difficult but not impossible, as demonstrated by the African Charter.

The African Charter on Human Rights and People's Rights

The process which led to the Charter gives some insight into how the convergence advocated by the New Zealand Report might be given effect.

Although the African Charter represents a regional convergence, some of the thinking and processes behind it could also be applied at national level to achieve the type of harmonisation envisaged in the New Zealand Report. Indeed, given the importance of customary law, traditional values and the plurality of legal systems, the 'Banjul Charter', as it is often referred to, might provide a useful model for the Pacific region. Certainly the African Charter was considered when the LAWASIA Draft Pacific Charter was being drawn up in 1989.

The African Charter came into force in October 1986 after being adopted by the Organisation of African Unity and Heads of States at its eighteenth assembly in 1981. It was drafted in the period 1979–1981. Its original inception was at a conference on the rule of law, held in Lagos in 1961. The Lagos conference recommended the adoption of an African Convention on Human Rights. Clearly the final outcome took a number of years. As is the case in the Pacific region, almost all of the African states experienced colonisation and the subsequent challenges of independence under structures not always of their own choosing. Often boundaries between states were demarcated by colonial authorities and sometimes people were divided. There were, and still are, the challenges of inter-tribal or inter-clan strife, under-development, inadequate infra-structure, inequality of access to education and health care and problems of discrimination. African countries, like Pacific Island countries, therefore have a shared colonial history, and much common contemporary experience in terms of economic, political and social concerns. They are also countries where customary law rests in oral traditions, where freedoms are constrained by consideration of duties and the welfare of the community and where traditional conflict resolution remains an important element in the lives of people who are predominantly still rural dwellers (Frémont 2008).

The Charter, however, is an attempt by those countries to give effect to the rights which they believe to be important within the African context, the while having regard to the international instruments of the United Nations, especially the Charter of the United Nations and the Universal Declaration of Human Rights. The Preamble to the Charter reflects the importance of the common history of African countries, the importance of African values and civilisation and the interrelationship of rights and duties, human and peoples' rights, and the right to development with other rights.

While many of the rights listed reflect those found in other rights' instruments, such as the International Covenant on Civil and Political Rights, what is distinctive about the Charter is its inclusion of individual rights and duties, especially the duties owed by individuals to family, society and the state, and the integration of civil and political rights with social, economic and cultural rights.

There are also some specific rights found in the Charter which may find some resonance in the Pacific. For example, Article 12 prohibits the mass expulsion of non-nationals from a territory. As this could include racial, ethnic or religious groups, such a right might be important in the Pacific region where there are small pockets of such groups scattered throughout the region, some of whom – as indicated in earlier chapters – have been subject to harassment, intimidation and – certainly in the case of religion – banishment or exclusion. Article 18 emphasises the importance of the family as the 'natural unit and basis of society' and 'the custodian of morals and traditional values'. This too may well find support in the Pacific region, where the articulation of family rights is remarkably weak despite the importance of the family to the structure of society and the economic well-being of most individuals. Article 29.1 emphasises the important duty of every individual to 'preserve the harmonious development of the family and to work for the cohesion and respect of the family'.

Significantly, by incorporating rights found in other international instruments and stating some of these even more strongly – for example, the rights of women and children not to be discriminated against,[3] the Charter gives effect to the scope of international instruments which a number of states may not have incorporated into domestic law or even ratified. Thus, states which become parties to the Charter become bound by those international instruments which they have chosen to ignore. Given the relatively low uptake of international rights' commitments in the Pacific region, this approach may have positive advantages, especially if member states – as with the Banjul Charter – feel a sense of ownership of the Charter.

The Charter also imposes a duty on member states to promote, through teaching, education and publicity, the provisions of the Charter.[4] Given that many people, especially in the Pacific region, and probably in Africa, are ignorant of their rights and certainly ignorant of any international rights instruments, this obligation to provide awareness is a positive feature of the Charter, although the extent to which there are resources or political will to do this of course may be very variable.

Also importantly, the Banjul Charter includes 'third generation' rights. These encompass the right to self-determination, the right to economic, social and cultural development, the right to peace and security, and the right to a 'general satisfactory environment favourable to their development'.[5] This suggests that not only is there an obligation on domestic government in its pursuit of development, but that foreign policy must be directed at achieving this as well. In other words, other countries dealing with African states which are parties to the Charter become subject to a rights régime which could impose obligations on that foreign state, particularly when pursuing certain development policies in the region. Arguably this dimension could be of considerable significance in the Pacific region, where there is international pressure on Pacific Island Countries to pursue development policies which may not be conducive to 'a general satisfactory environment favourable to ... development,' a point which has been highlighted in Chapter Four.

The African Charter is not, however, without its flaws. First, although there are no general derogation provisions, there is scope for derogating from particular rights where this is provided for by law. Given the plural nature of many legal systems in Africa, this may mean that considerations of customary law permit restrictions of freedom of conscience and religion, or expression and association, or that state laws may be passed to allow such restrictions. Second, the Charter makes no provision for a Court or tribunal to adjudicate on rights' infringements. This is a perceived weakness of the Charter. Instead there is a Commission composed of members elected by the Assembly of Heads of State and Government of the Organisation of African Unity, who serve in their individual capacity for a period of six years. The Commission's powers are set out under Article 45. Its role is to promote human rights and make recommendations to governments where the opportunity to do so arises and to formulate standards, principles and rules to guide national legislative bodies. It also serves an interpretative role, which is quasi-judicial, and can give authoritative interpretations on the provisions of the Charter. In its exercise of this power, the Commission is expected to draw on the many international models which are referred to in Articles 60 and 61. Although there is no court, the Commission is empowered to receive communications either by individuals or states who feel that their rights have been breached.

Where a matter arises inter-state, then this may be resolved bilaterally without involving the Commission, other than keeping it informed, or it may be resolved by way of reference to the Commission if no solution can be reached by the states concerned or one of the states wants the matter referred to the Commission. Because the Commission does not sit as a court its proceedings are in the nature of a general inquiry and it has wide powers to call for submissions, information and representations, including witnesses. The primary task of the Commission appears to be to broker an amicable solution.[6] If this cannot be achieved then a report is sent to the Organisation of African Unity Heads of State and Government together with the Commission's recommendations. The purpose presumably is to facilitate a political solution – rather than a legal one.

There is scope for non-state parties to complain to the Commission. It is not specified whether this is limited to individuals or whether group representations are also permitted.[7] An applicant, whether an individual or a group, does not have to be the victim of a breach of rights set out in the Charter. These communications must reveal a series of serious or massive violations of human and peoples' rights, and must be well-founded and not based solely on media reports. Domestic remedies have to be exhausted before such a communication to the Commission can be made. If the allegations are found to be well-founded and sufficiently widespread and serious, then the Commission communicates with the Organisation of African Unity Heads of State and Government. It is this political body which will then decide whether the Commission should undertake a study into the matter, or not. A majority of two-thirds is required before the matter can be referred back to the Commission to follow this course of action and make a report and recommendations. All reports remain confidential until considered by the Assembly.

The political dimension, the lack of judicial process, lack of publicity and obstacles for individuals seeking redress from the Commission where they are victims of rights violations, have all combined to undermine the perceived effectiveness of the Charter. But there are other problems. Language and legal literacy are one, especially where many people rely on oral tradition and have their own vernacular language which is different from that of official publications or the language used in the legal system. Competing claims between modern state laws and traditional customary law, which has not been addressed by discussion, negotiation or conciliation, means that the former is still seen as lacking both legitimacy and a relevance (Frémont 2008). There is also, more fundamentally, uncertainty about the identity of legal systems within African countries and the authoritative sources of the rule of law within plural systems which facilitate the shifting of normative boundaries.

The African Charter, therefore, offers a useful inspiration for how traditional and customary rights might be integrated with a range of intentionally sanctioned human rights, but also demonstrates how a charter which leaves too much power of derogation to sovereign states can become an empty statement, especially if it lacks a strong enforcement mechanism which operates in a transparent way and provides access to justice for individual grievances as well as group or collective rights. The African experience also highlights some of the challenges which are experienced in states emerging from colonial rule and where there are a number of normative systems which can inform legal development.

Initiatives from the Commonwealth

There are, however, alternatives to attempting to establish a regional charter which is both acceptable to all the countries of the region, and meets the demands of international organisations while satisfying those of Pacific Islanders. Many of the countries of the region are members of the Commonwealth.[8] Indeed, nearly half of all Commonwealth countries are small island states and many of them are relatively young independent states. The advancement of human rights is a core political value of the Commonwealth as indicated in the Harare Commonwealth Declaration of 1991 and the earlier Declaration of Commonwealth Principles of 1971. The Strategic Plan of the Commonwealth Secretariat 2004/2005 – 2007/2008 has two broad goals: to support member countries to prevent or resolve conflicts, strengthen democracy and the rule of law and achieve greater respect for human rights; to support pro-poor policies for economic growth and sustainable development in member countries. Both are relevant to Pacific Island countries.

Within its human rights programme, the Commonwealth has a number of key themes: developing best practices, with particular focus on the adoption and implementation of international human rights instruments; strengthening human rights mechanisms; increasing knowledge and awareness; mainstreaming human rights and the publication and dissemination of human rights information. This latter includes the publication of the Commonwealth Human Rights Law Digest and the Human Rights Update Newsletter. These publications enable human rights defenders and activists to keep up to date with developments elsewhere in the Commonwealth and to contribute to this body of knowledge. The Commonwealth Secretariat also has a legal education association (CLEA) which aims to foster research and best practice in legal education throughout the Commonwealth. Among other human rights initiatives this has produced a model human rights curriculum for member countries which could be drawn on in advancing human rights education in the Pacific Island member countries.

In 2007, the Commonwealth Forum of National Human Rights Institutions was formed. This provides an opportunity for all those member countries with National Human Rights Institutions to come together and share information, experiences and best practices and assist national institutions to fulfill their mandated activities. The Forum is also intended to complement and support other human rights organisations and to provide a platform for strengthening the capacity of national human rights institutions to protect and promote human rights in the Commonwealth.[9] This Forum met for the first time in Kampala in November 2007. It made a number of recommendations of relevance to Commonwealth Pacific Island countries. These included recommendations that: Commonwealth Heads of Government should strengthen NHRIS through increased funding, timely implementation of their recommendations and establishment of mechanisms of engagement; and that Commonwealth Heads of Government grant full recognition and participation of the Forum in CHOGM processes and related activities. The Forum also noted the expression of support by the Office of the UN High Commissioner of Human Rights towards Commonwealth national human rights institutions to assist them to effectively carry out their mandates. Although at present only Fiji has a National Human Rights Institution, the presence of an office of the United Nations High Commission for Human Rights in the region – in Fiji – together with the Commonwealth membership of most of the countries of the region, presents an opportunity to pursue these recommendations at national and regional level within the Pacific.

The Commonwealth Secretariat also has its own human rights division which was established in 1985 and became an independent unit in 2002. The aims of the unit are to: support member countries in their efforts to develop and comply with national and international human rights mandates;

to assist in the establishment or strengthening of in-country human rights institutions through the provision of technical assistance and policy advice; to advocate and promote human rights awareness; to assist, where requested, in the development of national plans of action on human rights; to disseminate best practice across the Commonwealth; to collaborate with other international agencies, especially the United Nations; to advise the Secretary General on human rights issues within the Commonwealth; to mainstream human rights in addressing issues of poverty and inequality within the Commonwealth and to integrate human rights into all the activities of the Commonwealth Secretariat.

In 2007, the Human Rights Unit of the Commonwealth Secretariat developed a Model National Plan of Action on Human Rights which was launched in 2008. This model is intended to assist Commonwealth member countries in developing their own national human rights plans while advancing Commonwealth values. As Pacific Island countries which are members of the United Nations will be subject to a Universal Periodic Review Mechanism being developed by the Human Rights Council of the United Nations, the launch of the model is timely, especially as some Pacific Island countries are due to report on their human rights record in the near future. Attending the 2008 symposium in Apia, Samoa, Dr Purna Sen, Head of the Human Rights Unit of the Commonwealth Secretariat, indicated in a news release that the recommendations of the delegates there would be useful in helping to tailor Commonwealth development assistance to the Pacific region.[10]

To date, Commonwealth initiatives in the region may appear to be limited. However, two of its key programmes are of considerable relevance to the Pacific region. These are its Commonwealth Youth Programme and its focus on the impact of climate change on Commonwealth Countries.

The Commonwealth Youth Programme Pacific Centre is located in Honiara in Solomon Islands. The Programme works with 14 Pacific countries, including Australia and New Zealand, and provides a focus for youth policy development, youth enterprise (job creation), youth participation, youth worker training and HIV/AIDS awareness. The programme works with national governments, tertiary education providers in the region and corporate bodies as well as development agencies such as UNICEF and the UNDP. The overarching aim of the programme is to empower young people by focusing on the development of entrepreneurial skills, the involvement of youth in governance, youth participation in society and social awareness and the education of young people as youth workers. The programme also aims to build strategic partnerships with other organisations at national, regional and international level and to link young people in Pacific Island countries with those elsewhere in the Commonwealth through the Commonwealth Youth Ministers Meeting and the Youth Caucus network. In December 2007, the Commonwealth Plan of Action for Youth Empowerment 2007–2015 was launched in Papua New Guinea. This provides the blueprint for the involvement of young people in the development and social transformation of their countries. Given the high percentage of young people in Pacific Island populations, acceptance of the Plan by ministers in Pacific Island countries may be an important step in working to ensure that their voice and their rights are taken into account in the development of human rights initiatives in the region.

Climate change first came onto the Commonwealth agenda in 1989. A number of Commonwealth countries are threatened by climate change and twenty-six of the forty-three members of the Alliance of Small Island States (AOSIS) are Commonwealth countries. For them, climate change may be the single most important threat facing the economic development, peace, security and the continuing existence of small island states. Climate change is inseparable from issues of sustainable development and the economic and social rights of island people. The Commonwealth reviewed its framework for action on climate change in 2007. Working with the Commonwealth Foundation, the Commonwealth Secretariat's climate change programme is based on helping vulnerable member states identify ways in which they can adapt socially and economically to these new challenges. It has commissioned a number of research projects to determine the needs and vulnerabilities of specific member countries. The Commonwealth Heads of Government meeting in Kampala in November 2007 issued the Commonwealth Climate Change Action Plan. Besides the lobbying weight of the Commonwealth in its dealings with other international organisations, the plan includes some provision of specific relevance to Pacific Island states. Resolution 12 (iii) advocates 'Support for improved land use management, including conservation and sustainable use of forest resources. This should comprise market-based mechanisms and compensatory measures for the preservation of standing forests; provisions for reforestation and afforestation; and measures to combat illegal logging and other causes of deforestation'. This initiative may be of particular significance for countries such as Papua New Guinea and Solomon Islands, while Resolution 12 (vi), which advocates 'The provision of technical assistance and other support, particularly to least developed countries and vulnerable small states, to assess the implications of climate change and the benefits of building adaptation into all aspects of national planning and budgeting, wherever feasible and practical,'[11] could be of considerable importance to those Pacific Island countries which are also Commonwealth members facing the direct challenges of climate change such as Tuvalu, Kiribati and parts of Papua New Guinea.

The current Commonwealth Plan ends in 2008 and the next four-year cycle will be considered in mid-2008. There is therefore an opportunity for the Pacific to engage more closely with the Commonwealth over the next four years to advance those dimensions of human rights which Pacific Islanders perceive as being priorities.

The Commonwealth Secretariat also works closely with the United Nations human rights system and has a Memorandum of Understanding with the

Office of the High Commissioner for Human Rights and the United Nations Development Programme (1998).

The offices of the United Nations

Throughout this book, there has been reference to the United Nations and the international conventions and treaties that have emanated from the UN. As a result of United Nations membership,[12] Pacific Island countries are brought within the umbrella of the United Nations' bodies for a variety of purposes and although they tend to have very little direct representation on the governing panels, do have the opportunity to be heard from time to time in a variety of ways. For example, through the International Coordinating Committee of National Institutions for the Protection and Promotion of Human Rights (ICC), National Human Rights institutions are provided with a collective body, voice and representation within the UN human rights mechanisms, facilitated by the Office of the UN High Commissioner for Human Rights (OHCHR).[13] Although at present only Fiji has a national human rights institution, should other Pacific Island countries establish similar bodies, they too would have the opportunity to be represented through this body. It is also the case that a number of non-governmental organisations have observer status at the United Nations. Although there are no organisations under this heading dedicated to the South Pacific region,[14] international organisations such as the International Committee of the Red Cross and the Commonwealth Secretariat do have such standing and maintain permanent offices at the headquarters of the United Nations. Moreover, the Commonwealth is well represented on the United Nations Human Rights Council, which replaced the Commission on Human Rights as the watchdog of human rights in the United Nations, in 2006 (Resolution 60/251). Of the forty-seven members who sit on the Council, thirteen are Commonwealth countries.[15] The mandate of this Council is to promote universal respect for the promotion and protection of human rights; to address situations where there are violations of human rights and to make recommendations regarding these. It is also to promote human rights education, capacity building and technical assistance. No Pacific Island countries are members of the Council, although there are representatives from the wider Asia-Pacific region. The Council has the power to adopt special procedures in respect of either specific themes or specific countries. While there are currently no special procedure mandates directed at Pacific Island countries, there have been visits to countries in the region in recent years by special procedure mandate holders, including for example, to Fiji in 1999 concerning the sale and prostitution of children and their involvement in pornography, and on the use of mercenaries. Visits have also been requested, for example for Nauru on arbitrary detention, for Papua New Guinea on torture, mercenaries, detention and education, and for Fiji on the independence of the judiciary. None of the Pacific Island countries have, however, extended a standing invitation to the Council to make such visits.

Significantly, the Council has recently announced a new system of universal periodic review under which the implementation of human rights obligations of each General Assembly Member State will be examined.[16] Pacific Island countries are brought within this review procedure. The purpose, as stated in the resolution, is to review 'the fulfillment by each State of its human rights obligations and commitments in a manner which ensures universality of coverage and equal treatment with respect to all States'. The review process is envisaged as being one of co-operation between the reviewing panel and the reviewed state and to complement rather than replace existing treaty monitoring processes. In 2007, further details of this process were published. States have to prepare and present reports, either orally or in writing, in Geneva. These reports are meant to be prepared in consultation with other stakeholders. The United Nations Office of the High Commissioner for Human Rights will also present information, drawing on reports of treaty bodies, any special procedures adopted in respect of the country under review, and any observations made by the State or other UN agencies. Additional information may be provided by non-state stakeholders such as academics, non-governmental organisations, human rights defenders and national human rights institutions. The amount of material which can be presented is limited by stipulated page limits.

Under the timetable of this review process Tonga will be reviewed in 2008; Vanuatu in 2009; Fiji, Kiribati, Marshall Islands and the Federated States of Micronesia in 2010; and Nauru, Papua New Guinea, Solomon Islands and Samoa in 2011.[17]

Within the OHCHR the Pacific Island countries fall under the much wider Asia-Pacific region. However, a more localised presence has been evident in the region for the past seven years. In 2001, the OCHR was involved in supporting the peace process in the Solomon Islands following the civil unrest of 1999–2000. In 2005, the OHCHR established a regional office in Suva, Fiji and the following year a sub-office was opened in Honiara, Solomon Islands. Under the 2008–2009 programme it is proposed to close the latter and to work through the Suva office and the Human Rights Adviser established in 2007 in Papua New Guinea. There are also United Nations Country Teams based in Fiji, Samoa and Papua New Guinea. The regional office covers the sixteen member countries of the Pacific Forum.

Increasingly, the United Nations is becoming more involved in the Pacific Island region. Not only has the Office of the United Nations High Commissioner for Human Rights (OHCHR) supported a number of regional human rights initiatives in recent years, but the establishment of a United Nations Commissioner for Human Rights in Fiji has meant that there is a visible, local presence in the region. Under the 2006–2007 programme of human rights action, regional priorities are to promote the ratification of the core human rights treaties and to support Pacific

Island countries in meeting their reporting and implementation obligations. The regional office also has as its priorities: assisting in initiatives to establish human rights institutions at a national level; to assist in strengthening national protection mechanisms; and to contribute to awareness raising and training so that a better understanding of human rights not only empowers rights holders but encourages a greater acceptance of international rights standards and norms. Over the next two years the OHCHR proposes to work more closely with the Pacific Forum and in particular to support those aspects of the Pacific Plan which are directed at human rights, including proposals within the Forum to 'establish regional judicial structures and develop national human rights institutions or other analogous mechanisms.'[18] The regional office also proposes to develop its co-operation with the different levels of stakeholders in the region who are engaged in the reporting process to UN treaty bodies, including the recently announced Universal Periodic Review, referred to above.

This review procedure offers an important opportunity to bring human rights issues in the region under the international spotlight. As the review process is not limited to specific treaty compliance and as potentially a wide range of stakeholders could be involved in the process, the next few years might see the role of the United Nations in the region acquiring greater visibility and publicity. Whether Pacific Island countries will comply with the review process, or involve the range of stakeholders potentially provided for, or make public the statements which are made or the observations of the reviewing panel remains to be seen. There is also the question of whether there will be sufficient resources not only to produce the reports but to travel to Geneva to present them. It may be the case that this new initiative of the United Nations encourages greater co-operation between organisations such as the Commonwealth Human Rights Unit, the Office of the High Commission for Human Rights in Fiji, the Pacific Forum and other stakeholders such as RRRT and the University of the South Pacific in order to produce the information required. Alternatively, this review process may go the same way as the reporting process under various international instruments; that is that Pacific Island countries fall behind in meeting their reporting obligations, concessions are made and reports attract little if any publicity, either in their countries of origin or in the international forum.

Conclusion

This brings us full circle but still leaves many questions unanswered. Who decides what is desirable in the field of human rights and who asserts that a particular *modus vivendi* is appropriate for a particular people? Is it the predominantly male government of a country, or the King, or the party which has won an election by buying the most votes? Is the challenge to universal rights on the grounds of legal imperialism a subterfuge for avoiding international or domestic criticism for the failure of governments to deliver human rights protection without discrimination to their own people? Is the claim of culture, custom and national uniqueness a way of avoiding charges of racism, bigotry, greed, or sheer apathy about human rights issues? Or does it reflect a deep-seated belief in the intrinsic value of what is local, known and proven?

There are no easy or single answers to these questions, nor do all people speak with one voice. Pacific Island countries adopted constitutions with bills of rights in them because at the time they had little choice. They may have signed up to, or succeeded to, international conventions on human rights without having as the prime motive a desire to implement a raft of measures to give effect to the rights contained therein. In many respects Pacific Island countries appear to be uneasily suspended between local and global cultural structures, with the consequence that human rights law struggles to find a secure footing. For this to happen, the focus of human rights law may have to shift towards greater emphasis on the democratic involvement of all sectors of society, and towards concentrating on those needs which are most important in developing countries. This will require political will at national level, assisted and supported by regional initiatives and agendas. The international community also has a role to play. If Pacific Island countries are to be urged to sign up to international conventions then the benefits of such commitments need to be clear. There also needs to be a realistic appreciation of the burden of complying with implementation and monitoring of international convention obligations in small island states. The initiatives which international organisations have commenced in the region need to be continued and enhanced so that not only can Pacific Islands benefit from these but also the wider international community acquires greater knowledge of Pacific Island countries. Better representation of Pacific Islands at Asia-Pacific and international forum would also assist this mutual process. At the same time, it needs to be appreciated that globalisation and internationalism can be insensitive and damaging to the interests of countries such as those in the Pacific region. It is therefore particularly important that Pacific Island countries are afforded the dignity and respect that the international community expects those countries to show to their own citizens, equally and without discrimination.

Notes

1 Criminal Code (Sexual Offences and Crimes against Children) Act 2002, incorporated into the Criminal Code Act (Cap 262).
2 It was proposed to include within this Hawaii and French Polynesia as well as Australia and New Zealand (Deklin 1992: 99).
3 Article 18(3).
4 Article 25.
5 Article 24.

6 Article 52.
7 Article 55 refers to 'other communications', that is, other than state.
8 Fiji (when not suspended), Kiribati, Nauru, Papua New Guinea, Solomon Islands, Samoa, Tonga, Tuvalu and Vanuatu.
9 Kampala Communiqué of the Commonwealth Forum of National Human Rights Institutions, 19 November 2007, http://www.thecommonwealth.org/shared_asp_files/GFSR.asp?NodeID=173604 (accessed 23 June 2008).
10 News Release, 1 May 2008, http://www.thecommonwealth.org/news/34580/178695/010508humanrightssamoa.htm. (accessed 9 May 2008).
11 http://www.thecommonwealth.org/document/34293/35144/173014/climateactionplan.htm (accessed 9 May 2008).
12 Although Cook Islands, Niue and Tokelau are not members of the United Nations General Assembly, membership of other countries of the region is as follows: Fiji (1970); Kiribati (1999); Marshall Islands (1991); Nauru (1999); Palau (1994); Papua New Guinea (1975); Samoa (1976); Solomon Islands (1978); Tonga (1999); Tuvalu (2000) and Vanuatu (1981). Most of these countries have representatives in New York.
13 Human Rights Unit scoping paper 'Towards a Commonwealth Forum of National Human Rights Institutions', Commonwealth Conference of National Human Rights Institutions, London, 26–28 February 2007. http://www.thecommonwealth.org/Shared_ASP_Files/UploadedFiles/D3C9CB10-98A7-4EC5-9D86-9E7700EFDFA2_HumanRightsUnitPaper.pdf (accessed 10 May 2008).
14 Compared to, for example, the League of Arab States or the Caribbean Community.
15 A/RES/60/251. None of the countries of the region under consideration in this book are members of the new Council, although interestingly Marshall Islands and Palau voted against the establishment of the Council – along with United States of America and Israel.
16 Resolution 60/251.
17 http://www2.ohchr.org/english/
18 OHCHR Pacific Regional Office (2008–2009), http://www.ohchr.org/EN/Countries/AsiaRegion/Pages/PacificSummary0809.aspx (accessed 24 May 2008).

Conclusion

Internationally, the contemporary human rights environment is a difficult one. On the one hand, an increasing number of international conventions, protocols and treaties are emerging. Inter-governmental agencies and non-governmental organisations are coming together at international, regional and national levels to implement practical measures and agree strategies for advancing human rights. At the same time, concerns about international terrorism, criminal activity and financial dealing have been used to justify the suppression of liberties and breaches of fundamental rights. Trade, the environment and health have become matters of global attention, while technology has meant that no country is now an island. Sovereignty, identity, culture and language are all under pressure. It is against this international background that the development and future of human rights in the Pacific region has to be considered.

Human rights have been part of the Pacific experience for some time. If it is accepted that traditional structures, institutions and mores reflected and gave effect to certain fundamental rights and core values, then human rights have been part of the history and culture of Pacific Island people since they first settled in the region. Certainly, some modern human rights were in place before independence and the constitutions of Pacific Island countries expressly incorporate what may be regarded as contemporary human rights from an international perspective.

It is clear however that, until the 1990s, very little attention had been given to rights advocacy or the enhanced protection and enforcement of rights expressed either in the written constitutions or international instruments to which Pacific Island countries were parties. The impetus for increasing attention may be attributable to a number of factors: individual advocates of human rights; initiatives by national and regional organisations, such as LAWASIA and RRT; increasing awareness by non-governmental organisations of rights issues, especially perhaps among women's groups of the rights stated under CEDAW; workshops and conferences supported by the Commonwealth and United Nations Agencies such as UNICEF and UNDP, as well as other aid donors; and in some cases legislative and judicial activism in asserting and enhancing human rights. Certainly, there is evidence to support the view that the climate for human rights in a region, which itself is experiencing rapid change and development, has changed considerably in a comparatively short space of time and continues to change. This changed climate is a cause for optimism.

There remain many obstacles, but there is considerable goodwill, support and expertise within Pacific Island countries, especially increasingly from national non-governmental organisations, from the judiciary and from a growing number of public sector organisations. There is also an increasing presence of international agencies in the region. The challenge is to ensure that the momentum is not lost as a result of lack of political will, poor governance or inappropriate foreign intervention. It is also important to ensure that human rights issues are seen as integral to all aspects of the lives and futures of Pacific islanders, whether the topic is the environment, economic growth, sustainable development or political stability, and not marginalised as a separate and distinct area of concern.

There are existing mechanisms which could be given an enhanced human rights dimension and role, whether this is through judicial training programmes, the office of the Ombudsman, the agencies of the Pacific Forum, the role and mandate of PIANGO, or the scope of the electronic information disseminated by PacLII. However, before this can be done, or the wider human rights environment strengthened, certain preliminary issues need to be addressed.

The first is to be clear what are the rights that Pacific islanders themselves value? To discover these, representatives from all sectors in each country need to get together to arrive at agreed fundamental rights which are not obscured by ritual, performance, or myth. This could be mandated by the Pacific Forum or by an agency established under its auspices to coordinate the necessary enquiry or research programme, or it could be mandated under one of the United Nations offices in the region, or by the Commonwealth Secretariat. In some countries of the region this type of exercise in itself will be a challenge because of a lack of cultural or linguistic homogeneity and difficulties in arriving at consensus. Nevertheless, if the argument is that traditional values are important and should not be trumped by what are perceived as introduced values, then this needs to be done. The New Zealand Law Commission's report on 'Converging Currents' (2006) suggests that this is possible. There are, however, two dangers. First, if this cannot be done then the argument for any particular Pacific human rights régime remains elusive and, when balanced against international human rights standards, unconvincing. Second, if it can be done, for example, by arriving at an agreed statement of customary values, then it commits to writing a value system which has survived – if it has survived – by being oral, changeable and malleable. There is the risk therefore that concretising traditional, customary values will change the nature and form of these and perhaps, over time, weaken them. This might provoke resistance.

If however, first this step can be taken, then there is a need to identify commonalties between these Pacific values and those found in international human rights instruments. There is therefore a need to negotiate a common space which, on the one hand does not derogate from international standards, but on the other facilitates the acceptance and recognition of these standards through the Pacific lens. To do otherwise would fail to overcome the current psychological and cultural barriers which are erected to defend breaches of human rights or simply failures to give positive effect to such rights.

If a common language and value system of rights can be found, then the next issue is how these rights can be best advanced and enhanced in the region. This is of course a matter for Pacific islanders to decide, but it would seem that there are many synergies and initiatives now present in the region which could be tasked with this. The important thing would be to foster co-operation between them, to disseminate knowledge of best practice and possible models of approach and to share setbacks and challenges. It would also be important to ensure that less well-resourced countries and agencies are not disempowered or ignored in this process and that the larger or more vocal countries of the region do not claim ownership of regional initiatives which are designed to support national ones.

Finally, if there is one human right above all others which is important for the region I would suggest that it is the freedom to give and receive information. Governments and others need to be accountable and transparent; judges need to be clear why they are reaching the decisions they do and the public needs to be aware of their rights and duties, avenues of redress and possible remedies for breaches of rights or derelictions of duties. The international community needs to be better educated about the Pacific region and its people, and the countries of the Pacific region need to build on the advances they have made in claiming the right to sit at the table of international discussions which impact on them. There is now human rights dialogue at all levels. Hopefully it will continue and lead to many positive outcomes.

Bibliography

Books

Arat, Z. (1991). *Democracy and Human Rights in Developing Countries*, Boulder, CO: Lynne Rienner.

Baehr, P., Flinterman, C. and Senders, M. (eds) (1999). *Innovation and Inspirations: fifty years of the Universal Declaration of Human Rights*, Amsterdam: Royal Netherlands Academy of Arts and Sciences.

Bauer, J. and Bell, D. (eds) (1999). *The East Asian Challenge for Human Rights*, Cambridge: Cambridge University Press.

Bainham, A. (ed.) (1997). *The International Survey of Family Law*, Bristol: Jordan Publishing Ltd.

Blanpain, R. (ed.) (2003). *International Encyclopaedia of Laws*, The Hague: Kluwer International.

Beitz, C. (1979). *Political Theory and International Relations*, Princeton, NJ: Princeton University Press.

Brölmann, C., Lefeber, R. and Zieck, M. (eds) (1993). *Peoples and Minorities in International Law*, Dordrecht: Martinus Nijhoff.

Campbell, T. *et al.* (eds) (1986). *Human Rights: From Rhetoric to Reality*, London: Blackwell.

Clarke, D. and McCoy, G. (2000). *Habeas Corpus: Australia; New Zealand; the South Pacific*, Sydney: Federation Press.

Commonwealth Lawyers Association (2004). *Report: Gender and Human Rights Workshop, Nadi, Fiji, 28–29 May 2004*, London: Commonwealth Secretariat.

Corrin Care, J., Newton, T. and Paterson, D. (1999). *Introduction to South Pacific Law*, London: Cavendish.

Corrin, J. and Zorn, J. (2001). *Proving Customary Law in the Common Law Courts of the South Pacific*, Occasional Paper 2, London, British Institute of International and Comparative Law.

Crocombe, R. (ed.) (1987). *Land Tenure in the Atolls*, Suva: Institute of Pacific Studies, University of the South Pacific.

Crocombe, R. and Meleisea, M. (eds) (1994). *Land Issues in the Pacific*, Christchurch: MacMillan Brown Centre for Pacific Studies, University of Canterbury and Institute of Pacific Studies, University of the South Pacific.

Crocombe, R. (ed.) (1987). *Land Tenure in the Pacific*, Suva: University of the South Pacific.

De Smith, S. A., Woolf, H. K. Lord and Jowell, J. L. (1995). *Judicial Review of Administrative Action*, 5th edition, London: Sweet and Maxwell.

Dicey, A. V. (1959). *Introduction to the Study of the Law of the Constitution*, 10th edition, London: Macmillan, St. Martin's Press.

Donnelly, J. (1985). *The Concept of Human Rights*, London: Croom Helm.

Douzinas, C. (2007). *Human Rights and Empire*, London: Routledge-Cavendish.

Farran, S. and Paterson D. (2004). *South Pacific Property Law*, London: Cavendish Publishing.

Filer, C. (ed.) (1999). *Dilemmas of Development: the social and economic impact of the Porgera gold mine 1989–1994*, Canberra: Asia Pacific Press; and Resource Management in Asia-Pacific; Boroko: The National Research Institute.

Freeman, M. (2002). *Human Rights: An Interdisciplinary Approach*, Cambridge: Polity Press.

Gallagher, P., Low, P. and Stoler, A. (eds) (2005). *Managing the Challenges of WTO Participation 45 Case Studies*, Geneva and Cambridge: WTO and Cambridge University Press.

Ghai, Y. (1988). *Law, Politics and Government in Pacific States*, Suva, Fiji: Institute of Pacific Studies, University of the South Pacific.

Held, D., McGew, A., Goldblatt, D. and Perraton J. (1999). *Global Transformations: Politics, Economics and Culture*, Cambridge: Polity Press.

Herdt, G. (1994). *Third Sex Third Gender*, New York: Zone Books.

Hoffman, D. and Rowe, J. (2006). *Human Rights in the UK*, 2nd edition, London: Pearson Longman.

Institute of Comparative Law in Japan (1998). *Towards Comparative Law in the 21st Century*, Tokyo: Institute of Comparative Law.

Institute of Pacific Studies (1986). *Land Rights of Pacific Women*, Fiji: University of the South Pacific.

Jalal, P. (1998). *Law for Pacific Women*, Suva: Fiji Women's Rights Movement.

Joseph, P. (2001). *Constitutional and Administrative Law in New Zealand*, 2nd edition, Wellington: Brookers.

Larmour, P., Crocombe, R. and Taungenga, A. (eds) (1981). *Land, People, and Government: Public Lands Policy in the South Pacific*, Suva: The Institute of Pacific Studies in association with the Lincoln Institute of Land Policy.

Laslett, P. (ed.) (1963). *Philosophy, Politics and Society*, Oxford: Basil Blackwell.

Leane, G. and von Tigerstrom, B. (eds) (2005). *International Law Issues in the South Pacific*, Aldershot: Ashgate.

Locke, J. (1946). *An Essay Concerning the True Original Extent of Civil Government (The Second treatise of Civil Government)*, Oxford: Blackwell.

Meron, T. (ed.) (1984). *Human Rights in International Law: Legal and Policy Issues*, Oxford: Clarendon.

Morsink, J. (1999). *The Universal Declaration of Human Rights: Origins, Drafting and Intent*, Philadelphia: University of Pennsylvania Press.

Naupa, A. (2006). *Youth and Land in 2015: Selections for Vanuatu's 2006 National Land Summit Youth Essay and Poster Competition*, Port Vila: Australian Government/AusAID.

Ntumy, M. (ed.) (1993). *South Pacific Islands Legal Systems*, Honolulu, Hawaii: University of Hawaii Press.

Paterson, D. (2000). *Selected Constitutions of the South Pacific*, Suva, Fiji: University of the South Pacific, Institute of Justice and Applied Legal Studies.

Powles, G. and Pulea, M. (eds) (1988). *Pacific Courts and Legal Systems*, Fiji: University of the South Pacific and Faculty of Law, Monash University.

Pulea, M. (1986). *The Family, Law and Population in the Pacific Islands*, Fiji: Institute of Pacific Studies, University of the South Pacific.

Risse, T., Ropp, S. and Sikink, K. (eds) (1999). *The Power of Human Rights: International Norms and Domestic Change*, Cambridge: Cambridge University Press.

Roberts Wray, K. Sir. (1966). *Commonwealth and Colonial Law*, London: Stevens.

Rousseau, J. J. (1762). *The Social Contract*, trans. Cranston, M. (1968). Hammondsworth: Penguin.

Sack, P. (ed.) (1982). *Pacific Constitutions: Proceedings of the Canberra Law Workshop VI*, Canberra: Australian National University.

Shorts, R. and de Than, C. (2001). *Human Rights Law in the United Kingdom*, London: Sweet and Maxwell.

Tesón, F. (1997). *Humanitarian Intervention: an inquiry into law and morality*, 3rd edition, New York: Transnational.

Thomas, N. (ed.) (1998). *Collective Human Rights of Pacific Peoples*, Auckland: International Research Unit for Maori and Indigenous Education, University of Auckland.

UNESCO (1949). *Human Rights Comments and Interpretations*, Westport CT: Greenwood Press.

Van Trease, H. (1987). *The Politics of Land in Vanuatu*, Suva: Institute of Pacific Studies, University of the South Pacific.

Vattel, E. De. (1834). *The Law of Nations*, trans. Chitty, J. (ed.), London: Sweet and Maxwell.

White, G. and Lindstrom, L. (eds) (1997). *Traditional Pacific Leadership and the Post Colonial State*, Stanford, CA: Stanford University Press.

Wolff, C. (1934). *Jus Gentium Methodo Scientifica per Tractum*, trans. Drake, J., Oxford: The Clarendon Press.

Chapters in books

Angelo, A. (1998). 'Nagol jumping should return to Pentecost: a conspectus of the French English and custom law of Vanuatu', in Institute of Comparative Law in Japan, 1011–1035.

Barutciski, M. (2005) 'Mass refugee flows and burden-sharing in the South Pacific', in Leane, G. and von Tigerstrom, B. (eds), 9–34.

Besnier, N. (1994). 'Polynesian gender liminality: through time and space', in Herdt (ed.), 285–328.

Boister, N. (2005). 'Regional cooperation in the suppression of transnational crime in the South Pacific', in Leane and von Tigerstrom (eds), 35–93.

Bolobola, C. (1986). 'Fiji: customary constraints and legal progress', in Institute of Pacific Studies, 1–15.

Crocombe, R. and Hide, R. (1987). 'New Guinea', in Crocombe (ed.), 324–359.

Donnelly, J. (1993). 'Third Generation Rights', in Brölmann, Lefeber and Zieck (eds), 119–150.

Farran, S. (2003). 'South Pacific Intellectual Property', Blanpain (ed.), Supplement 20.

Franco, R. (1997). 'The kingly-populist divergence in Tongan and Western Samoan Chiefly Systems', in Lindstrom and White (eds), 71–83.

Freeman, M. (1999). 'Fifty years of development of the concept and contents of human rights', in Baehr, Flinterman and Senders (eds), 27–47.

Gay, D. (2005). 'Vanuatu's Suspended Accession: Second thoughts?', in Gallagher, Low and Stoler, Case Study 43. http://www.wto.org/english/res_e/booksp_e/casestudies_e/case43_e.htm (accessed 4 June 2008).

Hicks, N. (1997). 'Divorce in Paradise – A south Pacific perspective', in Bainham (ed.), 379–404.

James, K. (1997). 'Rank and leadership in Tonga', in White and Lindstrom, 49–70.

Henare, M. (1998). 'Economic rights and Fish: Toward a Pacific Understanding of Economic Collective rights', in Thomas (ed.), 25–34.

Hooper, A. and Huntsman, J. (1997). 'Tenure, society and economy', in Crocombe, 127–131.

Keesing, R. (1997). 'Tuesday's chiefs revisited', in White and Lindstrom, 253–263.

Kepa, S. (1998). Justice 'Law-based and Culture-based Human Rights', in Thomas (ed.), 101–108.

Kotoisuva, E. (2004). 'Commonwealth plan of action: Critical area of concern to gender, human rights and law', in Commonwealth Lawyers Association Report, 33–37.

Laliet, L. (2006). 'Youth and Land in 2015', in Naupa, 26.

Lawson, S. (1997). 'Chiefs, Politics and the Power of tradition in Contemporary Fiji', in White and Lindstrom, 108–118.

Lillich, R. (1984). 'Civil Rights', in Meron, 115–170.

MacDonald, M. (1963). 'Natural Rights', in Laslett (ed.), 35–55.

Macpherson, C. (1997). 'The Persistence of Chiefly Authority in Western Samoa', in White and Lindstrom, 19–48.

Maenu'u, L. (1994). 'Solomon Islands: Recognising Traditional Landrights and Traditional Groups', in Crocombe and Meleisea (eds), 85–88.

Maritain, J. (1949). 'Introduction', UNESCO, 9–17.

Mason, L. (1987). 'Tenures from Subsistence to Star Wars', in Crocombe (ed.), 3–27.

McGrath, W. and Scott Wilson, W. (1987). 'The Marshall, Caroline and Mariana Islands: Too many foreign precedents', in Crocombe (ed.), 190–210.

Orücü, E. (1986). 'Core rights and Freedoms', in Campbell *et al.* (eds), 37–59.

Paterson, D. (1988). 'The Pacific Law Unit', in Powles and Pulea, 286–290.

Peteru, M. (2004). 'Domestic Violence in Samoa', in Commonwealth Lawyers Association Report, 26, 27.

Reeves, Sir Paul, (1998). 'Collective rights of Pacific Peoples', in Thomas (ed.), 11–16.

Scheffler, H. and Larmour, P. (1987). 'Solomon Islands: Evolving a new custom', in Crocombe (ed.), 303–323.

Sen, A. (1999). 'Human Rights and Economic Achievements', in Bauer and Bell (eds), 88–99.

Senituli, L. (1998). 'Economic rights and Fish', in Thomas (ed.), 17–24.

Shameen, N. Justice. (2004). 'Women and the Criminal Justice System', in Commonwealth Lawyers Association Report, 53–58.

Totorea, D. (1981). 'Decentralisation in Solomon Islands', in Larmour, Crocombe and Taungenga A. (eds), 119–122.

Thaman, K. H. (1998). 'A Pacific Island Perspective of Collective Human Rights', in Thomas (ed.), 1–9.

Journal articles

Ahmadu, M. (1998). 'Vanuatu's accession to the WTO and WIPO: A reflection on patent and pharmaceutical technology', **2**, *Journal of South Pacific Law*, http://www.paclii.org/journals/fJSPL/vol02/.

Amankwah, H. (1989). 'Fundamental human rights: roots, fruits, myths and realities', **17**, *Melanesian Law Review*, 43–66.

Amankwah, H. (2007). 'Traditional values and modern challenges in property law', **11**(1), *Journal of South Pacific Law*, http://www.paclii.org/journals/fJSPL/vol11no1/.

Angelo, A. (1992). 'Lo bilong yumi yet', **22**, *Victoria University of Wellington Law Review*, 33–48.

Angelo, A. (1995). 'Compulsory land acquisition in small Pacific communities – thoughts on land valuation' **23**, *Melanesian Law Journal*, 183–194.

Annandale, M. (1997). 'A comparison and contrast of the role of the Ombudsman in Vanuatu and Samoa: who, what and how can they investigate?', Working Paper 5, Vol 1, *Journal of South Pacific Law*, http://www.paclii.org/journals/fJSPL/vol01/ (accessed 7 January 2005).

Bhalla, R. (1981). 'Legal analysis of the right of property', **10**, *Anglo American Law Review*, 180–189.

Binder, G. (1999).'Cultural relativism and cultural imperialism in human rights law', **5**, *Buffalo Human Rights Law Review*, 211–221.

Bolton, L. (1998). 'Chief Willie Bongmatur Maldo and the role of chiefs in Vanuatu', **33**(2), *Journal of Pacific History*, 179–195.

Borovnik, M. (2006). 'Working overseas: seafarers' remittances and their distribution in Kiribati', **47**, *Asia Pacific Viewpoint*, 151–161.

Butler, P. (2005). 'A human rights charter for the Pacific', **3**, *Human Rights Research Journal*, 121–135.

Brinktrine, R. (2001). 'The horizontal effect of human rights in German constitutional law: the British debate on horizontality and the possible role model of the German doctrine of 'mittelbare Drittwirkung de Grundrechte', **4**, *European Human Rights Law Review*, 421–432.

Brown, K. (2000). 'The language of land: look before you leap', **4**, *Journal of South Pacific Law*, http://www.paclii.org/journals/fJSPL/vol04/.

Brown, R. and Connell, J. (2006). 'Occupation specific analysis of migration and remittance behaviour: Pacific Island nurses in Australia and New Zealand', **47**, *Asia Pacific Viewpoint*, 135–150.

Brown, K. and Corrin, J. (2004). 'Marit long kastom: marriage in the Solomon Islands', **18**, *International Journal of Law, Policy and the Family*, 52–75.

Brown, K. and Corrin, J. (1998). 'Conflict in Melanesia: Customary Law and the Rights of Women', *Commonwealth Law Bulletin*, 1334–1355.

Campbell, I. C. (2005). 'The quest for constitutional reform in Tonga', **40**(1), *The Journal of Pacific History*, 91–104.

Cerna, C. M. (1994). 'Universality of human rights and cultural diversity: implementation of human rights in different socio-cultural contexts', **16**(4), *Human Rights Quarterly*, 740–752.

Civic, M. A. (1995–1996). 'A comparative analysis of international and Chinese human rights law – universalism versus cultural relativism', **2**, *Buffalo Journal of International Law*, 285–322.

Cobbah, J. M. (1987). 'Africa values and the human rights debate: an African perspective', **9**(3), *Human Rights Quarterly*, 309–331.

Corrin, J. (2007). 'Breaking the mould: constitutional review in Solomon Islands', **13**, *Revue Juridique Polynésienne*, 143–168.

Corrin, J. (2000). 'The status of customary law in Fiji Islands after the Constitutional Amendment Act 1997', **4**, *Journal of South Pacific Law*, http://www.paclii.org/journals/fJSPL/vol04/.

Corrin, J. (1997). 'Colonial legacies? A study of received and adopted legislation in the University of the South Pacific region', **21**, *Journal of Pacific Studies*, 33–59.

Corrin, J. (1992). 'Abrogation of the rights of customary landowners by the Forest Resources and Timber Utilisation Act', **8**, *Queensland University of Technology Law Journal*, 131–140.

de Jonge, A. (1998). 'Ombudsmen and leadership codes in Papua New Guinea. Keeping government accountable in a rapidly changing world' [1998–1999], **26**, *Melanesian Law Journal*, 139, accessible via PacLII http://www.paclii.org/journals/MLJ/.

Deklin, T. (1992). 'Strongim hiumen raits: a proposal for a regional human rights charter and commission for the Pacific', **20**, *Melanesian Law Journal*, 93–106.

Donnolly, J. (1984). 'Cultural relativism and universal human rights', **6**, *Human Rights Quarterly*, 400–419.

du Plessis, M. and Ford, J. (2004). 'Developing the Common Law progressively – Horizontality, the Human Rights Act and the South African experience', **3**, *European Human Rights Law Review*, 286–313.

Farran, S. (2006). 'Is legal pluralism an obstacle to human rights? Considerations from the South Pacific', **52**, *Journal of Legal Pluralism*, 77–106.

Farran, S. (2005a). 'Human rights in the Pacific region – Challenges and solutions', *LAWASIA Journal*, 39–68.

Farran, S. (2005b). 'Land rights and gender equality in the Pacific region', **11**, *Australian Property Law Journal*, 131–140.

Farran, S. (2005c). 'A mother's care or land, but not both –*Tepulolo v Pou* [2005] TVHC 1', Case Note, **2**, *Journal of South Pacific Law*, http://law.vanuatu.usp.ac.fj/jspl.

Farran, S. and Su'a, A. (2005). 'Discrimination on the grounds of status: criminal law and *fa'afafine* and *fakaleiti* in the South Pacific', Working paper, **1**, *Journal of South Pacific Law*, http://www.vanuatu.usp.ac.fj/jspl.

Farran, S. (2004a). 'A microcosm of comparative law: the overlay of customary, French and English family law in present day Vanuatu', **4**, *Oxford University Comparative Law Forum*, http://ouclf.iuscomp.org/articles/farran.shtml.

Farran, S. (2004b). 'Transsexuals, fa'afafine, fakaleiti and marriage law in the Pacific: considerations for the future', **113**(2), *The Journal of the Polynesian Society*, 119–142.

Farran, S. (2004c). 'Pigs, mats and feathers: customary marriage in Vanuatu', **27**(2), *The Journal of Pacific Studies*, 245–276.

Farran, S. (2003). 'Ministerial leases in Vanuatu', Working Paper, **9**, *Journal of South Pacific Law*, http://www.vanuatu.usp.ac.fj/jspl.

Farran, S. (1997). 'Custom and constitutionally protected fundamental rights in the South Pacific region: the approach of the courts to potential conflicts', **21**, *Journal of Pacific Studies*, 103–122.

Field, R. (2005). 'Federal Family Law Reform in 2005: The Problems and Pitfalls for Women and Children of an Increased Emphasis on Post-Separation Informal

Dispute Resolution', **2**, *QUT Law and Justice Journal*, online at http://austlii.edu. au/journals/QUTLJJ/2005/2.html (accessed 30 May 2007).

Forsyth, M. (2005). 'Is there horizontal or vertical enforcement of constitutional rights in Vanuatu? *Family Kalontano v Duruaki Council of Chiefs*', Case Commentary', **9**(2), *Journal of South Pacific Law*, http://www.paclii.org/journals/ fJSPL/vol09no2/ (accessed 24 April 2006).

Forsyth, M. (2003). 'Intellectual property law in the South Pacific: friend of foe', **7**(1), *Journal of South Pacific Law*, http://www.paclii.org/jounrals/fJSPL/vol07no1/8. shtml (accessed 16 October 2007).

Frame, A. (1992). 'Property: some Pacific reflections', *Victoria University of Wellington Law Review*, 21–32.

George, N. (2008). 'Contending masculinities and the limits of tolerance: sexual minorities in Fiji', **20**(1), *The Contemporary Pacific*, 163–189.

Gatty, R. (1953). 'Fiji: colony in transition', **26**(2), *Pacific Affairs*, 118–130.

Gibbs, Sir Harry, (1982–1983). 'Eleventh Wilfred Fullagar Memorial Lecture: the constitutional protection of human rights', **9**(1), *Monash University Law Revue*, 1–13.

Graycar, R. (2000). 'Law Reform by Frozen Chook: Family Law Reform for the New Millennium?' **29**, *Melbourne University Law Review*, online at http://austlii.edu. au/cgi-bin/disp.pl/au/journals/MULR/2000/29.html (accessed 28 May 2007).

Hom, S. K. (1996–1997). 'Commentary: re-positioning human rights discourse on "Asian" perspective', **3**, *Buffalo Journal of International Law*, 209–234.

Howard, R. (1983). 'The full-belly thesis: should economic rights take priority over civil and political rights? Evidence for Sub-Saharan Africa', **4**, *Human Rights Quarterly*, 467–490.

Hughes, B. (2005). 'Report on the South Pacific countries', **2**, *New Zealand Yearbook of International Law*, 271–277.

Hyndman, P. (1992) *Essays and Documents on Human Rights in the Pacific*, Monograph, **4**(22):99–174, Wellington: Victoria University of Wellington Law Review.

Jacobs, R. (2005). 'Treading deep waters: substantive law issues in Tuvalu's threat to sue the United States in the International Court of Justice', **14**, *Pacific Rim Law and Policy Journal*, 103–128.

James, K. (1994). 'Effeminate males and changes to the construction of gender in Tonga', **17**(2), *Pacific Studies*, 39–69.

Jefferies, P. (2000). 'Human rights, foreign policy, and religious belief: an Asia/Pacific Perspective', *Brigham Young University Law Review*, 855–904.

Jowitt, A. (2005). 'Reconstructing custom: the politics of homophobia in Vanuatu', **30**(1), *Alternative Law Journal*, 10–14.

Kabui, F. (1997). 'Crown ownership of foreshores and seabed in Solomon Islands', *Journal of Pacific Studies*, 123–144.

Kaeppler, A. (1999). '*Kie Hingoa*: mats of power, rank, prestige and history', **108**(2), *Journal of the Polynesian Society*, 168–232.

Kalinoe, L. (2000). 'Ascertaining the nature of indigenous intellectual and cultural property and traditional knowledge and the search for legal options in regulating access in Papua New Guinea', **27**, *Melanesian Law Journal*, 1, accessed online via PacLII [2000] MLJ 1 http://www.paclii.org/cgi-bin/disp.pl/www/journals/ MLJ/2000/1.html (accessed 16 October 2007).

Kelsey, J. (2004–2005). 'World trade and small nations in the South Pacific region', **14**(2), *Kansas Journal of Law and Public Policy*, 247–306.

Lal, B. (2003). 'Heartbreak islands: reflections on Fiji in transition', **44**(3), *Asia Pacific Viewpoint*, 335–350.

Lal, R. (1997). 'The Diversified or Strict Role of an Ombudsman: A Comparison in the Roles of the Ombudsman in Vanuatu and Fiji', Working Paper, **1**, *Journal of South Pacific Law*, http://www.paclii.org/journals/fJSPL/vol01/ (accessed 7 January 2005).

Larmour, P. (1992). 'States and Societies in the Pacific Islands', **15**(1), *Pacific Studies*, 99–122.

Leigh, I. (1999). 'Horizontal rights, the Human Rights Act and privacy: lessons from the Commonwealth?', **48**(1), *International and Comparative Law Quarterly*, 57–87.

Lunabeck, Chief Justice V. (2004). 'Adjudication of customary law in the Pacific', **15**(4), *Commonwealth Judicial Journal*, 25–35.

Mageo, J. (1992). 'Male Transvestism and cultural change in Samoa', **19**, *American Ethnologist*, 443–459.

Marsters, E., Lewis, N. and Friesen, W. (2006). 'Pacific flows: the fluidity of remittances in the Cook Islands', **47**, *Asia Pacific Viewpoint*, 31–44.

McGuire, C. (1932). 'The Legislator's Interest in Comparative Legal Studies', *Tulane Law Review*, 171.

Mori, W. (2006). 'The protection of the interest of indigenous Fijians in the Senate and ethnically-based electoral system of Fiji: examples of racial discrimination?' **10**(2), *Journal of South Pacific Law*, http://www.paclii.org/journals.

Oluwu, D. (2005). 'When unwritten customary authority override the legal effect of Constitutional rights: a critical review of the Tuvaluan decision in *Mase Teonea v Pule O' Kaupule and another*', **9**(2), *Journal of South Pacific Law*, http://www.paclii.org/journals.

Paterson, D. (2003). 'New impulses in the interaction of law and religion: a South Pacific perspective', *Brigham Young University Law Review*, 593–624.

Paterson, D. (1995). 'South Pacific customary law and common law – their interrelationship', *Commonwealth Law Bulletin*, 661–671.

Peteru, C. (1996). 'The gay life', *Pacific Islands Monthly*, 43, 44.

Poasa, K. (1992). 'The Samoan Fa'afafine: one case study and discussion of transsexualism', **5**(3), *Journal of Psychology and Human Sexuality*, 39–51.

Powles, G. (1997). 'Common law at bay? The scope and status of customary law regimes in the Pacific', **21**, *Journal of Pacific Studies*, 61–82.

Rodman, K. (1998). '"Think globally, punish locally": nonstate actors, multinational corporations and human rights sanctions', **12**, *Ethics and International Affairs*, 19–41.

Sahlins, M. D. (1963). 'Poor man, rich man, Big-Man, Chief: political types in Melanesia and Polynesia', **5**(3), *Comparative Studies in Society and History*, 285–303.

Shameen, N. Justice. (2004). 'Women and the Criminal Justice System', *Report: Gender and Human Rights Workshop*, Commonwealth Lawyers Association, 53–58.

Sharma, S. (1999). 'The control and protection of native lands in Fiji', **3**, *Journal of South Pacific Law*, http://www.paclii.org/journals/fJSPL/vol03/ (accessed 12 June 2008).

Schmidt, J. (2001). 'Redefining fa'afafine: Western discourses and the construction of transgenderism in Samoa', **6**, *Intersections*, 1–16, http://www.she.murdoch.edu.au/intersections/issue6/schmidt.html (accessed 26 November 2003).

Schmidt, J. (2003). 'Paradise lost? Social change and *fa'afafine* in Samoa', **51**(3/4), *Current Sociology*, 417–432.

Serrano, K. (2007). 'Sweet like sugar: Does the EU's new sugar regime become Fiji's bitter reality or welcome oppurtunity?' 11(2), *Journal of South Pacific Law*, 169–193.

Tamata, L. (2000). 'Application of human rights conventions in the Pacific Islands courts', Working Paper, 4, *Journal of South Pacific Law*, http://www.paclii.org/journals/fJSPL/vol04/ (accessed 3 May 2004).

Tom'tavala, Y. D. (2000). 'Yam Gardens in the Sea: The Marine Claims of the Trobriand Islanders of Papua New Guinea', 27, *Melanesian Law Journal*, 77, http://www.paclii.org/journals/MLJ/2000/5.html.

Van Dyke, J., Smith, K. and Siwatibau, S. (1984). 'Nuclear activities and the Pacific islanders', 10, *The Journal of Pacific Studies*, 1–35.

Weisbrot, D. (1989). 'Custom, pluralism, and realism in Vanuatu: legal development and the role of customary law', 13(1), *Pacific Studies*, 65–97.

Unpublished papers

Baird, N. (2007). 'To ratify or not to ratify? An assessment of the case for ratification of international human rights treaties in the Pacific', unpublished paper presented at the 10th PIPSA Conference in Port Vila, Vanuatu, December 2007.

Corrin Care, J. (1999). 'Conflict between customary law and human rights in the South Pacific', paper presented at the 12th Commonwealth Law Conference at Kuala Lumpur 1999.

de Jonge, A. (1999). 'The Pacific ombudsman's complaints function: comparative perspectives of Fiji, Papua New Guinea and Vanuatu', paper presented at the State, society and governance in Melanesia Conference, 1999.

Frémont, J. (2008). 'Legal pluralism, customary law and human rights in francophone African countries', paper presented *in absentia* at 'Strategies for the Future: Protecting Rights in the Pacific', Apia, Samoa, 2008.

Maclellan, N. (2003) 'Australian neo-colonialism in the Pacific: human rights implications', Paper presented at the Castan Centre for Human Rights Law conference: 'Human rights 2003: the Year in review', December 2003, Melbourne, http://www.law.mnash.edu.au/castancentre/events/2003/macleelan-paper.pdf (accessed 12 June 2008).

McLean, G. (2008). Community Para-Legal Task Force 'Documenting the Treatment of Detainees and Prisoners by the Security Forces in the Kingdom of Tonga', Paper tabled at 'Strategies for the Future: Protecting Rights in the Pacific' Symposium, Apia, April 2008.

Vaá, U. (2008). 'Samoan Custom and Human Rights: an Indigenous View', paper presented at 'Strategies for the Future: Protecting Rights in the Pacific', Apia, Samoa, 2008.

Law Commission papers

Constitutional and Law Reform Commission of Papua New Guinea 'Final Report on Domestic Violence', Report No 14 1992, http://www.paclii.org/cgi-bin/disp.pl/pg/LRC/REP_14.htm?query=domestic%20violence (accessed 1 July 2008).

Fiji Law Reform Commission: Domestic Violence Review 2005, http://www.lawreform.gov.fj/common/Default.aspx?page=domesticRev (accessed 30 June 2008).

Law Commission New Zealand 'Converging Currents: Custom and Human Rights in the Pacific' (2006), Study Paper 17, Wellington, New Zealand.

Others

Amnesty International Report, September 1998, 'Vanuatu: No safe place for prisoners', http://www.amnesty.org/en/library/asset/ASA44/001/1998/en/dom-ASA440011998en.pdf (accessed 8 May 2008).

Amnesty International, 'Fiji: Justice must not be selective', 15 November 2002, http://www.amnesty.org.uk/news_details.asp?NewsID=13211 (accessed 8 May 2008).

Amnesty International, 'Papua New Guinea: Investigate Police Killings', 19 July 2001, http://www.amnesty.org.uk/news_details.asp?NewsID=13746 (accessed 8 May 2008).

Amnesty International (2006), 'Papua New Guinea: Violence Against Women: Not Inevitable, Never Acceptable', ASA 34/002/2006, http://www.amnesty.org/en/library/asset/ASA34/002/2006/en/dom-ASA340022006en.html (accessed 18 October 2006).

Asian Development Bank, *Annual Report 2006*, http://www.adb.org/Documents/Reports/Annual_Report/2006/ADB-AR2006-Pacific.pdf (accessed 6 June 2008).

AusAid, *Pacific 2020: Challenges and Opportunities for Growth*, http://www.ausaid.gov.au/publications/pdf/pacific2020.pdf (accessed 28 February 2008).

CIA, *World Fact Book on Pitcairn*, http://www.cia.gov/cia/publications/factbook/geos/pc.html#People (accessed 16 January 2006).

Commonwealth Forum of National Human Rights Institution (2007), Kampala Communiqué of the Commonwealth Forum of National Human Rights Institutions, 19 November 2007, http://www.thecommonwealth.org/shared_asp_files/GFSR.asp?NodeID=173604 (accessed 6 June 2008).

Commonwealth Secretariat, 'Highlighting Human Rights Issues Affecting Young People', 16 October 2007, http://www.thecommonwealth.org/news/152865/154172/170895/161007highlighting.htm (accessed 8 May 2008).

Commonwealth Secretariat Human Rights Unit Scoping paper (2007), 'Towards a Commonwealth Forum of National Human Rights Institutions', Commonwealth Conference of National Human Rights Institutions, London, 26–28 February 2007, http://www.thecommonwealth.org/Shared_ASP_Files/UploadedFiles/D3C9CB10-98A7-4EC5-9D86-9E7700EFDFA2_HumanRightsUnitPaper.pdf. Online at http://www.thecommonwealth.org/Internal/39448/161637/commonwealth_conference_of_national_human_rights/ (accessed 6 June 2008).

Cook, L., Didham, R. and Khawaja, M. (1999). 'On the demography of Pacific People in New Zealand', *Demographic Trends*, 1999, Statistics New Zealand, http://www.stats.govt.nz/NR/rdonlyres/D0B2A9AF-11E9-483C-8F65-A355C1AE3AB3/0/demtrends.pdf (accessed 15 March 2007).

Council Decision of 1 October 2007 on the conclusion of consultations with the Republic of the Fiji Islands under Article 96 of the ACP-EC Partnership Agreement and Article 37 of the Development Cooperation Instrument (2007/641/EC) Official Journal of the European Union 5.10.2007, L 260/15.

Department of Economic and Social Affairs of the United Nations Secretariat, 'The United Nations Development Agenda: Development for All', 1990–2005, http://www.un.org/esa/devagenda/UNDA_BW5_Final.pdf (accessed 29/05/08).

Duckworth, J. (2002). 'Custom, Law and Practice in Tuvalu: the relationship between law and custom in Tuvalu', International Center for Not-for-Profit Law.

'Elections Observer Group for the Vanuatu 2002 National Elections: the Common Interest in Ethical Politics', http://www.iipe.org/conference2002/papers/Randell.pdf (accessed 26 February 2008).

Farran, S. (2003). 'Approaches to Child Custody in the Pacific Region', *University of the South Pacific Law School Occasional Paper Series*, No. 3, Vanuatu: University of the South Pacific Law School. Fiji Government 'Extensions services offered in sugar mills', August 15 2005, http://www.fiji.gov.fj/publish/page_5226.shtml (accessed 14 June 2008).

Fiji Human Rights Commission Digest 2004, http://www.paclii.org/fj/indices/cases/Human%20Rights%20Digest%202004.htm (accessed 21 June 2008).

Fiji Women's Crisis Centre, *'National Research on Domestic Violence and Sexual Assault 1997/8'*, http://www.fijiwomen.com/index.php?id=1282 (accessed 8 May 2008).

Gill, I. (2003). 'Fiji Islands: Better harvest', Asian Development Bank, http://www.adb.org/Documents/Periodicals/ADB_Review/2003/vol35_5/better_harvest.asp (accessed 11 June 2008).

Grieco, E. (2003). Migration Information Source: Country Profiles, 'The Federated States of Micronesia: The "Push" to Migrate', Migration Policy Institute, http://www.migrationinformaiton.org/Profiles/display.cfm?ID=143 (accessed 12 March 2007).

Government of Western Samoa (1975). 'Report on Matai Titles, Customary Land and the Land and Titles Court', 2.

Hughes, R. (2004). 'Conference Report – 23rd Pacific Islands Law Officers Meeting, Nuku'alofa, Tonga, 27th–29th September 2004', 8(2), *Journal of South Pacific Law*, http://www.paclii.org/journals/fJSPL/vol08no2/9.shtml (accessed 19 June 2008).

Human Rights Watch Letter to Interim Prime Minister Voreqe Bainimarama and President Ratu Josefa Iloilo, 5 February 2007, http://hrw.org/english/docs/2007/02/05/fiji15266.htm (accessed 16 May 2008).

Hyndman, P. (1991). 'The Protection of Human Rights in the Pacific Region', Government Defence of Human Rights Series, London: Human Rights Unit, Commonwealth Secretariat.

Inglis, C. (2003). 'Australia Mulls Seasonal Migrant Labor Scheme', Migrations Information Source, 1 September 2003, http://www.migrationinformaiton.org/Feature/display.cfm?ID=161 (accessed 22 May 2008).

International Commission of Jurists, 'Fiji-ICJ calls on Fiji military to immediately restore rule of law and respect for human rights', 13 December 2006, http://www.icj.org/news.php3?id_article=4082&lang=en (accessed 19 May 2008).

International Committee of the Red Cross, *Annual Report 2006*, p. 224, http://www.icrc.org/Web/Eng/siteeng0.nsf/htmlall/738D7N/$FILE/icrc_ar_06_suva.pdf?OpenElement (accessed 8 May 2008).

Interights, 'Pacific judges affirm justiciability of Economic, Social and Cultural Rights', http://www.interights.org/suva (accessed 19 June 2008).

Jalal, I. P. (2006). 'Pacific culture and human rights: why Pacific island countries should ratify international human rights treaties', RRT/UNDP, April 2006.

Jalal, I. P. (2005). 'The situation of human rights defenders in the Pacific Islands', http://pacific.ohchr.org/docs/HRD_Pacific_2005.pdf (accessed 6 June 2008).

Kampala Communiqué of the Commonwealth Forum of National Human Rights Institutions, 19 November 2007, http://www.thecommonwealth.org/shared_asp_files/GFSR.asp?NodeID=173604 (accessed 8 May 2008).

Kelsey, J. (2004). 'Big brothers behaving badly. The implications for the Pacific Islands of the Pacific Agreement on Closer Economic Relations (PACER)', 2004 Pacific Network on Globalisation, http://www.pang.org.fj/doc/040401bigbrothersjanekelsey.pdf (accessed 4 June 2008).

Lal, B. 'Fiji Islands: From immigration to emigration', Migration Policy Institution web site, http://www.migrationinformation.org/Profiles/display.cfm?ID=110 (accessed 9 March 2006).

Levi, N. (2003). 'Pacific Islands Forum', Paper presented to the World Trade Organisation (WT/MIN(03)/ST/144) Ministerial Conference, Fifth Session, Cancún, 10–14 September 2003, http://www.wto.org/english/theWTO_e/minist_e/min03_e/statements_e/st144.doc (accessed 24 June 2008).

Magna Carta, British Library translation, http://www.bl.uk/treasures/magnacarta/translation.html (accessed 6 June 2008).

Mackenzie, T. (2000). 'The situation in the South Pacific Islands', World Council of Churches, http://www.wcc-coe.org/wcc/what/interreligious/cd35-20.html (accessed 12 June 2008).

McIntosh, T. (1999). 'Words and worlds of difference: homosexualities in the Pacific', Working papers on Sociology and Social Policy, University of the South Pacific.

Morgan, W. (2008) 'Trading away our rights? Free trade and human rights in the Pacific Islands', http://www.pang.org.fj/doc/110508_Dev-Zone-Access_to_Medicine.pdf (accessed 4 June 2008).

Migrant workers opportunities, http://www.premiers.qld.gov.au/About_the_department/publications/multicultural/Australian_South_Sea_Islander_Training_Package/history/australia/recruiting/ (accessed 15 March 2006).

Migration information, Source, http://www.migrationinformation.org/index.cfm (accessed 22 May 2008).

Muntarbhorn, V. (2005). 'In search of the right track: evolving a regional framework for the promotion and protection of human rights in the Asia-Pacific region', Discussion Paper, June 2005, http://pacific.ohchr.org/docs/VititDis.pdf (accessed 12 May 2008).

Musungu, Sisule F. (2007). 'An analysis of the EC Non-Paper on the Objectives and Possible Elements of an IP Section in the EC-Pacific EPA', CAFOD, London, UK; and ICTSD Programme on Intellectual Property Rights and Sustainable Development, International Centre for Trade and Sustainable Development, Geneva, Switzerland, http://www.pang.org.fj/doc/060807_Musungu_IP_Pacific-EPA.pdf (accessed 4 June 2008).

New Zealand Government Statistics, New Zealand Statistics, http://www.stats.govt.nz/cmsapp/templates/system/migration.aspx?NRMODE=Pubis (accessed 1 February 2006).

OHCHR Pacific Regional Office (2008–2009). http://www.ohchr.org/EN/Countries/AsiaRegion/Pages/PacificSummary0809.aspx (accessed 24 May 2008).

Pacific Centre for Public Integrity (2006). 'The challenge of freedom of information in Fiji and the Pacific' Commonwealth Human Rights Initiative Newsletter, Volume 13(3), http://www.humanrightsinitiaitve.org/publicaiotns/nl/newsletter_autumn_2006/article (accessed 13 November 2007).

Pacific Concerns Resource Centre, Suva Fiji Islands, 'Action Alert', August 1999, http://archives.pireport.org/archive/1999/august/08-05-19.html (accessed 16 March 2007).

Pacific Islands Forum Secretariat, 'Pacific Plan', http://www.forumsec.org/pages. cfm/about-us/the-pacific-plan/ (accessed 15 October 2008).

Pacific Islands Forum Secretariat, Annual Progress Report, 2007, http://www. forumsec.org/pages.cfm/about-us/the-pacific-plan/ (accessed 10 March 2008).

Pacific Islands Forum Secretariat (2007). *The Pacific Plan for Strengthening Regional Cooperation and Integration*, November 2007, http://www.forumsec. org/UserFiles/File/Pacific_Plan_Nov_2007_version.pdf (accessed 6 June 2008).

Pacific Islands Forum Secretariat, 'Vision Statement', http://www.forumsec.org/ pages.cfm/about-us/vision-statement (accessed 6 June 2008).

Pacific Islands Law Officers' Meeting (PILOM) Review, http://www.pilonsec.org/ www/pilon/rwpattach.nsf/PublicbySrc/Pacific+Islands+Law+Officers+Meeting+ (PILOM)+Review.pdf/$file/Pacific+Islands+Law+Officers+Meeting+(PILOM)+ Review.pdf (accessed 19 June 2008).

Pacific Judicial Development Program (PJDP) Newsletter, March 2007, Issue 1.

Poerio, L. (1995). 'Domestic Violence in Solomon Islands: Results of a Community Survey', Brisbane: Department of Health and Behavioural Sciences, Griffith University.

Population migrations statistics, http://www.tokelau.org.nz/ (accessed 2 November 2005).

Rigamoto, W. (2005). 'Ombudsman and the right to information: a case study from the Pacific' Commonwealth Human Rights Initiative Newsletter, Vol 12, Issue 1, http://www.humanrightsinitiative.org/publicaitons/nl/newsletter_spring_2005/ article 2 (accessed 13 November 2007).

RRRT (2005). 'The Big Seven: Human Rights Conventions and Judicial Declarations', Fiji: United Nations Development Programme.

SR International and Associates and Vanuatu Association of Women Graduates (2003). 'Awareness Raising on Court Rules Relating to Domestic Violence inVanuatu: Final Report', Port Vila: AusAid.

Secretariat of the Pacific Community (2004). Pacific Island Populations, Part 1.

Secretariat .of the Pacific Community, 'Estimated population growth rates 2006–2010', http://www.spc.int/demog/en/stats/2006/Pacific%20Island% 20Populations%202006-2015%20-%2030%20Oct%2006.xls (accessed 29 May 2007).

Secretariat of the Pacific Community, 'Vision and Mission', http://www.spc. int/corp/index.php?option=com_content&task=view&id=22&Itemid=73 (accessed 29 May 2008).

Sen, P. (2006). 'Papua New Guinea: women subject to gang rape, beatings and murder of female "sorcerers"', 4 September 2006, http://www.amnesty.org.uk/ news_details.asp?NewsID=17082 (accessed 8 May 2008).

Tahi, S. (2007). 'National Land Summit, Final Report', published by the Government of Vanuatu, 2007.

Tokelau Referendum, http://www.paclii.org/tk/government.html (accessed 2 November 2005).

Tor, R. and Toka, A. (2004). 'Gender, Kastom and Domestic Violence', Port Vila: Department of Women's Affairs.

Transparency International Annual Report, 2006–2007, http://www.transparencyfiji. org/docs/TIF%20Chairman%20Report%202006-07.pdf (accessed 27 February 2008).

Transparency International – Vanuatu Chapter, 'Elections observer group for the Vanuatu 2002 national elections: the common interest in ethical politics', http://www.iipe.org/conference2002/papers/Randell.pdf (accessed 26 February 2008).

United Nations Committee on the Elimination of Discrimination against Women, Thirty-eighth session, 14 May–1 June 2007, 'Concluding comments of the Committee on the Elimination of Discrimination against Women: Vanuatu', www.un.org/womenwatch/daw/cedaw/cdrom_cedaw/EN/files/cedaw 25years/content/english/CONCLUDING_COMMENTS_ENGLISH/Vanuatu/Vanuatu%20CO-3.pdf - 2008-01-10 (accessed 26 June 2008).

United Nations Report on the mission of the Special Rapporteur to the Republic of Fiji on the issue of commercial sexual exploitation of children (11–16 October 1991) GE.99-16549 (E), http://daccessdds.un.org/doc/UNDOC/GEN/G99/165/49/PDF/G9916549.pdf?OpenElement (accessed 16 May 2008).

United Nations Secretariat Department of Economic and Social Affairs, 'The United Nations Development Agenda: Development for All 1990–2005', http://www.un.org/esa/devagenda/UNDA_BW5_Final.pdf (accessed 29 May 2008).

UNICEF Information by Country: East Asia and the Pacific, http://www.unicef.org/infobycountry/index.html (accessed 6 June 2008).

UNPFII, http://www.un.org/esa/socdev/unpfii/ (accessed 19 June 2008).

US Department of State Country Reports on Human Rights Practices, http://www.state.gov/g/drl/rls/hrrpt/2007/index.htm (accessed 20 May 2008).

Vanuatu Ombudsman Reports 'Illegal and Unconstitutional Discrimination in the Citizenship Act' [1999] VUOM 8; 1999.08 (19 May 1999); 'Granting of Leases by the Former Minister of Lands Mr Paul Telukluk to Himself, Family Members and Wantoks' [1999] VUOM 6; 1999.06 (22 April 1999); 'Mismanagement of the Tender Sale of 10 Deportees' Properties by the Former Minister of Lands Mr Paul Telukluk' [1999] VUOM 9; 1999.09 (28 May 1999; 'Breaches of the Leadership Code by Sato Kilman, Minister of Lands' [1998] VUOM 5; 1998.05 (24 February 1998); 'Deportation of the Publisher of the Trading Post Marc-Neil Jones from Vanuatu' [2001] VUOM 5; 2001.08 (31 October 2001) accessible online at http://www.paclii.org/vu/ombudsman/

Vanuatu Ombudsman. (1995). 'First Annual Report', Office of the Ombudsman, Republic of Vanuatu.

'Wasdok', December 2006, Newsletter of the Papua New Guinea Ombudsman Commission, http://www.paclii.org/pg/OC/Newsletter/2006Dec_Wasdok.pdf (accessed 1 July 2008).

World Council of Churches, 'The Island of Hope: an alternative to economic globalisation', Dossier No 7 2001, http://www.oikoumene.org/fileadmin/files/wcc-main/documents/p3/dossier-7.pdf (accessed 10 June 2008).

WHO, 'Gender-based violence in the Western Pacific Region: a hidden epidemic?', Special Issue on Women's Health, World Health Organisation Western Pacific Region, 2006, 5, http://www.wpro.who.int/NR/rdonlyres/B2AFAFF0-F8A1-41DF-A02C-94B8DA789698/0/ViolenceBook.pdf (accessed 6 June 2008).

Newspapers and news sources

Adams, J. (2007). 'Rising sea levels threaten small Pacific island nations', *International Herald Tribune*, 3 May 2007, http://www.iht.com/articles/2007/05/03/asia/pacific.php (accessed 4 June 2008).

Aiavo, U. (2001). Forum Secretariat's Media Adviser, 'Letter to the Editor: "Pacific Islands Forum and nuclear issues"', *Pacific Islands Report*, 21 February 2001, http:// archives.pireport.org/archive/2001/february/02-28-24.htm (accessed 16 March 2007).

Anan, K. (2000). Secretary-General of the United Nations Statement on presenting his Millennium Report, 3 April 2000, http://www.unhchr.ch/minorities/ (accessed 19 June 2008).

Buchanan, S. (2005). 'Tongan government makes mad dash for the WTO', 11 November 2005, Aotearoa Independent Media Centre, http://indymedia.org. nz/newswire/display/39214/index.php (accessed 3 June 2008).

Buadromo, V. (2005). 'FWRM Congratulates Government on Establishment of Family Court' Press Release, 2 November 2005, Fiji Government, http://www. fiji.gov.fj/publish/page_5681.shtml (accessed 27 July 2007).

Dorney, S. (2006). 'China Evacuates Honiara Riot Victims', *ABC News* Online, 23 April 2006, www.abc.net.au/ra.

Faiparik, C. (2004). 'Culture Clash seen in PNG Killings of Chinese', *The National*, 2 September 2004, www.thenational.com.pg/.

Field, M. (2004). 'Fiji sugar turns sour', *Pacific Magazine*, 1 March 2004, http://www. pacificmagazine.net/issue/2004/03/01/fiji-sugar-turns-sour (accessed 14 June 2008).

Fiji Government. 'Vice President Ratu Joni opens new Family Law Court, 2 November 2005, http://www.fiji.gov.fj/publish/printer_5678.shtml (accessed 20 September 2007).

Gregory, A. (2006) 'Tokelau Votes To Stay With NZ', *New Zealand Herald*, 17 February 2006.

Hulsen, A. (2000). 'Pacific Islanders air nuclear shipping concerns at Japan Meeting', *Pacific Island Report*, 25 April 2000, http://archives.pireport.org/archive/2000/ april/04-27-01.htm (accessed 21 June 2008).

Jalal, I. (2004). 'State on Track with new Act', *The Fiji Times*, 27 July 2004, http:// rrrt.org/page.asp?active_page_id=172 (accessed 20 September 2007).

Jalal, I. (2003). 'A woman's quest for Equality', *The Fiji Times*, 25 November 2003, http://rrrt.org/page.asp?active_page_id=142 (accessed 20 September 2007).

Jalal, I. (2003). 'Why Fiji needs a Family Law Bill', *The Fiji Times*, 18 November 2003.

Johnson, G. (2006). 'Lawyer alleges abuse of Marshall Islands Chinese', *Marianas Variety*, 11 May 2006, www.mvariety.com.

Keith-Reid, R. and Pareti, S. (2006). 'China Stirs The Pot Of Divided Pacific Loyalties', *Islands Business*, 16 March 2006, http://www.islandsbusiness.com.

Lini-Gamali, L. (2005). 'Indigenous communities more secured economically: Motarilavoa', *Vanuatu Daily Post*, 25 June 2005: 5.

Macleod, F. (2008). 'Climate change talks to hammer out "son of Kyoto"', *Tuvalu News*, 2 June 2008, http://www.tuvaluislands.com/news/archives/2008/2008-06-02a.htm (accessed 24 June 2008).

Marango, T. (2008). 'Chiefs hold Summit to address crime', *Vanuatu Daily Post*, 1 March 2008.

Mamu, M. (2005). 'Foreign Loggers Taking Solomons for Ride', *Solomon Star*, 10 June 2005.

Misa, T. (2006). 'Warning signs were there for Tongan leader to see', *New Zealand Herald*, 22 November 2006, http://www.nzherald.co.nz/search/story.cfm? storyid=000DE107-8F90-1562-80CE830 (accessed 12 March 2007).

Neil-Jones, M. (2008). 'Crime is out of control – it is time to stop the talk and act', *Vanuatu Daily Post*, 12 January 2008.

Ong, T. (2006). 'SIRO muzzles climate scientists', *The Australian*, 13 February 2006.

OXFAM Australia 'Tonga set to join WTP today on worse terms ever', 15 December 2005, http://www.oxfam.org.au/media/article.php?id=187 (accessed 4 June 2008).

OXFAM New Zealand. 'Trading Away Pacific Nations' Livelihoods', 15 June 2007, http://www.oxfam.org.nz/news.asp?s1=news&aid=1471 (accessed 4 June 2008).

Pacific Islands Forum Secretariat Newsroom, 6 August 2006, 'Opening Statement By Mr. Peter Forau, Acting Secretary General, Pacific Islands Forum Secretariat, At The WTO/PIFS Advanced Programme For Senior Officials On The Doha Development Agenda Negotiation Issues For Pacific Economies Trade,' 7 August 2005, Fiji, http://www.forumsec.org/pages.cfm/speeches-2006/acting-sg-forauwto-course.html (accessed 29 May 2008).

Robie, D. (2003). 'Censoring Pacific Media', 16 April 2003, *Mediawatch*, http://archives.pireport.org/archive/2003/april/04-16-comm.htm (accessed 20 June 2008).

Seneviratne, K. (2000). 'Australia uneasy as Beijing woos South Pacific', 16 August 2000, *Inter Press Service/Asia Times*.

Seneviratne, K. (2002). 'Tuvalu Steps Up Threat to Sue Australia, U.S.', *Pacific Islands Report*, 8 September 2002 – IPS/PINA Nius Online.

Sevele, F. (2006). 'Aussie friendship not forgotten', *The Daily Telegraph*, 29 November 2006, http://www.news.com.au/dailytelegraph/opinion/story/0,22049,20836884-5001031,00 (accessed 12 March 2007).

Simms, A. (2001). 'Farewell Tuvalu', *The Guardian*, 29 October 2001.

Tupeni, L. Baba. (2004). 'Reflections on the role of Pacific media', 9 March 2004, *Pacific Islands Report*, http://archives.pireport.org/archive/2004/march/pjr_baba.htm (accessed 20 June 2008).

Yakham, H. (2007). 'Png Is China's Largest Pacific Trading Partner', *The National*, 20 February 2007, www.thenational.com.pg/.

Yombon, P-P. (1999). 'PNG needs Copyright law says Attorney Lomai', *The National*, 11 January 1999, http://arhives.pireport.org/archive/1999/january/01%2D12%2D17.html (accessed 10 June 2004).

Anonymous

ADB Press Release, 22 February 2008, 'Economic Report Indicates Some Optimism for Medium-Term Growth in Nauru', http://www.adb.org/Media/Articles/2008/12404-nauru-economics-reports/default.asp (accessed 28 January 2008).

Australian Government Media Release, Mr Vaile, Deputy Prime Minister and Minister for Trade 'Tonga and Saudi Arabia join the WTO', 15 December 2005. http://www.trademinister.gov.au/releases/2005/mvt093a_05.html (accessed 4 June 2008).

Commonwealth Secretariat News Release, 1 May 2008, http://www.thecommonwealth.org/news/34580/178695/010508humanrightssamoa.htm (accessed 9 May 2008).

Council of Europe Press Release by the Council of Europe Luxembourg, 1 October 2007, 13383/07 (Presse 214).

Greenpeace Press Released, 'Plutonium ships stranded off Japanese coast in bad weather, Greenpeace urge last chance rejection of plutonium fuel use in Japan', 22 September 1999, http://archives.pireport.org/archive/1999/september/09-23-22.htm (accessed 16 March 2007).

United Nations Press Release, UNPFII 15th and 16th meetings, http://www.un.org/News/Press/docs/2008/hr4953.doc.htm (accessed 19 June 2008).

Wansolwara News online, Vol. 6, No. 2, June 2001, 'Ethnic dilemmas' http://www.usp.ac.fj/journ/docs/wansol/62ethnic.html (accessed 14 June 2008).

WTO News, 'Talks Suspended "Today there are only losers"', 24 July 2006, http://www.wto.org/english/news_e/news06_e/mod06_summary_24july_e.htm (accessed 4 June 2008).

BBC News

'Pacific states step into the breach', 3 September 2001, http://news.bbc.co.uk/1/hi/world/asia-pacfiic/1520388.stm (accessed 12 March 2007).

'WTO accepts Tonga after ten years', 15 December 2005, http://news.bbc.co.uk/1/hi/business/4532698.stm (accessed 4 June 2008).

'Tonga becomes latest WTO member', 27 July 2007, http://news.bbc.co.uk/1/hi/business/6919215.stm (accessed 4 June 2008).

'Fiji police chief "should resign"', 7 November 2006, http://news.bbc.co.uk/2/hi/asia-pacific/6123688.stm (accessed 20 June 2008).

Cook Islands Herald

'Cook Islands have "issues" with Japan Largesse', 3 June 2006, *The Cook Islands Herald*, http://www.ciherlad.co.ck/Times.htm.

Cook Island News

'Politicians Hold Key to Rescuing Cook Islands' Culture', *Cook Islands News*, 21 August 2001, http://archives.pireport.org/archive/2001/august/08%2D24%2D19.htm (accessed 10 June 2004).

'Cook Islands lawmakers laud new Media Council', 7 December 2007, *Cook Islands News*, accessed through Pacific Islands Report, http://archives.pireport.org/archive/2007/december/12-07-09.htm (accessed 20 June 2008).

Fiji Times

'Fiji's Chinese Community concerned by Police Action', 1 April 1999, *Fiji Times*.

'Chinese farmers targeted in Fiji Attacks', 18 December 2005, *Fiji Times*, http://www.fijitimes.com/.

'Fiji Ag Disagrees with Court's View On Homosexuality', 30 August 2005, *Fiji Times*, http://www.fijitimes.com/ (accessed 10 June 2008).

'Fiji Methodists Seek Reversal of Gay Rights', 30 May 2006, *Fiji Times Online*, http://www.fijitimes.com

http://archives.pireport.org/archive/2006/may/05-31-04.htm (accessed 10 June 2008).

Fiji Live

'Chinese Premier Wen Jiabao To Visit Fiji', 24 January 2006, *Fijilive*, http://www. fijilive.com.

'Violence Against Gays On Rise In Fiji', 4 May 2005, *Fijilive*, http://www.fijilive. com http://archives.pireport.org/archive/2005/may/05-04-06.htm (accessed 10 June 2008).

'Bainimarama warns against "irresponsible reporting"', *Fijilive*, 27 February 2008. http://archives.pireport.org/archive/2008/february/02-27-fj2.htm (accessed 20 June 2008).

Fiji Sun

'Fiji Pastor Condemns Homosexuality', 25 April 2005, *Fiji Sun*, http://www. sun.com.fj/ Pacific Islands Report, http://archives.pireport.org/archive/2005/ april/04-25-14.htm (accessed 11 June 2008).

Islands Business Magazine

'Solomons Economy Based On Dwindling Forests', Editorial, 24 July 2007, http:// archives.pireport.org/archive/2007/july/07-24-ed2.htm (accessed 24 June 2008).

Matangi Tonga Magazine

'Tonga Seeks $29 Million Loan From China', 1 May 2006, www.matangitonga.to/ home/.

'Tonga King Cites $20 Million China Aid Package', 11 November 2004.

Pacific Magazine

'Marshall Islands: Training for Pacific judges', 10 February 2005, http://www. pacificmagazine.net/news/2005/02/10/marshall-islands-training-for-pacific-judges (accessed 19 June 2008).

PINA Nius

'PINA alert over threats to Cook Islands News Media', 24 September 2004, *PINA Nius online*, http://archives.pireport.org/archive/2002/september/09-24-20.htm (accessed 20 June 2008).

Solomon Islands Broadcasting Corporation

'Temotus in Solomon Islands Ban Logging', Solomon Islands Broadcasting Corporations, 27 June 2005, http://archives.pireport.org/archive/2005/june/ 06-27-12.htm (accessed 3 March 2008).

Solomon Star

'Solomons Revoke Logging Export Exemptions', *Solomon Star*, 20 July 2006, http:// archives.pireport.org/archive/2006/july/07-21-02.htm (accessed 24 June 2008).

'Solomons Timber Over-Harvest Threatens Economy', *Solomon Star*, 14 September 2007, http://archives.pireport.org/archive/2007/september/09-18-13.htm (accessed 24 June 2008).

'Former Solomon's Minister cites Illegal Logging', *Solomon Star*, 21 December 2006, http://archives.pireport.org/archive/2006/december/12-22-03.htm (accessed 24 June 2008).

'Solomons logging trend unsustainable', *Solomon Star*, 27 May 2005, http://archives.pireport.org/archive/2006/may/05-17-ed1.htm (accessed 24 June 2008).

The National (Papua New Guinea), www.thenational.com.pg/

'Png Must Keep Watchful Eye On China's Benevolence', *The National*, 25 April 2006, http://archives.pireport.org/archive/2006/april/04-25-ed.htm (accessed 24 June 2008).

'PNG Governor criticizes Somare over media threats', *The National*, 20 June 2008, http://pidp.eastwestcenter.org/pireport/2008/June/06-20-20.htm (accessed 21 June 2008).

Oceania Flash

'Homosexual Fears Harsh Treatment In Fiji', 25 January 2005, *Oceania Flash*, http://newspad-pacific.info/, Pacific Islands Report, http://archives.pireport.org/archive/2005/january/01-25-16.htm (accessed 10 June 2008).

Pacific Island News

'Tongans Challenge Gay Minister In New Zealand' 6 March 2003, *Pacific Islands News Association*, http://www.ifex.org/members/pina/ Pacific Islands Report, http://archives.pireport.org/archive/2003/march/03-06-19.htm (accessed 11 June 2008).

Pacific Islands Report

'Banned Tongan newspaper plans return', 14 October 2004, *Pacific Islands Report*, http://archives.pireport.org/archive/2004/october/10-14-01.htm (accessed 20 June 2008).

Post-Courier (Papua New Guinea)

'PNG: Demonic gays promote sex hatred', *Post-Courier*, quoted in *Pacific Magazine*, 28 August 2003, http://www.pacificmagazine.net/news/2003/08/28/png-demonic-gays-promoting-sex-hatred (accessed 10 June 2008).

'Png Deputy Prime Minister Denounces Gays', 28 August 2003, *Post-Courier*, www.postcourier.com.pg/ Pacific Islands Report, http://archives.pireport.org/archive/2003/august/08-28-06.htm (accessed 11 June 2008).

'PNG slams door on public's right to know', 9 January 2007, *PNG Post-Courier*, http://archives.pireport.org/archive/2007/january/01-09-ed2.htm (accessed 20 June 2008).

Radio Fiji

'Fiji's Top Prosecutor Exhorts Against Homosexuality', 4 May 2005, *Radio Fiji News*, http://www.radiofiji.org/news/current/currnews.htm (accessed 10 June 2008).

Radio New Zealand

'Samoa Church Leader Calls For Ban On Gays', 14 July 2006, *Radio New Zealand International*, www.rnzi.com Pacific Islands Report, http://archives.pireport.org/archive/2006/july/07-14-18.htm (accessed 10 June 2008).

'Tonga candidate protests broadcast blackout', *Radio New Zealand International*, 7 April 2008, http://archives.pireport.org/archive/2008/april/04-08-07.htm (accessed 20 June 2008).

'Landmark Fiji ruling: media free to publish', *Radio New Zealand International*, www.rnzi.com, accessed via Pacific Islands Report, 22 October 2007.

Vanuatu Daily Post

'Vanuatu praises China's Way of Giving Aid', 18 September 2001, *Vanuatu Trading Post*, http://www.pinanius.org.

Glossary of terms

Alii ma Faipule (Samoa) – chiefly heads of families who combine to represent the interests of a village.

Ariki (Cook Islands) – a person who has been invested with the title rank or office of *Ariki* in accordance with ancient custom prevailing in each of the Cook Islands.

Beqa (Fiji) – island in Fiji, famous for its fire-dance.

'Big-Man' (Solomon Islands, Papua New Guinea and Vanuatu) – male leader (often self-made) in Melanesia.

Bose Levu Vakaturaga (Fiji) – Great Council of Chiefs.

Bulubulu (Fiji) – customary apology made by the family or perpetrator of a wrong to the family of the victim.

Fa'afafine (Samoa) – gender liminal or trans-gender men.

Fa'kaleiti (Tonga) – as above.

Falekaupule (Tuvalu) – island council.

Fa'a Samoa (Samoa) – the Samoan way of doing things (customary).

Fono (Samoa) – village council.

Habeas corpus – (Latin) (Lit) 'Bring forth the body'.

i-Kiribati – people of Kiribati.

Indo-Fijian – person from Fiji of Indian descent or ancestry.

Ifoga (Samoan) – a ceremonial request for forgiveness made by the offender and his *aiga* (family) to those injured.

Iroij (Marshall Islands) – hereditary title of a person or representative of a group in district who has traditional or customary rights and obligations.

Kanaks (New Caledonia) – Melanesian people of New Caledonia.

Kava (Melanesia) – traditional drink made form a species of the pepper plant (known as *yaqona* in Fiji).

Magna Carta – (Latin) – the Great Charter.

Mahu (Hawaii) – see *fa'afafine*.

Malvatamauri (Vanuatu) – National Council of Chiefs.

Matai (Samoa) – customary title holders who represent the extended family – usually male but not only.

Mataqali (Fiji) – clan.

ni-Vanuatu – people of Vanuatu.

Nagol (Vanuatu) – land dive from the island of Pentecost.

Nakamal (Vanuatu) – meeting place where *kava* is traditionally drunk.

Nasara (Vanuatu) – meeting place or men's house, the building of which may be evidence of being the first to settle on land, but also a basic socio-political unit.

Nitijela (Marshall Islands) – legislative assembly of Marshall Islands.

Pinapinaaine (Tuvalu) – see *fa'afafine*.

Pro bono (Latin) – legal work or legal representation without a fee or charge.

Status quo (Latin) – the present state of affairs or position.

Tapa (Fiji) – cloth made from the bark of the mulberry tree, used for ceremonial occasions in Polynesian countries.

Tabu (General) – forbidden or prohibited.

Taupulega (Tokelau) – village council of elders.

Ulu Aliki (Tuvalu) – traditional chief.

Vakasalewalewa (Fiji) – see *fa'afafine*.

Vakavanua (Fiji) – informal arrangement relating to land use.

Vola ni Kawa Bula (Fiji) – register of names of those entitled by virtue of being Fijian or part-Fijian to Native land in Fiji.

Yavusa (Fiji) – social group descended from a shared ancestor, within which there are several *mataqali*.

Index

Page references followed by t indicate a table

For Product Safety Concerns and Information please contact our EU
representative GPSR@taylorandfrancis.com
Taylor & Francis Verlag GmbH, Kaufingerstraße 24, 80331 München, Germany